ALL GLORY TO ŚRĪ GURU AND GAURĀṄGA

ŚRĪMAD BHĀGAVATAM

of

KṚṢṆA-DVAIPĀYANA VYĀSA

तस्मात् सङ्कीर्तनं विष्णोर्जगन्मङ्गलमंहसाम् ।
महतामपि कौरव्य विद्ध्यैकान्तिकनिष्कृतम् ॥३१॥

tasmāt saṅkīrtanaṁ viṣṇor
jagan-maṅgalam aṁhasām
mahatām api kauravya
viddhy aikāntika-niṣkṛtam (p.182)

BOOKS by
His Divine Grace
A. C. Bhaktivedanta Swami Prabhupāda

Bhagavad-gītā As It Is
Śrīmad-Bhāgavatam, cantos 1-10 (12 vols.)
Śrī Caitanya-caritāmṛta (17 vols.)
Teachings of Lord Caitanya
The Nectar of Devotion
The Nectar of Instruction
Śrī Īśopaniṣad
Easy Journey to Other Planets
Kṛṣṇa Consciousness: The Topmost Yoga System
Kṛṣṇa, The Supreme Personality of Godhead
Perfect Questions, Perfect Answers
Teachings of Lord Kapila, the Son of Devahūti
Transcendental Teachings of Prahlāda Mahārāja
Teachings of Queen Kuntī
Kṛṣṇa, the Reservoir of Pleasure
The Science of Self-Realization
The Path of Perfection
Search for Liberation
The Journey of Self-Discovery
A Second Chance
Laws of Nature
Message of Godhead
Civilization and Transcendence
Life Comes From Life
The Perfection of Yoga
Beyond Birth and Death
On the Way to Kṛṣṇa
Rāja-vidyā: The King of Knowledge
Elevation to Kṛṣṇa Consciousness
Kṛṣṇa Consciousness: The Matchless Gift
Geetār-gan (Bengali)
Vairāgya-vidyā (Bengali)
Buddhi-yoga (Bengali)
Bhakti-ratna-bolī (Bengali)
Back to Godhead magazine (founder)

available from

The Bhaktivedanta Book Trust
P.O. Box 324, Borehamwood
Herts. WD6 1NB, England
Telephone: 081-905 1244

The Bhaktivedanta Book Trust
3764 Watseka Avenue
Los Angeles, California 90034
USA

The Bhaktivedanta Book Trust
P.O. Box 262
Botany, N.S.W. 2019
Australia

ŚRĪMAD BHĀGAVATAM

Sixth Canto

(Part One—Chapters 1-5)

"The Way of Universal Justice"

With the Original Sanskrit Text,
Its Roman Transliteration, Synonyms,
Translation and Elaborate Purports

by

His Divine Grace
A.C. Bhaktivedanta Swami Prabhupāda
Founder-*Ācārya* of the International Society for Krishna Consciousness

THE BHAKTIVEDANTA BOOK TRUST

Readers interested in the subject matter of this book are invited by the International Society for Krishna Consciousness to visit any ISKCON center worldwide (see address list in back of book) or to correspond with the secretary:

International Society for Krishna Consciousness
P.O. Box 324, Borehamwood, Herts,
WD6 1NB, U.K.

International Society for Krishna Consciousness
3764 Watseka Avenue
Los Angeles, California 90034, USA

International Society for Krishna Consciousness
P.O. Box 159, Kings Cross
N.S.W. 2011, Australia

1993 Edition: 50,000 copies

Printed in Germany

ISBN 0-912776-81-1

Table of Contents

CHAPTER TWO

Ajāmila Delivered by the Viṣṇudūtas 89

CHAPTER THREE

Yamarāja Instructs His Messengers 141

Appendixes

Preface

We must know the present need of human society. And what is that need? Human society is no longer bounded by geographical limits to particular countries or communities. Human society is broader than in the Middle Ages, and the world tendency is toward one state or one human society. The ideals of spiritual communism, according to *Śrīmad-Bhāgavatam,* are based more or less on the oneness of the entire human society, nay, on the entire energy of living beings. The need is felt by great thinkers to make this a successful ideology. *Śrīmad-Bhāgavatam* will fill this need in human society. It begins, therefore, with the aphorism of Vedānta philosophy (*janmādy asya yataḥ*) to establish the ideal of a common cause.

Human society, at the present moment, is not in the darkness of oblivion. It has made rapid progress in the field of material comforts, education and economic development throughout the entire world. But there is a pinprick somewhere in the social body at large, and therefore there are large-scale quarrels, even over less important issues. There is need of a clue as to how humanity can become one in peace, friendship and prosperity with a common cause. *Śrīmad-Bhāgavatam* will fill this need, for it is a cultural presentation for the re-spiritualization of the entire human society.

Śrīmad-Bhāgavatam should be introduced also in the schools and colleges, for it is recommended by the great student devotee Prahlāda Mahārāja in order to change the demonic face of society.

kaumāra ācaret prājño
dharmān bhāgavatān iha
durlabhaṁ mānuṣaṁ janma
tad apy adhruvam arthadam
(*Bhāg.* 7.6.1)

Disparity in human society is due to lack of principles in a godless civilization. There is God, or the Almighty One, from whom everything emanates, by whom everything is maintained and in whom everything is merged to rest. Material science has tried to find the ultimate source of creation very insufficiently, but it is a fact that there is one ultimate source of everything that be. This ultimate source is explained rationally and authoritatively in the beautiful *Bhāgavatam* or *Śrīmad-Bhāgavatam.*

Śrīmad-Bhāgavatam is the transcendental science not only for knowing the ultimate source of everything but also for knowing our relation with Him and our duty towards perfection of the human society on the basis of this perfect knowledge. It is powerful reading matter in the Sanskrit language, and it is now rendered into English elaborately so that simply by a careful reading one will know God perfectly well, so much so that the reader will be sufficiently educated to defend himself from the onslaught of atheists. Over and above this, the reader will be able to convert others to accept God as a concrete principle.

Śrīmad-Bhāgavatam begins with the definition of the ultimate source. It is a bona fide commentary on the *Vedānta-sūtra* by the same author, Śrīla Vyāsadeva, and gradually it develops into nine cantos up to the highest state of God realization. The only qualification one needs to study this great book of transcendental knowledge is to proceed step by step cautiously and not jump forward haphazardly as with an ordinary book. It should be gone through chapter by chapter, one after another. The reading matter is so arranged with its original Sanskrit text, its English transliteration, synonyms, translation and purports so that one is sure to become a God realized soul at the end of finishing the first nine cantos.

The Tenth Canto is distinct from the first nine cantos, because it deals directly with the transcendental activities of the Personality of Godhead Śrī Kṛṣṇa. One will be unable to capture the effects of the Tenth Canto without going through the first nine cantos. The book is complete in twelve cantos, each independent, but it is good for all to read them in small installments one after another.

I must admit my frailties in presenting *Śrīmad-Bhāgavatam,* but still I am hopeful of its good reception by the thinkers and leaders of society on the strength of the following statement of *Śrīmad-Bhāgavatam.*

tad vāg-visargo janatāgha-viplavo
yasmin pratiślokam abaddhavaty api

nāmāny anantasya yaśo 'ṅkitāni yac
chṛṇvanti gāyanti gṛṇanti sādhavaḥ
(*Bhāg.* 1.5.11)

"On the other hand, that literature which is full with descriptions of the transcendental glories of the name, fame, form and pastimes of the unlimited Supreme Lord is a transcendental creation meant to bring about a revolution in the impious life of a misdirected civilization. Such transcendental literatures, even though irregularly composed, are heard, sung and accepted by purified men who are thoroughly honest."

Oṁ tat sat

A. C. Bhaktivedanta Swami

Introduction

"This *Bhāgavata Purāṇa* is as brilliant as the sun, and it has arisen just after the departure of Lord Kṛṣṇa to His own abode, accompanied by religion, knowledge, etc. Persons who have lost their vision due to the dense darkness of ignorance in the age of Kali shall get light from this *Purāṇa.*" (*Śrīmad-Bhāgavatam* 1.3.43)

The timeless wisdom of India is expressed in the *Vedas*, ancient Sanskrit texts that touch upon all fields of human knowledge. Originally preserved through oral tradition, the *Vedas* were first put into writing five thousand years ago by Śrīla Vyāsadeva, the "literary incarnation of God." After compiling the *Vedas*, Vyāsadeva set forth their essence in the aphorisms known as *Vedānta-sūtras*. *Śrīmad-Bhāgavatam* is Vyāsadeva's commentary on his own *Vedānta-sūtras*. It was written in the maturity of his spiritual life under the direction of Nārada Muni, his spiritual master. Referred to as "the ripened fruit of the tree of Vedic literature," *Śrīmad-Bhāgavatam* is the most complete and authoritative exposition of Vedic knowledge.

After compiling the *Bhāgavatam*, Vyāsa impressed the synopsis of it upon his son, the sage Śukadeva Gosvāmī. Śukadeva Gosvāmī subsequently recited the entire *Bhāgavatam* to Mahārāja Parīkṣit in an assembly of learned saints on the bank of the Ganges at Hastināpura (now Delhi). Mahārāja Parīkṣit was the emperor of the world and was a great *rājarṣi* (saintly king). Having received a warning that he would die within a week, he renounced his entire kingdom and retired to the bank of the Ganges to fast until death and receive spiritual enlightenment. The *Bhāgavatam* begins with Emperor Parīkṣit's sober inquiry to Śukadeva Gosvāmī:

> "You are the spiritual master of great saints and devotees. I am therefore begging you to show the way of perfection for all persons, and especially for one who is about to die. Please let me know what a man should hear, chant, remember and worship, and also what he should not do. Please explain all this to me."

Śukadeva Gosvāmī's answer to this question, and numerous other questions posed by Mahārāja Parīkṣit, concerning everything from the nature of the self to the origin of the universe, held the assembled sages in rapt attention continuously for the seven days leading to the King's death. The sage Sūta Gosvāmī, who was present on the bank of the Ganges when Śukadeva Gosvāmī first recited *Śrīmad-Bhāgavatam,* later repeated the *Bhāgavatam* before a gathering of sages in the forest of Naimiṣāraṇya. Those sages, concerned about the spiritual welfare of the people in general, had gathered to perform a long, continuous chain of sacrifices to counteract the degrading influence of the incipient age of Kali. In response to the sages' request that he speak the essence of Vedic wisdom, Sūta Gosvāmī repeated from memory the entire eighteen thousand verses of *Śrīmad-Bhāgavatam,* as spoken by Śukadeva Gosvāmī to Mahārāja Parīkṣit.

The reader of *Śrīmad-Bhāgavatam* hears Sūta Gosvāmī relate the questions of Mahārāja Parīkṣit and the answers of Śukadeva Gosvāmī. Also, Sūta Gosvāmī sometimes responds directly to questions put by Śaunaka Ṛṣi, the spokesman for the sages gathered at Naimiṣāraṇya. One therefore simultaneously hears two dialogues: one between Mahārāja Parīkṣit and Śukadeva Gosvāmī on the bank of the Ganges, and another at Naimiṣāraṇya between Sūta Gosvāmī and the sages at Naimiṣāraṇya Forest, headed by Śaunaka Ṛṣi. Furthermore, while instructing King Parīkṣit, Śukadeva Gosvāmī often relates historical episodes and gives accounts of lengthy philosophical discussions between such great souls as the saint Maitreya and his disciple Vidura. With this understanding of the history of the *Bhāgavatam,* the reader will easily be able to follow its intermingling of dialogues and events from various sources. Since philosophical wisdom, not chronological order, is most important in the text, one need only be attentive to the subject matter of *Śrīmad-Bhāgavatam* to appreciate fully its profound message.

It should also be noted that the volumes of the *Bhāgavatam* need not be read consecutively, starting with the first and proceeding to the last. The translator of this edition compares the *Bhāgavatam* to sugar candy—wherever you taste it, you will find it equally sweet and relishable.

This edition of the *Bhāgavatam* is the first complete English translation of this important text with an elaborate commentary, and it is the first widely available to the English-speaking public. It is the product of the scholarly and devotional effort of His Divine Grace A. C. Bhaktivedanta Swami Prabhupāda, the world's most distinguished teacher of Indian religious and philosophical thought. His consummate Sanskrit scholarship and intimate familiarity with Vedic culture and thought as well as the modern way of life combine to reveal to the West a magnificent exposition of this important classic.

Readers will find this work of value for many reasons. For those interested in the classical roots of Indian civilization, it serves as a vast reservoir of detailed information on virtually every one of its aspects. For students of comparative philosophy and religion, the *Bhāgavatam* offers a penetrating view into the meaning of India's profound spiritual heritage. To sociologists and anthropologists, the *Bhāgavatam* reveals the practical workings of a peaceful and scientifically organized Vedic culture, whose institutions were integrated on the basis of a highly developed spiritual world view. Students of literature will discover the *Bhāgavatam* to be a masterpiece of majestic poetry. For students of psychology, the text provides important perspectives on the nature of consciousness, human behavior and the philosophical study of identity. Finally, to those seeking spiritual insight, the *Bhāgavatam* offers simple and practical guidance for attainment of the highest self-knowledge and realization of the Absolute Truth. The entire multivolume text, presented by the Bhaktivedanta Book Trust, promises to occupy a significant place in the intellectual, cultural and spiritual life of modern man for a long time to come.

—The Publishers

CHAPTER ONE

The History of the Life of Ajāmila

Throughout *Śrīmad-Bhāgavatam* there are descriptions of ten subject matters, including creation, subsequent creation and the planetary systems. Śukadeva Gosvāmī, the speaker of *Śrīmad-Bhāgavatam*, has already described creation, subsequent creation and the planetary systems in the Third, Fourth and Fifth Cantos. Now, in this Sixth Canto, which consists of nineteen chapters, he will describe *poṣaṇa*, or protection by the Lord.

The first chapter relates the history of Ajāmila, who was considered a greatly sinful man, but was liberated when four order carriers of Viṣṇu came to rescue him from the hands of the order carriers of Yamarāja. A full description of how he was liberated, having been relieved of the reactions of his sinful life, is given in this chapter. Sinful activities are painful both in this life and in the next. We should know for certain that the cause of all painful life is sinful action. On the path of fruitive work one certainly commits sinful activities, and therefore according to the considerations of *karma-kāṇḍa*, different types of atonement are recommended. Such methods of atonement, however, do not free one from ignorance, which is the root of sinful life. Consequently one is prone to commit sinful activities even after atonement, which is therefore very inadequate for purification. On the path of speculative knowledge one becomes free from sinful life by understanding things as they are. Therefore the acquirement of speculative knowledge is also considered a method of atonement. While performing fruitive activities one can become free from the actions of sinful life through austerity, penance, celibacy, control of the mind and senses, truthfulness and the practice of mystic *yoga*. By awakening knowledge one may also neutralize sinful reactions. Neither of these methods, however, can free one from the tendency to commit sinful activities.

By *bhakti-yoga* one can completely avoid the tendency for sinful life; other methods are not very feasible. Therefore the Vedic literature concludes that devotional service is more important than the methods of *karma-kāṇḍa* and *jñāna-kāṇḍa.* Only the path of devotional service is auspicious for everyone. Fruitive activities and speculative knowledge cannot independently liberate anyone, but devotional service, independent of *karma* and *jñāna,* is so potent that one who has fixed his mind at the lotus feet of Kṛṣṇa is guaranteed not to meet the Yamadūtas, the order carriers of Yamarāja, even in dreams.

To prove the strength of devotional service, Śukadeva Gosvāmī described the history of Ajāmila. Ajāmila was a resident of Kānyakubja (the modern Kanauj). He was trained by his parents to become a perfect *brāhmaṇa* by studying the *Vedas* and following the regulative principles, but because of his past, this youthful *brāhmaṇa* was somehow attracted by a prostitute, and because of her association he became most fallen and abandoned all regulative principles. Ajāmila begot in the womb of the prostitute ten sons, the last of whom was called Nārāyaṇa. At the time of Ajāmila's death, when the order carriers of Yamarāja came to take him, he loudly called the name Nārāyaṇa in fear because he was attached to his youngest son. Thus he remembered the original Nārāyaṇa, Lord Viṣṇu. Although he did not chant the holy name of Nārāyaṇa completely offenselessly, it acted nevertheless. As soon as he chanted the holy name of Nārāyaṇa, the order carriers of Lord Viṣṇu immediately appeared on the scene. A discussion ensued between the order carriers of Lord Viṣṇu and those of Yamarāja, and by hearing that discussion Ajāmila was liberated. He could then understand the bad effect of fruitive activities and could also understand how exalted is the process of devotional service.

TEXT 1

श्रीपरीक्षिदुवाच
निवृत्तिमार्गः कथित आदौ भगवता यथा ।
क्रमयोगोपलब्धेन ब्रह्मणा यदसंसृतिः ॥ १ ॥

śrī-parīkṣid uvāca
nivṛtti-mārgaḥ kathita
ādau bhagavatā yathā
krama-yogopalabdhena
brahmaṇā yad asaṁsṛtiḥ

śrī-parīkṣit uvāca—Mahārāja Parīkṣit said; *nivṛtti-mārgaḥ*—the path of liberation; *kathitaḥ*—described; *ādau*—in the beginning; *bhagavatā*—by Your Holiness; *yathā*—duly; *krama*—gradually; *yoga-upalabdhena*—obtained by the *yoga* process; *brahmaṇā*—along with Lord Brahmā (after reaching Brahmaloka); *yat*—by which way; *asaṁsṛtiḥ*—cessation of the repetition of birth and death.

TRANSLATION

Mahārāja Parīkṣit said: O my lord, O Śukadeva Gosvāmī, you have already described [in the Second Canto] the path of liberation [nivṛtti-mārga]. By following that path, one is certainly elevated gradually to the highest planetary system, Brahmaloka, from which one is promoted to the spiritual world along with Lord Brahmā. Thus one's repetition of birth and death in the material world ceases.

PURPORT

Since Mahārāja Parīkṣit was a Vaiṣṇava, when he heard the description, at the end of the Fifth Canto, of the different hellish conditions of life, he was very much concerned with how to liberate the conditioned souls from the clutches of *māyā* and take them back home, back to Godhead. Therefore he reminded his spiritual master, Śukadeva Gosvāmī, about the *nivṛtti-mārga*, or path of liberation, which he had described in the Second Canto. Mahārāja Parīkṣit, who at the time of death was fortunate to have met Śukadeva Gosvāmī, inquired from Śukadeva Gosvāmī about the path of liberation at that crucial time. Śukadeva Gosvāmī very much appreciated his question and congratulated him by saying:

varīyān eṣa te praśnaḥ
kṛto loka-hitaṁ nṛpa
ātmavit-sammataḥ puṁsāṁ
śrotavyādiṣu yaḥ paraḥ

"My dear King, your question is glorious because it is very beneficial for all kinds of people. The answer to this question is the prime subject matter for hearing, and it is approved by all transcendentalists." (*Bhāg.* 2.1.1)

Parīkṣit Mahārāja was astonished that the living entities in the conditional stage do not accept the path of liberation, devotional service, instead of suffering in so many hellish conditions. This is the symptom of a Vaiṣṇava. *Vāñchā-kalpa-tarubhyaś ca kṛpā-sindhubhya eva ca:* a Vaiṣṇava is an ocean of mercy. *Para-duḥkha-duḥkhī:* he is unhappy because of the unhappiness of others. Therefore Parīkṣit Mahārāja, being compassionate toward the conditioned souls suffering in hellish life, suggested that Śukadeva Gosvāmī continue describing the path of liberation, which he had explained in the beginning of *Śrīmad-Bhāgavatam.* The word *asaṁsṛti* is very important in this connection. *Saṁsṛti* refers to continuing on the path of birth and death. *Asaṁsṛti,* on the contrary, refers to *nivṛtti-mārga,* or the path of liberation, by which one's birth and death cease and one gradually progresses to Brahmaloka, unless one is a pure devotee who does not care about going to the higher planetary systems, in which case one immediately returns home, back to Godhead, by executing devotional service (*tyaktvā dehaṁ punar janma naiti*). Parīkṣit Mahārāja, therefore, was very eager to hear from Śukadeva Gosvāmī about the path of liberation for the conditioned soul.

According to the opinion of the *ācāryas,* the word *krama-yogopalabdhena* indicates that by first performing *karma-yoga* and then *jñāna-yoga* and finally coming to the platform of *bhakti-yoga,* one can be liberated. *Bhakti-yoga,* however, is so powerful that it does not depend on *karma-yoga* or *jñāna-yoga. Bhakti-yoga* itself is so powerful that even an impious man with no assets in *karma-yoga* or an illiterate with no assets in *jñāna-yoga* can undoubtedly be elevated to the spiritual world if he simply adheres to *bhakti-yoga. Mām evaiṣyasy asaṁśayaḥ.* Kṛṣṇa says in *Bhagavad-gītā* (8.7) that by the process of *bhakti-yoga* one undoubtedly goes back to Godhead, back home to the spiritual world. *Yogīs,* however, instead of going directly to the spiritual world, sometimes want to see other planetary systems, and therefore they ascend to the planetary system where Lord Brahmā lives, as indicated here by the word *brahmaṇā.* At the time of dissolution, Lord Brahmā, along with all the inhabitants of Brahmaloka, goes directly to the spiritual world. This is confirmed in the *Vedas* as follows:

brahmaṇā saha te sarve
samprāpte pratisañcare

parasyānte kṛtātmānaḥ
praviśanti paraṁ padam

"Because of their exalted position, those who are on Brahmaloka at the time of dissolution go directly back home, back to Godhead, along with Lord Brahmā."

TEXT 2

प्रवृत्तिलक्षणश्चैव त्रैगुण्यविषयो मुने ।
योऽसावलीनप्रकृतेर्गुणसर्गः पुनः पुनः ॥ २ ॥

pravṛtti-lakṣaṇaś caiva
traiguṇya-viṣayo mune
yo 'sāv alīna-prakṛter
guṇa-sargaḥ punaḥ punaḥ

pravṛtti—by inclination; *lakṣaṇaḥ*—symptomized; *ca*—also; *eva*—indeed; *trai-guṇya*—the three modes of nature; *viṣayaḥ*—possessing as objectives; *mune*—O great sage; *yaḥ*—which; *asau*—that; *alīna-prakṛteḥ*—of one who is not freed from the clutches of *māyā; guṇa-sargaḥ*—in which there is a creation of material bodies; *punaḥ punaḥ*—again and again.

TRANSLATION

O great sage Śukadeva Gosvāmī, unless the living entity is freed from the infection of the material modes of nature, he receives different types of bodies in which to enjoy or suffer, and according to the body, he is understood to have various inclinations. By following these inclinations he traverses the path called pravṛtti-mārga, by which one may be elevated to the heavenly planets, as you have already described [in the Third Canto].

PURPORT

As Lord Kṛṣṇa explains in *Bhagavad-gītā* (9.25):

yānti deva-vratā devān
pitṝn yānti pitṛ-vratāḥ

bhūtāni yānti bhūtejyā
yānti mad-yājino 'pi mām

"Those who worship the demigods will take birth among the demigods; those who worship ghosts and spirits will take birth among such beings; those who worship ancestors go to the ancestors; and those who worship Me will live with Me." Because of the influence of the various modes of nature, the living entities have various tendencies or propensities, and therefore they are qualified to achieve various destinations. As long as one is materially attached, he wants to be elevated to the heavenly planets because of his attraction to the material world. The Supreme Personality of Godhead declares, however, "Those who worship Me come to Me." If one has no information about the Supreme Lord and His abode, one tries to be elevated only to a higher material position, but when one concludes that in this material world there is nothing but repeated birth and death, he tries to return home, back to Godhead. If one attains that destination, he need never return to this material world (*yad gatvā na nivartante tad dhāma paramaṁ mama*). As Śrī Caitanya Mahāprabhu says in *Caitanya-caritāmṛta* (*Madhya* 19.151):

brahmāṇḍa bhramite kona bhāgyavān jīva
guru-kṛṣṇa-prasāde pāya bhakti-latā-bīja

"According to their *karma*, all living entities are wandering throughout the entire universe. Some of them are being elevated to the upper planetary systems, and some are going down into the lower planetary systems. Out of many millions of wandering living entities, one who is very fortunate gets an opportunity to associate with a bona fide spiritual master by the grace of Kṛṣṇa. By the mercy of both Kṛṣṇa and the spiritual master, such a person receives the seed of the creeper of devotional service." All living entities are rotating throughout the universe, going sometimes up to the higher planetary systems and sometimes down to the lower planets. This is the material disease, which is known as *pravṛtti-mārga*. When one becomes intelligent he takes to *nivṛtti-mārga*, the path of liberation, and thus instead of rotating within this material world, he returns home, back to Godhead. This is necessary.

TEXT 3

अधर्मलक्षणा नाना नरकाश्चानुवर्णिताः ।
मन्वन्तरश्च व्याख्यात आद्यः स्वायम्भुवो यतः॥ ३ ॥

adharma-lakṣaṇā nānā
narakāś cānuvarṇitāḥ
manvantaraś ca vyākhyāta
ādyaḥ svāyambhuvo yataḥ

adharma-lakṣaṇāḥ—symptomized by impious activities; *nānā*—various; *narakāḥ*—hells; *ca*—also; *anuvarṇitāḥ*—have been described; *manu-antaraḥ*—the change of Manus [in one day of Brahmā there are fourteen Manus]; *ca*—also; *vyākhyātaḥ*—has been described; *ādyaḥ*—the original; *svāyambhuvaḥ*—directly the son of Lord Brahmā; *yataḥ*—wherein.

TRANSLATION

You have also described [at the end of the Fifth Canto] the varieties of hellish life that result from impious activities, and you have described [in the Fourth Canto] the first manvantara, which was presided over by Svāyambhuva Manu, the son of Lord Brahmā.

TEXTS 4–5

प्रियव्रतोत्तानपदोर्वंशस्तच्चरितानि च ।
द्वीपवर्षसमुद्राद्रिनद्युद्यानवनस्पतीन् ॥ ४ ॥

धरामण्डलसंस्थानं भागलक्षणमानतः ।
ज्योतिषां विवराणां च यथेदमसृजद्विभुः ॥ ५ ॥

priyavratottānapador
vaṁśas tac-caritāni ca
dvīpa-varṣa-samudrādri-
nady-udyāna-vanaspatīn

dharā-maṇḍala-saṁsthānaṁ
bhāga-lakṣaṇa-mānataḥ
jyotiṣāṁ vivarāṇāṁ ca
yathedam asṛjad vibhuḥ

priyavrata—of Priyavrata; *uttānapadoḥ*—and of Uttānapāda; *vaṁśaḥ*—the dynasty; *tat-caritāni*—their characteristics; *ca*—also; *dvīpa*—different planets; *varṣa*—lands; *samudra*—oceans and seas; *adri*—mountains; *nadī*—rivers; *udyāna*—gardens; *vanaspatīn*—and trees; *dharā-maṇḍala*—of the planet earth; *saṁsthānam*—situation; *bhāga*—according to divisions; *lakṣaṇa*—different symptoms; *mānataḥ*—and measurements; *jyotiṣām*—of the sun and other luminaries; *vivarāṇām*—of the lower planetary systems; *ca*—and; *yathā*—as; *idam*—this; *asṛjat*—created; *vibhuḥ*—the Supreme Personality of Godhead.

TRANSLATION

My dear lord, you have described the dynasties and characteristics of King Priyavrata and King Uttānapāda. The Supreme Personality of Godhead created this material world with various universes, planetary systems, planets and stars, with varied lands, seas, oceans, mountains, rivers, gardens and trees, all with different characteristics. These are divided among this planet earth, the luminaries in the sky and the lower planetary systems. You have very clearly described these planets and the living entities who live on them.

PURPORT

Here the words *yathedam asṛjad vibhuḥ* clearly indicate that the Supreme, the great, almighty Personality of Godhead, created this entire material world with its different varieties of planets, stars and so forth. Atheists try to conceal the hand of God, which is present in every creation, but they cannot explain how all these creations could come into existence without a competent intelligence and almighty power behind them. Simply to imagine or speculate is a waste of time. In *Bhagavad-gītā* (10.8), the Lord says, *ahaṁ sarvasya prabhavo:* "I am the origin of everything." *Mattaḥ sarvaṁ pravartate:* "Whatever exists in the creation emanates from Me." *Iti matvā bhajante māṁ budhā bhāva-samanvitāḥ:* "When one fully understands that I create everything by My omnipotence, one becomes firmly situated in devotional service and fully surrenders at My lotus feet." Unfortunately, the unintelligent cannot immediately understand Kṛṣṇa's supremacy. Nonetheless, if they associate with devotees and read authorized books, they may gradually come to the proper understanding, although this may take many, many births. As Kṛṣṇa says in *Bhagavad-gītā* (7.19):

bahūnāṁ janmanām ante
jñānavān māṁ prapadyate
vāsudevaḥ sarvam iti
sa mahātmā sudurlabhaḥ

"After many births and deaths, he who is actually in knowledge surrenders unto Me, knowing Me to be the cause of all causes and all that is. Such a great soul is very rare." Vāsudeva, Kṛṣṇa, is the creator of everything, and His energy is displayed in various ways. As explained in *Bhagavad-gītā* (7.4–5), a combination of the material energy (*bhūmir āpo 'nalo vāyuḥ*) and the spiritual energy, the living entity, exists in every creation. Therefore the same principle, the combination of the supreme spirit and the material elements, is the cause of the cosmic manifestation.

TEXT 6

अधुनेह महाभाग यथैव नरकान्नरः ।
नानोग्रयातनान्नेयात्तन्मे व्याख्यातुमर्हसि ॥ ६ ॥

adhuneha mahā-bhāga
yathaiva narakān naraḥ
nānogra-yātanān neyāt
tan me vyākhyātum arhasi

adhunā—right now; *iha*—in this material world; *mahā-bhāga*—O greatly opulent and fortunate Śukadeva Gosvāmī; *yathā*—so that; *eva*—

indeed; *narakān*—all the hellish conditions into which the impious are put; *naraḥ*—human beings; *nānā*—varieties of; *ugra*—terrible; *yātanān*—conditions of suffering; *na īyāt*—may not undergo; *tat*—that; *me*—to me; *vyākhyātum arhasi*—please describe.

TRANSLATION

O greatly fortunate and opulent Śukadeva Gosvāmī, now kindly tell me how human beings may be saved from having to enter hellish conditions in which they suffer terrible pains.

PURPORT

In the Twenty-sixth Chapter of the Fifth Canto, Śukadeva Gosvāmī has explained that people who commit sinful acts are forced to enter hellish planets and suffer. Now Mahārāja Parīkṣit, being a devotee, is concerned with how this can be stopped. A Vaiṣṇava is *para-duḥkha-duḥkhī;* in other words, he has no personal troubles, but he is very unhappy to see others in trouble. Prahlāda Mahārāja said, "My Lord, I have no personal problems, for I have learned how to glorify Your transcendental qualities and thus enter a trance of ecstasy. I do have a problem, however, for I am simply thinking of these rascals and fools who are busy with *māyā-sukha,* temporary happiness, without knowledge of devotional service unto You." This is the problem faced by a Vaiṣṇava. Because a Vaiṣṇava fully takes shelter of the Supreme Personality of Godhead, he personally has no problems, but because he is compassionate toward the fallen, conditioned souls, he is always thinking of plans to save them from their hellish life in this body and the next. Parīkṣit Mahārāja, therefore, anxiously wanted to know from Śukadeva Gosvāmī how humanity can be saved from gliding down to hell. Śukadeva Gosvāmī had already explained how people enter hellish life, and he could also explain how they could be saved from it. Intelligent men must take advantage of these instructions. Unfortunately, however, the entire world is lacking Kṛṣṇa consciousness, and therefore people are suffering from the grossest ignorance and do not even believe in a life after this one. To convince them of their next life is very difficult because they have become almost mad in their pursuit of material enjoyment. Nevertheless, our duty, the duty of all sane men, is to save them. Mahārāja Parīkṣit is the representative of one who can save them.

TEXT 7

श्रीशुक उवाच
न चेदिहैवापचितिं यथांहसः
कृतस्य कुर्यान्मनउक्तपाणिभिः ।
ध्रुवं स वै प्रेत्य नरकानुपैति
ये कीर्तिता मे भवतस्तिग्मयातनाः ॥ ७ ॥

śrī-śuka uvāca
na ced ihaivāpacitiṁ yathāṁhasaḥ
kṛtasya kuryān mana-ukta-pāṇibhiḥ
dhruvaṁ sa vai pretya narakān upaiti
ye kīrtitā me bhavatas tigma-yātanāḥ

śrī-śukaḥ uvāca—Śrīla Śukadeva Gosvāmī said; *na*—not; *cet*—if; *iha*—within this life; *eva*—certainly; *apacitim*—counteraction, atonement; *yathā*—duly; *aṁhasaḥ kṛtasya*—when one has performed sinful activities; *kuryāt*—performs; *manaḥ*—with the mind; *ukta*—words; *pāṇibhiḥ*—and with the senses; *dhruvam*—undoubtedly; *saḥ*—that person; *vai*—indeed; *pretya*—after death; *narakān*—different varieties of hellish conditions; *upaiti*—attains; *ye*—which; *kīrtitāḥ*—were already described; *me*—by me; *bhavataḥ*—unto you; *tigma-yātanāḥ*—in which there is very terrible suffering.

TRANSLATION

Śukadeva Gosvāmī replied: My dear King, if before one's next death whatever impious acts one has performed in this life with his mind, words and body are not counteracted through proper atonement according to the description of the Manu-saṁhitā and other dharma-śāstras, one will certainly enter the hellish planets after death and undergo terrible suffering, as I have previously described to you.

PURPORT

Śrīla Viśvanātha Cakravartī Ṭhākura mentions that although Mahārāja Parīkṣit was a pure devotee, Śukadeva Gosvāmī did not immediately speak to him about the strength of devotional service. As stated in *Bhagavad-gītā* (14.26):

māṁ ca yo 'vyabhicāreṇa
bhakti-yogena sevate
sa guṇān samatītyaitān
brahma-bhūyāya kalpate

Devotional service is so strong that if one fully surrenders to Kṛṣṇa and takes fully to His devotional service, the reactions of his sinful life immediately stop.

Elsewhere in the *Gītā* (18.66), Lord Kṛṣṇa urges that one give up all other duties and surrender to Him, and He promises, *ahaṁ tvāṁ sarva-pāpebhyo mokṣayiṣyāmi:* "I shall free you from all sinful reactions and give you liberation." Therefore in response to the inquiries of Parīkṣit Mahārāja, Śukadeva Gosvāmī, his *guru,* could have immediately explained the principle of *bhakti,* but to test Parīkṣit Mahārāja's intelligence, he first prescribed atonement according to *karma-kāṇḍa,* the path of fruitive activities. For *karma-kāṇḍa* there are eighty authorized scriptures, such as *Manu-saṁhitā,* which are known as *dharma-śāstras.* In these scriptures one is advised to counteract his sinful acts by performing other types of fruitive action. This was the path first recommended by Śukadeva Gosvāmī to Mahārāja Parīkṣit, and actually it is a fact that one who does not take to devotional service must follow the decision of these scriptures by performing pious acts to counteract his impious acts. This is known as atonement.

TEXT 8

तस्मात्पुरैवाश्विह पापनिष्कृतौ
यतेत मृत्योरविपद्यतात्मना ।
दोषस्य दृष्ट्वा गुरुलाघवं यथा
भिषक् चिकित्सेत रुजां निदानवित् ॥ ८ ॥

tasmāt puraivāśv iha pāpa-niṣkṛtau
yateta mṛtyor avipadyatātmanā

doṣasya dṛṣṭvā guru-lāghavaṁ yathā
bhiṣak cikitseta rujāṁ nidānavit

tasmāt—therefore; *purā*—before; *eva*—indeed; *āśu*—very quickly; *iha*—in this life; *pāpa-niṣkṛtau*—to become free from the reaction of sinful activities; *yateta*—one should endeavor; *mṛtyoḥ*—death; *avipadyata*—not troubled by disease and old age; *ātmanā*—with a body; *doṣasya*—of the sinful activities; *dṛṣṭvā*—estimating; *guru-lāghavam*—the heaviness or lightness; *yathā*—just like; *bhiṣak*—a physician; *cikitseta*—would treat; *rujām*—of disease; *nidāna-vit*—one who is expert in diagnosis.

TRANSLATION

Therefore, before one's next death comes, as long as one's body is strong enough, one should quickly adopt the process of atonement according to śāstra; otherwise one's time will be lost, and the reactions of his sins will increase. As an expert physician diagnoses and treats a disease according to its gravity, one should undergo atonement according to the severity of one's sins.

PURPORT

The *dharma-śāstras* like the *Manu-saṁhitā* prescribe that a man who has committed murder should be hanged and his own life sacrificed in atonement. Previously this system was followed all over the world, but since people are becoming atheists, they are stopping capital punishment. This is not wise. Herein it is said that a physician who knows how to diagnose a disease prescribes medicine accordingly. If the disease is very serious, the medicine must be strong. The weight of a murderer's sin is very great, and therefore according to *Manu-saṁhitā* a murderer must be killed. By killing a murderer the government shows mercy to him because if a murderer is not killed in this life, he will be killed and forced to suffer many times in future lives. Since people do not know about the next life and the intricate workings of nature, they manufacture their own laws, but they should properly consult the established injunctions of the *śāstras* and act accordingly. In India even today the Hindu community often takes advice from expert scholars regarding how to counteract sinful activities. In Christianity also there is a process of confession and atonement. Therefore atonement is required, and atonement must be undergone according to the gravity of one's sinful acts.

TEXT 9

श्रीराजोवाच
दृष्टश्रुताभ्यां यत्पापं जानन्नप्यात्मनोऽहितम् ।
करोति भूयो विवशः प्रायश्चित्तमथो कथम् ॥ ९ ॥

śrī-rājovāca
dṛṣṭa-śrutābhyāṁ yat pāpaṁ
jānann apy ātmano 'hitam
karoti bhūyo vivaśaḥ
prāyaścittam atho katham

śrī-rājā uvāca—Parīkṣit Mahārāja replied; *dṛṣṭa*—by seeing; *śrutābhyām*—also by hearing (from the scriptures or lawbooks); *yat*—since; *pāpam*—sinful, criminal action; *jānan*—knowing; *api*—although; *ātmanaḥ*—of his self; *ahitam*—injurious; *karoti*—he acts; *bhūyaḥ*—again and again; *vivaśaḥ*—unable to control himself; *prāyaścittam*—atonement; *atho*—therefore; *katham*—what is the value of.

TRANSLATION

Mahārāja Parīkṣit said: One may know that sinful activity is injurious for him because he actually sees that a criminal is punished by the government and rebuked by people in general and because he hears from scriptures and learned scholars that one is thrown into hellish conditions in the next life for committing sinful acts. Nevertheless, in spite of such knowledge, one is forced to commit sins again and again, even after performing acts of atonement. Therefore, what is the value of such atonement?

PURPORT

In some religious sects a sinful man goes to a priest to confess his sinful acts and pay a fine, but then he again commits the same sins and returns to confess them again. This is the practice of a professional sinner. Parīkṣit Mahārāja's observations indicate that even five thousand years ago it was the practice of criminals to atone for their crimes but then commit the same crimes again, as if forced to do so. Therefore, owing to his practical experience, Parīkṣit Mahārāja saw that the process of repeatedly sinning and atoning is pointless. Regardless of how many times he is punished, one who is attached to sense enjoyment will commit sinful acts again and again until he is trained to refrain from enjoying his senses. The word *vivaśa* is used herein, indicating that even one who does not want to commit sinful acts will be forced to do so by habit. Parīkṣit Mahārāja therefore considered the process of atonement to have little value for saving one from sinful acts. In the following verse he further explains his rejection of this process.

TEXT 10

क्वचिन्निवर्ततेऽभद्रात्क्वचिच्चरति तत्पुनः ।
प्रायश्चित्तमथोऽपार्थं मन्ये कुञ्जरशौचवत् ॥१०॥

kvacin nivartate 'bhadrāt
kvacic carati tat punaḥ
prāyaścittam atho 'pārthaṁ
manye kuñjara-śaucavat

kvacit—sometimes; *nivartate*—ceases; *abhadrāt*—from sinful activity; *kvacit*—sometimes; *carati*—commits; *tat*—that (sinful activity); *punaḥ*—again; *prāyaścittam*—the process of atonement; *atho*—therefore; *apārtham*—useless; *manye*—I consider; *kuñjara-śauca-vat*—exactly like the bathing of an elephant.

TRANSLATION

Sometimes one who is very alert so as not to commit sinful acts is victimized by sinful life again. I therefore consider this process of repeated sinning and atoning to be useless. It is like the bathing of an elephant, for an elephant cleanses itself by taking a full bath, but then throws dust over its head and body as soon as it returns to the land.

PURPORT

When Parīkṣit Mahārāja inquired how a human being could free himself from sinful activities so as not to be forced to go to hellish planetary systems after death, Śukadeva Gosvāmī answered that the process of counteracting sinful life is atonement. In this way Śukadeva Gosvāmī tested the intelligence of Mahārāja Parīkṣit, who passed the examination by refusing to accept this process as genuine. Now Parīkṣit Mahārāja is expecting another answer from his spiritual master, Śukadeva Gosvāmī.

TEXT 11

श्रीबादरायणिरुवाच

कर्मणा कर्मनिर्हारो न ह्यात्यन्तिक इष्यते ।
अविद्वदधिकारित्वात्प्रायश्चित्तं विमर्शनम् ॥११॥

śrī-bādarāyaṇir uvāca
karmaṇā karma-nirhāro
na hy ātyantika iṣyate
avidvad-adhikāritvāt
prāyaścittaṁ vimarśanam

śrī-bādarāyaṇiḥ uvāca—Śukadeva Gosvāmī, the son of Vyāsadeva, replied; *karmaṇā*—by fruitive activities; *karma-nirhāraḥ*—counteraction of fruitive activities; *na*—not; *hi*—indeed; *ātyantikaḥ*—final; *iṣyate*—becomes possible; *avidvat-adhikāritvāt*—from being without knowledge; *prāyaścittam*—real atonement; *vimarśanam*—full knowledge of Vedānta.

TRANSLATION

Śukadeva Gosvāmī, the son of Vedavyāsa, answered: My dear King, since acts meant to neutralize impious actions are also fruitive, they will not release one from the tendency to act fruitively. Persons who subject themselves to the rules and regulations of atonement are not at all intelligent. Indeed, they are in the mode of darkness. Unless one is freed from the mode of ignorance, trying to counteract one action through another is useless because this will not uproot one's desires. Thus even though

one may superficially seem pious, he will undoubtedly be prone to act impiously. Therefore real atonement is enlightenment in perfect knowledge, Vedānta, by which one understands the Supreme Absolute Truth.

PURPORT

The *guru*, Śukadeva Gosvāmī, has examined Parīkṣit Mahārāja, and it appears that the King has passed one phase of the examination by rejecting the process of atonement because it involves fruitive activities. Now Śukadeva Gosvāmī is suggesting the platform of speculative knowledge. Progressing from *karma-kāṇḍa* to *jñāna-kāṇḍa*, he is proposing, *prāyaścittaṁ vimarśanam:* "Real atonement is full knowledge." *Vimarśana* refers to the cultivation of speculative knowledge. In *Bhagavad-gītā, karmīs*, who are lacking in knowledge, are compared to asses. Kṛṣṇa says in *Bhagavad-gītā* (7.15):

na māṁ duṣkṛtino mūḍhāḥ
prapadyante narādhamāḥ
māyayāpahṛta-jñānā
āsuraṁ bhāvam āśritāḥ

"Those miscreants who are grossly foolish, lowest among mankind, whose knowledge is stolen by illusion, and who partake of the atheistic nature of demons, do not surrender unto Me." Thus *karmīs* who engage in sinful acts and who do not know the true objective of life are called *mūḍhas*, asses. *Vimarśana*, however, is also explained in *Bhagavad-gītā* (15.15), where Kṛṣṇa says, *vedaiś ca sarvair aham eva vedyaḥ:* the purpose of Vedic study is to understand the Supreme Personality of Godhead. If one studies Vedānta but merely advances somewhat in speculative knowledge and does not understand the Supreme Lord, one remains the same *mūḍha*. As stated in *Bhagavad-gītā* (7.19), one attains real knowledge when he understands Kṛṣṇa and surrenders unto Him (*bahūnāṁ janmanām ante jñānavān māṁ prapadyate*). To become learned and free from material contamination, therefore, one should try to understand Kṛṣṇa, for thus one is immediately liberated from all pious and impious activities and their reactions.

TEXT 12

नाश्नतः पथ्यमेवान्नं व्याधयोऽभिभवन्ति हि ।
एवं नियमकृद्राजन् शनैः क्षेमाय कल्पते ॥१२॥

nāśnataḥ pathyam evānnaṁ
vyādhayo 'bhibhavanti hi
evaṁ niyamakṛd rājan
śanaiḥ kṣemāya kalpate

na—not; *aśnataḥ*—those who eat; *pathyam*—suitable; *eva*—indeed; *annam*—food; *vyādhayaḥ*—different types of disease; *abhibhavanti*—overcome; *hi*—indeed; *evam*—similarly; *niyama-kṛt*—one following regulative principles; *rājan*—O King; *śanaiḥ*—gradually; *kṣemāya*—for well-being; *kalpate*—becomes fit.

TRANSLATION

My dear King, if a diseased person eats the pure, uncontaminated food prescribed by a physician, he is gradually cured, and the infection of disease can no longer touch him. Similarly, if one follows the regulative principles of knowledge, he gradually progresses toward liberation from material contamination.

PURPORT

One is gradually purified if one cultivates knowledge, even through mental speculation, and strictly follows the regulative principles enjoined in the *śāstras* and explained in the next verse. Therefore the platform of *jñāna*, speculative knowledge, is better than the platform of *karma*, fruitive action. There is every chance of falling from the platform of *karma* to hellish conditions, but on the platform of *jñāna* one is saved from hellish life, although one is still not completely free from infection. The difficulty is that on the platform of *jñāna* one thinks that he has been liberated and has become Nārāyaṇa, or Bhagavān. This is another phase of ignorance.

ye 'nye 'ravindākṣa vimukta-māninas
tvayy asta-bhāvād aviśuddha-buddhayaḥ

āruhya kṛcchreṇa paraṁ padaṁ tataḥ
patanty adho 'nādṛta-yuṣmad-aṅghrayaḥ
(*Bhāg.* 10.2.32)

Because of ignorance, one speculatively thinks himself liberated from material contamination although actually he is not. Therefore even if one rises to *brahma-jñāna*, understanding of Brahman, one nevertheless falls down because of not taking shelter of the lotus feet of Kṛṣṇa. Nonetheless, *jñānīs* at least know what is sinful and what is pious, and they very cautiously act according to the injunctions of the *śāstras*.

TEXTS 13–14

तपसा ब्रह्मचर्येण शमेन च दमेन च ।
त्यागेन सत्यशौचाभ्यां यमेन नियमेन वा ॥१३॥
देहवाग्बुद्धिजं धीरा धर्मज्ञाः श्रद्धयान्विताः ।
क्षिपन्त्यघं महदपि वेणुगुल्ममिवानलः ॥१४॥

tapasā brahmacaryeṇa
śamena ca damena ca
tyāgena satya-śaucābhyāṁ
yamena niyamena vā

deha-vāg-buddhijaṁ dhīrā
dharmajñāḥ śraddhayānvitāḥ
kṣipanty aghaṁ mahad api
veṇu-gulmam ivānalaḥ

tapasā—by austerity or voluntary rejection of material enjoyment; *brahmacaryeṇa*—by celibacy (the first austerity); *śamena*—by controlling the mind; *ca*—and; *damena*—by fully controlling the senses; *ca*—also; *tyāgena*—by voluntarily giving charity to good causes; *satya*—by truthfulness; *śaucābhyām*—and by following regulative principles to keep oneself internally and externally clean; *yamena*—by avoiding cursing and violence; *niyamena*—by regularly chanting the holy name of the Lord; *vā*—and; *deha-vāk-buddhi-jam*—performed by the body, words and intelligence; *dhīrāḥ*—those who are sober; *dharma-jñāḥ*—fully imbued with knowledge of religious principles; *śraddhayā anvitāḥ*—endowed with faith; *kṣipanti*—destroy; *agham*—all kinds of sinful activities; *mahat api*—although very great and abominable; *veṇu-gulmam*—the dried creepers beneath a bamboo tree; *iva*—like; *analaḥ*—fire.

TRANSLATION

To concentrate the mind, one must observe a life of celibacy and not fall down. One must undergo the austerity of voluntarily giving up sense enjoyment. One must then control the mind and senses, give charity, be truthful, clean and nonviolent, follow the regulative principles and regularly chant the holy name of the Lord. Thus a sober and faithful person who knows the religious principles is temporarily purified of all sins performed with his body, words and mind. These sins are like the dried leaves of creepers beneath a bamboo tree, which may be burned by fire although their roots remain to grow again at the first opportunity.

PURPORT

Tapaḥ is explained in the *smṛti-śāstra* as follows: *manasaś cendriyāṇāṁ ca aikāgryaṁ paramaṁ tapaḥ.* "Complete control of the mind and senses and their complete concentration on one kind of activity is called *tapaḥ.*" Our Kṛṣṇa consciousness movement is teaching people how to concentrate the mind on devotional service. This is first-class *tapaḥ. Brahmacarya,* the life of celibacy, has eight aspects: one should not think of women, speak about sex life, dally with women, look lustfully at women, talk intimately with women or decide to engage in sexual intercourse, nor should one endeavor for sex life or engage in sex life. One should not even think of women or look at them, to say nothing of talking with them. This is called first-class *brahmacarya.* If a *brahmacārī* or *sannyāsī* talks with a woman in a secluded place, naturally there will be a possibility of sex life without anyone's knowledge. Therefore a complete *brahmacārī* practices just the opposite. If one is a perfect *brahmacārī,* he can very easily control the mind and senses, give charity, speak truthfully and so forth. To begin, however, one must control the tongue and the process of eating.

In the *bhakti-mārga*, the path of devotional service, one must strictly follow the regulative principles by first controlling the tongue (*sevon-mukhe hi jihvādau svayam eva sphuraty adaḥ*). The tongue (*jihvā*) can be controlled if one chants the Hare Kṛṣṇa *mahā-mantra*, does not speak of any subjects other than those concerning Kṛṣṇa and does not taste anything not offered to Kṛṣṇa. If one can control the tongue in this way, *brahmacarya* and other purifying processes will automatically follow. It will be explained in the next verse that the path of devotional service is completely perfect and is therefore superior to the path of fruitive activities and the path of knowledge. Quoting from the *Vedas*, Śrīla Vīrarāghava Ācārya explains that austerity involves observing fasts as fully as possible (*tapasānāśakena*). Śrīla Rūpa Gosvāmī has also advised that *atyāhāra*, too much eating, is an impediment to advancement in spiritual life. Also, in *Bhagavad-gītā* (6.17) Kṛṣṇa says:

yuktāhāra-vihārasya
yukta-ceṣṭasya karmasu
yukta-svapnāvabodhasya
yogo bhavati duḥkha-hā

"He who is temperate in his habits of eating, sleeping, working and recreation can mitigate all material pains by practicing the *yoga* system."

In text 14 the word *dhīrāḥ*, meaning "those who are undisturbed under all circumstances," is very significant. Kṛṣṇa tells Arjuna in *Bhagavad-gītā* (2.14):

mātrā-sparśās tu kaunteya
śītoṣṇa-sukha-duḥkha-dāḥ
āgamāpāyino 'nityās
tāṁs titikṣasva bhārata

"O son of Kuntī, the nonpermanent appearance of happiness and distress, and their disappearance in due course, are like the appearance and disappearance of winter and summer seasons. They arise from sense perception, O scion of Bharata, and one must learn to tolerate them without being disturbed." In material life there are many disturbances (*adhyātmika, adhidaivika* and *adhibhautika*). One who has learned to tolerate these disturbances under all circumstances is called *dhīra*.

TEXT 15

केचित्केवलया भक्त्या वासुदेवपरायणाः ।
अघं धुन्वन्ति कार्त्स्न्येन नीहारमिव भास्करः ॥१५॥

kecit kevalayā bhaktyā
vāsudeva-parāyaṇāḥ
aghaṁ dhunvanti kārtsnyena
nīhāram iva bhāskaraḥ

kecit—some people; *kevalayā bhaktyā*—by executing unalloyed devotional service; *vāsudeva*—to Lord Kṛṣṇa, the all-pervading Supreme Personality of Godhead; *parāyaṇāḥ*—completely attached (only to such service, without dependence on austerity, penance, cultivation of knowledge or pious activities); *agham*—all kinds of sinful reactions; *dhunvanti*—destroy; *kārtsnyena*—completely (with no possibility that sinful desires will revive); *nīhāram*—fog; *iva*—like; *bhāskaraḥ*—the sun.

TRANSLATION

Only a rare person who has adopted complete, unalloyed devotional service to Kṛṣṇa can uproot the weeds of sinful actions with no possibility that they will revive. He can do this simply by discharging devotional service, just as the sun can immediately dissipate fog by its rays.

PURPORT

In the previous verse Śukadeva Gosvāmī gave the example that the dried leaves of creepers beneath a bamboo tree may be completely burnt to ashes by a fire, although the creepers may sprout again because the root is still in the ground. Similarly, because the root of sinful desire is not destroyed in the heart of a person who is cultivating knowledge but who has no taste for devotional service, there is a possibility that his sinful desires will reappear. As stated in *Śrīmad-Bhāgavatam* (10.14.4):

śreyaḥ-sṛtiṁ bhaktim udasya te vibho
kliśyanti ye kevala-bodha-labdhaye

Speculators who undergo great labor to gain a meticulous understanding of the material world by distinguishing between sinful and pious activities, but who are not situated in devotional service, are prone to material activities. They may fall down and become implicated in fruitive activities. If one becomes attached to devotional service, however, his desires for material enjoyment are automatically vanquished without separate endeavor. *Bhaktiḥ pareśānubhavo viraktir anyatra ca:* if one is advanced in Kṛṣṇa consciousness, material activities, both sinful and pious, automatically become distasteful to him. That is the test of Kṛṣṇa consciousness. Both pious and impious activities are actually due to ignorance because a living entity, as an eternal servant of Kṛṣṇa, has no need to act for his personal sense gratification. Therefore as soon as one is reclaimed to the platform of devotional service, he relinquishes his attachment for pious and impious activities and is interested only in what will satisfy Kṛṣṇa. This process of *bhakti*, devotional service to Kṛṣṇa (*vāsudeva-parāyaṇa*), relieves one from the reactions of all activities.

Since Mahārāja Parīkṣit was a great devotee, the answers of his *guru*, Śukadeva Gosvāmī, concerning *karma-kāṇḍa* and *jñāna-kāṇḍa* could not satisfy him. Therefore Śukadeva Gosvāmī, knowing very well the heart of his disciple, explained the transcendental bliss of devotional service. The word *kecit*, which is used in this verse, means, "a few people but not all." Not everyone can become Kṛṣṇa conscious. As Kṛṣṇa explains in *Bhagavad-gītā* (7.3):

manuṣyāṇāṁ sahasreṣu
kaścid yatati siddhaye
yatatām api siddhānāṁ
kaścin māṁ vetti tattvataḥ

"Out of many thousands among men, one may endeavor for perfection, and of those who have achieved perfection, hardly one knows Me in truth." Practically no one understands Kṛṣṇa as He is, for Kṛṣṇa cannot be understood through pious activities or attainment of the most elevated speculative knowledge. Actually the highest knowledge consists of understanding Kṛṣṇa. Unintelligent men who do not understand Kṛṣṇa are grossly puffed up, thinking that they are liberated or have themselves become Kṛṣṇa or Nārāyaṇa. This is ignorance.

To indicate the purity of *bhakti*, devotional service, Śrīla Rūpa Gosvāmī says in *Bhakti-rasāmṛta-sindhu* (1.1.11):

anyābhilāṣitā-śūnyaṁ
jñāna-karmādy-anāvṛtam
ānukūlyena kṛṣṇānu-
śīlanaṁ bhaktir uttamā

"One should render transcendental loving service to the Supreme Lord Kṛṣṇa favorably and without desire for material profit or gain through fruitive activities or philosophical speculation. That is called pure devotional service." Śrīla Rūpa Gosvāmī further explains that *bhakti* is *kleśa-ghnī śubhadā*, which means if one takes to devotional service, all kinds of unnecessary labor and material distress cease entirely and one achieves all good fortune. *Bhakti* is so powerful that it is also said to be *mokṣa-laghutākṛt;* in other words, it minimizes the importance of liberation.

Nondevotees must undergo material hardships because they are prone to commit sinful fruitive activities. The desire to commit sinful actions continues in their hearts due to ignorance. These sinful actions are divided into three categories—*pātaka, mahā-pātaka* and *atipātaka*—and also into two divisions: *prārabdha* and *aprārabdha. Prārabdha* refers to sinful reactions from which one is suffering at the present, and *aprārabdha* refers to sources of potential suffering. When the seeds (*bīja*) of sinful reactions have not yet fructified, the reactions are called *aprārabdha.* These seeds of sinful action are unseen, but they are unlimited, and no one can trace when they were first planted. Because of *prārabdha*, sinful reactions that have already fructified, one is seen to have taken birth in a low family or to be suffering from other miseries.

When one takes to devotional service, however, all phases of sinful life, including *prārabdha, aprārabdha* and *bīja*, are vanquished. In *Śrīmad-Bhāgavatam* (11.14.19) Lord Kṛṣṇa tells Uddhava:

yathāgniḥ susamṛddhārciḥ
karoty edhāṁsi bhasmasāt
tathā mad-viṣayā bhaktir
uddhavaināṁsi kṛtsnaśaḥ

"My dear Uddhava, devotional service in relationship with Me is like a blazing fire that can burn to ashes all the fuel of sinful activities supplied to it." How devotional service vanquishes the reactions of sinful life is explained in *Śrīmad-Bhāgavatam* (3.33.6) in a verse spoken during Lord Kapiladeva's instructions to His mother, Devahūti. Devahūti said:

yan-nāmadheya-śravaṇānukīrtanād
yat-prahvaṇād yat-smaraṇād api kvacit
śvādo 'pi sadyaḥ savanāya kalpate
kutaḥ punas te bhagavan nu darśanāt

"My dear Lord, if even a person born in a family of dog-eaters hears and repeats the chanting of Your glories, offers respects to You and remembers You, he is immediately greater than a *brāhmaṇa* and is therefore eligible to perform sacrifices. Therefore, what is to be said of one who has seen You directly?"

In the *Padma Purāṇa* there is a statement that persons whose hearts are always attached to the devotional service of Lord Viṣṇu are immediately released from all the reactions of sinful life. These reactions generally exist in four phases. Some of them are ready to produce results immediately, some are in the form of seeds, some are unmanifested, and some are current. All such reactions are immediately nullified by devotional service. When devotional service is present in one's heart, desires to perform sinful activities have no place there. Sinful life is due to ignorance, which means forgetfulness of one's constitutional position as an eternal servant of God, but when one is fully Kṛṣṇa conscious he realizes that he is God's eternal servant.

In this regard, Śrīla Jīva Gosvāmī comments that *bhakti* may be divided into two divisions: (1) *santatā*, devotional service that continues incessantly with faith and love, and (2) *kādācitkī*, devotional service that does not continue incessantly but is sometimes awakened. Incessantly flowing devotional service (*santatā*) may also be divided into two categories: (1) service performed with slight attachment and (2) spontaneous devotional service. Intermittent devotional service (*kādācitkī*) may be divided into three categories: (1) *rāgābhāsamayī*, devotional service in which one is almost attached, (2) *rāgābhāsa-śūnya-svarūpa-bhūtā*, devotional service in which there is no spontaneous love but one likes the constitutional position of serving, and

(3) *ābhāsa-rūpā*, a slight glimpse of devotional service. As for atonement, if one has caught even a slight glimpse of devotional service, all needs to undergo *prāyaścitta*, atonement, are superseded. Therefore atonement is certainly unnecessary when one has achieved spontaneous love and, above that, attachment with love, which are signs of increasing advancement in *kādācitkī*. Even in the stage of *ābhāsa-rūpā bhakti*, all the reactions of sinful life are uprooted and vanquished. Śrīla Jīva Gosvāmī expresses the opinion that the word *kārtsnyena* means that even if one has a desire to commit sinful actions, the roots of that desire are vanquished merely by *ābhāsa-rūpā bhakti*. The example of *bhāskara*, the sun, is most appropriate. The *ābhāsa* feature of *bhakti* is compared to twilight, and the accumulation of one's sinful activities is compared to fog. Since fog does not spread throughout the sky, the sun need do no more than merely manifest its first rays, and the fog immediately disappears. Similarly, if one has even a slight relationship with devotional service, all the fog of his sinful life is immediately vanquished.

TEXT 16

न तथा ह्यघवान् राजन् पूयेत तपआदिभिः ।
यथा कृष्णार्पितप्राणस्तत्पुरुषनिषेवया ॥१६॥

na tathā hy aghavān rājan
pūyeta tapa-ādibhiḥ
yathā kṛṣṇārpita-prāṇas
tat-puruṣa-niṣevayā

na—not; *tathā*—so much; *hi*—certainly; *agha-vān*—a man full of sinful activities; *rājan*—O King; *pūyeta*—can become purified; *tapaḥ-ādibhiḥ*—by executing the principles of austerity, penance, *brahmacarya* and other purifying processes; *yathā*—as much as; *kṛṣṇa-arpita-prāṇaḥ*—the devotee whose life is fully Kṛṣṇa conscious; *tat-puruṣa-niṣevayā*—by engaging his life in the service of Kṛṣṇa's representative.

TRANSLATION

My dear King, if a sinful person engages in the service of a bona fide devotee of the Lord and thus learns how to dedicate his life

unto the lotus feet of Kṛṣṇa, he can be completely purified. One cannot be purified merely by undergoing austerity, penance, brahmacarya and the other methods of atonement I have previously described.

PURPORT

Tat-puruṣa refers to a preacher of Kṛṣṇa consciousness, such as the spiritual master. Śrīla Narottama dāsa Ṭhākura has said, *chāḍiyā vaiṣṇava-sevā nistāra pāyeche kebā:* "Without serving a bona fide spiritual master, an ideal Vaiṣṇava, who can be delivered from the clutches of *māyā?*" This idea is also expressed in many other places. *Śrīmad-Bhāgavatam* (5.5.2) says, *mahat-sevāṁ dvāram āhur vimukteḥ:* if one desires liberation from the clutches of *māyā*, one must associate with a pure devotee *mahātmā.* A *mahātmā* is one who engages twenty-four hours daily in the loving service of the Lord. As Kṛṣṇa says in *Bhagavad-gītā* (9.13):

mahātmānas tu māṁ pārtha
daivīṁ prakṛtim āśritāḥ
bhajanty ananya-manaso
jñātvā bhūtādim avyayam

"O son of Pṛthā, those who are not deluded, the great souls, are under the protection of the divine nature. They are fully engaged in devotional service because they know Me as the Supreme Personality of Godhead, original and inexhaustible." Thus the symptom of a *mahātmā* is that he has no engagement other than service to Kṛṣṇa. One must render service to a Vaiṣṇava in order to get freed from sinful reactions, revive one's original Kṛṣṇa consciousness and be trained in how to love Kṛṣṇa. This is the result of *mahātma-sevā.* Of course, if one engages in the service of a pure devotee, the reactions of one's sinful life are vanquished automatically. Devotional service is necessary not to drive away an insignificant stock of sins, but to awaken our dormant love for Kṛṣṇa. As fog is vanquished at the first glimpse of sunlight, one's sinful reactions are automatically vanquished as soon as one begins serving a pure devotee; no separate endeavor is required.

The word *kṛṣṇārpita-prāṇaḥ* refers to a devotee who dedicates his life to serving Kṛṣṇa, not to being saved from the path to hellish life. A devotee is *nārāyaṇa-parāyaṇa*, or *vāsudeva-parāyaṇa*, which means that the path of Vāsudeva, or the devotional path, is his life and soul. *Nārāyaṇa-parāḥ sarve na kutaścana bibhyati* (*Bhāg.* 6.17.28): such a devotee is not afraid of going anywhere. There is a path toward liberation in the higher planetary systems and a path toward the hellish planets, but a *nārāyaṇa-para* devotee is unafraid wherever he is sent; he simply wants to remember Kṛṣṇa, wherever he may be. Such a devotee is unconcerned with hell and heaven; he is simply attached to rendering service to Kṛṣṇa. When a devotee is put into hellish conditions, he accepts them as Kṛṣṇa's mercy: *tat te 'nukampāṁ susamīkṣamāṇaḥ* (*Bhāg.* 10.14.8). He does not protest, "Oh, I am such a great devotee of Kṛṣṇa. Why have I been put into this misery?" Instead he thinks, "This is Kṛṣṇa's mercy." Such an attitude is possible for a devotee who engages in the service of Kṛṣṇa's representative. This is the secret of success.

TEXT 17

सध्रीचीनो ह्ययं लोके पन्थाः क्षेमोऽकुतोभयः ।
सुशीलाः साधवो यत्र नारायणपरायणाः ॥१७॥

sadhrīcīno hy ayaṁ loke
panthāḥ kṣemo 'kuto-bhayaḥ
suśīlāḥ sādhavo yatra
nārāyaṇa-parāyaṇāḥ

sadhrīcīnaḥ—just appropriate; *hi*—certainly; *ayam*—this; *loke*—in the world; *panthāḥ*—path; *kṣemaḥ*—auspicious; *akutaḥ-bhayaḥ*—without fear; *su-śīlāḥ*—well-behaved; *sādhavaḥ*—saintly persons; *yatra*—wherein; *nārāyaṇa-parāyaṇāḥ*—those who have taken the path of Nārāyaṇa, devotional service, as their life and soul.

TRANSLATION

The path followed by pure devotees, who are well behaved and fully endowed with the best qualifications, is certainly the most auspicious path in this material world. It is free from fear, and it is authorized by the śāstras.

PURPORT

One should not think that the person who takes to *bhakti* is one who cannot perform the ritualistic ceremonies recommended in the *karma-kāṇḍa* section of the *Vedas* or is not sufficiently educated to speculate on spiritual subjects. Māyāvādīs generally allege that the *bhakti* path is for women and illiterates. This is a groundless accusation. The *bhakti* path is followed by the most learned scholars, such as the Gosvāmīs, Lord Caitanya Mahāprabhu and Rāmānujācārya. These are the actual followers of the *bhakti* path. Regardless of whether or not one is educated or aristocratic, one must follow in their footsteps. *Mahājano yena gataḥ sa panthāḥ:* one must follow the path of the *mahājanas*. The *mahājanas* are those who have taken to the path of devotional service (*suśīlāḥ sādhavo yatra nārāyaṇa-parāyaṇāḥ*), for these great personalities are the perfect persons. As stated in *Śrīmad-Bhāgavatam* (5.18.12):

yasyāsti bhaktir bhagavaty akiñcanā
sarvair guṇais tatra samāsate surāḥ

"One who has unflinching devotion to the Personality of Godhead has all the good qualities of the demigods." The less intelligent, however, misunderstand the *bhakti* path and therefore allege that it is for one who cannot execute ritualistic ceremonies or speculate. As confirmed here by the word *sadhrīcīnaḥ*, *bhakti* is the path that is appropriate, not the paths of *karma-kāṇḍa* and *jñāna-kāṇḍa*. Māyāvādīs may be *suśīlāḥ sādhavaḥ* (well-behaved saintly persons), but there is nevertheless some doubt about whether they are actually making progress, for they have not accepted the path of *bhakti*. On the other hand, those who follow the path of the *ācāryas* are *suśīlāḥ* and *sādhavaḥ*, but furthermore their path is *akuto-bhaya*, which means free from fear. One should fearlessly follow the twelve *mahājanas* and their line of disciplic succession and thus be liberated from the clutches of *māyā*.

TEXT 18

प्रायश्चित्तानि चीर्णानि नारायणपराङ्मुखम् ।
न निष्पुनन्ति राजेन्द्र सुराकुम्भमिवापगाः ॥१८॥

prāyaścittāni cīrṇāni
nārāyaṇa-parāṅmukham
na niṣpunanti rājendra
surā-kumbham ivāpagāḥ

prāyaścittāni—processes of atonement; *cīrṇāni*—very nicely performed; *nārāyaṇa-parāṅmukham*—a nondevotee; *na niṣpunanti*—cannot purify; *rājendra*—O King; *surā-kumbham*—a pot containing liquor; *iva*—like; *āpa-gāḥ*—the waters of the rivers.

TRANSLATION

My dear King, as a pot containing liquor cannot be purified even if washed in the waters of many rivers, nondevotees cannot be purified by processes of atonement even if they perform them very well.

PURPORT

To take advantage of the methods of atonement, one must be at least somewhat devoted; otherwise there is no chance of one's being purified. It is clear from this verse that even those who take advantage of *karma-kāṇḍa* and *jñāna-kāṇḍa*, but are not at least slightly devoted cannot be purified simply by following these other paths. The word *prāyaścittāni* is plural in number to indicate both *karma-kāṇḍa* and *jñāna-kāṇḍa.* Narottama dāsa Ṭhākura therefore says, *karma-kāṇḍa, jñāna-kāṇḍa, kevala viṣera bhāṇḍa.* Thus Narottama dāsa Ṭhākura compares the paths of *karma-kāṇḍa* and *jñāna-kāṇḍa* to pots of poison. Liquor and poison are in the same category. According to this verse from *Śrīmad-Bhāgavatam,* a person who has heard a good deal about the path of devotional service, but who is not attached to it, who is not Kṛṣṇa conscious, is like a pot of liquor. Such a person cannot be purified without at least a slight touch of devotional service.

TEXT 19

सकृन्मनः कृष्णपदारविन्दयो-
र्निवेशितं तद्गुणरागि यैरिह ।

न ते यमं पाशभृतश्च तद्भटान्
स्वप्नेऽपि पश्यन्ति हि चीर्णनिष्कृताः॥१९॥

sakṛn manaḥ kṛṣṇa-padāravindayor
niveśitaṁ tad-guṇa-rāgi yair iha
na te yamaṁ pāśa-bhṛtaś ca tad-bhaṭān
svapne 'pi paśyanti hi cīrṇa-niṣkṛtāḥ

sakṛt—once only; *manaḥ*—the mind; *kṛṣṇa-pada-aravindayoḥ*—unto the two lotus feet of Lord Kṛṣṇa; *niveśitam*—completely surrendered; *tat*—of Kṛṣṇa; *guṇa-rāgi*—which is somewhat attached to the qualities, name, fame and paraphernalia; *yaiḥ*—by whom; *iha*—in this world; *na*—not; *te*—such persons; *yamam*—Yamarāja, the superintendent of death; *pāśa-bhṛtaḥ*—those who carry ropes (to catch sinful persons); *ca*—and; *tat*—his; *bhaṭān*—order carriers; *svapne api*—even in dreams; *paśyanti*—see; *hi*—indeed; *cīrṇa-niṣkṛtāḥ*—who have performed the right type of atonement.

TRANSLATION

Although not having fully realized Kṛṣṇa, persons who have even once surrendered completely unto His lotus feet and who have become attracted to His name, form, qualities and pastimes are completely freed of all sinful reactions, for they have thus accepted the true method of atonement. Even in dreams, such surrendered souls do not see Yamarāja or his order carriers, who are equipped with ropes to bind the sinful.

PURPORT

Kṛṣṇa says in *Bhagavad-gītā* (18.66):

sarva-dharmān parityajya
māṁ ekaṁ śaraṇaṁ vraja
ahaṁ tvāṁ sarva-pāpebhyo
mokṣayiṣyāmi mā śucaḥ

"Abandon all varieties of religion and just surrender unto Me. I shall deliver you from all sinful reaction. Do not fear." This same principle is described here (*sakṛn manaḥ kṛṣṇa-padāravindayoḥ*). If by studying *Bhagavad-gītā* one decides to surrender to Kṛṣṇa, he is immediately freed from all sinful reactions. It is also significant that Śukadeva Gosvāmī, having several times repeated the words *vāsudeva-parāyaṇa* and *nārāyaṇa-parāyaṇa*, finally says *kṛṣṇa-padāravindayoḥ*. Thus he indicates that Kṛṣṇa is the origin of both Nārāyaṇa and Vāsudeva. Even though Nārāyaṇa and Vāsudeva are not different from Kṛṣṇa, simply by surrendering to Kṛṣṇa one fully surrenders to all His expansions, such as Nārāyaṇa, Vāsudeva and Govinda. As Kṛṣṇa says in *Bhagavad-gītā* (7.7), *mattaḥ parataraṁ nānyat:* "There is no truth superior to Me." There are many names and forms of the Supreme Personality of Godhead, but Kṛṣṇa is the supreme form (*kṛṣṇas tu bhagavān svayam*). Therefore Kṛṣṇa recommends to neophyte devotees that one should surrender unto Him only (*mām ekam*). Because neophyte devotees cannot understand what the forms of Nārāyaṇa, Vāsudeva and Govinda are, Kṛṣṇa directly says, *mām ekam*. Herein, this is also supported by the word *kṛṣṇa-padāravindayoḥ*. Nārāyaṇa does not speak personally, but Kṛṣṇa, or Vāsudeva, does, as in *Bhagavad-gītā* for example. Therefore, to follow the direction of *Bhagavad-gītā* means to surrender unto Kṛṣṇa, and to surrender in this way is the highest perfection of *bhakti-yoga*.

Parīkṣit Mahārāja had inquired from Śukadeva Gosvāmī how one can be saved from falling into the various conditions of hellish life. In this verse Śukadeva Gosvāmī answers that a soul who has surrendered to Kṛṣṇa certainly cannot go to *naraka*, hellish existence. To say nothing of going there, even in his dreams he does not see Yamarāja or his order carriers, who are able to take one there. In other words, if one wants to save himself from falling into *naraka*, hellish life, he should fully surrender to Kṛṣṇa. The word *sakṛt* is significant because it indicates that if one sincerely surrenders to Kṛṣṇa once, he is saved even if by chance he falls down by committing sinful activities. Therefore Kṛṣṇa says in *Bhagavad-gītā* (9.30):

api cet sudurācāro
bhajate mām ananya-bhāk

sādhur eva sa mantavyaḥ
samyag vyavasito hi saḥ

"Even if one commits the most abominable actions, if he is engaged in devotional service he is to be considered saintly because he is properly situated." If one never for a moment forgets Kṛṣṇa, he is safe even if by chance he falls down by committing sinful acts.

In the Second Chapter of *Bhagavad-gītā* (2.40) the Lord also says:

nehābhikrama-nāśo 'sti
pratyavāyo na vidyate
svalpam apy asya dharmasya
trāyate mahato bhayāt

"In this endeavor there is no loss or diminution, and a little advancement on this path can protect one from the most dangerous type of fear."

Elsewhere in the *Gītā* (6.40) the Lord says, *na hi kalyāṇa-kṛt kaścid durgatiṁ tāta gacchati:* "One who performs auspicious activity is never overcome by evil." The highest *kalyāṇa* (auspicious) activity is to surrender to Kṛṣṇa. That is the only path by which to save oneself from falling down into hellish life. Śrīla Prabodhānanda Sarasvatī has confirmed this as follows:

kaivalyaṁ narakāyate tri-daśa-pūr ākāśa-puṣpāyate
durdāntendriya-kāla-sarpa-paṭalī protkhāta-daṁṣṭrāyate
viśvaṁ pūrṇa-sukhāyate vidhi-mahendrādiś ca kīṭāyate
yat-kāruṇya-kaṭākṣa-vaibhavavatāṁ taṁ gauram eva stumaḥ

The sinful actions of one who has surrendered unto Kṛṣṇa are compared to a snake with its poison fangs removed (*protkhāta-daṁṣṭrāyate*). Such a snake is no longer to be feared. Of course, one should not commit sinful activities on the strength of having surrendered to Kṛṣṇa. However, even if one who has surrendered to Kṛṣṇa happens to do something sinful because of his former habits, such sinful actions no longer have a destructive effect. Therefore one should adhere to the lotus feet of Kṛṣṇa very tightly and serve Him under the direction of the spiritual master. Thus in all conditions one will be *akuto-bhaya,* free from fear.

TEXT 20

अत्र चोदाहरन्तीममितिहासं पुरातनम् ।
दूतानां विष्णुयमयोः संवादस्तं निबोध मे ॥२०॥

atra codāharantīmam
itihāsaṁ purātanam
dūtānāṁ viṣṇu-yamayoḥ
saṁvādas taṁ nibodha me

atra—in this connection; *ca*—also; *udāharanti*—they give as an example; *imam*—this; *itihāsam*—the history (of Ajāmila); *purātanam*—which is very old; *dūtānām*—of the order carriers; *viṣṇu*—of Lord Viṣṇu; *yamayoḥ*—and of Yamarāja; *saṁvādaḥ*—the discussion; *tam*—that; *nibodha*—try to understand; *me*—from me.

TRANSLATION

In this regard, learned scholars and saintly persons describe a very old historical incident involving a discussion between the order carriers of Lord Viṣṇu and those of Yamarāja. Please hear of this from me.

PURPORT

The *Purāṇas,* or old histories, are sometimes neglected by unintelligent men who consider their descriptions mythological. Actually, the descriptions of the *Purāṇas,* or the old histories of the universe, are factual, although not chronological. The *Purāṇas* record the chief incidents that have occurred over many millions of years, not only on this planet but also on other planets within the universe. Therefore all learned and realized Vedic scholars speak with references to the incidents in the *Purāṇas.* Śrīla Rūpa Gosvāmī accepts the *Purāṇas* to be as important as the *Vedas* themselves. Therefore in *Bhakti-rasāmṛta-sindhu* he quotes the following verse from the *Brahma-yāmala:*

śruti-smṛti-purāṇādi-
pañcarātra-vidhiṁ vinā
aikāntikī harer bhaktir
utpātāyaiva kalpate

"Devotional service of the Lord that ignores the authorized Vedic literatures like the *Upaniṣads, Purāṇas* and *Nārada-pañcarātra* is simply an unnecessary disturbance in society." A devotee of Kṛṣṇa must refer not only to the *Vedas,* but also to the *Purāṇas.* One should not foolishly consider the *Purāṇas* mythological. If they were mythological, Śukadeva Gosvāmī would not have taken the trouble to recite the old historical incidents concerning the life of Ajāmila. Now the history begins as follows.

TEXT 21

कान्यकुब्जे द्विजः कश्चिद्दासीपतिरजामिलः ।
नाम्ना नष्टसदाचारो दास्याः संसर्गदूषितः ॥२१॥

kānyakubje dvijaḥ kaścid
dāsī-patir ajāmilaḥ
nāmnā naṣṭa-sadācāro
dāsyāḥ saṁsarga-dūṣitaḥ

kānya-kubje—in the city of Kānyakubja (Kanauj, a town near Kanpur); *dvijaḥ—brāhmaṇa; kaścit*—some; *dāsī-patiḥ*—the husband of a low-class woman or prostitute; *ajāmilaḥ*—Ajāmila; *nāmnā*—by name; *naṣṭa-sat-ācāraḥ*—who lost all brahminical qualities; *dāsyāḥ*—of the prostitute or maidservant; *saṁsarga-dūṣitaḥ*—contaminated by the association.

TRANSLATION

In the city known as Kānyakubja there was a brāhmaṇa named Ajāmila who married a prostitute maidservant and lost all his brahminical qualities because of the association of that low-class woman.

PURPORT

The fault of illicit connection with women is that it makes one lose all brahminical qualities. In India there is still a class of servants, called *śūdras*, whose maidservant wives are called *śūdrāṇīs*. Sometimes people who are very lusty establish relationships with such maidservants and sweeping women, since in the higher statuses of society they cannot indulge in the habit of woman hunting, which is strictly prohibited by social convention. Ajāmila, a qualified *brāhmaṇa* youth, lost all his brahminical qualities because of his association with a prostitute, but he was ultimately saved because he had begun the process of *bhakti-yoga*. Therefore in the previous verse, Śukadeva Gosvāmī spoke of the person who has only once surrendered himself at the lotus feet of the Lord (*manaḥ kṛṣṇa-padāravindayoḥ*) or has just begun the *bhakti-yoga* process. *Bhakti-yoga* begins with *śravaṇaṁ kīrtanaṁ viṣṇoḥ*, hearing and chanting of Lord Viṣṇu's names, as in the *mahā-mantra*—Hare Kṛṣṇa, Hare Kṛṣṇa, Kṛṣṇa Kṛṣṇa, Hare Hare/ Hare Rāma, Hare Rāma, Rāma Rāma, Hare Hare. Chanting is the beginning of *bhakti-yoga*. Therefore Śrī Caitanya Mahāprabhu declares:

harer nāma harer nāma
harer nāmaiva kevalam
kalau nāsty eva nāsty eva
nāsty eva gatir anyathā

"In this age of quarrel and hypocrisy the only means of deliverance is chanting the holy name of the Lord. There is no other way. There is no other way. There is no other way." The process of chanting the holy name of the Lord is always superbly effective, but it is especially effective in this age of Kali. Its practical effectiveness will now be explained by Śukadeva Gosvāmī through the history of Ajāmila, who was freed from the hands of the Yamadūtas simply because of chanting the holy name of Nārāyaṇa. Parīkṣit Mahārāja's original question was how to be freed from falling down into hell or into the hands of the Yamadūtas. In reply, Śukadeva Gosvāmī is citing this old historical example to convince Parīkṣit Mahārāja of the potency of *bhakti-yoga*, which begins simply with the chanting of the Lord's name. All the great authorities of *bhakti-yoga* recommend the devotional process beginning with the chanting of the holy name of Kṛṣṇa (*tan-nāma-grahaṇādibhiḥ*).

TEXT 22

बन्द्यक्षैः कैतवैश्चौर्यैर्गर्हितां वृत्तिमास्थितः ।
बिभ्रत्कुटुम्बमशुचिर्यातयामास देहिनः ॥२२॥

bandy-akṣaiḥ kaitavaiś cauryair
garhitāṁ vṛttim āsthitaḥ
bibhrat kuṭumbam aśucir
yātayām āsa dehinaḥ

bandī-akṣaiḥ—by unnecessarily arresting someone; *kaitavaiḥ*—by cheating in gambling or throwing dice; *cauryaiḥ*—by committing theft; *garhitām*—condemned; *vṛttim*—professions; *āsthitaḥ*—who has undertaken (because of association with a prostitute); *bibhrat*—maintaining; *kuṭumbam*—his dependent wife and children; *aśuciḥ*—being most sinful; *yātayām āsa*—he gave trouble; *dehinaḥ*—to other living entities.

TRANSLATION

This fallen brāhmaṇa, Ajāmila, gave trouble to others by arresting them, by cheating them in gambling or by directly plundering them. This was the way he earned his livelihood and maintained his wife and children.

PURPORT

This verse indicates how degraded one becomes simply by indulging in illicit sex with a prostitute. Illicit sex is not possible with a chaste or aristocratic woman, but only with unchaste *śūdras.* The more society allows prostitution and illicit sex, the more impetus it gives to cheaters, thieves, plunderers, drunkards and gamblers. Therefore we first advise all the disciples in our Kṛṣṇa consciousness movement to avoid illicit sex, which is the beginning of all abominable life and which is followed by meat-eating, gambling and intoxication, one after another. Of course, restraint is very difficult, but it is quite possible if one fully surrenders to Kṛṣṇa, since all these abominable habits gradually become distasteful for a Kṛṣṇa conscious person. If illicit sex is allowed to increase in a society, however, the entire society will be condemned, for it will be full of rogues, thieves, cheaters and so forth.

TEXT 23

एवं निवसतस्तस्य लालयानस्य तत्सुतान् ।
कालोऽत्यगान्महान् राजन्नष्टाशीत्यायुषः समाः ॥ २३ ॥

evaṁ nivasatas tasya
lālayānasya tat-sutān
kālo 'tyagān mahān rājann
aṣṭāśītyāyuṣaḥ samāḥ

evam—in this way; *nivasataḥ*—living; *tasya*—of him (Ajāmila); *lālayānasya*—maintaining; *tat*—of her (the *śūdrāṇī*); *sutān*—sons; *kālaḥ*—time; *atyagāt*—passed away; *mahān*—a great amount; *rājan*—O King; *aṣṭāśītyā*—eighty-eight; *āyuṣaḥ*—of the duration of life; *samāḥ*—years.

TRANSLATION

My dear King, while he thus spent his time in abominable, sinful activities to maintain his family of many sons, eighty-eight years of his life passed by.

TEXT 24

तस्य प्रवयसः पुत्रा दश तेषां तु योऽवमः ।
बालो नारायणो नाम्ना पित्रोश्च दयितो भृशम् ॥२४॥

tasya pravayasaḥ putrā
daśa teṣāṁ tu yo 'vamaḥ
bālo nārāyaṇo nāmnā
pitroś ca dayito bhṛśam

tasya—of him (Ajāmila); *pravayasaḥ*—who was very old; *putrāḥ*—sons; *daśa*—ten; *teṣām*—of all of them; *tu*—but; *yaḥ*—the one who; *avamaḥ*—the youngest; *bālaḥ*—child; *nārāyaṇaḥ*—Nārāyaṇa; *nāmnā*—by name; *pitroḥ*—of the father and mother; *ca*—and; *dayitaḥ*—dear; *bhṛśam*—very.

TRANSLATION

That old man Ajāmila had ten sons, of whom the youngest was a baby named Nārāyaṇa. Since Nārāyaṇa was the youngest of all the sons, he was naturally very dear to both his father and his mother.

PURPORT

The word *pravayasaḥ* indicates Ajāmila's sinfulness because although he was eighty-eight years old, he had a very young child. According to Vedic culture, one should leave home as soon as he has reached fifty years of age; one should not live at home and go on producing children. Sex life is allowed for twenty-five years, between the ages of twenty-five and forty-five or, at the most, fifty. After that one should give up the habit of sex life and leave home as a *vānaprastha* and then properly take *sannyāsa*. Ajāmila, however, because of his association with a prostitute, lost all brahminical culture and became most sinful, even in his so-called household life.

TEXT 25

स बद्धहृदयस्तस्मिन्नर्भके कलभाषिणि ।
निरीक्षमाणस्तल्लीलां मुमुदे जरठो भृशम् ॥२५॥

sa baddha-hṛdayas tasminn
arbhake kala-bhāṣiṇi
nirīkṣamāṇas tal-līlāṁ
mumude jaraṭho bhṛśam

saḥ—he; *baddha-hṛdayaḥ*—being very attached; *tasmin*—to that; *arbhake*—small child; *kala-bhāṣiṇi*—who could not talk clearly but talked in broken language; *nirīkṣamāṇaḥ*—seeing; *tat*—his; *līlām*—

pastimes (such as walking and talking to his father); *mumude*—enjoyed; *jaraṭhaḥ*—the old man; *bhṛśam*—very much.

TRANSLATION

Because of the child's broken language and awkward movements, old Ajāmila was very much attached to him. He always took care of the child and enjoyed the child's activities.

PURPORT

Here it is clearly mentioned that the child Nārāyaṇa was so young that he could not even speak or walk properly. Since the old man was very attached to the child, he enjoyed the child's activities, and because the child's name was Nārāyaṇa, the old man always chanted the holy name of Nārāyaṇa. Although he was referring to the small child and not to the original Nārāyaṇa, the name of Nārāyaṇa is so powerful that even by chanting his son's name he was becoming purified (*harer nāma harer nāma harer nāmaiva kevalam*). Śrīla Rūpa Gosvāmī has therefore declared that if one's mind is somehow or other attracted by the holy name of Kṛṣṇa (*tasmāt kenāpy upāyena manaḥ kṛṣṇe niveśayet*), one is on the path of liberation. It is customary in Hindu society for parents to give their children names like Kṛṣṇadāsa, Govinda dāsa, Nārāyaṇa dāsa and Vṛndāvana dāsa. Thus they chant the names Kṛṣṇa, Govinda, Nārāyaṇa and Vṛndāvana and get the chance to be purified.

TEXT 26

भुञ्जानः प्रपिबन् खादन् बालकंस्नेहयन्त्रितः ।
भोजयन् पाययन्मूढो न वेदागतमन्तकम् ॥२६॥

bhuñjānaḥ prapiban khādan
bālakaṁ sneha-yantritaḥ
bhojayan pāyayan mūḍho
na vedāgatam antakam

bhuñjānaḥ—while eating; *prapiban*—while drinking; *khādan*—while chewing; *bālakam*—unto the child; *sneha-yantritaḥ*—being attached by affection; *bhojayan*—feeding; *pāyayan*—giving something to drink; *mūḍhaḥ*—the foolish man; *na*—not; *veda*—understood; *āgatam*—had arrived; *antakam*—death.

TRANSLATION

When Ajāmila chewed food and ate it, he called the child to chew and eat, and when he drank he called the child to drink also. Always engaged in taking care of the child and calling his name, Nārāyaṇa, Ajāmila could not understand that his own time was now exhausted and that death was upon him.

PURPORT

The Supreme Personality of Godhead is kind to the conditioned soul. Although this man completely forgot Nārāyaṇa, he was calling his child, saying, "Nārāyaṇa, please come eat this food. Nārāyaṇa, please come drink this milk." Somehow or other, therefore, he was attached to the name Nārāyaṇa. This is called *ajñāta-sukṛti.* Although calling for his son, he was unknowingly chanting the name of Nārāyaṇa, and the holy name of the Supreme Personality of Godhead is so transcendentally powerful that his chanting was being counted and recorded.

TEXT 27

स एवं वर्तमानोऽज्ञो मृत्युकाल उपस्थिते ।
मतिं चकार तनये बाले नारायणाह्वये ॥२७॥

sa evaṁ vartamāno 'jño
mṛtyu-kāla upasthite
matiṁ cakāra tanaye
bāle nārāyaṇāhvaye

saḥ—that Ajāmila; *evam*—thus; *vartamānaḥ*—living; *ajñaḥ*—foolish; *mṛtyu-kāle*—when the time of death; *upasthite*—arrived; *matim cakāra*—concentrated his mind; *tanaye*—on his son; *bāle*—the child; *nārāyaṇa-āhvaye*—whose name was Nārāyaṇa.

TRANSLATION

When the time of death arrived for the foolish Ajāmila, he began thinking exclusively of his son Nārāyaṇa.

PURPORT

In the Second Canto of the *Śrīmad-Bhāgavatam* (2.1.6) Śukadeva Gosvāmī says:

etāvān sāṅkhya-yogābhyāṁ
svadharma-pariniṣṭhayā
janma-lābhaḥ paraḥ puṁsām
ante nārāyaṇa-smṛtiḥ

"The highest perfection of human life, achieved either by complete knowledge of matter and spirit, by acquirement of mystic powers, or by perfect discharge of one's occupational duty, is to remember the Personality of Godhead at the end of life." Somehow or other, Ajāmila consciously or unconsciously chanted the name of Nārāyaṇa at the time of death (*ante nārāyaṇa-smṛtiḥ*), and therefore he became all-perfect simply by concentrating his mind on the name of Nārāyaṇa.

It may also be concluded that Ajāmila, who was the son of a *brāhmaṇa*, was accustomed to worshiping Nārāyaṇa in his youth because in every *brāhmaṇa's* house there is worship of the *nārāyaṇa-śilā*. This system is still present in India; in a rigid *brāhmaṇa's* house, there is *nārāyaṇa-sevā*, worship of Nārāyaṇa. Therefore, although the contaminated Ajāmila was calling for his son, by concentrating his mind on the holy name of Nārāyaṇa he remembered the Nārāyaṇa he had very faithfully worshiped in his youth.

In this regard Śrīla Śrīdhara Svāmī expressed his verdict as follows: *etac ca tad-upalālanādi-śrī-nārāyaṇa-namoccāraṇa-māhātmyena tad-bhaktir evābhūd iti siddhāntopayogitvenāpi draṣṭavyam.* "According to the *bhakti-siddhānta*, it is to be analyzed that because Ajāmila constantly chanted his son's name, Nārāyaṇa, he was elevated to the platform of *bhakti*, although he did not know it." Similarly, Śrīla Vīrarāghava Ācārya gives this opinion: *evaṁ vartamānaḥ sa dvijaḥ mṛtyu-kāle upasthite satyajño nārāyaṇākhye putra eva matiṁ cakāra matim āsak-*

tām akarod ity arthaḥ. "Although at the time of death he was chanting the name of his son, he nevertheless concentrated his mind upon the holy name of Nārāyaṇa." Śrīla Vijayadhvaja Tīrtha gives a similar opinion:

mṛtyu-kāle deha-viyoga-lakṣaṇa-kāle mṛtyoḥ sarva-doṣa-pāpa-harasya harer anugrahāt kāle datta-jñāna-lakṣaṇe upasthite hṛdi prakāśite tanaye pūrṇa-jñāne bāle pañca-varṣa-kalpe prādeśa-mātre nārāyaṇāhvaye mūrti-viśeṣe matiṁ smaraṇa-samarthaṁ cittaṁ cakāra bhaktyāsmarad ity arthaḥ.

Directly or indirectly, Ajāmila factually remembered Nārāyaṇa at the time of death (*ante nārāyaṇa-smṛtiḥ*).

TEXTS 28–29

स पाशहस्तांस्त्रीन्दृष्ट्वा पुरुषानतिदारुणान् ।
वक्रतुण्डानूर्ध्वरोम्ण आत्मानं नेतुमागतान् ॥२८॥
दूरे क्रीडनकासक्तं पुत्रं नारायणाह्वयम् ।
प्लावितेन स्वरेणोच्चैराजुहावाकुलेन्द्रियः ॥२९॥

sa pāśa-hastāṁs trīn dṛṣṭvā
puruṣān ati-dāruṇān
vakra-tuṇḍān ūrdhva-romṇa
ātmānaṁ netum āgatān

dūre krīḍanakāsaktaṁ
putraṁ nārāyaṇāhvayam
plāvitena svareṇoccair
ājuhāvākulendriyaḥ

saḥ—that person (Ajāmila); *pāśa-hastān*—having ropes in their hands; *trīn*—three; *dṛṣṭvā*—seeing; *puruṣān*—persons; *ati-dāruṇān*—very fearful in their features; *vakra-tuṇḍān*—with twisted faces; *ūrdhva-romṇaḥ*—with hair standing on the body; *ātmānam*—the self; *netum*—to take away; *āgatān*—arrived; *dūre*—a short distance away;

krīḍanaka-āsaktam—engaged in his play; *putram*—his child; *nārāyaṇa-āhvayam*—named Nārāyaṇa; *plāvitena*—with tearful eyes; *svareṇa*—with his voice; *uccaiḥ*—very loudly; *ājuhāva*—called; *ākula-indriyaḥ*—being full of anxiety.

TRANSLATION

Ajāmila then saw three awkward persons with deformed bodily features, fierce, twisted faces, and hair standing erect on their bodies. With ropes in their hands, they had come to take him away to the abode of Yamarāja. When he saw them he was extremely bewildered, and because of attachment to his child, who was playing a short distance away, Ajāmila began to call him loudly by his name. Thus with tears in his eyes he somehow or other chanted the holy name of Nārāyaṇa.

PURPORT

A person who performs sinful activities performs them with his body, mind and words. Therefore three order carriers from Yamarāja came to take Ajāmila to Yamarāja's abode. Fortunately, even though he was referring to his son, Ajāmila chanted the four syllables of the *hari-nāma* Nārāyaṇa, and therefore the order carriers of Nārāyaṇa, the Viṣṇudūtas, also immediately arrived there. Because Ajāmila was extremely afraid of the ropes of Yamarāja, he chanted the Lord's name with tearful eyes. Actually, however, he never meant to chant the holy name of Nārāyaṇa; he meant to call his son.

TEXT 30

निशम्य म्रियमाणस्य मुखतो हरिकीर्तनम् ।
भर्तुर्नाम महाराज पार्षदाः सहसापतन् ॥३०॥

niśamya mriyamāṇasya
mukhato hari-kīrtanam
bhartur nāma mahārāja
pārṣadāḥ sahasāpatan

niśamya—hearing; *mriyamāṇasya*—of the dying man; *mukhataḥ*—from the mouth; *hari-kīrtanam*—chanting of the holy name of the

Supreme Personality of Godhead; *bhartuḥ nāma*—the holy name of their master; *mahā-rāja*—O King; *pārṣadāḥ*—the order carriers of Viṣṇu; *sahasā*—immediately; *āpatan*—arrived.

TRANSLATION

My dear King, the order carriers of Viṣṇu, the Viṣṇudūtas, immediately arrived when they heard the holy name of their master from the mouth of the dying Ajāmila, who had certainly chanted without offense because he had chanted in complete anxiety.

PURPORT

Śrīla Viśvanātha Cakravartī Ṭhākura remarks, *hari-kīrtanaṁ niśamyāpatan, katham-bhūtasya bhartur nāma bruvataḥ:* the order carriers of Lord Viṣṇu came because Ajāmila had chanted the holy name of Nārāyaṇa. They did not consider why he was chanting. While chanting the name of Nārāyaṇa, Ajāmila was actually thinking of his son, but simply because they heard Ajāmila chanting the Lord's name, the order carriers of Lord Viṣṇu, the Viṣṇudūtas, immediately came for Ajāmila's protection. *Hari-kīrtana* is actually meant to glorify the holy name, form, pastimes and qualities of the Lord. Ajāmila, however, did not glorify the form, qualities or paraphernalia of the Lord; he simply chanted the holy name. Nevertheless, that chanting was sufficient to cleanse him of all sinful activities. As soon as the Viṣṇudūtas heard their master's name being chanted, they immediately came. In this regard Śrīla Vijayadhvaja Tīrtha remarks: *anena putra-sneham antareṇa prācīnādṛṣṭa-balād udbhūtayā bhaktyā bhagavan-nāma-saṅkīrtanaṁ kṛtam iti jñāyate.* "Ajāmila chanted the name of Nārāyaṇa because of his excessive attachment to his son. Nevertheless, because of his past good fortune in having rendered devotional service to Nārāyaṇa, he apparently chanted the holy name in full devotional service and without offenses."

TEXT 31

विकर्षतोऽन्तर्हृदयाद्दासीपतिमजामिलम् ।
यमप्रेष्यान् विष्णुदूता वारयामासुरोजसा ॥३१॥

vikarṣato 'ntar hṛdayād
dāsī-patim ajāmilam

yama-preṣyān viṣṇudūtā
vārayām āsur ojasā

vikarṣataḥ—snatching; *antaḥ hṛdayāt*—from within the heart; *dāsī-patim*—the husband of the prostitute; *ajāmilam*—Ajāmila; *yama-preṣyān*—the messengers of Yamarāja; *viṣṇu-dūtāḥ*—the order carriers of Lord Viṣṇu; *vārayām āsuḥ*—forbade; *ojasā*—with resounding voices.

TRANSLATION

The order carriers of Yamarāja were snatching the soul from the core of the heart of Ajāmila, the husband of the prostitute, but with resounding voices the messengers of Lord Viṣṇu, the Viṣṇudūtas, forbade them to do so.

PURPORT

A Vaiṣṇava, one who has surrendered to the lotus feet of Lord Viṣṇu, is always protected by Lord Viṣṇu's order carriers. Because Ajāmila had chanted the holy name of Nārāyaṇa, the Viṣṇudūtas not only immediately arrived on the spot but also at once ordered the Yamadūtas not to touch him. By speaking with resounding voices, the Viṣṇudūtas threatened to punish the Yamadūtas if they continued trying to snatch Ajāmila's soul from his heart. The order carriers of Yamarāja have jurisdiction over all sinful living entities, but the messengers of Lord Viṣṇu, the Viṣṇudūtas, are capable of punishing anyone, including Yamarāja, if he wrongs a Vaiṣṇava.

Materialistic scientists do not know where to find the soul within the body with their material instruments, but this verse clearly explains that the soul is within the core of the heart (*hṛdaya*); it is from the heart that the Yamadūtas were extracting the soul of Ajāmila. Similarly, we learn that the Supersoul, Lord Viṣṇu, is also situated within the heart (*īśvaraḥ sarva-bhūtānāṁ hṛd-deśe 'rjuna tiṣṭhati*). In the *Upaniṣads* it is said that the Supersoul and the individual soul are living in the same tree of the body as two friendly birds. The Supersoul is said to be friendly because the Supreme Personality of Godhead is so kind to the original soul that when the original soul transmigrates from one body to another, the Lord goes with him. Furthermore, according to the desire and *karma* of the individual soul, the Lord, through the agency of *māyā*, creates another body for him.

The heart of the body is a mechanical arrangement. As the Lord says in *Bhagavad-gītā* (18.61):

īśvaraḥ sarva-bhūtānāṁ
hṛd-deśe 'rjuna tiṣṭhati
bhrāmayan sarva-bhūtāni
yantrārūḍhāni māyayā

"The Supreme Lord is situated in everyone's heart, O Arjuna, and is directing the wanderings of all living entities, who are seated as on a machine, made of the material energy." *Yantra* means a machine, such as an automobile. The driver of the machine of the body is the individual soul, who is also its director or proprietor, but the supreme proprietor is the Supreme Personality of Godhead. One's body is created through the agency of *māyā* (*karmaṇā daiva-netreṇa*), and according to one's activities in this life, another vehicle is created, again under the supervision of *daivī māyā* (*daivī hy eṣā guṇamayī mama māyā duratyayā*). At the appropriate time, one's next body is immediately chosen, and both the individual soul and the Supersoul transfer to that particular bodily machine. This is the process of transmigration. During transmigration from one body to the next, the soul is taken away by the order carriers of Yamarāja and put into a particular type of hellish life (*naraka*) in order to become accustomed to the condition in which he will live in his next body.

TEXT 32

ऊचुर्निषेधितास्तांस्ते वैवस्वतपुरःसराः ।
के यूयं प्रतिषेद्धारो धर्मराजस्य शासनम् ॥३२॥

ūcur niṣedhitās tāṁs te
vaivasvata-puraḥsarāḥ
ke yūyaṁ pratiṣeddhāro
dharma-rājasya śāsanam

ūcuḥ—replied; *niṣedhitāḥ*—being forbidden; *tān*—to the order carriers of Lord Viṣṇu; *te*—they; *vaivasvata*—of Yamarāja; *puraḥ-sarāḥ*—the assistants or messengers; *ke*—who; *yūyam*—all of you; *pratiṣed-dhāraḥ*—who are opposing; *dharma-rājasya*—of the king of religious principles, Yamarāja; *śāsanam*—the ruling jurisdiction.

TRANSLATION

When the order carriers of Yamarāja, the son of the sun-god, were thus forbidden, they replied: Who are you, sirs, that have the audacity to challenge the jurisdiction of Yamarāja?

PURPORT

According to the sinful activities of Ajāmila, he was within the jurisdiction of Yamarāja, the supreme judge appointed to consider the sins of the living entities. When forbidden to touch Ajāmila, the order carriers of Yamarāja were surprised because they had never been hindered in the execution of their duty by anyone within the three worlds.

TEXT 33

कस्य वा कुत आयाताः कस्मादस्य निषेधथ ।
किं देवा उपदेवा या यूयं किं सिद्धसत्तमाः ॥३३॥

kasya vā kuta āyātāḥ
kasmād asya niṣedhatha
kiṁ devā upadevā yā
yūyaṁ kiṁ siddha-sattamāḥ

kasya—whose servants; *vā*—or; *kutaḥ*—from where; *āyātāḥ*—have you come; *kasmāt*—what is the reason; *asya*—(the taking away) of this Ajāmila; *niṣedhatha*—are you forbidding; *kim*—whether; *devāḥ*—demigods; *upadevāḥ*—sub-demigods; *yāḥ*—who; *yūyam*—all of you; *kim*—whether; *siddha-sat-tamāḥ*—the best of the perfect beings, the pure devotees.

TRANSLATION

Dear sirs, whose servants are you, where have you come from, and why are you forbidding us to touch the body of Ajāmila? Are

you demigods from the heavenly planets, are you sub-demigods, or are you the best of devotees?

PURPORT

The most significant word used in this verse is *siddha-sattamāḥ*, which means "the best of the perfect." In *Bhagavad-gītā* (7.3) it is said, *manuṣyāṇāṁ sahasreṣu kaścid yatati siddhaye:* out of millions of persons, one may try to become *siddha*, perfect—or, in other words, self-realized. A self-realized person knows that he is not the body but a spiritual soul (*ahaṁ brahmāsmi*). At the present moment practically everyone is unaware of this fact, but one who understands this has attained perfection and is therefore called *siddha*. When one understands that the soul is part and parcel of the supreme soul and one thus engages in the devotional service of the supreme soul, one becomes *siddha-sattama*. One is then eligible to live in the Vaikuṇṭha planets or Kṛṣṇaloka. The word *siddha-sattama*, therefore, refers to a liberated, pure devotee.

Since the Yamadūtas are servants of Yamarāja, who is also one of the *siddha-sattamas*, they knew that a *siddha-sattama* is above the demigods and sub-demigods and, indeed, above all the living entities within this material world. The Yamadūtas therefore inquired why the Viṣṇudūtas were present where a sinful man was going to die.

It should also be noted that Ajāmila was not yet dead, for the Yamadūtas were trying to snatch the soul from his heart. They could not take the soul, however, and therefore Ajāmila was not yet dead. This will be revealed in later verses. Ajāmila was simply in an unconscious state when the argument was in progress between the Yamadūtas and the Viṣṇudūtas. The conclusion of the argument was to be a decision regarding who would claim the soul of Ajāmila.

TEXTS 34–36

सर्वे पद्मपलाशाक्षाः पीतकौशेयवाससः ।
किरीटिनः कुण्डलिनो लसत्पुष्करमालिनः ॥३४॥
सर्वे च नूत्नवयसः सर्वे चारुचतुर्भुजाः ।
धनुर्निषङ्गासिगदाशङ्खचक्राम्बुजश्रियः ॥३५॥

दिशो वितिमिरालोकाः कुर्वन्तः स्वेन तेजसा ।
किमर्थं धर्मपालस्य किङ्करान्नो निषेधथ ॥३६॥

sarve padma-palāśākṣāḥ
pīta-kauśeya-vāsasaḥ
kirīṭinaḥ kuṇḍalino
lasat-puṣkara-mālinaḥ

sarve ca nūtna-vayasaḥ
sarve cāru-caturbhujāḥ
dhanur-niṣaṅgāsi-gadā-
śaṅkha-cakrāmbuja-śriyaḥ

diśo vitimirālokāḥ
kurvantaḥ svena tejasā
kim arthaṁ dharma-pālasya
kiṅkarān no niṣedhatha

sarve—all of you; *padma-palāśa-akṣāḥ*—with eyes like the petals of a lotus flower; *pīta*—yellow; *kauśeya*—silk; *vāsasaḥ*—wearing garments; *kirīṭinaḥ*—with helmets; *kuṇḍalinaḥ*—with earrings; *lasat*—glittering; *puṣkara-mālinaḥ*—with a garland of lotus flowers; *sarve*—all of you; *ca*—also; *nūtna-vayasaḥ*—very youthful; *sarve*—all of you; *cāru*—very beautiful; *catuḥ-bhujāḥ*—with four arms; *dhanuḥ*—bow; *niṣaṅga*—quiver of arrows; *asi*—sword; *gadā*—club; *śaṅkha*—conchshell; *cakra*—disc; *ambuja*—lotus flower; *śriyaḥ*—decorated with; *diśaḥ*—all directions; *vitimira*—without darkness; *ālokāḥ*—extraordinary illumination; *kurvantaḥ*—exhibiting; *svena*—by your own; *tejasā*—effulgence; *kim artham*—what is the purpose; *dharma-pālasya*—of Yamarāja, the maintainer of religious principles; *kiṅkarān*—servants; *naḥ*—us; *niṣedhatha*—you are forbidding.

TRANSLATION

The order carriers of Yamarāja said: Your eyes are just like the petals of lotus flowers. Dressed in yellow silken garments, deco-

rated with garlands of lotuses, and wearing very attractive helmets on your heads and earrings on your ears, you all appear fresh and youthful. Your four long arms are decorated with bows and quivers of arrows and with swords, clubs, conchshells, discs and lotus flowers. Your effulgence has dissipated the darkness of this place with extraordinary illumination. Now, sirs, why are you obstructing us?

PURPORT

Before even being introduced to a foreigner, one becomes acquainted with him through his dress, bodily features and behavior and can thus understand his position. Therefore when the Yamadūtas saw the Viṣṇudūtas for the first time, they were surprised. They said, "By your bodily features you appear to be very exalted gentlemen, and you have such celestial power that you have dissipated the darkness of this material world with your own effulgences. Why then should you endeavor to stop us from executing our duty?" It will be explained that the Yamadūtas, the order carriers of Yamarāja, mistakenly considered Ajāmila sinful. They did not know that although he was sinful throughout his entire life, he was purified by constantly chanting the holy name of Nārāyaṇa. In other words, unless one is a Vaiṣṇava, one cannot understand the activities of a Vaiṣṇava.

The dress and bodily features of the residents of Vaikuṇṭhaloka are properly described in these verses. The residents of Vaikuṇṭha, who are decorated with garlands and yellow silken garments, have four arms holding various weapons. Thus they conspicuously resemble Lord Viṣṇu. They have the same bodily features as Nārāyaṇa because they have attained the liberation of *sārūpya*, but they nevertheless act as servants. All the residents of Vaikuṇṭhaloka know perfectly well that their master is Nārāyaṇa, or Kṛṣṇa, and that they are all His servants. They are all self-realized souls who are *nitya-mukta*, everlastingly liberated. Although they could conceivably declare themselves Nārāyaṇa or Viṣṇu, they never do so; they always remain Kṛṣṇa conscious and serve the Lord faithfully. Such is the atmosphere of Vaikuṇṭhaloka. Similarly, one who learns the faithful service of Lord Kṛṣṇa through the Kṛṣṇa consciousness movement will always remain in Vaikuṇṭhaloka and have nothing to do with the material world.

TEXT 37

श्रीशुक उवाच
इत्युक्ते यमदूतैस्ते वासुदेवोक्तकारिणः ।
तान् प्रत्यूचुः प्रहस्येदं मेघनिर्ह्रादया गिरा ॥३७॥

śrī-śuka uvāca
ity ukte yamadūtais te
vāsudevokta-kāriṇaḥ
tān pratyūcuḥ prahasyedaṁ
megha-nirhrādayā girā

śrī-śukaḥ uvāca—Śrī Śukadeva Gosvāmī said; *iti*—thus; *ukte*—being addressed; *yamadūtaiḥ*—by the messengers of Yamarāja; *te*—they; *vāsudeva-ukta-kāriṇaḥ*—who are always ready to execute the orders of Lord Vāsudeva (being personal associates of Lord Viṣṇu who have obtained the liberation of *sālokya*); *tān*—unto them; *pratyūcuḥ*—replied; *prahasya*—smiling; *idam*—this; *megha-nirhrādayā*—resounding like a rumbling cloud; *girā*—with voices.

TRANSLATION

Śukadeva Gosvāmī continued: Being thus addressed by the messengers of Yamarāja, the servants of Vāsudeva smiled and spoke the following words in voices as deep as the sound of rumbling clouds.

PURPORT

The Yamadūtas were surprised to see that the Viṣṇudūtas, although polite, were hindering the rule of Yamarāja. Similarly, the Viṣṇudūtas were also surprised that the Yamadūtas, although claiming to be servants of Yamarāja, the supreme judge of religious principles, were unaware of the principles of religious action. Thus the Viṣṇudūtas smiled, thinking, "What is this nonsense they are speaking? If they are actually servants of Yamarāja they should know that Ajāmila is not a suitable candidate for them to carry off."

TEXT 38

श्रीविष्णुदूता ऊचुः
यूयं वै धर्मराजस्य यदि निर्देशकारिणः ।
ब्रूत धर्मस्य नस्तत्त्वं यच्चाधर्मस्य लक्षणम् ॥३८॥

śrī-viṣṇudūtā ūcuḥ
yūyaṁ vai dharma-rājasya
yadi nirdeśa-kāriṇaḥ
brūta dharmasya nas tattvaṁ
yac cādharmasya lakṣaṇam

śrī-viṣṇudūtāḥ ūcuḥ—the blessed messengers of Lord Viṣṇu spoke; *yūyam*—all of you; *vai*—indeed; *dharma-rājasya*—of King Yamarāja, who knows the religious principles; *yadi*—if; *nirdeśa-kāriṇaḥ*—order carriers; *brūta*—just speak; *dharmasya*—of religious principles; *naḥ*—unto us; *tattvam*—the truth; *yat*—that which; *ca*—also; *adharmasya*—of impious activities; *lakṣaṇam*—symptoms.

TRANSLATION

The blessed messengers of Lord Viṣṇu, the Viṣṇudūtas, said: If you are actually servants of Yamarāja, you must explain to us the meaning of religious principles and the symptoms of irreligion.

PURPORT

This inquiry by the Viṣṇudūtas to the Yamadūtas is most important. A servant must know the instructions of his master. The servants of Yamarāja claimed to be carrying out his orders, and therefore the Viṣṇudūtas very intelligently asked them to explain the symptoms of religious and irreligious principles. A Vaiṣṇava knows these principles perfectly well because he is well acquainted with the instructions of the Supreme Personality of Godhead. The Supreme Lord says, *sarva-dharmān parityajya mām ekaṁ śaraṇaṁ vraja:* "Give up all other varieties of religion and just surrender unto Me." Therefore surrender unto the Supreme Personality of Godhead is the actual principle of religion. Those who have surrendered to the principles of material nature instead of to

Kṛṣṇa are all impious, regardless of their material position. Unaware of the principles of religion, they do not surrender to Kṛṣṇa, and therefore they are considered sinful rascals, the lowest of men, and fools bereft of all knowledge. As Kṛṣṇa says in *Bhagavad-gītā* (7.15):

na māṁ duṣkṛtino mūḍhāḥ
prapadyante narādhamāḥ
māyayāpahṛta-jñānā
āsuraṁ bhāvam āśritāḥ

"Those miscreants who are grossly foolish, lowest among mankind, whose knowledge is stolen by illusion, and who partake of the atheistic nature of demons, do not surrender unto Me." One who has not surrendered to Kṛṣṇa does not know the true principle of religion; otherwise he would have surrendered.

The question posed by the Viṣṇudūtas was very suitable. One who represents someone else must fully know that person's mission. The devotees in the Kṛṣṇa consciousness movement must therefore be fully aware of the mission of Kṛṣṇa and Lord Caitanya; otherwise they will be considered foolish. All devotees, especially preachers, must know the philosophy of Kṛṣṇa consciousness so as not to be embarrassed and insulted when they preach.

TEXT 39

कथंस्विद् ध्रियते दण्डः किं वास्य स्थानमीप्सितम् ।
दण्ड्याः किं कारिणः सर्वे आहोस्वित्कतिचिन्नृणाम् ॥३९॥

kathaṁ svid dhriyate daṇḍaḥ
kiṁ vāsya sthānam īpsitam
daṇḍyāḥ kiṁ kāriṇaḥ sarve
āho svit katicin nṛṇām

katham svit—by which means; *dhriyate*—is imposed; *daṇḍaḥ*—punishment; *kim*—what; *vā*—or; *asya*—of this; *sthānam*—the place; *īpsitam*—desirable; *daṇḍyāḥ*—punishable; *kim*—whether; *kāriṇaḥ*—fruitive actors; *sarve*—all; *āho svit*—or whether; *katicit*—some; *nṛṇām*—of the human beings.

TRANSLATION

What is the process of punishing others? Who are the actual candidates for punishment? Are all karmīs engaged in fruitive activities punishable, or only some of them?

PURPORT

One who has the power to punish others should not punish everyone. There are innumerable living entities, the majority of whom are in the spiritual world and are *nitya-mukta,* everlastingly liberated. There is no question of judging these liberated living beings. Only a small fraction of the living entities, perhaps one fourth, are in the material world. And the major portion of the living entities in the material world—8,000,000 of the 8,400,000 forms of life—are lower than human beings. They are not punishable, for under the laws of material nature they are automatically evolving. Human beings, who are advanced in consciousness, are responsible, but not all of them are punishable. Those engaged in advanced pious activities are beyond punishment. Only those who engage in sinful activities are punishable. Therefore the Viṣṇudūtas particularly inquired about who is punishable and why Yamarāja has been designated to discriminate between who is punishable and who is not. How is one to be judged? What is the basic principle of authority? These are the questions raised by the Viṣṇudūtas.

TEXT 40

यमदूता ऊचुः

वेदप्रणिहितो धर्मो ह्यधर्मस्तद्विपर्ययः ।
वेदो नारायणः साक्षात्स्वयम्भूरिति शुश्रुम ॥४०॥

yamadūtā ūcuḥ
veda-praṇihito dharmo
hy adharmas tad-viparyayaḥ
vedo nārāyaṇaḥ sākṣāt
svayambhūr iti śuśruma

yamadūtāḥ ūcuḥ—the order carriers of Yamarāja said; *veda*—by the four *Vedas* (*Sāma, Yajur, Ṛg* and *Atharva*); *praṇihitaḥ*—prescribed;

dharmaḥ—religious principles; *hi*—indeed; *adharmaḥ*—irreligious principles; *tat-viparyayaḥ*—the opposite of that (that which is not supported by Vedic injunctions); *vedaḥ*—the *Vedas*, books of knowledge; *nārāyaṇaḥ sākṣāt*—directly the Supreme Personality of Godhead (being the words of Nārāyaṇa); *svayam-bhūḥ*—self-born, self-sufficient (appearing only from the breath of Nārāyaṇa and not being learned from anyone else); *iti*—thus; *śuśruma*—we have heard.

TRANSLATION

The Yamadūtas replied: That which is prescribed in the Vedas constitutes dharma, the religious principles, and the opposite of that is irreligion. The Vedas are directly the Supreme Personality of Godhead, Nārāyaṇa, and are self-born. This we have heard from Yamarāja.

PURPORT

The servants of Yamarāja replied quite properly. They did not manufacture principles of religion or irreligion. Instead, they explained what they had heard from the authority Yamarāja. *Mahājano yena gataḥ sa panthāḥ:* one should follow the *mahājana*, the authorized person. Yamarāja is one of twelve authorities. Therefore the servants of Yamarāja, the Yamadūtas, replied with perfect clarity when they said *śuśruma* ("we have heard"). The members of modern civilization manufacture defective religious principles through speculative concoction. This is not *dharma.* They do not know what is *dharma* and what is *adharma.* Therefore, as stated in the beginning of *Śrīmad-Bhāgavatam*, *dharmaḥ projjhita-kaitavo 'tra: dharma* not supported by the *Vedas* is rejected from *śrīmad-bhāgavata-dharma. Bhāgavata-dharma* comprises only that which is given by the Supreme Personality of Godhead. *Bhāgavata-dharma* is *sarva-dharmān parityajya mām ekaṁ śaraṇaṁ vraja:* one must accept the authority of the Supreme Personality of Godhead and surrender to Him and whatever He says. That is *dharma.* Arjuna, for example, thinking that violence was *adharma*, was declining to fight, but Kṛṣṇa urged him to fight. Arjuna abided by the orders of Kṛṣṇa, and therefore he is actually a *dharmī* because the order of Kṛṣṇa is *dharma.* Kṛṣṇa says in *Bhagavad-gītā* (15.15), *vedaiś ca sarvair aham eva vedyaḥ:* "The real purpose of *veda*, knowledge, is to know

Me." One who knows Kṛṣṇa perfectly is liberated. As Kṛṣṇa says in *Bhagavad-gītā* (4.9):

janma karma ca me divyam
evaṁ yo vetti tattvataḥ
tyaktvā dehaṁ punar janma
naiti mām eti so 'rjuna

"One who knows the transcendental nature of My appearance and activities does not, upon leaving the body, take his birth again in this material world, but attains My eternal abode, O Arjuna." One who understands Kṛṣṇa and abides by His order is a candidate for returning home, back to Godhead. It may be concluded that *dharma*, religion, refers to that which is ordered in the *Vedas*, and *adharma*, irreligion, refers to that which is not supported in the *Vedas*.

Dharma is not actually manufactured by Nārāyaṇa. As stated in the *Vedas*, *asya mahato bhūtasya niśvasitam etad yad ṛg-vedaḥ iti:* the injunctions of *dharma* emanate from the breathing of Nārāyaṇa, the supreme living entity. Nārāyaṇa exists eternally and breathes eternally, and therefore *dharma*, the injunctions of Nārāyaṇa, also exist eternally. Śrīla Madhvācārya, the original *ācārya* for those who belong to the Mādhva-Gauḍīya-sampradāya, says:

vedānāṁ prathamo vaktā
harir eva yato vibhuḥ
ato viṣṇv-ātmakā vedā
ity āhur veda-vādinaḥ

The transcendental words of the *Vedas* emanated from the mouth of the Supreme Personality of Godhead. Therefore the Vedic principles should be understood to be Vaiṣṇava principles because Viṣṇu is the origin of the *Vedas*. The *Vedas* contain nothing besides the instructions of Viṣṇu, and one who follows the Vedic principles is a Vaiṣṇava. The Vaiṣṇava is not a member of a manufactured community of this material world. A Vaiṣṇava is a real knower of the *Vedas*, as confirmed in *Bhagavad-gītā* (*vedaiś ca sarvair aham eva vedyaḥ*).

TEXT 41

येन स्वधाम्न्यमी भावा रजःसत्त्वतमोमयाः ।
गुणनामक्रियारूपैर्विभाव्यन्ते यथातथम् ॥४१॥

yena sva-dhāmny amī bhāvā
rajaḥ-sattva-tamomayāḥ
guṇa-nāma-kriyā-rūpair
vibhāvyante yathā-tatham

yena—by whom (Nārāyaṇa); *sva-dhāmni*—although in His own place, the spiritual world; *amī*—all these; *bhāvāḥ*—manifestations; *rajaḥ-sattva-tamaḥ-mayāḥ*—created by the three modes of material nature (passion, goodness and ignorance); *guṇa*—qualities; *nāma*—names; *kriyā*—activities; *rūpaiḥ*—and with forms; *vibhāvyante*—are variously manifested; *yathā-tatham*—exactly to the right point.

TRANSLATION

The supreme cause of all causes, Nārāyaṇa, is situated in His own abode in the spiritual world, but nevertheless He controls the entire cosmic manifestation according to the three modes of material nature—sattva-guṇa, rajo-guṇa and tamo-guṇa. In this way all living entities are awarded different qualities, different names [such as brāhmaṇa, kṣatriya and vaiśya], different duties according to the varṇāśrama institution, and different forms. Thus Nārāyaṇa is the cause of the entire cosmic manifestation.

PURPORT

The *Vedas* inform us:

na tasya kāryaṁ karaṇaṁ ca vidyate
na tat-samaś cābhyadhikaś ca dṛśyate
parāsya śaktir vividhaiva śrūyate
svābhāvikī jñāna-bala-kriyā ca
(*Śvetāśvatara Upaniṣad* 6.8)

Nārāyaṇa, the Supreme Personality of Godhead, is almighty, omnipotent. He has multifarious energies, and therefore He is able to remain in His own abode and without endeavor supervise and manipulate the entire cosmic manifestation through the interaction of the three modes of material nature—*sattva-guṇa, rajo-guṇa* and *tamo-guṇa.* These interactions create different forms, bodies, activities and changes, which all occur perfectly. Because the Lord is perfect, everything works as if He were directly supervising and taking part in it. Atheistic men, however, being covered by the three modes of material nature, cannot see Nārāyaṇa to be the supreme cause behind all activities. As Kṛṣṇa says in *Bhagavad-gītā* (7.13):

tribhir guṇamayair bhāvair
ebhiḥ sarvam idaṁ jagat
mohitaṁ nābhijānāti
mām ebhyaḥ param avyayam

"Deluded by the three modes, the whole world does not know Me, who am above the modes and inexhaustible." Because unintelligent agnostics are *mohita,* illusioned by the three modes of material nature, they cannot understand that Nārāyaṇa, Kṛṣṇa, is the supreme cause of all activities. As stated in *Brahma-saṁhitā* (5.1):

īśvaraḥ paramaḥ kṛṣṇaḥ
sac-cid-ānanda-vigrahaḥ
anādir ādir govindaḥ
sarva-kāraṇa-kāraṇam

"Kṛṣṇa, who is known as Govinda, is the supreme controller. He has an eternal, blissful, spiritual body. He is the origin of all. He has no other origin, for He is the prime cause of all causes."

TEXT 42

सूर्योऽग्निः खं मरुद्देवः सोमः सन्ध्याहनी दिशः ।
कं कुः स्वयं धर्म इति ह्येते दैह्यस्य साक्षिणः ॥४२॥

sūryo 'gniḥ khaṁ marud devaḥ
somaḥ sandhyāhanī diśaḥ

kaṁ kuḥ svayaṁ dharma iti
hy ete daihyasya sākṣiṇaḥ

sūryaḥ—the sun-god; *agniḥ*—the fire; *kham*—the sky; *marut*—the air; *devaḥ*—the demigods; *somaḥ*—the moon; *sandhyā*—evening; *ahanī*—the day and night; *diśaḥ*—the directions; *kam*—the water; *kuḥ*—the land; *svayam*—personally; *dharmaḥ*—Yamarāja or the Supersoul; *iti*—thus; *hi*—indeed; *ete*—all of these; *daihyasya*—of a living entity embodied in the material elements; *sākṣiṇaḥ*—witnesses.

TRANSLATION

The sun, fire, sky, air, demigods, moon, evening, day, night, directions, water, land and Supersoul Himself all witness the activities of the living entity.

PURPORT

The members of some religious sects, especially Christians, do not believe in the reactions of *karma.* We once had a discussion with a learned Christian professor who argued that although people are generally punished after the witnesses of their misdeeds are examined, where are the witnesses responsible for one's suffering the reactions of past *karma?* To such a person the answer by the Yamadūtas is given here. A conditioned soul thinks that he is working stealthily and that no one can see his sinful activities, but we can understand from the *śāstras* that there are many witnesses, including the sun, fire, sky, air, moon, demigods, evening, day, night, directions, water, land and the Supersoul Himself, who sits with the individual soul within his heart. Where is the dearth of witnesses? The witnesses and the Supreme Lord both exist, and therefore so many living entities are elevated to higher planetary systems or degraded to lower planetary systems, including the hellish planets. There are no discrepancies, for everything is arranged perfectly by the management of the Supreme God (*svābhāvikī jñāna-bala-kriyā ca*). The witnesses mentioned in this verse are also mentioned in other Vedic literatures:

āditya-candrāv anilo 'nalaś ca
dyaur bhūmir āpo hṛdayaṁ yamaś ca

ahaś ca rātriś ca ubhe ca sandhye
dharmo 'pi jānāti narasya vṛttam

TEXT 43

एतैरधर्मो विज्ञातः स्थानं दण्डस्य युज्यते ।
सर्वे कर्मानुरोधेन दण्डमर्हन्ति कारिणः ॥४३॥

etair adharmo vijñātaḥ
sthānaṁ daṇḍasya yujyate
sarve karmānurodhena
daṇḍam arhanti kāriṇaḥ

etaiḥ—by all these (witnesses, beginning from the sun-god); *adharmaḥ*—deviation from the regulative principles; *vijñātaḥ*—is known; *sthānam*—the proper place; *daṇḍasya*—of punishment; *yujyate*—is accepted as; *sarve*—all; *karma-anurodhena*—with consideration of the activities performed; *daṇḍam*—punishment; *arhanti*—deserve; *kāriṇaḥ*—the performers of sinful activities.

TRANSLATION

The candidates for punishment are those who are confirmed by these many witnesses to have deviated from their prescribed regulative duties. Everyone engaged in fruitive activities is suitable to be subjected to punishment according to his sinful acts.

TEXT 44

सम्भवन्ति हि भद्राणि विपरीतानि चानघाः ।
कारिणां गुणसङ्गोऽस्ति देहवान् न ह्यकर्मकृत् ॥४४॥

sambhavanti hi bhadrāṇi
viparītāni cānaghāḥ
kāriṇāṁ guṇa-saṅgo 'sti
dehavān na hy akarma-kṛt

sambhavanti—there are; *hi*—indeed; *bhadrāṇi*—auspicious, pious activities; *viparītāni*—just the opposite (inauspicious, sinful activities);

ca—also; *anaghāḥ*—O sinless inhabitants of Vaikuṇṭha; *kāriṇām*—of the fruitive workers; *guṇa-saṅgaḥ*—contamination of the three modes of nature; *asti*—there is; *deha-vān*—anyone who has accepted this material body; *na*—not; *hi*—indeed; *akarma-kṛt*—without performing action.

TRANSLATION

O inhabitants of Vaikuṇṭha, you are sinless, but those within this material world are all karmīs, whether acting piously or impiously. Both kinds of action are possible for them because they are contaminated by the three modes of nature and must act accordingly. One who has accepted a material body cannot be inactive, and sinful action is inevitable for one acting under the modes of material nature. Therefore all the living entities within this material world are punishable.

PURPORT

The difference between human beings and nonhuman beings is that a human is supposed to act according to the direction of the *Vedas*. Unfortunately, men manufacture their own ways of acting, without reference to the *Vedas*. Therefore all of them commit sinful actions and are punishable.

TEXT 45

येन यावान् यथाधर्मो धर्मो वेह समीहितः ।
स एव तत्फलं भुङ्क्ते तथा तावदमुत्र वै ॥४५॥

yena yāvān yathādharmo
dharmo veha samīhitaḥ
sa eva tat-phalaṁ bhuṅkte
tathā tāvad amutra vai

yena—by which person; *yāvān*—to which extent; *yathā*—in which manner; *adharmaḥ*—irreligious activities; *dharmaḥ*—religious activities; *vā*—or; *iha*—in this life; *samīhitaḥ*—performed; *saḥ*—that person; *eva*—indeed; *tat-phalam*—the particular result of that;

bhuṅkte—enjoys or suffers; *tathā*—in that way; *tāvat*—to that extent; *amutra*—in the next life; *vai*—indeed.

TRANSLATION

In proportion to the extent of one's religious or irreligious actions in this life, one must enjoy or suffer the corresponding reactions of his karma in the next.

PURPORT

As stated in *Bhagavad-gītā* (14.18):

ūrdhvaṁ gacchanti sattva-sthā
madhye tiṣṭhanti rājasāḥ
jaghanya-guṇa-vṛtti-sthā
adho gacchanti tāmasāḥ

Those who act in the mode of goodness are promoted to higher planetary systems to become demigods, those who act in an ordinary way and do not commit excessively sinful acts remain within this middle planetary system, and those who perform abominable sinful actions must go down to hellish life.

TEXT 46

यथेह देवप्रवरास्त्रैविध्यमुपलभ्यते ।
भूतेषु गुणवैचित्र्यात्तथान्यत्रानुमीयते ॥४६॥

yatheha deva-pravarās
trai-vidhyam upalabhyate
bhūteṣu guṇa-vaicitryāt
tathānyatrānumīyate

yathā—just as; *iha*—in this life; *deva-pravarāḥ*—O best of the demigods; *trai-vidhyam*—three kinds of attributes; *upalabhyate*—are achieved; *bhūteṣu*—among all living entities; *guṇa-vaicitryāt*—because of the diversity of the contamination by the three modes of nature; *tathā*—similarly; *anyatra*—in other places; *anumīyate*—it is inferred.

TRANSLATION

O best of the demigods, we can see three different varieties of life, which are due to the contamination of the three modes of nature. The living entities are thus known as peaceful, restless and foolish; as happy, unhappy or in-between; or as religious, irreligious and semireligious. We can deduce that in the next life these three kinds of material nature will similarly act.

PURPORT

The actions and reactions of the three modes of material nature are visible in this life. For example, some people are very happy, some are very distressed, and some are in mixed happiness and distress. This is the result of past association with the modes of material nature—goodness, passion and ignorance. Since these varieties are visible in this life, we may assume that the living entities, according to their association with the different modes of material nature, will be happy, distressed or between the two in their next lives also. Therefore the best policy is to disassociate oneself from the three modes of material nature and be always transcendental to their contamination. This is possible only when one fully engages in the devotional service of the Lord. As Kṛṣṇa confirms in *Bhagavad-gītā* (14.26):

māṁ ca yo 'vyabhicāreṇa
bhakti-yogena sevate
sa guṇān samatītyaitān
brahma-bhūyāya kalpate

"One who engages in full devotional service, who does not fall down under any circumstance, at once transcends the modes of material nature and thus comes to the spiritual platform." Unless one is fully absorbed in the service of the Lord, one is subject to the contamination of the three modes of material nature and must therefore suffer from distress or mixed happiness and distress.

TEXT 47

वर्तमानोऽन्ययोः कालो गुणाभिज्ञापको यथा ।
एवं जन्मान्ययोरेतद्धर्माधर्मनिदर्शनम् ॥४७॥

vartamāno 'nyayoḥ kālo
guṇābhijñāpako yathā
evaṁ janmānyayor etad
dharmādharma-nidarśanam

vartamānaḥ—the present; *anyayoḥ*—of the past and future; *kālaḥ*—time; *guṇa-abhijñāpakaḥ*—making known the qualities; *yathā*—just as; *evam*—thus; *janma*—birth; *anyayoḥ*—of the past and future births; *etat*—this; *dharma*—religious principles; *adharma*—irreligious principles; *nidarśanam*—indicating.

TRANSLATION

Just as springtime in the present indicates the nature of springtimes in the past and future, so this life of happiness, distress or a mixture of both gives evidence concerning the religious and irreligious activities of one's past and future lives.

PURPORT

Our past and future are not very difficult to understand, for time is under the contamination of the three modes of material nature. As soon as spring arrives, the usual exhibition of various types of fruits and flowers automatically becomes manifest, and therefore we may conclude that spring in the past was adorned with similar fruits and flowers and will be so adorned in the future also. Our repetition of birth and death is taking place within time, and according to the influence of the modes of nature, we are receiving various types of bodies and being subjected to various conditions.

TEXT 48

मनसैव पुरे देवः पूर्वरूपं विपश्यति ।
अनुमीमांसतेऽपूर्वं मनसा भगवानजः ॥४८॥

manasaiva pure devaḥ
pūrva-rūpaṁ vipaśyati
anumīmāṁsate 'pūrvaṁ
manasā bhagavān ajaḥ

manasā—by the mind; *eva*—indeed; *pure*—in his abode, or within everyone's heart like the Supersoul; *devaḥ*—the demigod Yamarāja (*dīvyatīti devaḥ*, one who is always brilliant and illuminated is called *deva*); *pūrva-rūpam*—the past religious or irreligious condition; *vipaśyati*—completely observes; *anumīmāṁsate*—he considers; *apūrvam*—the future condition; *manasā*—with his mind; *bhagavān*—who is omnipotent; *ajaḥ*—as good as Lord Brahmā.

TRANSLATION

The omnipotent Yamarāja is as good as Lord Brahmā, for while situated in his own abode or in everyone's heart like the Paramātmā, he mentally observes the past activities of a living entity and thus understands how the living entity will act in future lives.

PURPORT

One should not consider Yamarāja an ordinary living being. He is as good as Lord Brahmā. He has the complete cooperation of the Supreme Lord, who is situated in everyone's heart, and therefore, by the grace of the Supersoul, he can see the past, present and future of a living being from within. The word *anumīmāṁsate* means that he can decide in consultation with the Supersoul. *Anu* means "following." The actual decisions concerning the next lives of the living entities are made by the Supersoul, and they are carried out by Yamarāja.

TEXT 49

यथाज्ञस्तमसा युक्त उपास्ते व्यक्तमेव हि ।
न वेद पूर्वमपरं नष्टजन्मस्मृतिस्तथा ॥४९॥

yathājñas tamasā yukta
upāste vyaktam eva hi
na veda pūrvam aparaṁ
naṣṭa-janma-smṛtis tathā

yathā—just as; *ajñaḥ*—an ignorant living being; *tamasā*—in sleep; *yuktaḥ*—engaged; *upāste*—acts according to; *vyaktam*—a body manifested in a dream; *eva*—certainly; *hi*—indeed; *na veda*—does not know; *pūrvam*—the past body; *aparam*—the next body; *naṣṭa*—lost; *janma-smṛtiḥ*—the remembrance of birth; *tathā*—similarly.

TRANSLATION

As a sleeping person acts according to the body manifested in his dreams and accepts it to be himself, so one identifies with his present body, which he acquired because of his past religious or irreligious actions, and is unable to know his past or future lives.

PURPORT

A man engages in sinful activities because he does not know what he did in his past life to get his present materially conditioned body, which is subjected to the threefold miseries. As stated by Ṛṣabhadeva in *Śrīmad-Bhāgavatam* (5.5.4), *nūnaṁ pramattaḥ kurute vikarma:* a human being who is mad after sense gratification does not hesitate to act sinfully. *Yad indriya-prītaya āpṛṇoti:* he performs sinful actions simply for sense gratification. *Na sādhu manye:* this is not good. *Yata ātmano 'yam asann api kleśada āsa dehaḥ:* because of such sinful actions, one receives another body in which to suffer as he is suffering in his present body because of his past sinful activities.

It should be understood that a person who does not have Vedic knowledge always acts in ignorance of what he has done in the past, what he is doing at the present and how he will suffer in the future. He is completely in darkness. Therefore the Vedic injunction is, *tamasi mā:* "Don't remain in darkness." *Jyotir gama:* "Try to go to the light." The light or illumination is Vedic knowledge, which one can understand when he is elevated to the mode of goodness or when he transcends the mode of goodness by engaging in devotional service to the spiritual master and the Supreme Lord. This is described in the *Śvetāśvatara Upaniṣad* (6.23):

yasya deve parā bhaktir
yathā deve tathā gurau
tasyaite kathitā hy arthāḥ
prakāśante mahātmanaḥ

"Unto those great souls who have implicit faith in both the Lord and the spiritual master, all the imports of Vedic knowledge are automatically revealed." The *Vedas* enjoin, *tad-vijñānārthaṁ sa gurum evābhigacchet:* one must approach a spiritual master who has full knowledge of the *Vedas* and be faithfully directed by him in order to become a devotee of the Lord. Then the knowledge of the *Vedas* will be revealed. When the Vedic knowledge is revealed, one need no longer remain in the darkness of material nature.

According to his association with the material modes of nature—goodness, passion and ignorance—a living entity gets a particular type of body. The example of one who associates with the mode of goodness is a qualified *brāhmaṇa.* Such a *brāhmaṇa* knows past, present and future because he consults the Vedic literature and sees through the eyes of *śāstra* (*śāstra-cakṣuḥ*). He can understand what his past life was, why he is in the present body, and how he can obtain liberation from the clutches of *māyā* and not accept another material body. This is all possible when one is situated in the mode of goodness. Generally, however, the living entities are engrossed in the modes of passion and ignorance.

In any case, one receives an inferior or superior body at the discretion of the Supreme Personality of Godhead, Paramātmā. As stated in the previous verse:

manasaiva pure devaḥ
pūrva-rūpaṁ vipaśyati
anumīmāṁsate 'pūrvaṁ
manasā bhagavān ajaḥ

Everything depends on *bhagavān,* or *ajaḥ,* the unborn. Why doesn't one please Bhagavān to receive a better body? The answer is *ajñas tamasā:* because of gross ignorance. One who is in complete darkness cannot know what his past life was or what his next life will be; he is simply interested in his present body. Even though he has a human body, a person in the mode of ignorance and interested only in his present body is like an animal, for an animal, being covered by ignorance, thinks that the ultimate goal of life and happiness is to eat as much as possible. A human being must be educated to understand his past life and how he can endeavor for a better life in the future. There is even a book, called *Bhṛgu-*

saṁhitā, which reveals information about one's past, present and future lives according to astrological calculations. Somehow or other one must be enlightened about his past, present and future. One who is interested only in his present body and who tries to enjoy his senses to the fullest extent is understood to be engrossed in the mode of ignorance. His future is very, very dark. Indeed, the future is always dark for one who is grossly covered by ignorance. Especially in this age, human society is covered by the mode of ignorance, and therefore everyone thinks his present body to be everything, without consideration of the past or future.

TEXT 50

पञ्चभिः कुरुते स्वार्थान् पञ्च वेदाथ पञ्चभिः ।
एकस्तु षोडशेन त्रीन् स्वयं सप्तदशोऽश्नुते ॥५०॥

pañcabhiḥ kurute svārthān
pañca vedātha pañcabhiḥ
ekas tu ṣoḍaśena trīn
svayaṁ saptadaśo 'śnute

pañcabhiḥ—with the five working senses (voice, arms, legs, anus and genitals); *kurute*—performs; *sva-arthān*—his desired interests; *pañca*—the five objects of the senses (sound, form, touch, aroma and taste); *veda*—knows; *atha*—thus; *pañcabhiḥ*—by the five senses of perception (hearing, seeing, smelling, tasting and feeling); *ekaḥ*—the one; *tu*—but; *ṣoḍaśena*—by these fifteen items and the mind; *trīn*—the three categories of experience (happiness, distress and a mixture of both); *svayam*—he, the living entity himself; *saptadaśaḥ*—the seventeenth item; *aśnute*—enjoys.

TRANSLATION

Above the five senses of perception, the five working senses and the five objects of the senses is the mind, which is the sixteenth element. Above the mind is the seventeenth element, the soul, the living being himself, who, in cooperation with the other sixteen, enjoys the material world alone. The living being enjoys three kinds of situations, namely happy, distressful and mixed.

PURPORT

Everyone engages in work with his hands, legs and other senses just to achieve a certain goal according to his concocted ideas. One tries to enjoy the five sense objects, namely form, sound, taste, aroma and touch, not knowing the actual goal of life, which is to satisfy the Supreme Lord. Because of disobeying the Supreme Lord, one is put into material conditions, and he then tries to improve his situation in a concocted way, not desiring to follow the instructions of the Supreme Personality of Godhead. Nevertheless, the Supreme Lord is so kind that He comes Himself to instruct the bewildered living entity how to act obediently and then gradually return home, back to Godhead, where he can attain an eternal, peaceful life of bliss and knowledge. The living entity has a body, which is a very complicated combination of the material elements, and with this body he struggles alone, as indicated in this verse by the words *ekas tu.* For example, if one is struggling in the ocean, he must swim through it alone. Although many other men and aquatics are swimming in the ocean, he must take care of himself because no one else will help him. Therefore this verse indicates that the seventeenth item, the soul, must work alone. Although he tries to create society, friendship and love, no one will be able to help him but Kṛṣṇa, the Supreme Lord. Therefore his only concern should be how to satisfy Kṛṣṇa. That is also what Kṛṣṇa wants (*sarva-dharmān parityajya mām ekaṁ śaraṇaṁ vraja*). People bewildered by material conditions try to be united, but although they strive for unity among men and nations, all their attempts are futile. Everyone must struggle alone for existence with the many elements of nature. Therefore one's only hope, as Kṛṣṇa advises, is to surrender to Him, for He can help one become free from the ocean of nescience. Śrī Caitanya Mahāprabhu therefore prayed:

ayi nanda-tanuja kiṅkaraṁ
patitaṁ māṁ viṣame bhavāmbudhau
kṛpayā tava pāda-paṅkaja-
sthita-dhūlī-sadṛśaṁ vicintaya

"O Kṛṣṇa, beloved son of Nanda Mahārāja, I am Your eternal servant, but somehow or other I have fallen into this ocean of nescience, and although I am struggling very hard, there is no way I can save myself. If

You kindly pick me up and fix me as one of the particles of dust at Your lotus feet, that will save me."

In a similar way, Bhaktivinoda Ṭhākura sang:

anādi karama-phale, paḍi' bhavārṇava-jale,
taribāre nā dekhi upāya

"My dear Lord, I cannot remember when I somehow or other fell into this ocean of nescience, and now I can find no way to rescue myself." We should remember that everyone is responsible for his own life. If an individual becomes a pure devotee of Kṛṣṇa, he is then delivered from the ocean of nescience.

TEXT 51

तदेतत् षोडशकलं लिङ्गं शक्तित्रयं महत् ।
धत्तेऽनुसंसृतिं पुंसि हर्षशोकभयार्तिदाम् ॥५१॥

tad etat ṣoḍaśa-kalaṁ
liṅgaṁ śakti-trayaṁ mahat
dhatte 'nusaṁsṛtiṁ puṁsi
harṣa-śoka-bhayārtidām

tat—therefore; *etat*—this; *ṣoḍaśa-kalam*—made of sixteen parts (namely the ten senses, the mind and the five sense objects); *liṅgam*—the subtle body; *śakti-trayam*—the effect of the three modes of material nature; *mahat*—insurmountable; *dhatte*—gives; *anusaṁsṛtim*—almost perpetual rotation and transmigration in different types of bodies; *puṁsi*—unto the living entity; *harṣa*—jubilation; *śoka*—lamentation; *bhaya*—fear; *ārti*—misery; *dām*—which gives.

TRANSLATION

The subtle body is endowed with sixteen parts—the five knowledge-acquiring senses, the five working senses, the five objects of sense gratification, and the mind. This subtle body is an effect of the three modes of material nature. It is composed of insurmountably strong desires, and therefore it causes the living entity

to transmigrate from one body to another in human life, animal life and life as a demigod. When the living entity gets the body of a demigod, he is certainly very jubilant, when he gets a human body he is always in lamentation, and when he gets the body of an animal, he is always afraid. In all conditions, however, he is actually miserable. His miserable condition is called saṁsṛti, or transmigration in material life.

PURPORT

The sum and substance of material conditional life is explained in this verse. The living entity, the seventeenth element, is struggling alone, life after life. This struggle is called *saṁsṛti,* or material conditional life. In *Bhagavad-gītā* it is said that the force of material nature is insurmountably strong (*daivī hy eṣā guṇamayī mama māyā duratyayā*). Material nature harasses the living entity in different bodies, but if the living entity surrenders to the Supreme Personality of Godhead, he becomes free from this entanglement, as confirmed in *Bhagavad-gītā* (*mām eva ye prapadyante māyām etāṁ taranti te*). Thus his life becomes successful.

TEXT 52

देह्यज्ञोऽजितषड्वर्गो नेच्छन् कर्माणि कार्यते ।
कोशकार इवात्मानं कर्मणाच्छाद्य मुह्यति ॥५२॥

dehy ajño 'jita-ṣaḍ-vargo
necchan karmāṇi kāryate
kośakāra ivātmānaṁ
karmaṇācchādya muhyati

dehī—the embodied soul; *ajñaḥ*—without perfect knowledge; *ajita-ṣaṭ-vargaḥ*—who has not controlled the senses of perception and the mind; *na icchan*—without desiring; *karmāṇi*—activities for material benefit; *kāryate*—is caused to perform; *kośakāraḥ*—the silkworm; *iva*—like; *ātmānam*—himself; *karmaṇā*—by fruitive activities; *ācchādya*—covering; *muhyati*—becomes bewildered.

TRANSLATION

The foolish embodied living entity, inept at controlling his senses and mind, is forced to act according to the influence of the modes of material nature, against his desires. He is like a silkworm that uses its own saliva to create a cocoon and then becomes trapped in it, with no possibility of getting out. The living entity traps himself in a network of his own fruitive activities and then can find no way to release himself. Thus he is always bewildered, and repeatedly he dies.

PURPORT

As already explained, the influence of the modes of nature is very strong. The living entity entangled in different types of fruitive activity is like a silkworm trapped in a cocoon. Getting free is very difficult unless he is helped by the Supreme Personality of Godhead.

TEXT 53

न हि कश्चित्क्षणमपि जातु तिष्ठत्यकर्मकृत् ।
कार्यते ह्यवशः कर्म गुणैः स्वाभाविकैर्बलात् ॥५३॥

na hi kaścit kṣaṇam api
jātu tiṣṭhaty akarma-kṛt
kāryate hy avaśaḥ karma
guṇaiḥ svābhāvikair balāt

na—not; *hi*—indeed; *kaścit*—anyone; *kṣaṇam api*—even for a moment; *jātu*—at any time; *tiṣṭhati*—remains; *akarma-kṛt*—without doing anything; *kāryate*—he is caused to perform; *hi*—indeed; *avaśaḥ*—automatically; *karma*—fruitive activities; *guṇaiḥ*—by the three modes of nature; *svābhāvikaiḥ*—which are produced by his own tendencies in previous lives; *balāt*—by force.

TRANSLATION

Not a single living entity can remain unengaged even for a moment. One must act by his natural tendency according to the

three modes of material nature because this natural tendency forcibly makes him work in a particular way.

PURPORT

The *svābhāvika*, or one's natural tendency, is the most important factor in action. One's natural tendency is to serve because a living entity is an eternal servant of God. The living entity wants to serve, but because of his forgetfulness of his relationship with the Supreme Lord, he serves under the modes of material nature and manufactures various modes of service, such as socialism, humanitarianism and altruism. However, one should be enlightened in the tenets of *Bhagavad-gītā* and accept the instruction of the Supreme Personality of Godhead that one give up all natural tendencies for material service under different names and take to the service of the Lord. One's original natural tendency is to act in Kṛṣṇa consciousness because one's real nature is spiritual. The duty of a human being is to understand that since he is essentially spirit, he must abide by the spiritual tendency and not be carried away by material tendencies. Śrīla Bhaktivinoda Ṭhākura has therefore sung:

(miche) māyāra vaśe, yāccha bhese',
khāccha hābuḍubu, bhāi

"My dear brothers, you are being carried away by the waves of material energy and are suffering in many miserable conditions. Sometimes you are drowning in the waves of material nature, and sometimes you are tossed like a swimmer struggling in the ocean." As confirmed by Bhaktivinoda Ṭhākura, this tendency to be battered by the waves of *māyā* can be changed to one's original, natural tendency, which is spiritual, when the living entity comes to understand that he is eternally *kṛṣṇa-dāsa*, a servant of God, Kṛṣṇa.

(jīva) kṛṣṇa-dāsa, ei viśvāsa,
karle ta' āra duḥkha nāi

If instead of serving *māyā* under different names, one turns his service attitude toward the Supreme Lord, he is then safe, and there is no more difficulty. If one returns to his original, natural tendency in the human form of life by understanding the perfect knowledge given by Kṛṣṇa Himself in the Vedic literature, one's life is successful.

TEXT 54

लब्ध्वा निमित्तमव्यक्तं व्यक्ताव्यक्तं भवत्युत ।
यथायोनि यथाबीजं स्वभावेन बलीयसा ॥५४॥

labdhvā nimittam avyaktaṁ
vyaktāvyaktaṁ bhavaty uta
yathā-yoni yathā-bījaṁ
svabhāvena balīyasā

labdhvā—having gotten; *nimittam*—the cause; *avyaktam*—unseen or unknown to the person; *vyakta-avyaktam*—manifested and unmanifested, or the gross body and the subtle body; *bhavati*—come into being; *uta*—certainly; *yathā-yoni*—exactly like the mother; *yathā-bījam*—exactly like the father; *sva-bhāvena*—by the natural tendency; *balīyasā*—which is very powerful.

TRANSLATION

The fruitive activities a living being performs, whether pious or impious, are the unseen cause for the fulfillment of his desires. This unseen cause is the root for the living entity's different bodies. Because of his intense desire, the living entity takes birth in a particular family and receives a body which is either like that of his mother or like that of his father. The gross and subtle bodies are created according to his desire.

PURPORT

The gross body is a product of the subtle body. As stated in *Bhagavad-gītā* (8.6):

yaṁ yaṁ vāpi smaran bhāvaṁ
tyajaty ante kalevaram
taṁ tam evaiti kaunteya
sadā tad-bhāva-bhāvitaḥ

"Whatever state of being one remembers when he quits his body, that state he will attain without fail." The atmosphere of the subtle body at the time of death is created by the activities of the gross body. Thus the gross body acts during one's lifetime, and the subtle body acts at the time of death. The subtle body, which is called *liṅga,* the body of desire, is the background for the development of a particular type of gross body, which is either like that of one's mother or like that of one's father. According to the *Ṛg Veda,* if at the time of sex the secretions of the mother are more profuse than those of the father, the child will receive a female body, and if the secretions of the father are more profuse than those of the mother, the child will receive a male body. These are the subtle laws of nature, which act according to the desire of the living entity. If a human being is taught to change his subtle body by developing a consciousness of Kṛṣṇa, at the time of death the subtle body will create a gross body in which he will be a devotee of Kṛṣṇa, or if he is still more perfect, he will not take another material body but will immediately get a spiritual body and thus return home, back to Godhead. This is the process of the transmigration of the soul. Therefore instead of trying to unite human society through pacts for sense gratification that can never be achieved, it is clearly desirable to teach people how to become Kṛṣṇa conscious and return home, back to Godhead. This is true now and, indeed, at any time.

TEXT 55

एष प्रकृतिसङ्गेन पुरुषस्य विपर्ययः ।
आसीत् स एव नचिरादीशसङ्गाद्विलीयते ॥५५॥

eṣa prakṛti-saṅgena
puruṣasya viparyayaḥ
āsīt sa eva na cirād
īśa-saṅgād vilīyate

eṣaḥ—this; *prakṛti-saṅgena*—because of association with the material nature; *puruṣasya*—of the living entity; *viparyayaḥ*—a situation of forgetfulness or an awkward position; *āsīt*—came to be; *saḥ*—that position; *eva*—indeed; *na*—not; *cirāt*—taking a long time; *īśa-saṅgāt*—from the association of the Supreme Lord; *vilīyate*—is vanquished.

TRANSLATION

Since the living entity is associated with material nature, he is in an awkward position, but if in the human form of life he is taught how to associate with the Supreme Personality of Godhead or His devotee, this position can be overcome.

PURPORT

The word *prakṛti* means material nature, and *puruṣa* may also refer to the Supreme Personality of Godhead. If one wants to continue his association with *prakṛti*, the female energy of Kṛṣṇa, and be separated from Kṛṣṇa by the illusion that he is able to enjoy *prakṛti*, he must continue in his conditional life. If he changes his consciousness, however, and associates with the supreme, original person (*puruṣaṁ śāśvatam*), or with His associates, he can get out of the entanglement of material nature. As confirmed in *Bhagavad-gītā* (4.9), *janma karma ca me divyam evaṁ yo vetti tattvataḥ:* one must simply understand the Supreme Person, Kṛṣṇa, in terms of His form, name, activities and pastimes. This will keep one always in the association of Kṛṣṇa. *Tyaktvā dehaṁ punar janma naiti mām eti so 'rjuna:* thus after giving up his gross material body, one accepts not another gross body but a spiritual body in which to return home, back to Godhead. Thus one ends the tribulation caused by his association with the material energy. In summary, the living entity is an eternal servant of God, but he comes to the material world and is bound by material conditions because of his desire to lord it over matter. Liberation means giving up this false consciousness and reviving one's original service to the Lord. This return to one's original life is called *mukti*, as confirmed in *Śrīmad-Bhāgavatam* (*muktir hitvānyathā rūpaṁ svarūpeṇa vyavasthitiḥ*).

TEXTS 56–57

अयं हि श्रुतसम्पन्नः शीलवृत्तगुणालयः ।
धृतव्रतो मृदुर्दान्तः सत्यवाङ्मन्त्रविच्छुचिः ॥५६॥
गुर्वग्न्यतिथिवृद्धानां शुश्रूषुरनहङ्कृतः ।
सर्वभूतसुहृत्साधुर्मितवागनसूयकः ॥५७॥

ayaṁ hi śruta-sampannaḥ
śīla-vṛtta-guṇālayaḥ
dhṛta-vrato mṛdur dāntaḥ
satya-vāṅ mantra-vic chuciḥ

gurv-agny-atithi-vṛddhānāṁ
śuśrūṣur anahaṅkṛtaḥ
sarva-bhūta-suhṛt sādhur
mita-vāg anasūyakaḥ

ayam—this person (known as Ajāmila); *hi*—indeed; *śruta-sampannaḥ*—well educated in Vedic knowledge; *śīla*—of good character; *vṛtta*—good conduct; *guṇa*—and good qualities; *ālayaḥ*—the reservoir; *dhṛta-vrataḥ*—fixed in the execution of the Vedic injunctions; *mṛduḥ*—very mild; *dāntaḥ*—completely controlling the mind and senses; *satya-vāk*—always truthful; *mantra-vit*—knowing how to chant the Vedic hymns; *śuciḥ*—always very neat and clean; *guru*—the spiritual master; *agni*—the fire-god; *atithi*—guests; *vṛddhānām*—and of the old household members; *śuśrūṣuḥ*—very respectfully engaged in the service; *anahaṅkṛtaḥ*—without pride or false prestige; *sarva-bhūta-suhṛt*—friendly to all living entities; *sādhuḥ*—well behaved (no one could find any fault in his character); *mita-vāk*—talking with great care not to speak nonsense; *anasūyakaḥ*—not envious.

TRANSLATION

In the beginning this brāhmaṇa named Ajāmila studied all the Vedic literatures. He was a reservoir of good character, good conduct and good qualities. Firmly established in executing all the Vedic injunctions, he was very mild and gentle, and he kept his mind and senses under control. Furthermore, he was always truthful, he knew how to chant the Vedic mantras, and he was also very pure. Ajāmila was very respectful to his spiritual master, the fire-god, guests, and the elderly members of his household. Indeed, he was free from false prestige. He was upright, benevolent to all living entities, and well behaved. He would never speak nonsense or envy anyone.

PURPORT

The order carriers of Yamarāja, the Yamadūtas, are explaining the factual position of piety and impiety and how a living entity is entangled in this material world. Describing the history of Ajāmila's life, the Yamadūtas relate that in the beginning he was a learned scholar of the Vedic literature. He was well behaved, neat and clean, and very kind to everyone. In fact, he had all good qualities. In other words, he was like a perfect *brāhmaṇa.* A *brāhmaṇa* is expected to be perfectly pious, to follow all the regulative principles and to have all good qualities. The symptoms of piety are explained in these verses. Śrīla Vīrarāghava Ācārya comments that *dhṛta-vrata* means *dhṛtaṁ vrataṁ strī-saṅga-rāhityātmaka-brahmacarya-rūpam.* In other words, Ajāmila followed the rules and regulations of celibacy as a perfect *brahmacārī* and was very softhearted, truthful, clean and pure. How he fell down in spite of all these qualities and thus came to be threatened with punishment by Yamarāja will be described in the following verses.

TEXTS 58-60

एकदासौ वनं यातः पितृसन्देशकृद् द्विजः ।
आदाय तत आवृत्तः फलपुष्पसमित्कुशान् ॥५८॥
ददर्श कामिनं कञ्चिच्छूद्रं सह भुजिष्यया ।
पीत्वा च मधु मैरेयं मदाघूर्णितनेत्रया ॥५९॥
मत्तया विश्लथन्नीव्या व्यपेतं निरपत्रपम् ।
क्रीडन्तमनुगायन्तं हसन्तमनयान्तिके ॥६०॥

ekadāsau vanaṁ yātaḥ
pitṛ-sandeśa-kṛd dvijaḥ
ādāya tata āvṛttaḥ
phala-puṣpa-samit-kuśān

dadarśa kāminaṁ kañcic
chūdraṁ saha bhujiṣyayā

pītvā ca madhu maireyaṁ
madāghūrṇita-netrayā

mattayā viślathan-nīvyā
vyapetaṁ nirapatrapam
krīḍantam anugāyantaṁ
hasantam anayāntike

ekadā—once upon a time; *asau*—this Ajāmila; *vanam yātaḥ*—went to the forest; *pitṛ*—of his father; *sandeśa*—the order; *kṛt*—carrying out; *dvijaḥ*—the *brāhmaṇa; ādāya*—collecting; *tataḥ*—from the forest; *āvṛttaḥ*—returning; *phala-puṣpa*—fruits and flowers; *samit-kuśān*—two kinds of grass, known as *samit* and *kuśa; dadarśa*—saw; *kāminam*—very lusty; *kañcit*—someone; *śūdram*—a fourth-class man, a *śūdra; saha*—along with; *bhujiṣyayā*—an ordinary maidservant or prostitute; *pītvā*—after drinking; *ca*—also; *madhu*—nectar; *maireyam*—made of the *soma* flower; *mada*—by intoxication; *āghūrṇita*—moving; *netrayā*—her eyes; *mattayā*—intoxicated; *viślathat-nīvyā*—whose dress was slackened; *vyapetam*—fallen from proper behavior; *nirapatrapam*—without fear of public opinion; *krīḍantam*—engaged in enjoyment; *anugāyantam*—singing; *hasantam*—smiling; *anayā*—with her; *antike*—close by.

TRANSLATION

Once this brāhmaṇa Ajāmila, following the order of his father, went to the forest to collect fruit, flowers and two kinds of grass, called samit and kuśa. On the way home, he came upon a śūdra, a very lusty, fourth-class man, who was shamelessly embracing and kissing a prostitute. The śūdra was smiling, singing and enjoying as if this were proper behavior. Both the śūdra and the prostitute were drunk. The prostitute's eyes were rolling in intoxication, and her dress had become loose. Such was the condition in which Ajāmila saw them.

PURPORT

While traveling along the public way, Ajāmila came upon a fourth-class man and a prostitute, who are vividly described here. Drunkenness was sometimes manifest even in bygone ages, although not very frequently. In this age of Kali, however, such sin is to be seen everywhere, for people all over the world have become shameless. Long ago, when he saw the scene of the drunken *śūdra* and the prostitute, Ajāmila, who was a perfect *brahmacārī*, was affected. Nowadays such sin is visible in so many places, and we must consider the position of a *brahmacārī* student who sees such behavior. For such a *brahmacārī* to remain steady is very difficult unless he is extremely strong in following the regulative principles. Nevertheless, if one takes to Kṛṣṇa consciousness very seriously, he can withstand the provocation created by sin. In our Kṛṣṇa consciousness movement we prohibit illicit sex, intoxication, meat-eating and gambling. In Kali-yuga, a drunk, half-naked woman embracing a drunk man is a very common sight, especially in the Western countries, and restraining oneself after seeing such things is very difficult. Nevertheless, if by the grace of Kṛṣṇa one adheres to the regulative principles and chants the Hare Kṛṣṇa *mantra*, Kṛṣṇa will certainly protect him. Indeed, Kṛṣṇa says that His devotee is never vanquished (*kaunteya pratijānīhi na me bhaktaḥ praṇaśyati*). Therefore all the disciples practicing Kṛṣṇa consciousness should obediently follow the regulative principles and remain fixed in chanting the holy name of the Lord. Then there need be no fear. Otherwise one's position is very dangerous, especially in this Kali-yuga.

TEXT 61

दृष्ट्वा तां कामलिप्तेन बाहुना परिरम्भिताम् ।
जगाम हृच्छयवशं सहसैव विमोहितः ॥६१॥

dṛṣṭvā tāṁ kāma-liptena
bāhunā parirambhitām
jagāma hṛc-chaya-vaśaṁ
sahasaiva vimohitaḥ

dṛṣṭvā—by seeing; *tām*—her (the prostitute); *kāma-liptena*—decorated with turmeric to incite lusty desires; *bāhunā*—with the arm; *parirambhitām*—embraced; *jagāma*—went; *hṛt-śaya*—of lusty desires within the heart; *vaśam*—under the control; *sahasā*—suddenly; *eva*—indeed; *vimohitaḥ*—being illusioned.

TRANSLATION

The śūdra, his arm decorated with turmeric powder, was embracing the prostitute. When Ajāmila saw her, the dormant lusty desires in his heart awakened, and in illusion he fell under their control.

PURPORT

It is said that if one's body is smeared with turmeric, it attracts the lusty desires of the opposite sex. The word *kāma-liptena* indicates that the *śūdra* was decorated with turmeric smeared on his body.

TEXT 62

स्तम्भयन्नात्मनात्मानं यावत्सत्त्वं यथाश्रुतम् ।
न शशाक समाधातुं मनो मदनवेपितम् ॥६२॥

stambhayann ātmanātmānaṁ
yāvat sattvaṁ yathā-śrutam
na śaśāka samādhātuṁ
mano madana-vepitam

stambhayan—trying to control; *ātmanā*—by the intelligence; *ātmānam*—the mind; *yāvat sattvam*—as far as possible for him; *yathā-śrutam*—by remembering the instruction (of celibacy, *brahmacarya,* not even to see a woman); *na*—not; *śaśāka*—was able; *samādhātum*—to restrain; *manaḥ*—the mind; *madana-vepitam*—agitated by Cupid or lusty desire.

TRANSLATION

As far as possible he patiently tried to remember the instructions of the śāstras not even to see a woman. With the help of this knowledge and his intellect, he tried to control his lusty desires, but because of the force of Cupid within his heart, he failed to control his mind.

PURPORT

Unless one is very strong in knowledge, patience and proper bodily, mental and intellectual behavior, controlling one's lusty desires is extremely difficult. Thus after seeing a man embracing a young woman and practically doing everything required for sex life, even a fully qualified *brāhmaṇa*, as described above, could not control his lusty desires and restrain himself from pursuing them. Because of the force of materialistic life, to maintain self-control is extremely difficult unless one is specifically under the protection of the Supreme Personality of Godhead through devotional service.

TEXT 63

तन्निमित्तस्मरव्याजग्रहग्रस्तो विचेतनः ।
तामेव मनसा ध्यायन् स्वधर्माद्विरराम ह ॥६३॥

tan-nimitta-smara-vyāja-
graha-grasto vicetanaḥ
tām eva manasā dhyāyan
sva-dharmād virarāma ha

tat-nimitta—caused by the sight of her; *smara-vyāja*—taking advantage of his thinking of her always; *graha-grastaḥ*—being caught by an eclipse; *vicetanaḥ*—having completely forgotten his real position; *tām*—her; *eva*—certainly; *manasā*—by the mind; *dhyāyan*—meditating upon; *sva-dharmāt*—from the regulative principles executed by a *brāhmaṇa; virarāma ha*—he completely ceased.

TRANSLATION

In the same way that the sun and moon are eclipsed by a low planet, the brāhmaṇa lost all his good sense. Taking advantage of this situation, he always thought of the prostitute, and within a short time he took her as a servant in his house and abandoned all the regulative principles of a brāhmaṇa.

PURPORT

By speaking this verse, Śukadeva Gosvāmī wants to impress upon the mind of the reader that Ajāmila's exalted position as a *brāhmaṇa* was vanquished by his association with the prostitute, so much so that he forgot all his brahminical activities. Nevertheless, at the end of his life, by chanting the four syllables of the name Nārāyaṇa, he was saved from the gravest danger of falling down. *Svalpam apy asya dharmasya trāyate mahato bhayāt:* even a little devotional service can save one from the greatest danger. Devotional service, which begins with chanting of the holy name of the Lord, is so powerful that even if one falls down from the exalted position of a *brāhmaṇa* through sexual indulgence, he can be saved from all calamities if he somehow or other chants the holy name of the Lord. This is the extraordinary power of the Lord's holy name. Therefore in *Bhagavad-gītā* it is advised that one not forget the chanting of the holy name even for a moment (*satataṁ kīrtayanto māṁ yatantaś ca dṛḍha-vratāḥ*). There are so many dangers in this material world that one may fall down from an exalted position at any time. Yet if one keeps himself always pure and steady by chanting the Hare Kṛṣṇa *mahā-mantra*, he will be safe without a doubt.

TEXT 64

तामेव तोषयामास पित्र्येणार्थेन यावता ।
ग्राम्यैर्मनोरमैः कामैः प्रसीदेत यथा तथा ॥६४॥

tām eva toṣayām āsa
pitryeṇārthena yāvatā
grāmyair manoramaiḥ kāmaiḥ
prasīdeta yathā tathā

tām—her (the prostitute); *eva*—indeed; *toṣayām āsa*—he tried to please; *pitryeṇa*—he got from his father's hard labor; *arthena*—by the money; *yāvatā*—as long as possible; *grāmyaiḥ*—material; *manaḥ-ramaiḥ*—pleasing to her mind; *kāmaiḥ*—by presentations for sense enjoyment; *prasīdeta*—she would be satisfied; *yathā*—so that; *tathā*—in that way.

TRANSLATION

Thus Ajāmila began spending whatever money he had inherited from his father to satisfy the prostitute with various material presentations so that she would remain pleased with him. He gave up all his brahminical activities to satisfy the prostitute.

PURPORT

There are many instances throughout the world in which even a purified person, being attracted by a prostitute, spends all the money he has inherited. Prostitute hunting is so abominable that the desire for sex with a prostitute can ruin one's character, destroy one's exalted position and plunder all one's money. Therefore illicit sex is strictly prohibited. One should be satisfied with his married wife, for even a slight deviation will create havoc. A Kṛṣṇa conscious *gṛhastha* should always remember this. He should always be satisfied with one wife and be peaceful simply by chanting the Hare Kṛṣṇa *mantra.* Otherwise at any moment he may fall down from his good position, as exemplified in the case of Ajāmila.

TEXT 65

विप्रां स्वभार्यामप्रौढां कुले महति लम्भिताम् ।
विससर्जाचिरात्पापः स्वैरिण्यापाङ्गविद्धधीः ॥६५॥

viprāṁ sva-bhāryām apraudhāṁ
kule mahati lambhitām
visasarjācirāt pāpaḥ
svairiṇyāpāṅga-viddha-dhīḥ

viprām—the daughter of a *brāhmaṇa; sva-bhāryām*—his wife; *apraudhām*—not very old (youthful); *kule*—from a family; *mahati*—very respectable; *lambhitām*—married; *visasarja*—he gave up; *acirāt*—very soon; *pāpaḥ*—being sinful; *svairiṇyā*—of the prostitute; *apāṅga-viddha-dhīḥ*—his intelligence pierced by the lustful glance.

TRANSLATION

Because his intelligence was pierced by the lustful glance of the prostitute, the victimized brāhmaṇa Ajāmila engaged in sinful acts in her association. He even gave up the company of his very beautiful young wife, who came from a very respectable brāhmaṇa family.

PURPORT

Customarily everyone is eligible to inherit his father's property, and Ajāmila also inherited the money of his father. But what did he do with the money? Instead of engaging the money in the service of Kṛṣṇa, he engaged it in the service of a prostitute. Therefore he was condemned and was punishable by Yamarāja. How did this happen? He was victimized by the dangerous lustful glance of a prostitute.

TEXT 66

यतस्ततश्चोपनिन्ये न्यायतोऽन्यायतो धनम् ।
बभारास्याः कुटुम्बिन्याः कुटुम्बं मन्दधीरयम् ॥६६॥

yatas tataś copaninye
nyāyato 'nyāyato dhanam
babhārāsyāḥ kuṭumbinyāḥ
kuṭumbaṁ manda-dhīr ayam

yataḥ tataḥ—wherever possible, however possible; *ca*—and; *upaninye*—he got; *nyāyataḥ*—properly; *anyāyataḥ*—improperly; *dhanam*—money; *babhāra*—he maintained; *asyāḥ*—of her; *kuṭum-binyāḥ*—possessing many sons and daughters; *kuṭumbam*—the family; *manda-dhīḥ*—bereft of all intelligence; *ayam*—this person (Ajāmila).

TRANSLATION

Although born of a brāhmaṇa family, this rascal, bereft of intelligence because of the prostitute's association, earned money somehow or other, regardless of whether properly or improperly, and used it to maintain the prostitute's sons and daughters.

TEXT 67

यदसौ शास्त्रमुल्लङ्घ्य स्वैरचार्यतिगर्हितः ।
अवर्तत चिरं कालमघायुरशुचिर्मलात् ॥६७॥

yad asau śāstram ullaṅghya
svaira-cāry ati-garhitaḥ
avartata ciraṁ kālam
aghāyur aśucir malāt

yat—because; *asau*—this *brāhmaṇa; śāstram ullaṅghya*—transgressing the laws of *śāstra; svaira-cārī*—acting irresponsibly; *ati-garhitaḥ*—very much condemned; *avartata*—passed; *ciram kālam*—a long time; *agha-āyuḥ*—whose life was full of sinful activities; *aśuciḥ*—unclean; *malāt*—because of impurity.

TRANSLATION

This brāhmaṇa irresponsibly spent his long lifetime transgressing all the rules and regulations of the holy scripture, living extravagantly and eating food prepared by a prostitute. Therefore he is full of sins. He is unclean and is addicted to forbidden activities.

PURPORT

Food prepared by an unclean, sinful man or woman, especially a prostitute, is extremely infectious. Ajāmila ate such food, and therefore he was subject to be punished by Yamarāja.

TEXT 68

तत एनं दण्डपाणेः सकाशं कृतकिल्बिषम् ।
नेष्यामोऽकृतनिर्वेशं यत्र दण्डेन शुद्‌ध्यति ॥६८॥

tata enaṁ daṇḍa-pāṇeḥ
sakāśaṁ kṛta-kilbiṣam
neṣyāmo 'kṛta-nirveśaṁ
yatra daṇḍena śuddhyati

tataḥ—therefore; *enam*—him; *daṇḍa-pāṇeḥ*—of Yamarāja, who is authorized to punish; *sakāśam*—in the presence; *kṛta-kilbiṣam*—who has regularly committed all sinful activities; *neṣyāmaḥ*—we shall take; *akṛta-nirveśam*—who has not undergone atonement; *yatra*—where; *daṇḍena*—by punishment; *śuddhyati*—he will be purified.

TRANSLATION

This man Ajāmila did not undergo atonement. Therefore because of his sinful life, we must take him into the presence of

Yamarāja for punishment. There, according to the extent of his sinful acts, he will be punished and thus purified.

PURPORT

The Viṣṇudūtas had forbidden the Yamadūtas to take Ajāmila to Yamarāja, and therefore the Yamadūtas explained that taking such a man to Yamarāja was appropriate. Since Ajāmila had not undergone atonement for his sinful acts, he was to be taken to Yamarāja to be purified. When a man commits murder he becomes sinful, and therefore he also must be killed; otherwise after death he must suffer many sinful reactions. Similarly, punishment by Yamarāja is a process of purification for the most abominable sinful persons. Therefore the Yamadūtas requested the Viṣṇudūtas not to obstruct their taking Ajāmila to Yamarāja.

Thus end the Bhaktivedanta purports of the Sixth Canto, First Chapter, of the Śrīmad-Bhāgavatam, *entitled "The History of the Life of Ajāmila."*

CHAPTER TWO

Ajāmila Delivered by the Viṣṇudūtas

In this chapter the messengers from Vaikuṇṭha explain to the Yamadūtas the glories of chanting the holy name of the Lord. The Viṣṇudūtas said, "Now impious acts are being performed even in an assembly of devotees, for a person who is not punishable is going to be punished in the assembly of Yamarāja. The mass of people are helpless and must depend upon the government for their safety and security, but if the government takes advantage of this to harm the citizens, where will they go? We see perfectly that Ajāmila should not be punished, although you are attempting to take him to Yamarāja for punishment."

It was due to Ajāmila's glorifying the holy name of the Supreme Lord that he was not punishable. The Viṣṇudūtas explained this as follows: "Simply by once chanting the holy name of Nārāyaṇa, this *brāhmaṇa* has become free from the reactions of sinful life. Indeed, he has been freed not only from the sins of this life, but from the sins of many, many thousands of other lives. He has already undergone true atonement for all his sinful actions. If one atones according to the directions of the *śāstras*, one does not actually become free from sinful reactions, but if one chants the holy name of the Lord, even a glimpse of such chanting can immediately free one from all sins. Chanting the glories of the Lord's holy name awakens all good fortune. Therefore there is no doubt that Ajāmila, being completely free from all sinful reactions, should not be punished by Yamarāja."

As they were saying this, the Viṣṇudūtas released Ajāmila from the ropes of the Yamadūtas and left for their own abode. The *brāhmaṇa* Ajāmila, however, offered his respectful obeisances to the Viṣṇudūtas. He could understand how fortunate he was to have chanted the holy name of Nārāyaṇa at the end of his life. Indeed, he could realize the full significance of this good fortune. Having thoroughly understood the discussion between the Yamadūtas and the Viṣṇudūtas, he became a pure devotee of the Supreme Personality of Godhead. He lamented very much for how very sinful he had been, and he condemned himself again and again.

Finally, because of his association with the Viṣṇudūtas, Ajāmila, his original consciousness aroused, gave up everything and went to Hardwar, where he engaged in devotional service without deviation, always thinking of the Supreme Personality of Godhead. Thus the Viṣṇudūtas went there, seated him on a golden throne and took him away to Vaikuṇṭhaloka.

In summary, although the sinful Ajāmila meant to call his son, the holy name of Lord Nārāyaṇa, even though chanted in the preliminary stage, *nāmābhāsa*, was able to give him liberation. Therefore one who chants the holy name of the Lord with faith and devotion is certainly exalted. He is protected even in his material, conditional life.

TEXT 1

श्रीबादरायणिरुवाच

एवं ते भगवद्दूता यमदूताभिभाषितम् ।

उपधार्याथ तान् राजन् प्रत्याहुर्नयकोविदाः ॥ १ ॥

śrī-bādarāyaṇir uvāca
evaṁ te bhagavad-dūtā
yamadūtābhibhāṣitam
upadhāryātha tān rājan
pratyāhur naya-kovidāḥ

śrī-bādarāyaṇiḥ uvāca—Śukadeva Gosvāmī, the son of Vyāsadeva, said; *evam*—thus; *te*—they; *bhagavat-dūtāḥ*—the servants of Lord Viṣṇu; *yamadūta*—by the servants of Yamarāja; *abhibhāṣitam*—what was spoken; *upadhārya*—hearing; *atha*—then; *tān*—unto them; *rājan*—O King; *pratyāhuḥ*—replied properly; *naya-kovidāḥ*—being conversant in good arguments or good logic.

TRANSLATION

Śukadeva Gosvāmī said: My dear King, the servants of Lord Viṣṇu are always very expert in logic and arguments. After hearing the statements of the Yamadūtas, they replied as follows.

TEXT 2

श्रीविष्णुदूता ऊचुः
अहो कष्टं धर्मदृशामधर्मः स्पृशते सभाम् ।
यत्रादण्ड्येष्वपापेषु दण्डो यैर्ध्रियते वृथा ॥ २ ॥

śrī-viṣṇudūtā ūcuḥ
aho kaṣṭaṁ dharma-dṛśām
adharmaḥ spṛśate sabhām
yatrādaṇḍyeṣv apāpeṣu
daṇḍo yair dhriyate vṛthā

śrī-viṣṇudūtāḥ ūcuḥ—the Viṣṇudūtas said; *aho*—alas; *kaṣṭam*—how painful it is; *dharma-dṛśām*—of persons interested in maintaining religion; *adharmaḥ*—irreligion; *spṛśate*—is affecting; *sabhām*—the assembly; *yatra*—wherein; *adaṇḍyeṣu*—upon persons not to be punished; *apāpeṣu*—who are sinless; *daṇḍaḥ*—punishment; *yaiḥ*—by whom; *dhriyate*—is being allotted; *vṛthā*—unnecessarily.

TRANSLATION

The Viṣṇudūtas said: Alas, how painful it is that irreligion is being introduced into an assembly where religion should be maintained. Indeed, those in charge of maintaining the religious principles are needlessly punishing a sinless, unpunishable person.

PURPORT

The Viṣṇudūtas accused the Yamadūtas of violating the religious principles by attempting to drag Ajāmila to Yamarāja for punishment. Yamarāja is the officer appointed by the Supreme Personality of Godhead to judge religious and irreligious principles and to punish people who are irreligious. However, if completely sinless people are punished, the entire assembly of Yamarāja is contaminated. This principle applies not only in the assembly of Yamarāja, but throughout human society also.

In human society, properly maintaining religious principles is the duty of the king's court or the government. Unfortunately, in this *yuga*, Kali-yuga, the religious principles are tampered with, and the government cannot properly judge who is to be punished and who is not. It is said that in the Kali-yuga if one cannot spend money in court, one cannot get justice. Indeed, in courts of justice it is often found that magistrates are bribed for favorable judgments. Sometimes religious men who preach the Kṛṣṇa consciousness movement for the benefit of the entire populace are arrested and harassed by the police and courts. The Viṣṇudūtas, who are Vaiṣṇavas, lamented for these very regrettable facts. Because of their spiritual compassion for all the fallen souls, Vaiṣṇavas go out to preach according to the standard method of all religious principles, but unfortunately, because of the influence of Kali-yuga, Vaiṣṇavas who have dedicated their lives to preaching the glories of the Lord are sometimes harassed and punished by courts on false charges of disturbing the peace.

TEXT 3

प्रजानां पितरो ये च शास्तारः साधवः समाः ।
यदि स्यात्तेषु वैषम्यं कं यान्ति शरणं प्रजाः ॥ ३ ॥

prajānāṁ pitaro ye ca
śāstāraḥ sādhavaḥ samāḥ
yadi syāt teṣu vaiṣamyaṁ
kaṁ yānti śaraṇaṁ prajāḥ

prajānām—of the citizens; *pitaraḥ*—protectors, guardians (kings or government servants); *ye*—they who; *ca*—and; *śāstāraḥ*—give instructions concerning law and order; *sādhavaḥ*—endowed with all good qualities; *samāḥ*—equal to everyone; *yadi*—if; *syāt*—there is; *teṣu*—among them; *vaiṣamyam*—partiality; *kam*—what; *yānti*—will go to; *śaraṇam*—shelter; *prajāḥ*—the citizens.

TRANSLATION

A king or governmental official should be so well qualified that he acts as a father, maintainer and protector of the citizens because of affection and love. He should give the citizens good advice and instructions according to the standard scriptures and should be equal to everyone. Yamarāja does this, for he is the supreme master of justice, and so do those who follow in his footsteps.

However, if such persons become polluted and exhibit partiality by punishing an innocent, blameless person, where will the citizens go to take shelter for their maintenance and security?

PURPORT

The king, or in modern times the government, should act as the guardian of the citizens by teaching them the proper goal of life. The human form of life is especially meant for realization of one's self and one's relationship with the Supreme Personality of Godhead because this cannot be realized in animal life. The duty of the government, therefore, is to take charge of training all the citizens in such a way that by a gradual process they will be elevated to the spiritual platform and will realize the self and his relationship with God. This principle was followed by kings like Mahārāja Yudhiṣṭhira, Mahārāja Parīkṣit, Lord Rāmacandra, Mahārāja Ambarīṣa and Prahlāda Mahārāja. The leaders of the government must be very honest and religious because otherwise all the affairs of the state will suffer. Unfortunately, in the name of democracy, rogues and thieves are electing other rogues and thieves to the most important posts in the government. Recently this has been proven in America, where the President had to be condemned and dragged down from his post by the citizens. This is only one case, but there are many others. Because of the importance of the Kṛṣṇa consciousness movement, people should be Kṛṣṇa conscious and should not vote for anyone who is not Kṛṣṇa conscious. Then there will be actual peace and prosperity in the state. When a Vaiṣṇava sees mismanagement in the government, he feels great compassion in his heart and tries his best to purify the situation by spreading the Hare Kṛṣṇa movement.

TEXT 4

यद्यदाचरति श्रेयानितरस्तत्तदीहते ।
स यत्प्रमाणं कुरुते लोकस्तदनुवर्तते ॥ ४ ॥

yad yad ācarati śreyān
itaras tat tad īhate
sa yat pramāṇaṁ kurute
lokas tad anuvartate

yat yat—whatever; *ācarati*—executes; *śreyān*—a first-class man with full knowledge of religious principles; *itaraḥ*—the subordinate man; *tat tat*—that; *īhate*—performs; *saḥ*—he (the great man); *yat*—whatever; *pramāṇam*—as evidence or as the right thing; *kurute*—accepts; *lokaḥ*—the general public; *tat*—that; *anuvartate*—follows.

TRANSLATION

The mass of people follow the example of a leader in society and imitate his behavior. They accept as evidence whatever the leader accepts.

PURPORT

Although Ajāmila was not punishable, the Yamadūtas were insisting on taking him away to Yamarāja for punishment. This was *adharma*, contrary to religious principles. The Viṣṇudūtas feared that if such irreligious acts were allowed, the management of human society would be spoiled. In modern times, the Kṛṣṇa consciousness movement is trying to introduce the right principles of management for human society, but unfortunately the governments of Kali-yuga do not properly support the Hare Kṛṣṇa movement because they do not appreciate its valuable service. The Hare Kṛṣṇa movement is the right movement for ameliorating the fallen condition of human society, and therefore governments and public leaders in every part of the world should support this movement to completely rectify humanity's sinful condition.

TEXTS 5–6

यस्याङ्के शिर आधाय लोकः स्वपिति निर्वृतः ।
स्वयं धर्ममधर्मं वा न हि वेद यथा पशुः ॥ ५ ॥
स कथं न्यर्पितात्मानं कृतमैत्रमचेतनम् ।
विस्रम्भणीयो भूतानां सघृणो दोग्धुमर्हति ॥ ६ ॥

yasyāṅke śira ādhāya
lokaḥ svapiti nirvṛtaḥ
svayaṁ dharmam adharmaṁ vā
na hi veda yathā paśuḥ

sa kathaṁ nyarpitātmānaṁ
kṛta-maitram acetanam
visrambhaṇīyo bhūtānāṁ
saghṛṇo dogdhum arhati

yasya—of whom; *aṅke*—on the lap; *śiraḥ*—the head; *ādhāya*—placing; *lokaḥ*—the general mass of people; *svapiti*—sleep; *nirvṛtaḥ*—in peace; *svayam*—personally; *dharmam*—religious principles or the goal of life; *adharmam*—irreligious principles; *vā*—or; *na*—not; *hi*—indeed; *veda*—know; *yathā*—exactly like; *paśuḥ*—an animal; *saḥ*—such a person; *katham*—how; *nyarpita-ātmānam*—unto the living entity who has fully surrendered; *kṛta-maitram*—endowed with good faith and friendship; *acetanam*—with undeveloped consciousness, foolish; *visrambhaṇīyaḥ*—deserving to be the object of faith; *bhūtānām*—of the living entities; *sa-ghṛṇaḥ*—who has a soft heart for the good of all people; *dogdhum*—to give pain; *arhati*—is able.

TRANSLATION

People in general are not very advanced in knowledge by which to discriminate between religion and irreligion. The innocent, unenlightened citizen is like an ignorant animal sleeping in peace with its head on the lap of its master, faithfully believing in the master's protection. If a leader is actually kindhearted and deserves to be the object of a living entity's faith, how can he punish or kill a foolish person who has fully surrendered in good faith and friendship?

PURPORT

The Sanskrit word *viśvasta-ghāta* refers to one who breaks faith or causes a breach of trust. The mass of people should always feel security because of the government's protection. Therefore, how regrettable it is for the government itself to cause a breach of trust and put the citizens in difficulty for political reasons. We actually saw during the partition days in India that although Hindus and Muslims were living together peacefully, manipulation by politicians suddenly aroused feelings of hatred between them, and thus the Hindus and Muslims killed one another over politics. This is a sign of Kali-yuga. In this age, animals are kept nicely sheltered, completely confident that their masters will protect them, but unfortunately as soon as the animals are fat, they are immediately sent for slaughter. Such cruelty is condemned by Vaiṣṇavas like the Viṣṇudūtas. Indeed, the hellish conditions already described await the sinful men responsible for such suffering. One who betrays the confidence of a living entity who takes shelter of him in good faith, whether that living entity be a human being or an animal, is extremely sinful. Because such betrayals now go unpunished by the government, all of human society is terribly contaminated. The people of this age are therefore described as *mandāḥ sumanda-matayo manda-bhāgyā hy upadrutāḥ*. As a consequence of such sinfulness, men are condemned (*mandāḥ*), their intelligence is unclear (*sumanda-matayaḥ*), they are unfortunate (*manda-bhāgyāḥ*), and therefore they are always disturbed by many problems (*upadrutāḥ*). This is their situation in this life, and after death they are punished in hellish conditions.

TEXT 7

अयं हि कृतनिर्वेशो जन्मकोट्यंहसामपि ।
यद् व्याजहार विवशो नाम स्वस्त्ययनं हरेः ॥ ७ ॥

ayaṁ hi kṛta-nirveśo
janma-koṭy-aṁhasām api
yad vyājahāra vivaśo
nāma svasty-ayanaṁ hareḥ

ayam—this person (Ajāmila); *hi*—indeed; *kṛta-nirveśaḥ*—has undergone all kinds of atonement; *janma*—of births; *koṭi*—of millions; *aṁhasām*—for the sinful activities; *api*—even; *yat*—because; *vyājahāra*—he has chanted; *vivaśaḥ*—in a helpless condition; *nāma*—the holy name; *svasti-ayanam*—the means of liberation; *hareḥ*—of the Supreme Personality of Godhead.

TRANSLATION

Ajāmila has already atoned for all his sinful actions. Indeed, he has atoned not only for sins performed in one life but for those performed in millions of lives, for in a helpless condition he

chanted the holy name of Nārāyaṇa. Even though he did not chant purely, he chanted without offense, and therefore he is now pure and eligible for liberation.

PURPORT

The Yamadūtas had considered only the external situation of Ajāmila. Since he was extremely sinful throughout his life, they thought he should be taken to Yamarāja and did not know that he had become free from the reactions of all his sins. The Viṣṇudūtas therefore instructed that because he had chanted the four syllables of the name Nārāyaṇa at the time of his death, he was freed from all sinful reactions. In this regard Śrīla Viśvanātha Cakravartī Ṭhākura quotes the following verses from the *smṛti-śāstra:*

nāmno hi yāvatī śaktiḥ
pāpa-nirharaṇe hareḥ
tāvat kartuṁ na śaknoti
pātakaṁ pātakī naraḥ

"Simply by chanting one holy name of Hari, a sinful man can counteract the reactions to more sins than he is able to commit." (*Bṛhad-viṣṇu Purāṇa*)

avaśenāpi yan-nāmni
kīrtite sarva-pātakaiḥ
pumān vimucyate sadyaḥ
siṁha-trastair mṛgair iva

"If one chants the holy name of the Lord, even in a helpless condition or without desiring to do so, all the reactions of his sinful life depart, just as when a lion roars, all the small animals flee in fear." (*Garuḍa Purāṇa*)

sakṛd uccāritaṁ yena
harir ity akṣara-dvayam
baddha-parikaras tena
mokṣāya gamanaṁ prati

"By once chanting the holy name of the Lord, which consists of the two syllables *ha-ri*, one guarantees his path to liberation." (*Skanda Purāṇa*)

These are some of the reasons why the Viṣṇudūtas objected to the Yamadūtas' taking Ajāmila to the court of Yamarāja.

TEXT 8

एतेनैव ह्यघोनोऽस्य कृतं स्यादघनिष्कृतम् ।
यदा नारायणायेति जगाद चतुरक्षरम् ॥ ८ ॥

etenaiva hy aghono 'sya
kṛtaṁ syād agha-niṣkṛtam
yadā nārāyaṇāyeti
jagāda catur-akṣaram

etena—by this (chanting); *eva*—indeed; *hi*—certainly; *aghonaḥ*—who possesses sinful reactions; *asya*—of this (Ajāmila); *kṛtam*—performed; *syāt*—is; *agha*—of sins; *niṣkṛtam*—complete atonement; *yadā*—when; *nārāyaṇa*—O Nārāyaṇa (the name of his son); *āya*—please come; *iti*—thus; *jagāda*—he chanted; *catuḥ-akṣaram*—the four syllables (*nā-rā-ya-ṇa*).

TRANSLATION

The Viṣṇudūtas continued: Even previously, while eating and at other times, this Ajāmila would call his son, saying, "My dear Nārāyaṇa, please come here." Although calling the name of his son, he nevertheless uttered the four syllables nā-rā-ya-ṇa. Simply by chanting the name of Nārāyaṇa in this way, he sufficiently atoned for the sinful reactions of millions of lives.

PURPORT

Previously, when engaged in sinful activities to maintain his family, Ajāmila chanted the name of Nārāyaṇa without offenses. To chant the holy name of the Lord just to counteract one's sinful activities, or to commit sinful activities on the strength of chanting the holy name, is offensive (*nāmno balād yasya hi pāpa-buddhiḥ*). But although Ajāmila engaged in sinful activities, he never chanted the holy name of Nārāyaṇa to counteract them; he simply chanted the name Nārāyaṇa to call his son. Therefore his chanting was effective. Because of chanting the holy name of Nārāyaṇa in this way, he had already vanquished the accumulated sinful reactions of many, many lives. In the beginning he was pure, but although he later committed many sinful acts, he was offenseless because he did not chant the holy name of Nārāyaṇa to counteract them. One who always chants the holy name of the Lord without offenses is always pure. As confirmed in this verse Ajāmila was already sinless, and because he chanted the name of Nārāyaṇa he remained sinless. It did not matter that he was calling his son; the name itself was effective.

TEXTS 9–10

स्तेनः सुरापो मित्रध्रुग् ब्रह्महा गुरुतल्पगः ।
स्त्रीराजपितृगोहन्ता ये च पातकिनोऽपरे ॥ ९ ॥
सर्वेषामप्यघवतामिदमेव सुनिष्कृतम् ।
नामव्याहरणं विष्णोर्यतस्तद्विषया मतिः ॥१०॥

stenaḥ surā-po mitra-dhrug
brahma-hā guru-talpa-gaḥ
strī-rāja-pitṛ-go-hantā
ye ca pātakino 'pare

sarveṣām apy aghavatām
idam eva suniṣkṛtam
nāma-vyāharaṇaṁ viṣṇor
yatas tad-viṣayā matiḥ

stenaḥ—one who steals; *surā-paḥ*—a drunkard; *mitra-dhruk*—one who turns against a friend or relative; *brahma-hā*—one who kills a *brāhmaṇa; guru-talpa-gaḥ*—one who indulges in sex with the wife of his teacher or *guru; strī*—women; *rāja*—king; *pitṛ*—father; *go*—of cows; *hantā*—the killer; *ye*—those who; *ca*—also; *pātakinaḥ*—committed sinful activities; *apare*—many others; *sarveṣām*—of all of them; *api*—although; *agha-vatām*—persons who have committed many sins; *idam*—this; *eva*—certainly; *su-niṣkṛtam*—perfect atonement; *nāma-*

vyāharaṇam—chanting of the holy name; *viṣṇoḥ*—of Lord Viṣṇu; *yataḥ*—because of which; *tat-viṣayā*—on the person who chants the holy name; *matiḥ*—His attention.

TRANSLATION

The chanting of the holy name of Lord Viṣṇu is the best process of atonement for a thief of gold or other valuables, for a drunkard, for one who betrays a friend or relative, for one who kills a brāhmaṇa, or for one who indulges in sex with the wife of his guru or another superior. It is also the best method of atonement for one who murders women, the king or his father, for one who slaughters cows, and for all other sinful men. Simply by chanting the holy name of Lord Viṣṇu, such sinful persons may attract the attention of the Supreme Lord, who therefore considers, "Because this man has chanted My holy name, My duty is to give him protection."

TEXT 11

न निष्कृतैरुदितैर्ब्रह्मवादिभि-
स्तथा विशुद्ध्यत्यघवान् व्रतादिभिः ।
यथा हरेर्नामपदैरुदाहृतै-
स्तदुत्तमश्लोकगुणोपलम्भकम् ॥११॥

na niṣkṛtair uditair brahma-vādibhis
tathā viśuddhyaty aghavān vratādibhiḥ
yathā harer nāma-padair udāhṛtais
tad uttamaśloka-guṇopalambhakam

na—not; *niṣkṛtaiḥ*—by the processes of atonement; *uditaiḥ*—prescribed; *brahma-vādibhiḥ*—by learned scholars such as Manu; *tathā*—to that extent; *viśuddhyati*—becomes purified; *agha-vān*—a sinful man; *vrata-ādibhiḥ*—by observing the vows and regulative principles; *yathā*—as; *hareḥ*—of Lord Hari; *nāma-padaiḥ*—by the syllables of the holy name; *udāhṛtaiḥ*—chanted; *tat*—that; *uttamaśloka*—of the

Supreme Personality of Godhead; *guṇa*—of the transcendental qualities; *upalambhakam*—reminding one.

TRANSLATION

By following the Vedic ritualistic ceremonies or undergoing atonement, sinful men do not become as purified as by chanting once the holy name of Lord Hari. Although ritualistic atonement may free one from sinful reactions, it does not awaken devotional service, unlike the chanting of the Lord's names, which reminds one of the Lord's fame, qualities, attributes, pastimes and paraphernalia.

PURPORT

Śrīla Viśvanātha Cakravartī Ṭhākura comments that the chanting of the holy name of the Lord has special significance that distinguishes it from the Vedic ritualistic ceremonies of atonement for severe, more severe or most severe sinful actions. There are twenty types of religious scriptures called *dharma-śāstras*, beginning with the *Manu-saṁhitā* and *Parāśara-saṁhitā*, but herein it is stressed that although one may become free from the reactions of the most sinful activities by following the religious principles of these scriptures, this cannot promote a sinful man to the stage of loving service to the Lord. On the other hand, chanting the holy name of the Lord even once not only frees one immediately from the reactions of the greatest sins, but also raises one to the platform of rendering loving service to the Supreme Personality of Godhead, who is described as *uttamaśloka* because He is famous for His glorious activities. Thus one serves the Lord by remembering His form, His attributes and pastimes. Śrīla Viśvanātha Cakravartī Ṭhākura explains that this is all possible simply by chanting the Lord's holy name because of the Lord's omnipotence. What cannot be achieved through the performance of Vedic rituals can be easily achieved through the chanting of the Lord's holy name. To chant the holy name and dance in ecstasy is so easy and sublime that one can achieve all the benefits of spiritual life simply by following this process. Therefore Śrī Caitanya Mahāprabhu declares, *paraṁ vijayate śrī-kṛṣṇa-saṅkīrtanam:* "All glories to Śrī Kṛṣṇa *saṅkīrtana!*" The *saṅkīrtana* movement we have started offers the best process for becoming purified of all sinful reactions and coming immediately to the platform of spiritual life.

TEXT 12

नैकान्तिकं तद्धि कृतेऽपि निष्कृते
मनः पुनर्धावति चेदसत्पथे ।
तत्कर्मनिर्हारमभीप्सतां हरे-
र्गुणानुवादः खलु सत्त्वभावनः ॥१२॥

naikāntikaṁ tad dhi kṛte 'pi niṣkṛte
manaḥ punar dhāvati ced asat-pathe
tat karma-nirhāram abhīpsatāṁ harer
guṇānuvādaḥ khalu sattva-bhāvanaḥ

na—not; *aikāntikam*—absolutely cleansed; *tat*—the heart; *hi*—because; *kṛte*—very nicely performed; *api*—although; *niṣkṛte*—atonement; *manaḥ*—the mind; *punaḥ*—again; *dhāvati*—runs; *cet*—if; *asat-pathe*—on the path of material activities; *tat*—therefore; *karma-nirhāram*—cessation of the fruitive reactions of material activities; *abhīpsatām*—for those who seriously want; *hareḥ*—of the Supreme Personality of Godhead; *guṇa-anuvādaḥ*—constant chanting of the glories; *khalu*—indeed; *sattva-bhāvanaḥ*—actually purifying one's existence.

TRANSLATION

The ritualistic ceremonies of atonement recommended in the religious scriptures are insufficient to cleanse the heart absolutely because after atonement one's mind again runs toward material activities. Consequently, for one who wants liberation from the fruitive reactions of material activities, the chanting of the Hare Kṛṣṇa mantra, or glorification of the name, fame and pastimes of the Lord, is recommended as the most perfect process of atonement because such chanting eradicates the dirt from one's heart completely.

PURPORT

The statements in this verse have been confirmed previously in *Śrīmad-Bhāgavatam* (1.2.17):

śṛṇvatāṁ sva-kathāḥ kṛṣṇaḥ
puṇya-śravaṇa-kīrtanaḥ
hṛdy antaḥ-stho hy abhadrāṇi
vidhunoti suhṛt satām

"Śrī Kṛṣṇa, the Personality of Godhead, who is the Paramātmā [Supersoul] in everyone's heart and the benefactor of the truthful devotee, cleanses desire for material enjoyment from the heart of the devotee who relishes His messages, which are in themselves virtuous when properly heard and chanted." It is the special mercy of the Supreme Lord that as soon as He knows that one is glorifying His name, fame and attributes, He personally helps cleanse the dirt from one's heart. Therefore simply by such glorification one not only becomes purified, but also achieves the results of pious activities (*puṇya-śravaṇa-kīrtana*). *Puṇya-śravaṇa-kīrtana* refers to the process of devotional service. Even if one does not understand the meaning of the Lord's name, pastimes or attributes, one is purified simply by hearing or chanting of them. Such purification is called *sattva-bhāvana.*

One's main purpose in human life should be to purify his existence and achieve liberation. As long as one has a material body, one is understood to be impure. In such an impure, material condition, one cannot enjoy a truly blissful life, although everyone seeks it. Therefore *Śrīmad-Bhāgavatam* (5.5.1) says, *tapo divyaṁ putrakā yena sattvaṁ śuddhyet:* one must perform *tapasya,* austerity, to purify his existence in order to come to the spiritual platform. The *tapasya* of chanting and glorifying the name, fame and attributes of the Lord is a very easy purifying process by which everyone can be happy. Therefore everyone who desires the ultimate cleansing of his heart must adopt this process. Other processes, such as *karma, jñāna* and *yoga,* cannot cleanse the heart absolutely.

TEXT 13

अथैनं मापनयत कृताशेषाघनिष्कृतम् ।
यदसौ भगवन्नाम म्रियमाणः समग्रहीत् ॥१३॥

athainaṁ māpanayata
kṛtāśeṣāgha-niṣkṛtam
yad asau bhagavan-nāma
mriyamāṇaḥ samagrahīt

atha—therefore; *enam*—him (Ajāmila); *mā*—do not; *apanayata*—try to take; *kṛta*—already done; *aśeṣa*—unlimited; *agha-niṣkṛtam*—atonement for his sinful actions; *yat*—because; *asau*—he; *bhagavat-nāma*—the holy name of the Supreme Personality of Godhead; *mriyamāṇaḥ*—while dying; *samagrahīt*—perfectly chanted.

TRANSLATION

At the time of death, this Ajāmila helplessly and very loudly chanted the holy name of the Lord, Nārāyaṇa. That chanting alone has already freed him from the reactions of all sinful life. Therefore, O servants of Yamarāja, do not try to take him to your master for punishment in hellish conditions.

PURPORT

The Viṣṇudūtas, who are superior authorities, gave orders to the Yamadūtas, who did not know that Ajāmila was no longer subject to tribulation in hellish life for his past sins. Although he had chanted the holy name Nārāyaṇa to indicate his son, the holy name is so transcendentally powerful that he was automatically freed because he had chanted the holy name while dying (*ante nārāyaṇa-smṛtiḥ*). As Kṛṣṇa confirms in *Bhagavad-gītā* (7.28):

yeṣāṁ tv anta-gataṁ pāpaṁ
janānāṁ puṇya-karmaṇām
te dvandva-moha-nirmuktā
bhajante māṁ dṛḍha-vratāḥ

"Persons who have acted piously in previous lives and in this life, whose sinful actions are completely eradicated and who are freed from the duality of delusion, engage themselves in My service with determination." Unless one is freed from all sinful reactions, one cannot be promoted to the platform of devotional service. Elsewhere in *Bhagavad-gītā* (8.5) it is stated:

anta-kāle ca mām eva
smaran muktvā kalevaram
yaḥ prayāti sa mad-bhāvaṁ
yāti nāsty atra saṁśayaḥ

If one remembers Kṛṣṇa, Nārāyaṇa, at the time of death, one is certainly eligible to return immediately home, back to Godhead.

TEXT 14

साङ्केत्यं पारिहास्यं वा स्तोभं हेलनमेव वा ।
वैकुण्ठनामग्रहणमशेषाघहरं विदुः ॥१४॥

sāṅketyaṁ pārihāsyaṁ vā
stobhaṁ helanam eva vā
vaikuṇṭha-nāma-grahaṇam
aśeṣāgha-haraṁ viduḥ

sāṅketyam—as an assignation; *pārihāsyam*—jokingly; *vā*—or; *stobham*—as musical entertainment; *helanam*—neglectfully; *eva*—certainly; *vā*—or; *vaikuṇṭha*—of the Lord; *nāma-grahaṇam*—chanting the holy name; *aśeṣa*—unlimited; *agha-haram*—neutralizing the effect of sinful life; *viduḥ*—advanced transcendentalists know.

TRANSLATION

One who chants the holy name of the Lord is immediately freed from the reactions of unlimited sins, even if he chants indirectly [to indicate something else], jokingly, for musical entertainment, or even neglectfully. This is accepted by all the learned scholars of the scriptures.

TEXT 15

पतितः स्खलितो भग्नः सन्दष्टस्तप्त आहतः ।
हरिरित्यवशेनाह पुमान्नार्हति यातनाः ॥१५॥

patitaḥ skhalito bhagnaḥ
sandaṣṭas tapta āhataḥ

harir ity avaśenāha
pumān nārhati yātanāḥ

patitaḥ—fallen down; *skhalitaḥ*—slipped; *bhagnaḥ*—having broken his bones; *sandaṣṭaḥ*—bitten; *taptaḥ*—severely attacked by fever or similar painful conditions; *āhataḥ*—injured; *hariḥ*—Lord Kṛṣṇa; *iti*—thus; *avaśena*—accidentally; *āha*—chants; *pumān*—a person; *na*—not; *arhati*—deserves; *yātanāḥ*—hellish conditions.

TRANSLATION

If one chants the holy name of Hari and then dies because of an accidental misfortune, such as falling from the top of a house, slipping and suffering broken bones while traveling on the road, being bitten by a serpent, being afflicted with pain and high fever, or being injured by a weapon, one is immediately absolved from having to enter hellish life, even though he is sinful.

PURPORT

As stated in *Bhagavad-gītā* (8.6):

yaṁ yaṁ vāpi smaran bhāvaṁ
tyajaty ante kalevaram
taṁ tam evaiti kaunteya
sadā tad-bhāva-bhāvitaḥ

"Whatever state of being one remembers when he quits his body, that state he will attain without fail." If one practices chanting the Hare Kṛṣṇa *mantra*, he is naturally expected to chant Hare Kṛṣṇa when he meets with some accident. Even without such practice, however, if one somehow or other chants the holy name of the Lord (Hare Kṛṣṇa) when he meets with an accident and dies, he will be saved from hellish life after death.

TEXT 16

गुरूणां च लघूनां च गुरूणि च लघूनि च ।
प्रायश्चित्तानि पापानां ज्ञात्वोक्तानि महर्षिभिः ॥१६॥

gurūṇāṁ ca laghūnāṁ ca
gurūṇi ca laghūni ca
prāyaścittāni pāpānāṁ
jñātvoktāni maharṣibhiḥ

gurūṇām—heavy; *ca*—and; *laghūnām*—light; *ca*—also; *gurūṇi*—heavy; *ca*—and; *laghūni*—light; *ca*—also; *prāyaścittāni*—the processes of atonement; *pāpānām*—of sinful activities; *jñātvā*—knowing perfectly well; *uktāni*—have been prescribed; *mahā-ṛṣibhiḥ*—by great sages.

TRANSLATION

Authorities who are learned scholars and sages have carefully ascertained that one should atone for the heaviest sins by undergoing a heavy process of atonement and one should atone for lighter sins by undergoing lighter atonement. Chanting the Hare Kṛṣṇa mantra, however, vanquishes all the effects of sinful activities, regardless of whether heavy or light.

PURPORT

In this regard, Śrīla Viśvanātha Cakravartī Ṭhākura describes an incident that took place when Sāmba was rescued from the punishment of the Kauravas. Sāmba fell in love with the daughter of Duryodhana, and since according to *kṣatriya* custom one is not offered a *kṣatriya's* daughter unless he displays his chivalrous valor, Sāmba abducted her. Consequently Sāmba was arrested by the Kauravas. Later, when Lord Balarāma came to rescue him, there was an argument about Sāmba's release. Since the argument was not settled, Balarāma showed His power in such a way that all of Hastināpura trembled and would have been vanquished as if by a great earthquake. Then the matter was settled, and Sāmba married Duryodhana's daughter. The purport is that one should take shelter of Kṛṣṇa-Balarāma, the Supreme Personality of Godhead, whose protective power is so great that it cannot be equaled in the material world. However powerful the reactions of one's sins, they will immediately be vanquished if one chants the name of Hari, Kṛṣṇa, Balarāma or Nārāyaṇa.

TEXT 17

तैस्तान्यघानि पूयन्ते तपोदानव्रतादिभिः ।
नाधर्मजं तद्धृदयं तदपीशाङ्घ्रिसेवया ॥१७॥

tais tāny aghāni pūyante
tapo-dāna-vratādibhiḥ
nādharmajaṁ tad-dhṛdayaṁ
tad apīśāṅghri-sevayā

taiḥ—by those; *tāni*—all those; *aghāni*—sinful activities and their results; *pūyante*—become vanquished; *tapaḥ*—austerity; *dāna*—charity; *vrata-ādibhiḥ*—by vows and other such activities; *na*—not; *adharma-jam*—produced from irreligious actions; *tat*—of that; *hṛdayam*—the heart; *tat*—that; *api*—also; *īśa-aṅghri*—of the lotus feet of the Lord; *sevayā*—by service.

TRANSLATION

Although one may neutralize the reactions of sinful life through austerity, charity, vows and other such methods, these pious activities cannot uproot the material desires in one's heart. However, if one serves the lotus feet of the Personality of Godhead, he is immediately freed from all such contaminations.

PURPORT

As stated in *Śrīmad-Bhāgavatam* (11.2.42), *bhaktiḥ pareśānubhavo viraktir anyatra ca:* devotional service is so powerful that one who performs devotional service is immediately freed from all sinful desires. All desires within this material world are sinful because material desire means sense gratification, which always involves action that is more or less sinful. Pure *bhakti,* however, is *anyābhilāṣitā-śūnya;* in other words, it is free from material desires, which result from *karma* and *jñāna.* One who is situated in devotional service no longer has material desires, and therefore he is beyond sinful life. Material desires should be completely stopped. Otherwise, although one's austerities, penances and charity may free one from sin for the time being, one's desires will reappear because his heart is impure. Thus he will act sinfully and suffer.

TEXT 18

अज्ञानादथवा ज्ञानादुत्तमश्लोकनाम यत् ।
सङ्कीर्तितमघं पुंसो दहेदेधो यथानलः ॥१८॥

ajñānād athavā jñānād
uttamaśloka-nāma yat
saṅkīrtitam aghaṁ puṁso
dahed edho yathānalaḥ

ajñānāt—out of ignorance; *athavā*—or; *jñānāt*—with knowledge; *uttamaśloka*—of the Supreme Personality of Godhead; *nāma*—the holy name; *yat*—that which; *saṅkīrtitam*—chanted; *agham*—sin; *puṁsaḥ*—of a person; *dahet*—burns to ashes; *edhaḥ*—dry grass; *yathā*—just as; *analaḥ*—fire.

TRANSLATION

As a fire burns dry grass to ashes, so the holy name of the Lord, whether chanted knowingly or unknowingly, burns to ashes, without fail, all the reactions of one's sinful activities.

PURPORT

Fire will act, regardless of whether handled by an innocent child or by someone well aware of its power. For example, if a field of straw or dry grass is set afire, either by an elderly man who knows the power of fire or by a child who does not, the grass will be burned to ashes. Similarly, one may or may not know the power of chanting the Hare Kṛṣṇa *mantra*, but if one chants the holy name he will become free from all sinful reactions.

TEXT 19

यथागदं वीर्यतममुपयुक्तं यदृच्छया ।
अजानतोऽप्यात्मगुणं कुर्यान्मन्त्रोऽप्युदाहृतः ॥१९॥

yathāgadaṁ vīryatamam
upayuktaṁ yadṛcchayā
ajānato 'py ātma-guṇaṁ
kuryān mantro 'py udāhṛtaḥ

yathā—just like; *agadam*—medicine; *vīrya-tamam*—very powerful; *upayuktam*—properly taken; *yadṛcchayā*—somehow or other; *ajānataḥ*—by a person without knowledge; *api*—even; *ātma-guṇam*—its own potency; *kuryāt*—manifests; *mantraḥ*—the Hare Kṛṣṇa *mantra;* *api*—also; *udāhṛtaḥ*—chanted.

TRANSLATION

If a person unaware of the effective potency of a certain medicine takes that medicine or is forced to take it, it will act even without his knowledge because its potency does not depend on the patient's understanding. Similarly, even though one does not know the value of chanting the holy name of the Lord, if one chants knowingly or unknowingly, the chanting will be very effective.

PURPORT

In the Western countries, where the Hare Kṛṣṇa movement is spreading, learned scholars and other thoughtful men are realizing its effectiveness. For example, Dr. J. Stillson Judah, a learned scholar, has been very much attracted to this movement because he has actually seen that it is turning hippies addicted to drugs into pure Vaiṣṇavas who voluntarily become servants of Kṛṣṇa and humanity. Even a few years ago, such hippies did not know the Hare Kṛṣṇa *mantra,* but now they are chanting it and becoming pure Vaiṣṇavas. Thus they are becoming free from all sinful activities, such as illicit sex, intoxication, meat-eating and gambling. This is practical proof of the effectiveness of the Hare Kṛṣṇa movement, which is supported in this verse. One may or may not know the value of chanting the Hare Kṛṣṇa *mantra,* but if one somehow or other chants it, he will immediately be purified, just as one who takes a potent medicine will feel its effects, regardless of whether he takes it knowingly or unknowingly.

TEXT 20

श्रीशुक उवाच
त एवं सुविनिर्णीय धर्मं भागवतं नृप ।
तं याम्यपाशान्निर्मुच्य विप्रं मृत्योरमूमुचन् ॥२०॥

śrī-śuka uvāca
ta evaṁ suvinirṇīya
dharmaṁ bhāgavataṁ nṛpa
taṁ yāmya-pāśān nirmucya
vipraṁ mṛtyor amūmucan

śrī-śukaḥ uvāca—Śrī Śukadeva Gosvāmī said; *te*—they (the order carriers of Lord Viṣṇu); *evam*—thus; *su-vinirṇīya*—perfectly ascertaining; *dharmam*—real religion; *bhāgavatam*—in terms of devotional service; *nṛpa*—O King; *tam*—him (Ajāmila); *yāmya-pāśāt*—from the bondage of the order carriers of Yamarāja; *nirmucya*—releasing; *vipram*—the *brāhmaṇa; mṛtyoḥ*—from death; *amūmucan*—rescued.

TRANSLATION

Śrī Śukadeva Gosvāmī continued: My dear King, having thus perfectly judged the principles of devotional service with reasoning and arguments, the order carriers of Lord Viṣṇu released the brāhmaṇa Ajāmila from the bondage of the Yamadūtas and saved him from imminent death.

TEXT 21

इति प्रत्युदिता याम्या दूता यात्वा यमान्तिकम् ।
यमराज्ञे यथा सर्वमाचचक्षुररिन्दम ॥२१॥

iti pratyuditā yāmyā
dūtā yātvā yamāntikam
yama-rājñe yathā sarvam
ācacakṣur arindama

iti—thus; *pratyuditāḥ*—having been replied to (by the order carriers of Viṣṇu); *yāmyāḥ*—the servants of Yamarāja; *dūtāḥ*—the messengers; *yātvā*—going; *yama-antikam*—to the abode of Lord Yamarāja; *yama-rājñe*—unto King Yamarāja; *yathā*—duly; *sarvam*—everything; *ācacakṣuḥ*—informed in full detail; *arindama*—O subduer of the enemies.

TRANSLATION

My dear Mahārāja Parīkṣit, O subduer of all enemies, after the servants of Yamarāja had been answered by the order carriers of Lord Viṣṇu, they went to Yamarāja and explained to him everything that had happened.

PURPORT

In this verse the word *pratyuditāḥ* is very significant. The servants of Yamarāja are so powerful that they can never be hindered anywhere, but this time they were baffled and disappointed in their attempt to take away a man they considered sinful. Therefore they immediately returned to Yamarāja and described to him everything that had happened.

TEXT 22

द्विजः पाशाद्विनिर्मुक्तो गतभीः प्रकृतिं गतः ।
ववन्दे शिरसा विष्णोः किङ्करान् दर्शनोत्सवः ॥२२॥

dvijaḥ pāśād vinirmukto
gata-bhīḥ prakṛtiṁ gataḥ
vavande śirasā viṣṇoḥ
kiṅkarān darśanotsavaḥ

dvijaḥ—the *brāhmaṇa* (Ajāmila); *pāśāt*—from the noose; *vinirmuktaḥ*—being released; *gata-bhīḥ*—freed from fear; *prakṛtim gataḥ*—came to his senses; *vavande*—offered his respectful obeisances; *śirasā*—by bowing his head; *viṣṇoḥ*—of Lord Viṣṇu; *kiṅkarān*—unto the servants; *darśana-utsavaḥ*—very pleased by seeing them.

TRANSLATION

Having been released from the nooses of Yamarāja's servants, the brāhmaṇa Ajāmila, now free from fear, came to his senses and immediately offered obeisances to the Viṣṇudūtas by bowing his head at their lotus feet. He was extremely pleased by their presence, for he had seen them save his life from the hands of the servants of Yamarāja.

PURPORT

Vaiṣṇavas are also Viṣṇudūtas because they carry out the orders of Kṛṣṇa. Lord Kṛṣṇa is very eager for all the conditioned souls rotting in this material world to surrender to Him and be saved from material pangs in this life and punishment in hellish conditions after death. A Vaiṣṇava therefore tries to bring conditioned souls to their senses. Those who are fortunate like Ajāmila are saved by the Viṣṇudūtas, or Vaiṣṇavas, and thus they return back home, back to Godhead.

TEXT 23

तं विवक्षुमभिप्रेत्य महापुरुषकिङ्कराः ।
सहसा पश्यतस्तस्य तत्रान्तर्दधिरेऽनघ ॥२३॥

taṁ vivakṣum abhipretya
mahāpuruṣa-kiṅkarāḥ
sahasā paśyatas tasya
tatrāntardadhire 'nagha

tam—him (Ajāmila); *vivakṣum*—desiring to speak; *abhipretya*—understanding; *mahāpuruṣa-kiṅkarāḥ*—the order carriers of Lord Viṣṇu; *sahasā*—suddenly; *paśyataḥ tasya*—while he looked on; *tatra*—there; *antardadhire*—disappeared; *anagha*—O sinless Mahārāja Parīkṣit.

TRANSLATION

O sinless Mahārāja Parīkṣit, the order carriers of the Supreme Personality of Godhead, the Viṣṇudūtas, saw that Ajāmila was attempting to say something, and thus they suddenly disappeared from his presence.

PURPORT

The *śāstras* say:

pāpiṣṭhā ye durācārā
deva-brāhmaṇa-nindakāḥ
apathya-bhojanās teṣām
akāle maraṇaṁ dhruvam

"For persons who are *pāpiṣṭha*, very sinful, and *durācāra*, misbehaved or very unclean in their habits, who are against the existence of God, who disrespect Vaiṣṇavas and *brāhmaṇas*, and who eat anything and everything, untimely death is sure." It is said that in Kali-yuga one has a maximum lifetime of one hundred years, but as people become degraded, the duration of their lives decreases (*prāyeṇālpāyuṣaḥ*). Because Ajāmila was now free from all sinful reactions, his lifetime was extended, even though he was to have died immediately. When the Viṣṇudūtas saw Ajāmila trying to say something to them, they disappeared to give him a chance to glorify the Supreme Lord. Since all his sinful reactions had been vanquished, he was now prepared to glorify the Lord. Indeed, one cannot glorify the Lord unless one is completely free from all sinful activities. This is confirmed by Kṛṣṇa Himself in *Bhagavad-gītā* (7.28):

yeṣāṁ tv anta-gataṁ pāpaṁ
janānāṁ puṇya-karmaṇām
te dvanda-moha-nirmuktā
bhajante māṁ dṛḍha-vratāḥ

"Persons who have acted piously in previous lives and in this life, whose sinful actions are completely eradicated and who are freed from the duality of delusion, engage themselves in My service with determination." The Viṣṇudūtas made Ajāmila aware of devotional service so that He might immediately become fit to return home, back to Godhead. To increase his eagerness to glorify the Lord, they disappeared so that he would feel separation in their absence. In the mode of separation, glorification of the Lord is very intense.

TEXTS 24–25

अजामिलोऽप्यथाकर्ण्य दूतानां यमकृष्णयोः ।
धर्मं भागवतं शुद्धं त्रैवेद्यं च गुणाश्रयम् ॥२४॥
भक्तिमान् भगवत्याशु माहात्म्यश्रवणाद्धरेः ।
अनुतापो महानासीत्स्मरतोऽशुभमात्मनः ॥२५॥

ajāmilo 'py athākarṇya
dūtānāṁ yama-kṛṣṇayoḥ
dharmaṁ bhāgavataṁ śuddhaṁ
trai-vedyaṁ ca guṇāśrayam

bhaktimān bhagavaty āśu
māhātmya-śravaṇād dhareḥ
anutāpo mahān āsīt
smarato 'śubham ātmanaḥ

ajāmilaḥ—Ajāmila; *api*—also; *atha*—thereafter; *ākarṇya*—hearing; *dūtānām*—of the order carriers; *yama-kṛṣṇayoḥ*—of Yamarāja and Lord Kṛṣṇa; *dharmam*—actual religious principles; *bhāgavatam*—as described in *Śrīmad-Bhāgavatam*, or concerning the relationship between the living being and the Supreme Personality of Godhead; *śuddham*—pure; *trai-vedyam*—mentioned in three *Vedas; ca*—also; *guṇa-āśrayam*—material religion, under the modes of material nature; *bhakti-mān*—a pure devotee (cleansed of the modes of material nature); *bhagavati*—unto the Supreme Personality of Godhead; *āśu*—immediately; *māhātmya*—glorification of the name, fame, etc.; *śravaṇāt*—because of hearing; *hareḥ*—of Lord Hari; *anutāpaḥ*—regret; *mahān*—very great; *āsīt*—there was; *smarataḥ*—remembering; *aśubham*—all the inglorious activities; *ātmanaḥ*—done by himself.

TRANSLATION

After hearing the discourses between the Yamadūtas and the Viṣṇudūtas, Ajāmila could understand the religious principles that act under the three modes of material nature. These principles are mentioned in the three Vedas. He could also understand the transcendental religious principles, which are above the modes of material nature and which concern the relationship between the living being and the Supreme Personality of Godhead. Furthermore, Ajāmila heard glorification of the name, fame, qualities and pastimes of the Supreme Personality of Godhead. He thus became a perfectly pure devotee. He could then remember his past sinful activities, which he greatly regretted having performed.

PURPORT

In *Bhagavad-gītā* (2.45) Lord Kṛṣṇa told Arjuna:

traiguṇya-viṣayā vedā
nistraiguṇyo bhavārjuna
nirdvandvo nitya-sattva-stho
niryoga-kṣema ātmavān

"The *Vedas* mainly deal with the subject of the three modes of material nature. Rise above these modes, O Arjuna. Be transcendental to all of them. Be free from all dualities and from all anxieties for gain and safety, and be established in the Self." The Vedic principles certainly prescribe a gradual process for rising to the spiritual platform, but if one remains attached to the Vedic principles, there is no chance of his being elevated to spiritual life. Kṛṣṇa therefore advised Arjuna to perform devotional service, which is the process of transcendental religion. The transcendental position of devotional service is also confirmed in *Śrīmad-Bhāgavatam* (1.2.6). *Sa vai puṁsāṁ paro dharmo yato bhaktir adhokṣaje. Bhakti,* devotional service, is *paro dharmaḥ,* transcendental *dharma;* it is not material *dharma.* People generally think that religion should be pursued for material profit. This may be suitable for persons interested in material life, but one who is interested in spiritual life should be attached to *paro dharmaḥ,* the religious principles by which one becomes a devotee of the Supreme Lord (*yato bhaktir adhokṣaje*). The *bhāgavata* religion teaches that the Lord and the living entity are eternally related and that the duty of the living entity is to surrender to the Lord. When one is situated on the platform of devotional service, one is freed from impediments and completely satisfied (*ahaituky apratihatā yayātmā suprasīdati*). Having been elevated to that platform, Ajāmila began to lament for his past materialistic activities and glorify the name, fame, form and pastimes of the Supreme Personality of Godhead.

TEXT 26

अहो मे परमं कष्टमभूदविजितात्मनः ।
येन विप्लावितं ब्रह्म वृषल्यां जायतात्मना ॥२६॥

aho me paramaṁ kaṣṭam
abhūd avijitātmanaḥ
yena viplāvitaṁ brahma
vṛṣalyāṁ jāyatātmanā

aho—alas; *me*—my; *paramam*—extreme; *kaṣṭam*—miserable condition; *abhūt*—became; *avijita-ātmanaḥ*—because my senses were uncontrolled; *yena*—by which; *viplāvitam*—destroyed; *brahma*—all my brahminical qualifications; *vṛṣalyām*—through a *śūdrāṇī,* a maidservant; *jāyatā*—being born; *ātmanā*—by me.

TRANSLATION

Ajāmila said: Alas, being a servant of my senses, how degraded I became! I fell down from my position as a duly qualified brāhmaṇa and begot children in the womb of a prostitute.

PURPORT

The men of the higher classes—the *brāhmaṇas, kṣatriyas* and *vaiśyas*—do not beget children in the wombs of lower-class women. Therefore the custom in Vedic society is to examine the horoscopes of a girl and boy being considered for marriage to see whether their combination is suitable. Vedic astrology reveals whether one has been born in the *vipra-varṇa, kṣatriya-varṇa, vaiśya-varṇa* or *śūdra-varṇa,* according to the three qualities of material nature. This must be examined because a marriage between a boy of the *vipra-varṇa* and a girl of the *śūdra-varṇa* is incompatible; married life would be miserable for both husband and wife. Consequently a boy should marry a girl of the same category. Of course, this is *trai-guṇya,* a material calculation according to the *Vedas,* but if the boy and girl are devotees there need be no such considerations. A devotee is transcendental, and therefore in a marriage between devotees, the boy and girl form a very happy combination.

TEXT 27

धिङ्मां विगर्हितं सद्भिर्दुष्कृतं कुलकज्जलम् ।
हित्वा बालां सतीं योऽहं सुरापीमसतीमगाम् ॥२७॥

dhiṅ māṁ vigarhitaṁ sadbhir
duṣkṛtaṁ kula-kajjalam
hitvā bālāṁ satīṁ yo 'haṁ
surā-pīm asatīm agām

dhik mām—all condemnation upon me; *vigarhitam*—condemned; *sadbhiḥ*—by honest men; *duṣkṛtam*—who has committed sinful acts; *kula-kajjalam*—who has defamed the family tradition; *hitvā*—giving up; *bālām*—a young wife; *satīm*—chaste; *yaḥ*—who; *aham*—I; *surā-pīm*—with a woman accustomed to drinking wine; *asatīm*—unchaste; *agām*—I had sexual intercourse.

TRANSLATION

Alas, all condemnation upon me! I acted so sinfully that I degraded my family tradition. Indeed, I gave up my chaste and beautiful young wife to have sexual intercourse with a fallen prostitute accustomed to drinking wine. All condemnation upon me!

PURPORT

This is the mentality of one who is becoming a pure devotee. When one is elevated to the platform of devotional service by the grace of the Lord and the spiritual master, one first regrets his past sinful activities. This helps one advance in spiritual life. The Viṣṇudūtas had given Ajāmila the chance to become a pure devotee, and the duty of a pure devotee is to regret his past sinful activities in illicit sex, intoxication, meat-eating and gambling. Not only should one give up his past bad habits, but he must always regret his past sinful acts. This is the standard of pure devotion.

TEXT 28

वृद्धावनाथौ पितरौ नान्यबन्धू तपस्विनौ ।
अहो मयाधुना त्यक्तावकृतज्ञेन नीचवत् ॥२८॥

vṛddhāv anāthau pitarau
nānya-bandhū tapasvinau
aho mayādhunā tyaktāv
akṛtajñena nīcavat

vṛddhau—old; *anāthau*—who had no other person to look after their comforts; *pitarau*—my father and mother; *na anya-bandhū*—who had no other friend; *tapasvinau*—who underwent great difficulties; *aho*—alas; *mayā*—by me; *adhunā*—at that moment; *tyaktau*—were given up; *akṛta-jñena*—ungrateful; *nīca-vat*—like the most abominable low-class person.

TRANSLATION

My father and mother were old and had no other son or friend to look after them. Because I did not take care of them, they lived with great difficulty. Alas, like an abominable lower-class man, I ungratefully left them in that condition.

PURPORT

According to Vedic civilization, everyone has the responsibility for taking care of *brāhmaṇas*, old men, women, children and cows. This is the duty of everyone, especially an upper-class person. Because of his association with a prostitute, Ajāmila abandoned all his duties. Regretting this, Ajāmila now considered himself quite fallen.

TEXT 29

सोऽहं व्यक्तं पतिष्यामि नरके भृशदारुणे ।
धर्मघ्नाः कामिनो यत्र विन्दन्ति यमयातनाः ॥२९॥

so 'haṁ vyaktaṁ patiṣyāmi
narake bhṛśa-dāruṇe
dharma-ghnāḥ kāmino yatra
vindanti yama-yātanāḥ

saḥ—such a person; *aham*—I; *vyaktam*—it is now clear; *patiṣyāmi*—will fall down; *narake*—in hell; *bhṛśa-dāruṇe*—most miserable; *dharma-ghnāḥ*—they who break the principles of religion; *kāminaḥ*—who are too lusty; *yatra*—where; *vindanti*—undergo; *yama-yātanāḥ*—the miserable conditions imposed by Yamarāja.

TRANSLATION

It is now clear that as a consequence of such activities, a sinful person like me must be thrown into hellish conditions meant for those who have broken religious principles and must there suffer extreme miseries.

TEXT 30

किमिदं स्वप्न आहोस्वित् साक्षाद् दृष्टमिहाद्भुतम् ।
क्व याता अद्य ते ये मां व्यकर्षन् पाशपाणयः ॥३०॥

kim idaṁ svapna āho svit
sākṣād dṛṣṭam ihādbhutam
kva yātā adya te ye māṁ
vyakarṣan pāśa-pāṇayaḥ

kim—whether; *idam*—this; *svapne*—in a dream; *āho svit*—or; *sākṣāt*—directly; *dṛṣṭam*—seen; *iha*—here; *adbhutam*—wonderful; *kva*—where; *yātāḥ*—have gone; *adya*—now; *te*—all of them; *ye*—who; *mām*—me; *vyakarṣan*—were dragging; *pāśa-pāṇayaḥ*—with ropes in their hands.

TRANSLATION

Was this a dream I saw, or was it reality? I saw fearsome men with ropes in their hands coming to arrest me and drag me away. Where have they gone?

TEXT 31

अथ ते क्व गताः सिद्धाश्चत्वारश्चारुदर्शनाः ।
व्यामोचयन्नीयमानं बद्ध्वा पाशैरधो भुवः ॥३१॥

atha te kva gatāḥ siddhāś
catvāraś cāru-darśanāḥ
vyāmocayan nīyamānaṁ
baddhvā pāśair adho bhuvaḥ

atha—thereafter; *te*—those persons; *kva*—where; *gatāḥ*—went; *siddhāḥ*—liberated; *catvāraḥ*—four personalities; *cāru-darśanāḥ*—extremely beautiful to see; *vyāmocayan*—they released; *nīyamānam*—me, who was being carried away; *baddhvā*—being arrested; *pāśaiḥ*—by ropes; *adhaḥ bhuvaḥ*—downward to the hellish region.

TRANSLATION

And where have those four liberated and very beautiful persons gone who released me from arrest and saved me from being dragged down to the hellish regions?

PURPORT

As we have learned from the descriptions in the Fifth Canto, the hellish planets are situated in the lower portions of this universe. Therefore they are called *adho bhuvaḥ.* Ajāmila could understand that the Yamadūtas had come from that region.

TEXT 32

अथापि मे दुर्भगस्य विबुधोत्तमदर्शने ।
भवितव्यं मङ्गलेन येनात्मा मे प्रसीदति ॥३२॥

athāpi me durbhagasya
vibudhottama-darśane
bhavitavyaṁ maṅgalena
yenātmā me prasīdati

atha—therefore; *api*—although; *me*—of me; *durbhagasya*—so unfortunate; *vibudha-uttama*—exalted devotees; *darśane*—because of seeing; *bhavitavyam*—there must be; *maṅgalena*—auspicious activities; *yena*—by which; *ātmā*—self; *me*—my; *prasīdati*—actually becomes happy.

TRANSLATION

I am certainly most abominable and unfortunate to have merged in an ocean of sinful activities, but nevertheless, because of my

previous spiritual activities, I could see those four exalted personalities who came to rescue me. Now I feel exceedingly happy because of their visit.

PURPORT

As stated in *Caitanya-caritāmṛta* (*Madhya* 22.54):

'sādhu-saṅga', 'sādhu-saṅga'—sarva-śāstre kaya
lava-mātra sādhu-saṅge sarva-siddhi haya

"Association with devotees is recommended by all the *śāstras* because by even a moment of such association one can receive the seed for all perfection." In the beginning of his life Ajāmila was certainly very pure, and he associated with devotees and *brāhmaṇas;* because of that pious activity, even though he was fallen, he was inspired to name his son Nārāyaṇa. Certainly this was due to good counsel given from within by the Supreme Personality of Godhead. As the Lord says in *Bhagavad-gītā* (15.15), *sarvasya cāhaṁ hṛdi sanniviṣṭo mattaḥ smṛtir jñānam apohanaṁ ca:* "I am seated in everyone's heart, and from Me come remembrance, knowledge and forgetfulness." The Lord, who is situated in everyone's heart, is so kind that if one has ever rendered service to Him, the Lord never forgets him. Thus the Lord, from within, gave Ajāmila the opportunity to name his youngest son Nārāyaṇa so that in affection he would constantly call "Nārāyaṇa! Nārāyaṇa!" and thus be saved from the most fearful and dangerous condition at the time of his death. Such is the mercy of Kṛṣṇa. *Guru-kṛṣṇa-prasāde pāya bhakti-latā-bīja:* by the mercy of the *guru* and Kṛṣṇa, one receives the seed of *bhakti.* This association saves a devotee from the greatest fear. In our Kṛṣṇa consciousness movement we therefore change a devotee's name to a form that reminds him of Viṣṇu. If at the time of death the devotee can remember his own name, such as Kṛṣṇadāsa or Govinda dāsa, he can be saved from the greatest danger. Therefore the change of names at the time of initiation is essential. The Kṛṣṇa consciousness movement is so meticulous that it gives one a good opportunity to remember Kṛṣṇa somehow or other.

TEXT 33

अन्यथा म्रियमाणस्य नाशुचेर्वृषलीपतेः ।
वैकुण्ठनामग्रहणं जिह्वा वक्तुमिहार्हति ॥३३॥

anyathā mriyamāṇasya
nāśucer vṛṣalī-pateḥ
vaikuṇṭha-nāma-grahaṇaṁ
jihvā vaktum ihārhati

anyathā—otherwise; *mriyamāṇasya*—of a person who is just ready for death; *na*—not; *aśuceḥ*—most unclean; *vṛṣalī-pateḥ*—the keeper of a prostitute; *vaikuṇṭha*—of the Lord of Vaikuṇṭha; *nāma-grahaṇam*—the chanting of the holy name; *jihvā*—the tongue; *vaktum*—to speak; *iha*—in this situation; *arhati*—is able.

TRANSLATION

Were it not for my past devotional service, how could I, a most unclean keeper of a prostitute, have gotten an opportunity to chant the holy name of Vaikuṇṭhapati when I was just ready to die? Certainly it could not have been possible.

PURPORT

The name Vaikuṇṭhapati, which means "the master of the spiritual world," is not different from the name Vaikuṇṭha. Ajāmila, who was now a realized soul, could understand that because of his past spiritual activities in devotional service, he had gotten this opportunity to chant the holy name of Vaikuṇṭhapati in his horrible condition at the time of death.

TEXT 34

क्व चाहं कितवः पापो ब्रह्मघ्नो निरपत्रपः ।
क्व च नारायणेत्येतद्भगवन्नाम मङ्गलम् ॥३४॥

kva cāhaṁ kitavaḥ pāpo
brahma-ghno nirapatrapaḥ

kva ca nārāyaṇety etad
bhagavan-nāma maṅgalam

kva—where; *ca*—also; *aham*—I; *kitavaḥ*—a cheater; *pāpaḥ*—all sins personified; *brahma-ghnaḥ*—the killer of my brahminical culture; *nirapatrapaḥ*—shameless; *kva*—where; *ca*—also; *nārāyaṇa*—Nārāyaṇa; *iti*—thus; *etat*—this; *bhagavat-nāma*—the holy name of the Supreme Personality of Godhead; *maṅgalam*—all-auspicious.

TRANSLATION

Ajāmila continued: I am a shameless cheater who has killed his brahminical culture. Indeed, I am sin personified. Where am I in comparison to the all-auspicious chanting of the holy name of Lord Nārāyaṇa?

PURPORT

Those engaged in broadcasting the holy name of Nārāyaṇa, Kṛṣṇa, through the Kṛṣṇa consciousness movement should always consider what our position was before we came and what it is now. We had fallen into abominable lives as meat-eaters, drunkards and woman hunters who performed all kinds of sinful activities, but now we have been given the opportunity to chant the Hare Kṛṣṇa *mantra*. Therefore we should always appreciate this opportunity. By the grace of the Lord we are opening many branches, and we should use this good fortune to chant the holy name of the Lord and serve the Supreme Personality of Godhead directly. We must be conscious of the difference between our present and past conditions and should always be very careful not to fall from the most exalted life.

TEXT 35

सोऽहं तथा यतिष्यामि यतचित्तेन्द्रियानिलः ।
यथा न भूय आत्मानमन्धे तमसि मज्जये ॥३५॥

so 'haṁ tathā yatiṣyāmi
yata-cittendriyānilaḥ
yathā na bhūya ātmānam
andhe tamasi majjaye

saḥ—such a person; *aham*—I; *tathā*—in that way; *yatiṣyāmi*—I shall endeavor; *yata-citta-indriya*—controlling the mind and senses; *anilaḥ*—and the internal airs; *yathā*—so that; *na*—not; *bhūyaḥ*—again; *ātmānam*—my soul; *andhe*—in darkness; *tamasi*—in ignorance; *majjaye*—I drown.

TRANSLATION

I am such a sinful person, but since I have now gotten this opportunity, I must completely control my mind, life and senses and always engage in devotional service so that I may not fall again into the deep darkness and ignorance of material life.

PURPORT

Every one of us should have this determination. We have been elevated to an exalted position by the mercy of Kṛṣṇa and the spiritual master, and if we remember that this is a great opportunity and pray to Kṛṣṇa that we will not fall again, our lives will be successful.

TEXT 36–37

विमुच्य तमिमं बन्धमविद्याकामकर्मजम् ।
सर्वभूतसुहृच्छान्तो मैत्रः करुण आत्मवान् ॥३६॥
मोचये ग्रस्तमात्मानं योषिन्मय्यात्ममायया ।
विक्रीडितो ययैवाहं क्रीडामृग इवाधमः ॥३७॥

vimucya tam imaṁ bandham
avidyā-kāma-karmajam
sarva-bhūta-suhṛc chānto
maitraḥ karuṇa ātmavān

mocaye grastam ātmānaṁ
yoṣin-mayyātma-māyayā
vikrīḍito yayaivāhaṁ
krīḍā-mṛga ivādhamaḥ

vimucya—having become free from; *tam*—that; *imam*—this; *bandham*—bondage; *avidyā*—due to ignorance; *kāma*—due to lusty desire; *karma-jam*—caused by activities; *sarva-bhūta*—of all living entities; *suhṛt*—friend; *śāntaḥ*—very peaceful; *maitraḥ*—friendly; *karuṇaḥ*—merciful; *ātma-vān*—self-realized; *mocaye*—I shall disentangle; *grastam*—encaged; *ātmānam*—my soul; *yoṣit-mayyā*—in the form of woman; *ātma-māyayā*—by the illusory energy of the Lord; *vikrīḍitaḥ*—played with; *yayā*—by which; *eva*—certainly; *aham*—I; *krīḍā-mṛgaḥ*—a controlled animal; *iva*—like; *adhamaḥ*—so fallen.

TRANSLATION

Because of identifying oneself with the body, one is subjected to desires for sense gratification, and thus one engages in many different types of pious and impious action. This is what constitutes material bondage. Now I shall disentangle myself from my material bondage, which has been caused by the Supreme Personality of Godhead's illusory energy in the form of a woman. Being a most fallen soul, I was victimized by the illusory energy and have become like a dancing dog led around by a woman's hand. Now I shall give up all lusty desires and free myself from this illusion. I shall become a merciful, well-wishing friend to all living entities and always absorb myself in Kṛṣṇa consciousness.

PURPORT

This should be the standard of determination for all Kṛṣṇa conscious persons. A Kṛṣṇa conscious person should free himself from the clutches of *māyā*, and he should also be compassionate to all others suffering in those clutches. The activities of the Kṛṣṇa consciousness movement are meant not only for oneself but for others also. This is the perfection of Kṛṣṇa consciousness. One who is interested in his own salvation is not as advanced in Kṛṣṇa consciousness as one who feels compassion for others and who therefore propagates the Kṛṣṇa consciousness movement. Such an advanced devotee will never fall down, for Kṛṣṇa will give him special protection. That is the sum and substance of the Kṛṣṇa consciousness movement. Everyone is like a play toy in the hands of the illusory energy and is acting as she moves him. One should come to Kṛṣṇa consciousness to release oneself and also to release others.

TEXT 38

ममाहमिति देहादौ हित्वामिथ्यार्थधीर्मतिम् ।
धास्ये मनो भगवति शुद्धं तत्कीर्तनादिभिः ॥३८॥

mamāham iti dehādau
hitvāmithyārtha-dhīr matim
dhāsye mano bhagavati
śuddhaṁ tat-kīrtanādibhiḥ

mama—my; *aham*—I; *iti*—thus; *deha-ādau*—in the body and things related to the body; *hitvā*—giving up; *amithyā*—not false; *artha*—on values; *dhīḥ*—with my consciousness; *matim*—the attitude; *dhāsye*—I shall engage; *manaḥ*—my mind; *bhagavati*—on the Supreme Personality of Godhead; *śuddham*—pure; *tat*—His name; *kīrtana-ādibhiḥ*—by chanting, hearing and so on.

TRANSLATION

Simply because I chanted the holy name of the Lord in the association of devotees, my heart is now becoming purified. Therefore I shall not fall victim again to the false lures of material sense gratification. Now that I have become fixed in the Absolute Truth, henceforward I shall not identify myself with the body. I shall give up false conceptions of "I" and "mine" and fix my mind on the lotus feet of Kṛṣṇa.

PURPORT

How a living entity becomes a victim of the material condition is lucidly explained in this verse. The beginning is to misidentify the body as one's self. Therefore *Bhagavad-gītā* begins with the spiritual instruction that one is not the body, but is within the body. This consciousness can be possible only if one chants the holy name of Kṛṣṇa, the Hare Kṛṣṇa *mahā-mantra*, and always keeps oneself in the association of devotees. This is the secret of success. Therefore we stress that one should chant the holy name of the Lord and keep oneself free from the contaminations of this material world, especially the contaminations of lusty desires for illicit sex, meat-eating, intoxication and gambling. With determination, one should vow to follow these principles and thus be saved from the miserable condition of material existence. The first necessity is to become freed from the bodily concept of life.

TEXT 39

इति जातसुनिर्वेदः क्षणसङ्गेन साधुषु ।
गङ्गाद्वारमुपेयाय मुक्तसर्वानुबन्धनः ॥३९॥

iti jāta-sunirvedaḥ
kṣaṇa-saṅgena sādhuṣu
gaṅgā-dvāram upeyāya
mukta-sarvānubandhanaḥ

iti—thus; *jāta-sunirvedaḥ*—(Ajāmila) who had become detached from the material conception of life; *kṣaṇa-saṅgena*—by a moment's association; *sādhuṣu*—with devotees; *gaṅgā-dvāram*—to Hardwar (*hari-dvāra*), the doorway to Hari (because the Ganges begins there, Hardwar is also called *gaṅgā-dvāra*); *upeyāya*—went; *mukta*—being freed from; *sarva-anubandhanaḥ*—all kinds of material bondage.

TRANSLATION

Because of a moment's association with devotees [the Viṣṇudūtas], Ajāmila detached himself from the material conception of life with determination. Thus freed from all material attraction, he immediately started for Hardwar.

PURPORT

The word *mukta-sarvānubandhanaḥ* indicates that after this incident, Ajāmila, not caring for his wife and children, went straight to Hardwar for further advancement in his spiritual life. Our Kṛṣṇa consciousness movement now has centers in Vṛndāvana and Navadvīpa so that those who want to live a retired life, whether they be devotees or not, can go there and with determination give up the bodily concept of life. One is welcome to live in those holy places for the rest of his life in order to achieve the highest success by the very simple method of chanting the holy name of the Lord and taking *prasāda.* Thus one may return home, back to Godhead. We do not have a center in Hardwar, but Vṛndāvana and Śrīdhāma Māyāpur are better for devotees than any other places. The Caitanya Candrodaya temple offers one a good opportunity to associate with devotees. Let us all take advantage of this opportunity.

TEXT 40

स तस्मिन् देवसदन आसीनो योगमास्थितः ।
प्रत्याहृतेन्द्रियग्रामो युयोज मन आत्मनि ॥४०॥

sa tasmin deva-sadana
āsīno yogam āsthitaḥ
pratyāhṛtendriya-grāmo
yuyoja mana ātmani

saḥ—he (Ajāmila); *tasmin*—at that place (Hardwar); *deva-sadane*—in one Viṣṇu temple; *āsīnaḥ*—being situated; *yogam āsthitaḥ*—performed *bhakti-yoga; pratyāhṛta*—withdrawn from all activities of sense gratification; *indriya-grāmaḥ*—his senses; *yuyoja*—he fixed; *manaḥ*—the mind; *ātmani*—on the self or the Supersoul, the Supreme Personality of Godhead.

TRANSLATION

In Hardwar, Ajāmila took shelter at a Viṣṇu temple, where he executed the process of bhakti-yoga. He controlled his senses and fully applied his mind in the service of the Lord.

PURPORT

The devotees who have joined the Kṛṣṇa consciousness movement may live comfortably in our many temples and engage in the devotional service of the Lord. Thus they can control the mind and senses and achieve the highest success in life. This is the process descending from time immemorial. Learning from the life of Ajāmila, we should vow with determination to do what is necessary to follow this path.

TEXT 41

ततो गुणेभ्य आत्मानं वियुज्यात्मसमाधिना ।
युयुजे भगवद्धाम्नि ब्रह्मण्यनुभवात्मनि ॥४१॥

tato guṇebhya ātmānaṁ
viyujyātma-samādhinā
yuyuje bhagavad-dhāmni
brahmaṇy anubhavātmani

tataḥ—thereafter; *guṇebhyaḥ*—from the modes of material nature; *ātmānam*—the mind; *viyujya*—detaching; *ātma-samādhinā*—by being fully engaged in devotional service; *yuyuje*—engaged; *bhagavat-dhāmni*—in the form of the Lord; *brahmaṇi*—which is Parabrahman (not idol worship); *anubhava-ātmani*—which is always thought of (beginning from the lotus feet and gradually progressing upward).

TRANSLATION

Ajāmila fully engaged in devotional service. Thus he detached his mind from the process of sense gratification and became fully absorbed in thinking of the form of the Lord.

PURPORT

If one worships the Deity in the temple, one's mind will naturally be absorbed in thought of the Lord and His form. There is no distinction between the form of the Lord and the Lord Himself. Therefore *bhakti-yoga* is the most easy system of *yoga. Yogīs* try to concentrate their minds upon the form of the Supersoul, Viṣṇu, within the heart, but this same objective is easily achieved when one's mind is absorbed in the Deity worshiped in the temple. In every temple there is a transcendental form of the Lord, and one may easily think of this form. By seeing the Lord during *ārati*, by offering *bhoga* and by constantly thinking of the form of the Deity, one becomes a first-class *yogī*. This is the best process of *yoga*, as confirmed by the Supreme Personality of Godhead in *Bhagavad-gītā* (6.47):

yogināṁ api sarveṣāṁ
mad-gatenāntarātmanā
śraddhāvān bhajate yo māṁ
sa me yuktatamo mataḥ

"Of all *yogīs*, he who always abides in Me with great faith, worshiping Me in transcendental loving service, is most intimately united with Me in *yoga* and is the highest of all." The first-class *yogī* is he who controls his senses and detaches himself from material activities by always thinking of the form of the Lord.

TEXT 42

यर्ह्युपारतधीस्तस्मिन्नद्राक्षीत्पुरुषान् पुरः ।
उपलभ्योपलब्धान् प्राग् ववन्दे शिरसा द्विजः ॥४२॥

yarhy upārata-dhīs tasminn
adrākṣīt puruṣān puraḥ
upalabhyopalabdhān prāg
vavande śirasā dvijaḥ

yarhi—when; *upārata-dhīḥ*—his mind and intelligence were fixed; *tasmin*—at that time; *adrākṣīt*—had seen; *puruṣān*—the persons (the order carriers of Lord Viṣṇu); *puraḥ*—before him; *upalabhya*—getting; *upalabdhān*—who were gotten; *prāk*—previously; *vavande*—offered obeisances; *śirasā*—by the head; *dvijaḥ*—the *brāhmaṇa*.

TRANSLATION

When his intelligence and mind were fixed upon the form of the Lord, the brāhmaṇa Ajāmila once again saw before him four celestial persons. He could understand that they were those he had seen previously, and thus he offered them his obeisances by bowing down before them.

PURPORT

The Viṣṇudūtas who had rescued Ajāmila came before him again when his mind was firmly fixed upon the form of the Lord. The

Viṣṇudūtas had gone away for some time to give Ajāmila a chance to become firmly fixed in meditation upon the Lord. Now that his devotion had matured, they returned to take him. Understanding that the same Viṣṇudūtas had returned, Ajāmila offered them his obeisances by bowing down before them.

TEXT 43

हित्वा कलेवरं तीर्थे गङ्गायां दर्शनादनु ।
सद्यः स्वरूपं जगृहे भगवत्पार्श्ववर्तिनाम् ॥४३॥

hitvā kalevaraṁ tīrthe
gaṅgāyāṁ darśanād anu
sadyaḥ svarūpaṁ jagṛhe
bhagavat-pārśva-vartinām

hitvā—giving up; *kalevaram*—the material body; *tīrthe*—in the holy place; *gaṅgāyām*—on the bank of the Ganges; *darśanāt anu*—after seeing; *sadyaḥ*—immediately; *sva-rūpam*—his original spiritual form; *jagṛhe*—he assumed; *bhagavat-pārśva-vartinām*—which is fit for an associate of the Lord.

TRANSLATION

Upon seeing the Viṣṇudūtas, Ajāmila gave up his material body at Hardwar on the bank of the Ganges. He regained his original spiritual body, which was a body appropriate for an associate of the Lord.

PURPORT

The Lord says in *Bhagavad-gītā* (4.9):

janma karma ca me divyam
evaṁ yo vetti tattvataḥ
tyaktvā dehaṁ punar janma
naiti mām eti so 'rjuna

"One who knows the transcendental nature of My appearance and activities does not, upon leaving the body, take his birth again in this material world, but attains My eternal abode, O Arjuna."

The result of perfection in Kṛṣṇa consciousness is that after giving up one's material body, one is immediately transferred to the spiritual world in one's original spiritual body to become an associate of the Supreme Personality of Godhead. Some devotees go to Vaikuṇṭhaloka, and others go to Goloka Vṛndāvana to become associates of Kṛṣṇa.

TEXT 44

साकं विहायसा विप्रो महापुरुषकिङ्करैः ।
हैमं विमानमारुह्य ययौ यत्र श्रियः पतिः ॥४४॥

sākaṁ vihāyasā vipro
mahāpuruṣa-kiṅkaraiḥ
haimaṁ vimānam āruhya
yayau yatra śriyaḥ patiḥ

sākam—along; *vihāyasā*—by the path in the sky, or the airways; *vipraḥ*—the *brāhmaṇa* (Ajāmila); *mahāpuruṣa-kiṅkaraiḥ*—with the order carriers of Lord Viṣṇu; *haimam*—made of gold; *vimānam*—an airplane; *āruhya*—boarding; *yayau*—went; *yatra*—where; *śriyaḥ patiḥ*—Lord Viṣṇu, the husband of the goddess of fortune.

TRANSLATION

Accompanied by the order carriers of Lord Viṣṇu, Ajāmila boarded an airplane made of gold. Passing through the airways, he went directly to the abode of Lord Viṣṇu, the husband of the goddess of fortune.

PURPORT

For many years, material scientists have tried to go to the moon, but they are still unable to go there. However, the spiritual airplanes from the spiritual planets can take one back home, back to Godhead, in a second. The speed of such a spiritual plane can only be imagined. Spirit is finer than the mind, and everyone has experience of how swiftly the mind travels from one place to another. Therefore one can imagine the swiftness of the spiritual form by comparing it to the speed of the mind.

In less than even a moment, a perfect devotee can return home, back to Godhead, immediately after giving up his material body.

TEXT 45

एवं स विप्लावितसर्वधर्मा
दास्याः पतिः पतितो गर्ह्यकर्मणा ।
निपात्यमानो निरये हतव्रतः
सद्यो विमुक्तो भगवन्नाम गृह्णन् ॥४५॥

evaṁ sa viplāvita-sarva-dharmā
dāsyāḥ patiḥ patito garhya-karmaṇā
nipātyamāno niraye hata-vrataḥ
sadyo vimukto bhagavan-nāma gṛhṇan

evam—in this way; *saḥ*—he (Ajāmila); *viplāvita-sarva-dharmāḥ*—who gave up all religious principles; *dāsyāḥ patiḥ*—the husband of a prostitute; *patitaḥ*—fallen; *garhya-karmaṇā*—by being engaged in abominable activities; *nipātyamānaḥ*—falling; *niraye*—in hellish life; *hata-vrataḥ*—who broke all his vows; *sadyaḥ*—immediately; *vimuktaḥ*—liberated; *bhagavat-nāma*—the holy name of the Lord; *gṛhṇan*—chanting.

TRANSLATION

Ajāmila was a brāhmaṇa who because of bad association had given up all brahminical culture and religious principles. Becoming most fallen, he stole, drank and performed other abominable acts. He even kept a prostitute. Thus he was destined to be carried away to hell by the order carriers of Yamarāja, but he was immediately rescued simply by a glimpse of the chanting of the holy name Nārāyaṇa.

TEXT 46

नातः परं कर्मनिबन्धकृन्तनं
मुमुक्षतां तीर्थपदानुकीर्तनात् ।

न यत्पुनः कर्मसु सज्जते मनो
रजस्तमोभ्यां कलिलं ततोऽन्यथा ॥४६॥

nātaḥ paraṁ karma-nibandha-kṛntanaṁ
mumukṣatāṁ tīrtha-padānukīrtanāt
na yat punaḥ karmasu sajjate mano
rajas-tamobhyāṁ kalilaṁ tato 'nyathā

na—not; *ataḥ*—therefore; *param*—better means; *karma-nibandha*—the obligation to suffer or undergo tribulations as a result of fruitive activities; *kṛntanam*—that which can completely cut off; *mumukṣatām*—of persons desiring to get out of the clutches of material bondage; *tīrtha-pada*—about the Supreme Personality of Godhead, at whose feet all the holy places stand; *anukīrtanāt*—than constantly chanting under the direction of the bona fide spiritual master; *na*—not; *yat*—because; *punaḥ*—again; *karmasu*—in fruitive activities; *sajjate*—becomes attached; *manaḥ*—the mind; *rajaḥ-tamobhyām*—by the modes of passion and ignorance; *kalilam*—contaminated; *tataḥ*—thereafter; *anyathā*—by any other means.

TRANSLATION

Therefore one who desires freedom from material bondage should adopt the process of chanting and glorifying the name, fame, form and pastimes of the Supreme Personality of Godhead, at whose feet all the holy places stand. One cannot derive the proper benefit from other methods, such as pious atonement, speculative knowledge and meditation in mystic yoga, because even after following such methods one takes to fruitive activities again, unable to control his mind, which is contaminated by the base qualities of nature, namely passion and ignorance.

PURPORT

It has actually been seen that even after achieving so-called perfection, many *karmīs*, *jñānīs* and *yogīs* become attached to material activities again. Many so-called *svāmīs* and *yogīs* give up material activities as false (*jagan mithyā*), but after some time they nevertheless resume material activities by opening hospitals and schools or performing other activities for the benefit of the public. Sometimes they participate in politics, although still falsely declaring themselves *sannyāsīs*, members of the renounced order. The perfect conclusion, however, is that if one actually desires to get out of the material world, he must take to devotional service, which begins with *śravaṇaṁ kīrtanaṁ viṣṇoḥ:* chanting and hearing the glories of the Lord. The Kṛṣṇa consciousness movement has actually proved this. In the Western countries, many young boys who were addicted to drugs and who had many other bad habits, which they could not give up, abandoned all those propensities and very seriously engaged in chanting the glories of the Lord as soon as they joined the Kṛṣṇa consciousness movement. In other words, this process is the perfect method of atonement for actions performed in *rajaḥ* and *tamaḥ* (passion and ignorance). As stated in *Śrīmad-Bhāgavatam* (1.2.19):

tadā rajas-tamo-bhāvāḥ
kāma-lobhādayaś ca ye
ceta etair anāviddhaṁ
sthitaṁ sattve prasīdati

As a result of *rajaḥ* and *tamaḥ*, one becomes increasingly lusty and greedy, but when one takes to the process of chanting and hearing, one comes to the platform of goodness and becomes happy. As he advances in devotional service, all his doubts are completely eradicated (***bhidyate hṛdaya-granthiś chidyante sarva-saṁśayāḥ***). Thus the knot of his desire for fruitive activities is cut to pieces.

TEXTS 47–48

य एतं परमं गुह्यमितिहासमघापहम् ।
शृणुयाच्छ्रद्धया युक्तो यश्च भक्त्यानुकीर्तयेत् ॥४७॥
न वै स नरकं याति नेक्षितो यमकिङ्करैः ।
यद्यप्यमङ्गलो मर्त्यो विष्णुलोके महीयते ॥४८॥

ya etaṁ paramaṁ guhyam
itihāsam aghāpaham

śṛṇuyāc chraddhayā yukto
yaś ca bhaktyānukīrtayet

na vai sa narakaṁ yāti
nekṣito yama-kiṅkaraiḥ
yady apy amaṅgalo martyo
viṣṇu-loke mahīyate

yaḥ—anyone who; *etam*—this; *paramam*—very; *guhyam*—confidential; *itihāsam*—historical narration; *agha-apaham*—which frees one from all reactions to sins; *śṛṇuyāt*—hears; *śraddhayā*—with faith; *yuktaḥ*—endowed; *yaḥ*—one who; *ca*—also; *bhaktyā*—with great devotion; *anukīrtayet*—repeats; *na*—not; *vai*—indeed; *saḥ*—such a person; *narakam*—to hell; *yāti*—goes; *na*—not; *īkṣitaḥ*—is observed; *yama-kiṅkaraiḥ*—by the order carriers of Yamarāja; *yadi api*—although; *amaṅgalaḥ*—inauspicious; *martyaḥ*—a living entity with a material body; *viṣṇu-loke*—in the spiritual world; *mahīyate*—is welcomed and respectfully received.

TRANSLATION

Because this very confidential historical narration has the potency to vanquish all sinful reactions, one who hears or describes it with faith and devotion is no longer doomed to hellish life, regardless of his having a material body and regardless of how sinful he may have been. Indeed, the Yamadūtas, who carry out the orders of Yamarāja, do not approach him even to see him. After giving up his body, he returns home, back to Godhead, where he is very respectfully received and worshiped.

TEXT 49

म्रियमाणो हरेर्नाम गृणन् पुत्रोपचारितम् ।
अजामिलोऽप्यगाद्धाम किमुत श्रद्धया गृणन्॥४९॥

mriyamāṇo harer nāma
gṛṇan putropacāritam
ajāmilo 'py agād dhāma
kim uta śraddhayā gṛṇan

mriyamāṇaḥ—at the time of death; *hareḥ nāma*—the holy name of Hari; *gṛṇan*—chanting; *putra-upacāritam*—indicating his son; *ajāmilaḥ*—Ajāmila; *api*—even; *agāt*—went; *dhāma*—to the spiritual world; *kim uta*—what to speak of; *śraddhayā*—with faith and love; *gṛṇan*—chanting.

TRANSLATION

While suffering at the time of death, Ajāmila chanted the holy name of the Lord, and although the chanting was directed toward his son, he nevertheless returned home, back to Godhead. Therefore if one faithfully and inoffensively chants the holy name of the Lord, where is the doubt that he will return to Godhead?

PURPORT

At the time of death one is certainly bewildered because his bodily functions are in disorder. At that time, even one who throughout his life has practiced chanting the holy name of the Lord may not be able to chant the Hare Kṛṣṇa *mantra* very distinctly. Nevertheless, such a person receives all the benefits of chanting the holy name. While the body is fit, therefore, why should we not chant the holy name of the Lord loudly and distinctly? If one does so, it is quite possible that even at the time of death he will be properly able to chant the holy name of the Lord with love and faith. In conclusion, one who chants the holy name of the Lord constantly is guaranteed to return home, back to Godhead, without a doubt.

Supplementary note to this chapter.

Śrīla Viśvanātha Cakravartī Ṭhākura's commentary to texts 9 and 10 of this chapter form a dialogue concerning how one can become free from all sinful reactions simply by chanting the holy name of the Lord.

Someone may say, "It may be accepted that by chanting the holy name of the Lord one becomes freed from all the reactions of sinful life. However, if one commits sinful acts in full consciousness, not only once but many, many times, he is unable to free himself from the reactions of such sins even after atoning for them for twelve years or more. How is it possible, then, that simply by once chanting the holy name of the Lord one immediately becomes freed from the reactions of such sins?"

Śrīla Viśvanātha Cakravartī Ṭhākura replies by quoting verses 9 and 10 of this chapter: "The chanting of the holy name of Lord Viṣṇu is the best process of atonement for a thief of gold or other valuables, for a drunkard, for one who betrays a friend or relative, for one who kills a *brāhmaṇa,* or for one who indulges in sex with the wife of his *guru* or another superior. It is also the best method of atonement for one who murders women, the king or his father, for one who slaughters cows, and for all other sinful men. Simply by chanting the holy name of Lord Viṣṇu, such sinful persons may attract the attention of the Supreme Lord, who therefore considers, 'Because this man has chanted My holy name, My duty is to give him protection.' "

One may atone for sinful life and vanquish all sinful reactions by chanting the holy name, although this is not called atonement. Ordinary atonement may temporarily protect a sinful person, but it does not completely cleanse his heart of the deep-rooted desire to commit sinful acts. Therefore atonement is not as powerful as the chanting of the holy name of the Lord. In the *śāstras* it is said that if a person only once chants the holy name and completely surrenders unto the lotus feet of the Lord, the Lord immediately considers him His ward and is always inclined to give him protection. This is confirmed by Śrīdhara Svāmī. Thus when Ajāmila was in great danger of being carried off by the order carriers of Yamarāja, the Lord immediately sent His personal order carriers to protect him, and because Ajāmila was freed from all sinful reactions, the Viṣṇudūtas spoke on his behalf.

Ajāmila had named his son Nārāyaṇa, and because he loved the boy very much, he would call him again and again. Although he was calling for his son, the name itself was powerful because the name Nārāyaṇa is not different from the Supreme Lord Nārāyaṇa. When Ajāmila named his son Nārāyaṇa, all the reactions of his sinful life were neutralized, and as he continued calling his son and thus chanting the holy name of Nārāyaṇa thousands of times, he was actually unconsciously advancing in Kṛṣṇa consciousness.

One may argue, "Since he was constantly chanting the name of Nārāyaṇa, how was it possible for him to be associating with a prostitute and thinking of wine?" By his sinful actions he was bringing suffering upon himself again and again, and therefore one may say that his ultimate chanting of Nārāyaṇa was the cause of his being freed. However, his chanting would then have been a *nāma-aparādha. Nāmno balād yasya hi pāpa-buddhiḥ:* one who continues to act sinfully and tries to neutralize his sins by chanting the holy name of the Lord is a *nāma-aparādhī*, an offender to the holy name. In response it may be said that Ajāmila's chanting was inoffensive because he did not chant the name of Nārāyaṇa with the purpose of counteracting his sins. He did not know that he was addicted to sinful actions, nor did he know that his chanting of the name of Nārāyaṇa was neutralizing them. Thus he did not commit a *nāma-aparādha*, and his repeated chanting of the holy name of Nārāyaṇa while calling his son may be called pure chanting. Because of this pure chanting, Ajāmila unconsciously accumulated the results of *bhakti.* Indeed, even his first utterance of the holy name was sufficient to nullify all the sinful reactions of his life. To cite a logical example, a fig tree does not immediately yield fruits, but in time the fruits are available. Similarly, Ajāmila's devotional service grew little by little, and therefore although he committed very sinful acts, the reactions did not affect him. In the *śāstras* it is said that if one chants the holy name of the Lord even once, the reactions of past, present or future sinful life do not affect him. To give another example, if one extracts the poison fangs of a serpent, this saves the serpent's future victims from poisonous effects, even if the serpent bites repeatedly. Similarly, if a devotee chants the holy name even once inoffensively, this protects him eternally. He need only wait for the results of the chanting to mature in due course of time.

Thus end the Bhaktivedanta purports of the Sixth Canto, Second Chapter, of the Śrīmad-Bhāgavatam, *entitled "Ajāmila Delivered by the Viṣṇudūtas."*

CHAPTER THREE

Yamarāja Instructs His Messengers

As related in this chapter, the Yamadūtas approached Yamarāja, who very exhaustively explained *bhāgavata-dharma*, the religious principle of devotional service. Yamarāja thus satisfied the Yamadūtas, who had been very disappointed. Yamarāja said, "Although Ajāmila was calling for his son, he chanted the holy name of the Lord, Nārāyaṇa, and simply by a glimpse of the chanting of the holy name, he immediately achieved the association of Lord Viṣṇu's order carriers, who saved him from your attempt to arrest him. This is quite all right. It is a fact that even a chronically sinful person who chants the holy name of the Lord, although not completely without offenses, does not take another material birth."

By chanting the holy name of the Lord, Ajāmila had met four order carriers of Lord Viṣṇu. They were very beautiful and had quickly come to rescue him. Yamarāja now described them. "The Viṣṇudūtas are all pure devotees of the Lord, the Supreme Person in regard to the creation, maintenance and annihilation of this cosmic manifestation. Neither King Indra, Varuṇa, Śiva, Brahmā, the seven *ṛṣis* nor I myself can understand the transcendental activities of the Supreme Lord, who is self-sufficient and beyond the reach of the material senses. With material senses, no one can attain enlightenment about Him. The Lord, the master of the illusory energy, possesses transcendental qualities for the good fortune of everyone, and His devotees are also qualified in that way. The devotees, concerned only with rescuing the fallen souls from this material world, apparently take birth in different places in the material world just to save the conditioned souls. If one is somewhat interested in spiritual life, the devotees of the Lord protect him in many ways."

Yamarāja continued, "The essence of *sanātana-dharma*, or eternal religion, is extremely confidential. No one but the Lord Himself can deliver that confidential religious system to human society. It is by the mercy of the Lord that the transcendental system of religion can be understood by His pure devotees, and specifically by the twelve *mahājanas*—Lord Brahmā, Nārada Muni, Lord Śiva, the Kumāras, Kapila,

Manu, Prahlāda, Janaka, Bhīṣma, Bali, Śukadeva Gosvāmī and me. Other learned scholars, headed by Jaimini, are almost always covered by the illusory energy, and therefore they are more or less attracted by the flowery language of the three *Vedas*, namely *Ṛg*, *Yajur* and *Sāma*, which are called *trayī*. Instead of becoming pure devotees, people captivated by the flowery words of these three *Vedas* are interested in the Vedic ritualistic ceremonies. They cannot understand the glories of chanting the holy name of the Lord. Intelligent persons, however, take to the devotional service of the Lord. When they chant the holy name of the Lord without offenses, they are no longer subject to my rulings. If by chance they commit some sinful act, they are protected by the holy name of the Lord because that is where their interest lies. The four weapons of the Lord, especially the club and the Sudarśana *cakra*, always protect the devotees. One who chants, hears or remembers the holy name of the Lord without duplicity, or who prays or offers obeisances to the Lord, becomes perfect, whereas even a learned person may be called to hell if he is bereft of devotional service."

After Yamarāja thus described the glories of the Lord and His devotees, Śukadeva Gosvāmī further explained the potency of chanting the holy name and the futility of performing Vedic ritualistic ceremonies and pious activities for atonement.

TEXT 1

श्रीराजोवाच
निशम्य देवः स्वभटोपवर्णितं
प्रत्याह किं तानपि धर्मराजः ।
एवं हताज्ञो विहतान्मुरारे-
र्नैदेशिकैर्यस्य वशे जनोऽयम् ॥ १ ॥

śrī-rājovāca
niśamya devaḥ sva-bhaṭopavarṇitaṁ
pratyāha kiṁ tān api dharmarājaḥ
evaṁ hatājño vihatān murārer
naideśikair yasya vaśe jano 'yam

śrī-rājā uvāca—the King said; *niśamya*—after hearing; *devaḥ*—Lord Yamarāja; *sva-bhaṭa*—of his own servants; *upavarṇitam*—the statements; *pratyāha*—replied; *kim*—what; *tān*—unto them; *api*—also; *dharma-rājaḥ*—Yamarāja, the superintendent of death and the judge of religious and irreligious activities; *evam*—thus; *hata-ājñaḥ*—whose order was foiled; *vihatān*—who were defeated; *murāreḥ naideśikaiḥ*—by the order carriers of Murāri, Kṛṣṇa; *yasya*—of whom; *vaśe*—under the subjugation; *janaḥ ayam*—all the people of the world.

TRANSLATION

King Parīkṣit said: O my lord, O Śukadeva Gosvāmī, Yamarāja is the controller of all living entities in terms of their religious and irreligious activities, but his order had been foiled. When his servants, the Yamadūtas, informed him of their defeat by the Viṣṇudūtas, who had stopped them from arresting Ajāmila, what did he reply?

PURPORT

Śrīla Viśvanātha Cakravartī Ṭhākura says that although the statements of the Yamadūtas were fully upheld by Vedic principles, the statements of the Viṣṇudūtas were triumphant. This was confirmed by Yamarāja himself.

TEXT 2

यमस्य देवस्य न दण्डभङ्गः
कुतश्चनर्षे श्रुतपूर्व आसीत् ।
एतन्मुने वृश्चति लोकसंशयं
न हि त्वदन्य इति मे विनिश्चितम् ॥ २ ॥

yamasya devasya na daṇḍa-bhaṅgaḥ
kutaścanarṣe śruta-pūrva āsīt
etan mune vṛścati loka-saṁśayaṁ
na hi tvad-anya iti me viniścitam

yamasya—of Yamarāja; *devasya*—the demigod in charge of judgment; *na*—not; *daṇḍa-bhaṅgaḥ*—the breaking of the order;

kutaścana—from anywhere; *ṛṣe*—O great sage; *śruta-pūrvaḥ*—heard before; *āsīt*—was; *etat*—this; *mune*—O great sage; *vṛścati*—can eradicate; *loka-saṁśayam*—the doubt of people; *na*—not; *hi*—indeed; *tvat-anyaḥ*—anyone other than you; *iti*—thus; *me*—by me; *viniścitam*—concluded.

TRANSLATION

O great sage, never before has it been heard anywhere that an order from Yamarāja has been baffled. Therefore I think that people will have doubts about this that no one but you can eradicate. Since that is my firm conviction, kindly explain the reasons for these events.

TEXT 3

श्रीशुक उवाच
भगवत्पुरुषै राजन् याम्याः प्रतिहतोद्यमाः ।
पतिं विज्ञापयामासुर्यमं संयमनीपतिम् ॥ ३ ॥

śrī-śuka uvāca
bhagavat-puruṣai rājan
yāmyāḥ pratihatodyamāḥ
patiṁ vijñāpayām āsur
yamaṁ saṁyamanī-patim

śrī-śukaḥ uvāca—Śukadeva Gosvāmī said; *bhagavat-puruṣaiḥ*—by the order carriers of the Lord, the Viṣṇudūtas; *rājan*—O King; *yāmyāḥ*—the order carriers of Yamarāja; *pratihata-udyamāḥ*—whose efforts were defeated; *patim*—their master; *vijñāpayām āsuḥ*—informed; *yamam*—Yamarāja; *saṁyamanī-patim*—the master of the city Saṁyamanī.

TRANSLATION

Śrī Śukadeva Gosvāmī replied: My dear King, when the order carriers of Yamarāja were baffled and defeated by the order carriers of Viṣṇu, they approached their master, the controller of Saṁyamanī-purī and master of sinful persons, to tell him of this incident.

TEXT 4

यमदूता ऊचुः
कति सन्तीह शास्तारो जीवलोकस्य वै प्रभो ।
त्रैविध्यं कुर्वतः कर्म फलाभिव्यक्तिहेतवः ॥ ४ ॥

yamadūtā ūcuḥ
kati santīha śāstāro
jīva-lokasya vai prabho
trai-vidhyaṁ kurvataḥ karma
phalābhivyakti-hetavaḥ

yamadūtāḥ ūcuḥ—the order carriers of Yamarāja said; *kati*—how many; *santi*—are there; *iha*—in this world; *śāstāraḥ*—controllers or rulers; *jīva-lokasya*—of this material world; *vai*—indeed; *prabho*—O master; *trai-vidhyam*—under the three modes of material nature; *kurvataḥ*—performing; *karma*—activity; *phala*—of the results; *abhi-vyakti*—of the manifestation; *hetavaḥ*—causes.

TRANSLATION

The Yamadūtas said: Our dear lord, how many controllers or rulers are there in this material world? How many causes are responsible for manifesting the various results of activities performed under the three modes of material nature [sattva-guṇa, rajo-guṇa and tamo-guṇa]?

PURPORT

Śrīla Viśvanātha Cakravartī Ṭhākura says that the Yamadūtas, the order carriers of Yamarāja, were so disappointed that they asked their master, almost in great anger, whether there were many masters other than him. Furthermore, because the Yamadūtas had been defeated and their master could not protect them, they were inclined to say that there was no need to serve such a master. If a servant cannot carry out the orders of his master without being defeated, what is the use of serving such a powerless master?

TEXT 5

यदि स्युर्बहवो लोके शास्तारो दण्डधारिणः ।
कस्य स्यातां न वा कस्य मृत्युश्चामृतमेव वा ॥ ५ ॥

yadi syur bahavo loke
śāstāro daṇḍa-dhāriṇaḥ
kasya syātāṁ na vā kasya
mṛtyuś cāmṛtam eva vā

yadi—if; *syuḥ*—there are; *bahavaḥ*—many; *loke*—in this world; *śāstāraḥ*—rulers or controllers; *daṇḍa-dhāriṇaḥ*—who punish the sinful men; *kasya*—of whom; *syātām*—there may be; *na*—not; *vā*—or; *kasya*—of whom; *mṛtyuḥ*—distress or unhappiness; *ca*—and; *amṛtam*—happiness; *eva*—certainly; *vā*—or.

TRANSLATION

If in this universe there are many rulers and justices who disagree about punishment and reward, their contradictory actions will neutralize each other, and no one will be punished or rewarded. Otherwise, if their contradictory acts fail to neutralize each other, everyone will have to be both punished and rewarded.

PURPORT

Because the Yamadūtas had been unsuccessful in carrying out the order of Yamarāja, they doubted whether Yamarāja actually had the power to punish the sinful. Although they had gone to arrest Ajāmila, following Yamarāja's order, they found themselves unsuccessful because of the order of some higher authority. Therefore they were unsure of whether there were many authorities or only one. If there were many authorities who gave different judgments, which could be contradictory, a person might be wrongly punished or wrongly rewarded, or he might be neither punished nor rewarded. According to our experience in the material world, a person punished in one court may appeal to another. Thus the same man may be either punished or rewarded according to different judgments. However, in the law of nature or the court of the Supreme

Personality of Godhead there cannot be such contradictory judgments. The judges and their judgments must be perfect and free from contradictions. Actually the position of Yamarāja was very awkward in the case of Ajāmila because the Yamadūtas were right in attempting to arrest Ajāmila, but the Viṣṇudūtas had baffled them. Although Yamarāja, under these circumstances, was accused by both the Viṣṇudūtas and the Yamadūtas, he is perfect in administering justice because he is empowered by the Supreme Personality of Godhead. Therefore he will explain what his real position is and how everyone is controlled by the supreme controller, the Personality of Godhead.

TEXT 6

किन्तु शास्तृबहुत्वे स्याद्बहूनामिह कर्मिणाम् ।
शास्तृत्वमुपचारो हि यथा मण्डलवर्तिनाम् ॥ ६ ॥

kintu śāstṛ-bahutve syād
bahūnām iha karmiṇām
śāstṛtvam upacāro hi
yathā maṇḍala-vartinām

kintu—but; *śāstṛ*—of governors or judges; *bahutve*—in the plurality; *syāt*—there may be; *bahūnām*—of many; *iha*—in this world; *karmiṇām*—persons performing actions; *śāstṛtvam*—departmental management; *upacāraḥ*—administration; *hi*—indeed; *yathā*—just like; *maṇḍala-vartinām*—of the departmental heads.

TRANSLATION

The Yamadūtas continued: Since there are many different karmīs, or workers, there may be different judges or rulers to give them justice, but just as one central emperor controls different departmental rulers, there must be one supreme controller to guide all the judges.

PURPORT

In governmental management there may be departmental officials to give justice to different persons, but the law must be one, and that central law must control everyone. The Yamadūtas could not imagine that two judges would give two different verdicts in the same case, and therefore they wanted to know who the central judge is. The Yamadūtas were certain that Ajāmila was a most sinful man, but although Yamarāja wanted to punish him, the Viṣṇudūtas excused him. This was a puzzling situation that the Yamadūtas wanted Yamarāja to clarify.

TEXT 7

अतस्त्वमेको भूतानां सेश्वराणामधीश्वरः ।
शास्ता दण्डधरो नृणां शुभाशुभविवेचनः ॥ ७ ॥

atas tvam eko bhūtānāṁ
seśvarāṇām adhīśvaraḥ
śāstā daṇḍa-dharo nṛṇāṁ
śubhāśubha-vivecanaḥ

ataḥ—as such; *tvam*—you; *ekaḥ*—one; *bhūtānām*—of all living beings; *sa-īśvarāṇām*—including all the demigods; *adhīśvaraḥ*—the supreme master; *śāstā*—the supreme ruler; *daṇḍa-dharaḥ*—the supreme administrator of punishment; *nṛṇām*—of human society; *śubha-aśubha-vivecanaḥ*—who discriminates between what is auspicious and inauspicious.

TRANSLATION

The supreme judge must be one, not many. It was our understanding that you are that supreme judge and that you have jurisdiction even over the demigods. Our impression was that you are the master of all living entities, the supreme authority who discriminates between the pious and impious activities of all human beings.

TEXT 8

तस्य ते विहितो दण्डो न लोके वर्ततेऽधुना ।
चतुर्भिरद्भुतैः सिद्धैराज्ञा ते विप्रलम्भिता ॥ ८ ॥

tasya te vihito daṇḍo
na loke vartate 'dhunā
caturbhir adbhutaiḥ siddhair
ājñā te vipralambhitā

tasya—of the influence; *te*—of you; *vihitaḥ*—ordained; *daṇḍaḥ*—punishment; *na*—not; *loke*—within this world; *vartate*—exists; *adhunā*—now; *caturbhiḥ*—by four; *adbhutaiḥ*—very wonderful; *siddhaiḥ*—perfected persons; *ājñā*—the order; *te*—your; *vipralambhitā*—surpassed.

TRANSLATION

But now we see that the punishment ordained under your authority is no longer effective, since your order has been transgressed by four wonderful and perfect persons.

PURPORT

The Yamadūtas had been under the impression that Yamarāja was the only person in charge of administering justice. They were fully confident that no one could counteract his judgments, but now, to their surprise, his order had been violated by the four wonderful persons from Siddhaloka.

TEXT 9

नीयमानं तवादेशादस्माभिर्यातनागृहान् ।
व्यामोचयन् पातकिनं छित्त्वा पाशान् प्रसह्य ते ॥ ९ ॥

nīyamānaṁ tavādeśād
asmābhir yātanā-gṛhān
vyāmocayan pātakinaṁ
chittvā pāśān prasahya te

nīyamānam—being brought; *tava ādeśāt*—by your order; *asmābhiḥ*—by us; *yātanā-gṛhān*—to the torture chambers, the hellish planets; *vyāmocayan*—released; *pātakinam*—the sinful Ajāmila; *chittvā*—cutting; *pāśān*—the ropes; *prasahya*—by force; *te*—they.

TRANSLATION

We were bringing the most sinful Ajāmila toward the hellish planets, following your order, when those beautiful persons from Siddhaloka forcibly cut the knots of the ropes with which we were arresting him.

PURPORT

Śrīla Viśvanātha Cakravartī Ṭhākura remarks that the Yamadūtas wanted to bring the Viṣṇudūtas before Yamarāja. If Yamarāja could then have punished the Viṣṇudūtas, the Yamadūtas would have been satisfied.

TEXT 10

तांस्ते वेदितुमिच्छामो यदि नो मन्यसे क्षमम् ।
नारायणेत्यभिहिते मा भैरित्याययुर्द्रुतम् ॥१०॥

tāṁs te veditum icchāmo
yadi no manyase kṣamam
nārāyaṇety abhihite
mā bhair ity āyayur drutam

tān—about them; *te*—from you; *veditum*—to know; *icchāmaḥ*—we wish; *yadi*—if; *naḥ*—for us; *manyase*—you think; *kṣamam*—suitable; *nārāyaṇa*—Nārāyaṇa; *iti*—thus; *abhihite*—being uttered; *mā*—do not; *bhaiḥ*—fear; *iti*—thus; *āyayuḥ*—they arrived; *drutam*—very soon.

TRANSLATION

As soon as the sinful Ajāmila uttered the name Nārāyaṇa, these four beautiful men immediately arrived and reassured him, saying, "Do not fear. Do not fear." We wish to know about them from Your Lordship. If you think we are able to understand them, kindly describe who they are.

PURPORT

The order carriers of Yamarāja, being very much aggrieved because of their defeat by the four Viṣṇudūtas, wanted to bring them before

Yamarāja and, if possible, punish them. Otherwise they desired to commit suicide. Before pursuing either course, however, they wanted to know about the Viṣṇudūtas from Yamarāja, who is also omniscient.

TEXT 11

श्रीबादरायणिरुवाच
इति देवः स आपृष्टः प्रजासंयमनो यमः ।
प्रीतः स्वदूतान् प्रत्याह स्मरन् पादाम्बुजं हरेः ॥११॥

śrī-bādarāyaṇir uvāca
iti devaḥ sa āpṛṣṭaḥ
prajā-saṁyamano yamaḥ
prītaḥ sva-dūtān pratyāha
smaran pādāmbujaṁ hareḥ

śrī-bādarāyaṇiḥ uvāca—Śukadeva Gosvāmī said; *iti*—thus; *devaḥ*—the demigod; *saḥ*—he; *āpṛṣṭaḥ*—being questioned; *prajā-saṁyamanaḥ yamaḥ*—Lord Yamarāja, who controls the living entities; *prītaḥ*—being pleased; *sva-dūtān*—to his own servants; *pratyāha*—replied; *smaran*—remembering; *pāda-ambujam*—the lotus feet; *hareḥ*—of Hari, the Personality of Godhead.

TRANSLATION

Śrī Śukadeva Gosvāmī said: Thus having been questioned, Lord Yamarāja, the supreme controller of the living entities, was very pleased with his order carriers because of hearing from them the holy name of Nārāyaṇa. He remembered the lotus feet of the Lord and began to reply.

PURPORT

Śrīla Yamarāja, the supreme controller of the living entities in terms of their pious and impious activities, was very pleased with his servants because they had chanted the holy name of Nārāyaṇa in his dominion. Yamarāja has to deal with men who are all sinful and who can hardly understand Nārāyaṇa. Consequently when his order carriers uttered the name of Nārāyaṇa, he was extremely pleased, for he also is a Vaiṣṇava.

TEXT 12

यम उवाच
परो मदन्यो जगतस्तस्थुषश्च
ओतं प्रोतं पटवद्यत्र विश्वम् ।
यदंशतोऽस्य स्थितिजन्मनाशा
नस्योतवद् यस्य वशे च लोकः ॥१२॥

yama uvāca
paro mad-anyo jagatas tasthuṣaś ca
otaṁ protaṁ paṭavad yatra viśvam
yad-aṁśato 'sya sthiti-janma-nāśā
nasy otavad yasya vaśe ca lokaḥ

yamaḥ uvāca—Yamarāja replied; *paraḥ*—superior; *mat*—than me; *anyaḥ*—another; *jagataḥ*—of all moving things; *tasthuṣaḥ*—of non-moving things; *ca*—and; *otam*—crosswise; *protam*—lengthwise; *paṭa-vat*—like a woven cloth; *yatra*—in whom; *viśvam*—the cosmic manifestation; *yat*—of whom; *aṁśataḥ*—from the partial expansions; *asya*—of this universe; *sthiti*—the maintenance; *janma*—the creation; *nāśāḥ*—the annihilation; *nasi*—in the nose; *ota-vat*—like the rope; *yasya*—of whom; *vaśe*—under the control; *ca*—and; *lokaḥ*—the whole creation.

TRANSLATION

Yamarāja said: My dear servants, you have accepted me as the Supreme, but factually I am not. Above me, and above all the other demigods, including Indra and Candra, is the one supreme master and controller. The partial manifestations of His personality are Brahmā, Viṣṇu and Śiva, who are in charge of the creation, maintenance and annihilation of this universe. He is like the two threads that form the length and breadth of a woven cloth. The entire world is controlled by Him just as a bull is controlled by a rope in its nose.

PURPORT

The order carriers of Yamarāja suspected that there was a ruler even above Yamarāja. To eradicate their doubts, Yamarāja immediately replied, "Yes, there is one supreme controller above everything." Yamarāja is in charge of some of the moving living entities, namely the human beings, but the animals, who also move, are not under his control. Only human beings have consciousness of right and wrong, and among them only those who perform sinful activities come under the control of Yamarāja. Therefore although Yamarāja is a controller, he is only a departmental controller of a few living entities. There are other demigods who control many other departments, but above them all is one supreme controller, Kṛṣṇa. *Īśvaraḥ paramaḥ kṛṣṇaḥ sac-cid-ānanda-vigrahaḥ:* the supreme controller is Kṛṣṇa. Others, who control their own departments in the affairs of the universe, are insignificant in comparison to Kṛṣṇa, the supreme controller. Kṛṣṇa says in *Bhagavad-gītā* (7.7), *mattaḥ parataraṁ nānyat kiñcid asti dhanañjaya:* "My dear Dhanañjaya [Arjuna], no one is superior to Me." Therefore Yamarāja immediately cleared away the doubts of his assistants, the Yamadūtas, by confirming that there is a supreme controller above all others.

Śrīla Madhvācārya explains that the words *otaṁ protam* refer to the cause of all causes. The Supreme Lord is both vertical and horizontal to the cosmic manifestation. This is confirmed by the following verse from the *Skanda Purāṇa:*

yathā kanthā-paṭāḥ sūtra
otāḥ protāś ca sa sthitāḥ
evaṁ viṣṇāv idaṁ viśvam
otaṁ protaṁ ca saṁsthitam

Like the two threads, horizontal and vertical, of which a quilt is manufactured, Lord Viṣṇu is situated as the vertical and horizontal cause of the cosmic manifestation.

TEXT 13

यो नामभिर्वाचि जनं निजायां
बध्नाति तन्त्यामिव दामभिर्गाः ।
यस्मै बलिं त इमे नामकर्म-
निबन्धबद्धाश्चकिता वहन्ति ॥१३॥

yo nāmabhir vāci janaṁ nijāyāṁ
badhnāti tantryām iva dāmabhir gāḥ
yasmai baliṁ ta ime nāma-karma-
nibandha-baddhāś cakitā vahanti

yaḥ—He who; *nāmabhiḥ*—by different names; *vāci*—to the Vedic language; *janam*—all people; *nijāyām*—which has emanated from Himself; *badhnāti*—binds; *tantryām*—to a rope; *iva*—like; *dāmabhiḥ*—by cords; *gāḥ*—bulls; *yasmai*—unto whom; *balim*—a small presentation of taxes; *te*—all of them; *ime*—these; *nāma-karma*—of names and different activities; *nibandha*—by the obligations; *baddhāḥ*—bound; *cakitāḥ*—being fearful; *vahanti*—carry.

TRANSLATION

Just as the driver of a bullock cart ties ropes through the nostrils of his bulls to control them, the Supreme Personality of Godhead binds all men through the ropes of His words in the Vedas, which set forth the names and activities of the distinct orders of human society [brāhmaṇa, kṣatriya, vaiśya and śūdra]. In fear, the members of these orders all worship the Supreme Lord by offering Him presentations according to their respective activities.

PURPORT

In this material world, everyone is conditioned, regardless of who he is. One may be a human being, a demigod or an animal, tree or plant, but everything is controlled by the laws of nature, and behind this natural control is the Supreme Personality of Godhead. This is confirmed by *Bhagavad-gītā* (9.10), wherein Kṛṣṇa says, *mayādhyakṣeṇa prakṛtiḥ sūyate sa-carācaram:* "The material nature is working under My direction and producing all moving and nonmoving beings." Thus Kṛṣṇa is behind the natural machine, which works under His control.

Apart from other living entities, the living being in the human form of body is systematically controlled by the Vedic injunctions in terms of the divisions of *varṇa* and *āśrama*. A human being is expected to follow the rules and regulations of *varṇa* and *āśrama;* otherwise he cannot escape punishment by Yamarāja. The point is that every human being is expected to elevate himself to the position of a *brāhmaṇa*, the most intelligent man, and then one must transcend that position to become a Vaiṣṇava. This is the perfection of life. The *brāhmaṇa, kṣatriya, vaiśya* and *śūdra* can elevate themselves by worshiping the Lord according to their activities (*sve sve karmaṇy abhirataḥ saṁsiddhiṁ labhate naraḥ*). The divisions of *varṇa* and *āśrama* are necessary to insure the proper execution of duties and peaceful existence for everyone, but everyone is directed to worship the Supreme Lord, who is all-pervading (*yena sarvam idaṁ tatam*). The Supreme Lord exists vertically and horizontally (*otaṁ protam*), and therefore if one follows the Vedic injunctions by worshiping the Supreme Lord according to one's ability, his life will be perfect. As stated in *Śrīmad-Bhāgavatam* (1.2.13):

ataḥ pumbhir dvija-śreṣṭhā
varṇāśrama-vibhāgaśaḥ
svanuṣṭhitasya dharmasya
saṁsiddhir hari-toṣaṇam

"O best among the twice-born, it is therefore concluded that the highest perfection one can achieve, by discharging his prescribed duties [*dharma*] according to caste divisions and orders of life, is to please the Lord Hari." The *varṇāśrama* institution offers the perfect process for making one eligible to return home, back to Godhead, because the aim of every *varṇa* and *āśrama* is to please the Supreme Lord. One can please the Lord under the direction of a bona fide spiritual master, and if one does so his life is perfect. The Supreme Lord is worshipable, and everyone worships Him directly or indirectly. Those who worship Him directly get the results of liberation quickly, whereas the liberation of those who serve Him indirectly is delayed.

The words *nāmabhir vāci* are very important. In the *varṇāśrama* institution, there are different names—*brāhmaṇa, kṣatriya, vaiśya, śūdra, brahmacārī, gṛhastha, vānaprastha* and *sannyāsī*. The *vāk*, or Vedic injunctions, give directions for all these divisions. Everyone is expected to offer obeisances to the Supreme Lord and perform duties as indicated in the *Vedas*.

TEXTS 14–15

अहं महेन्द्रो निर्ऋतिः प्रचेताः
सोमोऽग्निरीशः पवनो विरिञ्चिः ।
आदित्यविश्वे वसवोऽथ साध्या
मरुद्गणा रुद्रगणाः ससिद्धाः ॥१४॥
अन्ये च ये विश्वसृजोऽमरेशा
भृग्वादयोऽस्पृष्टरजस्तमस्काः ।
यस्येहितं न विदुः स्पृष्टमायाः
सत्त्वप्रधाना अपि किं ततोऽन्ये ॥१५॥

ahaṁ mahendro nirṛtiḥ pracetāḥ
somo 'gnir īśaḥ pavano viriñciḥ
āditya-viśve vasavo 'tha sādhyā
marud-gaṇā rudra-gaṇāḥ sasiddhāḥ

anye ca ye viśva-sṛjo 'mareśā
bhṛgv-ādayo 'spṛṣṭa-rajas-tamaskāḥ
yasyehitaṁ na viduḥ spṛṣṭa-māyāḥ
sattva-pradhānā api kiṁ tato 'nye

aham—I, Yamarāja; *mahendraḥ*—Indra, the King of heaven; *nirṛtiḥ*—Nirṛti; *pracetāḥ*—Varuṇa, the controller of water; *somaḥ*—the moon; *agniḥ*—fire; *īśaḥ*—Lord Śiva; *pavanaḥ*—the demigod of the air; *viriñciḥ*—Lord Brahmā; *āditya*—the sun; *viśve*—Viśvāsu; *vasavaḥ*—the eight Vasus; *atha*—also; *sādhyāḥ*—the demigods; *marut-gaṇāḥ*—masters of the wind; *rudra-gaṇāḥ*—the expansions of Lord Śiva; *sa-siddhāḥ*—with the inhabitants of Siddhaloka; *anye*—others; *ca*—and; *ye*—who; *viśva-sṛjaḥ*—Marīci and the other creators of the universal affairs; *amara-īśāḥ*—the demigods like Bṛhaspati; *bhṛgu-ādayaḥ*—the great sages headed by Bhṛgu; *aspṛṣṭa*—who have not been contaminated; *rajaḥ-tamaskāḥ*—by the lower modes of material nature (*rajo-guṇa* and *tamo-guṇa*); *yasya*—of whom; *īhitam*—the activity; *na viduḥ*—do not know; *spṛṣṭa-māyāḥ*—who are illusioned by the illusory energy; *sattva-*

pradhānāḥ—chiefly in the mode of goodness; *api*—although; *kim*—what to speak of; *tataḥ*—than them; *anye*—others.

TRANSLATION

I, Yamarāja; Indra, the King of heaven; Nirṛti; Varuṇa; Candra, the moon-god; Agni; Lord Śiva; Pavana; Lord Brahmā; Sūrya, the sun-god; Viśvāsu; the eight Vasus; the Sādhyas; the Maruts; the Rudras; the Siddhas; and Marīci and the other great ṛṣis engaged in maintaining the departmental affairs of the universe, as well as the best of the demigods headed by Bṛhaspati, and the great sages headed by Bhṛgu are all certainly freed from the influence of the two base material modes of nature, namely passion and ignorance. Nevertheless, although we are in the mode of goodness, we cannot understand the activities of the Supreme Personality of Godhead. What, then, is to be said of others, who, under illusion, merely speculate to know God?

PURPORT

The men and other living entities within this cosmic manifestation are controlled by the three modes of nature. For the living entities controlled by the base qualities of nature, passion and ignorance, there is no possibility of understanding God. Even those in the mode of goodness, like the many demigods and great *ṛṣis* described in these verses, cannot understand the activities of the Supreme Personality of Godhead. As stated in *Bhagavad-gītā*, one who is situated in the devotional service of the Lord is transcendental to all the material qualities. Therefore the Lord personally says that no one can understand Him but the *bhaktas*, who are transcendental to all material qualities (*bhaktyā mām abhijānāti*). As stated by Bhīṣmadeva to Mahārāja Yudhiṣṭhira in *Śrīmad-Bhāgavatam* (1.9.16):

na hy asya karhicid rājan
pumān veda vidhitsitam
yad-vijijñāsayā yuktā
muhyanti kavayo 'pi hi

"O King, no one can know the plan of the Lord [Śrī Kṛṣṇa]. Even though great philosophers inquire exhaustively, they are bewildered." No one, therefore, can understand God by speculative knowledge. Indeed, by speculation one will be bewildered (*muhyanti*). This is also confirmed by the Lord Himself in *Bhagavad-gītā* (7.3):

manuṣyāṇāṁ sahasreṣu
kaścid yatati siddhaye
yatatām api siddhānāṁ
kaścin māṁ vetti tattvataḥ

Among many thousands of men, one may endeavor for perfection, and even among the *siddhas*, those who have already become perfect, only one who adopts the process of *bhakti*, devotional service, can understand Kṛṣṇa.

TEXT 16

यं वै न गोभिर्मनसासुभिर्वा
हृदा गिरा वासुभृतो विचक्षते ।
आत्मानमन्तर्हृदि सन्तमात्मनां
चक्षुर्यथैवाकृतयस्ततः परम् ॥१६॥

yaṁ vai na gobhir manasāsubhir vā
hṛdā girā vāsu-bhṛto vicakṣate
ātmānam antar-hṛdi santam ātmanāṁ
cakṣur yathaivākṛtayas tataḥ param

yam—whom; *vai*—indeed; *na*—not; *gobhiḥ*—by the senses; *manasā*—by the mind; *asubhiḥ*—by the life breath; *vā*—or; *hṛdā*—by thoughts; *girā*—by words; *vā*—or; *asu-bhṛtaḥ*—the living entities; *vicakṣate*—see or know; *ātmānam*—the Supersoul; *antaḥ-hṛdi*—within the core of the heart; *santam*—existing; *ātmanām*—of the living entities; *cakṣuḥ*—the eyes; *yathā*—just like; *eva*—indeed; *ākṛtayaḥ*—the different parts or limbs of the body; *tataḥ*—than them; *param*—higher.

TRANSLATION

As the different limbs of the body cannot see the eyes, the living entities cannot see the Supreme Lord, who is situated as the Super-

soul in everyone's heart. Not by the senses, by the mind, by the life air, by thoughts within the heart, or by the vibration of words can the living entities ascertain the real situation of the Supreme Lord.

PURPORT

Although the different parts of the body do not have the power to see the eyes, the eyes direct the movements of the body's different parts. The legs move forward because the eyes see what is in front of them, and the hand touches because the eyes see touchable entities. Similarly, every living being acts according to the direction of the Supersoul, who is situated within the heart. As the Lord Himself confirms in *Bhagavad-gītā* (15.15), *sarvasya cāhaṁ hṛdi sanniviṣṭo mattaḥ smṛtir jñānam apohanaṁ ca:* "I am sitting in everyone's heart and giving directions for remembrance, knowledge and forgetfulness." Elsewhere in *Bhagavad-gītā* it is stated, *īśvaraḥ sarva-bhūtānāṁ hṛd-deśe 'rjuna tiṣṭhati:* "The Supreme Lord, as the Supersoul, is situated within the heart." The living entity cannot do anything without the sanction of the Supersoul. The Supersoul is acting at every moment, but the living entity cannot understand the form and activities of the Supersoul by manipulating his senses. The example of the eyes and the bodily limbs is very appropriate. If the limbs could see, they could walk forward without the help of the eyes, but that is impossible. Although one cannot see the Supersoul in one's heart through sensual activities, His direction is necessary.

TEXT 17

तस्यात्मतन्त्रस्य हरेरधीशितुः
परस्य मायाधिपतेर्महात्मनः ।
प्रायेण दूता इह वै मनोहरा-
श्चरन्ति तद्रूपगुणस्वभावाः ॥१७॥

tasyātma-tantrasya harer adhīśituḥ
parasya māyādhipater mahātmanaḥ
prāyeṇa dūtā iha vai manoharāś
caranti tad-rūpa-guṇa-svabhāvāḥ

tasya—of Him; *ātma-tantrasya*—being self-sufficient, not dependent on any other person; *hareḥ*—the Supreme Personality of Godhead; *adhīśituḥ*—who is the master of everything; *parasya*—the Transcendence; *māyā-adhipateḥ*—the master of the illusory energy; *mahā-ātmanaḥ*—of the Supreme Soul; *prāyeṇa*—almost; *dūtāḥ*—the order carriers; *iha*—in this world; *vai*—indeed; *manoharāḥ*—pleasing in their dealings and bodily features; *caranti*—they move; *tat*—of Him; *rūpa*—possessing the bodily features; *guṇa*—the transcendental qualities; *sva-bhāvāḥ*—and nature.

TRANSLATION

The Supreme Personality of Godhead is self-sufficient and fully independent. He is the master of everyone and everything, including the illusory energy. He has His form, qualities and features; and similarly His order carriers, the Vaiṣṇavas, who are very beautiful, possess bodily features, transcendental qualities and a transcendental nature almost like His. They always wander within this world with full independence.

PURPORT

Yamarāja was describing the Supreme Personality of Godhead, the supreme controller, but the order carriers of Yamarāja were very eager to know about the Viṣṇudūtas, who had defeated them in their encounter with Ajāmila. Yamarāja therefore stated that the Viṣṇudūtas resemble the Supreme Personality of Godhead in their bodily features, transcendental qualities and nature. In other words, the Viṣṇudūtas, or Vaiṣṇavas, are almost as qualified as the Supreme Lord. Yamarāja informed the Yamadūtas that the Viṣṇudūtas are no less powerful than Lord Viṣṇu. Since Viṣṇu is above Yamarāja, the Viṣṇudūtas are above the Yamadūtas. Persons protected by the Viṣṇudūtas, therefore, cannot be touched by the Yamadūtas.

TEXT 18

भूतानि विष्णोः सुरपूजितानि
दुर्दर्शलिङ्गानि महाद्भुतानि ।

रक्षन्ति तद्भक्तिमतः परेभ्यो
मत्तश्च मर्त्यानथ सर्वतश्च ॥१८॥

bhūtāni viṣṇoḥ sura-pūjitāni
durdarśa-liṅgāni mahādbhutāni
rakṣanti tad-bhaktimataḥ parebhyo
mattaś ca martyān atha sarvataś ca

bhūtāni—living entities or servants; *viṣṇoḥ*—of Lord Viṣṇu; *sura-pūjitāni*—who are worshiped by the demigods; *durdarśa-liṅgāni*—possessing forms not easily seen; *mahā-adbhutāni*—greatly wonderful; *rakṣanti*—they protect; *tat-bhakti-mataḥ*—the devotees of the Lord; *parebhyaḥ*—from others who are inimical; *mattaḥ*—from me (Yamarāja) and my order carriers; *ca*—and; *martyān*—the human beings; *atha*—thus; *sarvataḥ*—from everything; *ca*—and.

TRANSLATION

The order carriers of Lord Viṣṇu, who are worshiped even by the demigods, possess wonderful bodily features exactly like those of Viṣṇu and are very rarely seen. The Viṣṇudūtas protect the devotees of the Lord from the hands of enemies, from envious persons and even from my jurisdiction, as well as from natural disturbances.

PURPORT

Yamarāja has specifically described the qualities of the Viṣṇudūtas to convince his own servants not to be envious of them. Yamarāja warned the Yamadūtas that the Viṣṇudūtas are worshiped with respectful obeisances by the demigods and are always very alert to protect the devotees of the Lord from the hands of enemies, from natural disturbances and from all dangerous conditions in this material world. Sometimes the members of the Kṛṣṇa Consciousness Society are afraid of the impending danger of world war and ask what would happen to them if a war should occur. In all kinds of danger, they should be confident of their protection by the Viṣṇudūtas or the Supreme Personality of Godhead, as confirmed in *Bhagavad-gītā* (*kaunteya pratijānīhi na me bhaktaḥ praṇaśyati*). Material danger is not meant for devotees. This is also confirmed in *Śrīmad-Bhāgavatam. Padaṁ padaṁ yad vipadāṁ na teṣām:* in this material world there are dangers at every step, but they are not meant for devotees who have fully surrendered unto the lotus feet of the Lord. The pure devotees of Lord Viṣṇu may rest assured of the Lord's protection, and as long as they are in this material world they should fully engage in devotional service by preaching the cult of Śrī Caitanya Mahāprabhu and Lord Kṛṣṇa, namely the Hare Kṛṣṇa movement of Kṛṣṇa consciousness.

TEXT 19

धर्मं तु साक्षाद्भगवत्प्रणीतं
न वै विदुरृषयो नापि देवाः ।
न सिद्धमुख्या असुरा मनुष्याः
कुतो नु विद्याधरचारणादयः ॥१९॥

dharmaṁ tu sākṣād bhagavat-praṇītaṁ
na vai vidur ṛṣayo nāpi devāḥ
na siddha-mukhyā asurā manuṣyāḥ
kuto nu vidyādhara-cāraṇādayaḥ

dharmam—real religious principles, or bona fide laws of religion; *tu*—but; *sākṣāt*—directly; *bhagavat*—by the Supreme Personality of Godhead; *praṇītam*—enacted; *na*—not; *vai*—indeed; *viduḥ*—they know; *ṛṣayaḥ*—the great *ṛṣis* such as Bhṛgu; *na*—not; *api*—also; *devāḥ*—the demigods; *na*—nor; *siddha-mukhyāḥ*—the chief leaders of Siddhaloka; *asurāḥ*—the demons; *manuṣyāḥ*—the inhabitants of Bhūrloka, the human beings; *kutaḥ*—where; *nu*—indeed; *vidyā-dhara*—the lesser demigods known as Vidyādharas; *cāraṇa*—the residents of the planets where people are by nature great musicians and singers; *ādayaḥ*—and so on.

TRANSLATION

Real religious principles are enacted by the Supreme Personality of Godhead. Although fully situated in the mode of goodness,

even the great ṛṣis who occupy the topmost planets cannot ascertain the real religious principles, nor can the demigods or the leaders of Siddhaloka, to say nothing of the asuras, ordinary human beings, Vidyādharas and Cāraṇas.

PURPORT

When challenged by the Viṣṇudūtas to describe the principles of religion, the Yamadūtas said, *veda-praṇihito dharmaḥ:* the religious principles are the principles enacted in the Vedic literature. They did not know, however, that the Vedic literature contains ritualistic ceremonies that are not transcendental, but are meant to keep peace and order among materialistic persons in the material world. Real religious principles are *nistraiguṇya*, above the three modes of material nature, or transcendental. The Yamadūtas did not know these transcendental religious principles, and therefore when prevented from arresting Ajāmila they were surprised. Materialistic persons who attach all their faith to the Vedic rituals are described in *Bhagavad-gītā* (2.42), wherein Kṛṣṇa says, *veda-vāda-ratāḥ pārtha nānyad astīti vādinaḥ:* the supposed followers of the *Vedas* say that there is nothing beyond the Vedic ceremonies. Indeed, there is a group of men in India who are very fond of the Vedic rituals, not understanding the meaning of these rituals, which are intended to elevate one gradually to the transcendental platform of knowing Kṛṣṇa (*vedaiś ca sarvair aham eva vedyaḥ*). Those who do not know this principle but who simply attach their faith to the Vedic rituals are called *veda-vāda-ratāḥ.*

Herein it is stated that the real religious principle is that which is given by the Supreme Personality of Godhead. That principle is stated in *Bhagavad-gītā. Sarva-dharmān parityajya mām ekaṁ śaraṇaṁ vraja:* one should give up all other duties and surrender unto the lotus feet of Kṛṣṇa. That is the real religious principle everyone should follow. Even though one follows Vedic scriptures, one may not know this transcendental principle, for it is not known to everyone. To say nothing of human beings, even the demigods in the upper planetary systems are unaware of it. This transcendental religious principle must be understood from the Supreme Personality of Godhead directly or from His special representative, as stated in the next verses.

TEXTS 20–21

स्वयम्भूर्नारदः शम्भुः कुमारः कपिलो मनुः ।
प्रह्लादो जनको भीष्मो बलिर्वैयासकिर्वयम् ॥२०॥
द्वादशैते विजानीमो धर्मं भागवतं भटाः ।
गुह्यं विशुद्धं दुर्बोधं यं ज्ञात्वामृतमश्नुते ॥२१॥

svayambhūr nāradaḥ śambhuḥ
kumāraḥ kapilo manuḥ
prahlādo janako bhīṣmo
balir vaiyāsakir vayam

dvādaśaite vijānīmo
dharmaṁ bhāgavataṁ bhaṭāḥ
guhyaṁ viśuddhaṁ durbodhaṁ
yaṁ jñātvāmṛtam aśnute

svayambhūḥ—Lord Brahmā; *nāradaḥ*—the great saint Nārada; *śambhuḥ*—Lord Śiva; *kumāraḥ*—the four Kumāras; *kapilaḥ*—Lord Kapila; *manuḥ*—Svāyambhuva Manu; *prahlādaḥ*—Prahlāda Mahārāja; *janakaḥ*—Janaka Mahārāja; *bhīṣmaḥ*—Grandfather Bhīṣma; *baliḥ*—Bali Mahārāja; *vaiyāsakiḥ*—Śukadeva, the son of Vyāsadeva; *vayam*—we; *dvādaśa*—twelve; *ete*—these; *vijānīmaḥ*—know; *dharmam*—real religious principles; *bhāgavatam*—which teach a person how to love the Supreme Personality of Godhead; *bhaṭāḥ*—O my dear servants; *guhyam*—very confidential; *viśuddham*—transcendental, not contaminated by the material modes of nature; *durbodham*—not easily understood; *yam*—which; *jñātvā*—understanding; *amṛtam*—eternal life; *aśnute*—he enjoys.

TRANSLATION

Lord Brahmā, Bhagavān Nārada, Lord Śiva, the four Kumāras, Lord Kapila [the son of Devahūti], Svāyambhuva Manu, Prahlāda Mahārāja, Janaka Mahārāja, Grandfather Bhīṣma, Bali Mahārāja, Śukadeva Gosvāmī and I myself know the real religious principle. My dear servants, this transcendental religious principle, which is known as bhāgavata-dharma, or surrender unto the Supreme Lord

and love for Him, is uncontaminated by the material modes of nature. It is very confidential and difficult for ordinary human beings to understand, but if by chance one fortunately understands it, he is immediately liberated, and thus he returns home, back to Godhead.

PURPORT

In *Bhagavad-gītā* Lord Kṛṣṇa refers to *bhāgavata-dharma* as the most confidential religious principle (*sarva-guhyatamam, guhyād guhyataram*). Kṛṣṇa says to Arjuna, "Because you are My very dear friend, I am explaining to you the most confidential religion." *Sarva-dharmān parityajya mām ekaṁ śaraṇaṁ vraja:* "Give up all other duties and surrender unto Me." One may ask, "If this principle is very rarely understood, what is the use of it?" In answer, Yamarāja states herein that this religious principle is understandable if one follows the *paramparā* system of Lord Brahmā, Lord Śiva, the four Kumāras and the other standard authorities. There are four lines of disciplic succession: one from Lord Brahmā, one from Lord Śiva, one from Lakṣmī, the goddess of fortune, and one from the Kumāras. The disciplic succession from Lord Brahmā is called the Brahma-sampradāya, the succession from Lord Śiva (Śambhu) is called the Rudra-sampradāya, the one from the goddess of fortune, Lakṣmījī, is called the Śrī-sampradāya, and the one from the Kumāras is called the Kumāra-sampradāya. One must take shelter of one of these four *sampradāyas* in order to understand the most confidential religious system. In the *Padma Purāṇa* it is said, *sampradāya-vihīnā ye mantrās te niṣphalā matāḥ:* if one does not follow the four recognized disciplic successions, his *mantra* or initiation is useless. In the present day there are many *apasampradāyas*, or *sampradāyas* which are not bona fide, which have no link to authorities like Lord Brahmā, Lord Śiva, the Kumāras or Lakṣmī. People are misguided by such *sampradāyas*. The *śāstras* say that being initiated in such a *sampradāya* is a useless waste of time, for it will never enable one to understand the real religious principles.

TEXT 22

एतावानेव लोकेऽस्मिन् पुंसां धर्मः परः स्मृतः ।
भक्तियोगो भगवति तन्नामग्रहणादिभिः ॥२२॥

etāvān eva loke 'smin
puṁsāṁ dharmaḥ paraḥ smṛtaḥ
bhakti-yogo bhagavati
tan-nāma-grahaṇādibhiḥ

etāvān—this much; *eva*—indeed; *loke asmin*—in this material world; *puṁsām*—of the living entities; *dharmaḥ*—the religious principles; *paraḥ*—transcendental; *smṛtaḥ*—recognized; *bhakti-yogaḥ*—*bhakti-yoga*, or devotional service; *bhagavati*—to the Supreme Personality of Godhead (not to the demigods); *tat*—His; *nāma*—of the holy name; *grahaṇa-ādibhiḥ*—beginning with chanting.

TRANSLATION

Devotional service, beginning with the chanting of the holy name of the Lord, is the ultimate religious principle for the living entity in human society.

PURPORT

As stated in the previous verse, *dharmaṁ bhāgavatam*, real religious principles, are *bhāgavata-dharma*, the principles described in *Śrīmad-Bhāgavatam* itself or in *Bhagavad-gītā*, the preliminary study of the *Bhāgavatam.* What are these principles? The *Bhāgavatam* says, *dharmaḥ projjhita-kaitavo 'tra:* in *Śrīmad-Bhāgavatam* there are no cheating religious systems. Everything in the *Bhāgavatam* is directly connected with the Supreme Personality of Godhead. The *Bhāgavatam* further says, *sa vai puṁsāṁ paro dharmo yato bhaktir adhokṣaje:* the supreme religion is that which teaches its followers how to love the Supreme Personality of Godhead, who is beyond the reach of experimental knowledge. Such a religious system begins with *tan-nāma-grahaṇa*, chanting of the holy name of the Lord (*śravaṇaṁ kīrtanaṁ viṣṇoḥ smaraṇaṁ pāda-sevanam*). After chanting the holy name of the Lord and dancing in ecstasy, one gradually sees the form of the Lord, the pastimes of the Lord and the transcendental qualities of the Lord. This way one fully understands the situation of the Personality of Godhead. One can come to this understanding of the Lord, how He descends into the material world, how He takes His births and what activities He performs, but one can know this only by executing devotional service. As stated in *Bhagavad-*

gītā, bhaktyā mām abhijānāti: simply by devotional service one can understand everything about the Supreme Lord. If one fortunately understands the Supreme Lord in this way, the result is *tyaktvā dehaṁ punar janma naiti:* after giving up his material body, he no longer has to take birth in this material world. Instead, he returns home, back to Godhead. That is the ultimate perfection. Therefore Kṛṣṇa says in *Bhagavad-gītā* (8.15):

mām upetya punar janma
duḥkhālayam aśāśvatam
nāpnuvanti mahātmānaḥ
saṁsiddhiṁ paramāṁ gatāḥ

"After attaining Me, the great souls, who are *yogīs* in devotion, never return to this temporary world, which is full of miseries, because they have attained the highest perfection."

TEXT 23

नामोच्चारणमाहात्म्यं हरेः पश्यत पुत्रकाः ।
अजामिलोऽपि येनैव मृत्युपाशादमुच्यत ॥२३॥

nāmoccāraṇa-māhātmyaṁ
hareḥ paśyata putrakāḥ
ajāmilo 'pi yenaiva
mṛtyu-pāśād amucyata

nāma—of the holy name; *uccāraṇa*—of the pronouncing; *māhātmyam*—the exalted position; *hareḥ*—of the Supreme Lord; *paśyata*—just see; *putrakāḥ*—O my dear servants, who are like my sons; *ajāmilaḥ api*—even Ajāmila (who was considered greatly sinful); *yena*—by the chanting of which; *eva*—certainly; *mṛtyu-pāśāt*—from the ropes of death; *amucyata*—was delivered.

TRANSLATION

My dear servants, who are as good as my sons, just see how glorious is the chanting of the holy name of the Lord. The greatly

sinful Ajāmila chanted only to call his son, not knowing that he was chanting the Lord's holy name. Nevertheless, by chanting the holy name of the Lord, he remembered Nārāyaṇa, and thus he was immediately saved from the ropes of death.

PURPORT

There is no need to conduct research into the significance of the chanting of the Hare Kṛṣṇa *mantra.* The history of Ajāmila is sufficient proof of the power of the Lord's holy name and the exalted position of a person who chants the holy name incessantly. Therefore Śrī Caitanya Mahāprabhu advised:

harer nāma harer nāma
harer nāmaiva kevalam
kalau nāsty eva nāsty eva
nāsty eva gatir anyathā.

In this age of Kali, no one can perform all the ritualistic ceremonies for becoming liberated; that is extremely difficult. Therefore all the *śāstras* and all the *ācāryas* have recommended that in this age one chant the holy name.

TEXT 24

एतावतालमघनिर्हरणाय पुंसां
सङ्कीर्तनं भगवतो गुणकर्मनाम्नाम् ।
विक्रुश्य पुत्रमघवान् यदजामिलोऽपि
नारायणेति म्रियमाण इयाय मुक्तिम् ॥२४॥

etāvatālam agha-nirharaṇāya puṁsāṁ
saṅkīrtanaṁ bhagavato guṇa-karma-nāmnām
vikruśya putram aghavān yad ajāmilo 'pi
nārāyaṇeti mriyamāṇa iyāya muktim

etāvatā—with this much; *alam*—sufficient; *agha-nirharaṇāya*—for taking away the reactions of sinful activities; *puṁsām*—of human beings; *saṅkīrtanam*—the congregational chanting; *bhagavataḥ*—of the

Supreme Personality of Godhead; *guṇa*—of the transcendental qualities; *karma-nāmnām*—and of His names according to His activities and pastimes; *vikruśya*—crying to without offense; *putram*—his son; *agha-vān*—the sinful; *yat*—since; *ajāmilaḥ api*—even Ajāmila; *nārāyaṇa*—the Lord's name, Nārāyaṇa; *iti*—thus; *mriyamāṇaḥ*—dying; *iyāya*—achieved; *muktim*—liberation.

TRANSLATION

Therefore it should be understood that one is easily relieved from all sinful reactions by chanting the holy name of the Lord and chanting of His qualities and activities. This is the only process recommended for relief from sinful reactions. Even if one chants the holy name of the Lord with improper pronunciation, he will achieve relief from material bondage if he chants without offenses. Ajāmila, for example, was extremely sinful, but while dying he merely chanted the holy name, and although calling his son, he achieved complete liberation because he remembered the name of Nārāyaṇa.

PURPORT

In the assembly of Raghunātha dāsa Gosvāmī's father, Haridāsa Ṭhākura confirmed that simply by chanting the holy name of the Lord one is liberated, even if he does not chant completely inoffensively. *Smārta-brāhmaṇas* and Māyāvādīs do not believe that one can achieve liberation in this way, but the truth of Haridāsa Ṭhākura's statement is supported by many quotations from *Śrīmad-Bhāgavatam.*

In his commentary on this verse, for example, Śrīdhara Svāmī gives the following quotation:

sāyaṁ prātar gṛṇan bhaktyā
duḥkha-grāmād vimucyate

"If one always chants the holy name of the Lord with great devotion in the evening and in the morning, one can become free from all material miseries." Another quotation confirms that one can achieve liberation if one hears the holy name of the Lord constantly, every day with great respect (*anudinam idam ādareṇa śṛṇvan*). Another quotation says:

śravaṇaṁ kīrtanaṁ dhyānaṁ
harer adbhuta-karmaṇaḥ
janma-karma-guṇānāṁ ca
tad-arthe 'khila-ceṣṭitam

"One should always chant and hear about the extraordinarily wonderful activities of the Lord, one should meditate upon these activities, and one should endeavor to please the Lord." (*Bhāg.* 11.3.27)

Śrīdhara Svāmī also quotes from the *Purāṇas, pāpa-kṣayaś ca bhavati smaratāṁ tam ahar-niśam:* "One can become free from all sinful reactions simply by remembering the lotus feet of the Lord day and night [*ahar-niśam*]." Furthermore, he quotes from *Bhāgavatam* (6.3.31):

tasmāt saṅkīrtanaṁ viṣṇor
jagan-maṅgalam aṁhasām
mahatām api kauravya
viddhy aikāntika-niṣkṛtam

All these quotations prove that one who constantly engages in chanting and hearing of the holy activities, name, fame and form of the Lord is liberated. As stated wonderfully in this verse, *etāvatālam agha-nirharaṇāya puṁsām:* simply by uttering the name of the Lord, one is freed from all sinful reactions.

The word *alam*, which is used in this verse, indicates that simply uttering the holy name of the Lord is sufficient. This word is used with different imports. As stated in the *Amara-kośa*, the most authorized dictionary in the Sanskrit language, *alaṁ bhūṣaṇa-paryāpti-śakti-vāraṇa-vācakam:* the word *alam* is used to mean "ornament," "sufficiency," "power" and "restraint." Here the word *alam* is used to indicate that there is no need of any other process, for the chanting of the holy name of the Lord is sufficient. Even if one chants imperfectly, one becomes free from all sinful reactions by chanting.

This power of chanting the holy name was proved by the liberation of Ajāmila. When Ajāmila chanted the holy name of Nārāyaṇa, he did not precisely remember the Supreme Lord; instead, he remembered his own son. At the time of death, Ajāmila certainly was not very clean; indeed, he was famous as a great sinner. Furthermore, one's physiological condition is completely disturbed at the time of death, and in such an awkward condition it would certainly have been very difficult for Ajāmila to have chanted clearly. Nevertheless, Ajāmila achieved liberation simply by chanting the holy name of the Lord. Therefore, what is to be said of those who are not sinful like Ajāmila? It is to be concluded that with a strong vow one should chant the holy name of the Lord—Hare Kṛṣṇa, Hare Kṛṣṇa, Kṛṣṇa Kṛṣṇa, Hare Hare/ Hare Rāma, Hare Rāma, Rāma Rāma, Hare Hare—for thus one will certainly be delivered from the clutches of *māyā* by the grace of Kṛṣṇa.

The chanting of the Hare Kṛṣṇa *mantra* is recommended even for persons who commit offenses, because if they continue chanting they will gradually chant offenselessly. By chanting the Hare Kṛṣṇa *mantra* without offenses, one increases his love for Kṛṣṇa. As stated by Śrī Caitanya Mahāprabhu, *premā pum-artho mahān:* one's main concern should be to increase one's attachment to the Supreme Personality of Godhead and to increase one's love for Him.

In this regard Śrīla Viśvanātha Cakravartī Ṭhākura quotes the following verse from *Śrīmad-Bhāgavatam* (11.19.24):

evaṁ dharmair manuṣyāṇām
uddhavātmani vedinām
mayi sañjāyate bhaktiḥ
ko 'nyo 'rtho 'syāvaśiṣyate

"My dear Uddhava, the supreme religious system for human society is that by which one can awaken his dormant love for Me." Commenting on this verse, Śrīla Viśvanātha Cakravartī Ṭhākura describes the word *bhakti* by saying *premaivoktaḥ. Kaḥ anyaḥ arthaḥ asya:* in the presence of *bhakti*, what is the necessity of liberation?

Śrīla Viśvanātha Cakravartī Ṭhākura also quotes this verse from the *Padma Purāṇa:*

nāmāparādha-yuktānāṁ
nāmāny eva haranty agham
aviśrānti-prayuktāni
tāny evārtha-karāṇi ca

Even if in the beginning one chants the Hare Kṛṣṇa *mantra* with offenses, one will become free from such offenses by chanting again and again. *Pāpa-kṣayaś ca bhavati smaratāṁ tam ahar-niśam:* one becomes free from all sinful reactions if one chants day and night, following the recommendation of Śrī Caitanya Mahāprabhu. It was Śrī Caitanya Mahāprabhu who quoted the following verse:

harer nāma harer nāma
harer nāmaiva kevalam
kalau nāsty eva nāsty eva
nāsty eva gatir anyathā

"In this age of quarrel and hypocrisy the only means of deliverance is chanting the holy name of the Lord. There is no other way. There is no other way. There is no other way." If the members of the Kṛṣṇa consciousness movement strictly follow this recommendation of Śrī Caitanya Mahāprabhu, their position will always be secure.

TEXT 25

प्रायेण वेद तदिदं न महाजनोऽयं
देव्या विमोहितमतिर्बत माययालम् ।
त्रय्यां जडीकृतमतिर्मधुपुष्पितायां
वैतानिके महति कर्मणि युज्यमानः ॥२५॥

prāyeṇa veda tad idaṁ na mahājano 'yaṁ
devyā vimohita-matir bata māyayālam
trayyāṁ jaḍī-kṛta-matir madhu-puṣpitāyāṁ
vaitānike mahati karmaṇi yujyamānaḥ

prāyeṇa—almost always; *veda*—know; *tat*—that; *idam*—this; *na*—not; *mahājanaḥ*—great personalities besides Svayambhū, Śambhu and the other ten; *ayam*—this; *devyā*—by the energy of the Supreme Personality of Godhead; *vimohita-matiḥ*—whose intelligence is bewildered; *bata*—indeed; *māyayā*—by the illusory energy; *alam*—greatly; *trayyām*—in the three *Vedas; jaḍī-kṛta-matiḥ*—whose intelligence has been dulled; *madhu-puṣpitāyām*—in the flowery Vedic language describing the results of ritualistic performances; *vaitānike*—in the performances mentioned in the *Vedas; mahati*—very great; *karmaṇi*—fruitive activities; *yujyamānaḥ*—being engaged.

TRANSLATION

Because they are bewildered by the illusory energy of the Supreme Personality of Godhead, Yājñavalkya and Jaimini and other compilers of the religious scriptures cannot know the secret, confidential religious system of the twelve mahājanas. They cannot understand the transcendental value of performing devotional service or chanting the Hare Kṛṣṇa mantra. Because their minds are attracted to the ritualistic ceremonies mentioned in the Vedas—especially the Yajur Veda, Sāma Veda and Ṛg Veda—their intelligence has become dull. Thus they are busy collecting the ingredients for ritualistic ceremonies that yield only temporary benefits, such as elevation to Svargaloka for material happiness. They are not attracted to the saṅkīrtana movement; instead, they are interested in dharma, artha, kāma and mokṣa.

PURPORT

Since one may easily achieve the highest success by chanting the holy name of the Lord, one may ask why there are so many Vedic ritualistic ceremonies and why people are attracted to them. This verse answers that question. As stated in *Bhagavad-gītā* (15.15), *vedaiś ca sarvair aham eva vedyaḥ:* the real purpose of studying the *Vedas* is to approach the lotus feet of Lord Kṛṣṇa. Unfortunately, unintelligent people bewildered by the grandeur of Vedic *yajñas* want to see gorgeous sacrifices performed. They want Vedic *mantras* chanted and huge amounts of money spent for such ceremonies. Sometimes we have to observe the Vedic ritualistic ceremonies to please such unintelligent men. Recently, when we established a large Kṛṣṇa-Balarāma temple in Vṛndāvana, we were obliged to have Vedic ceremonies enacted by *brāhmaṇas* because the inhabitants of Vṛndāvana, especially the *smārta-brāhmaṇas,* would not accept Europeans and Americans as bona fide *brāhmaṇas.* Thus we had to engage *brāhmaṇas* to perform costly *yajñas.*

In spite of these *yajñas*, the members of our Society performed *saṅkīrtana* loudly with *mṛdaṅgas*, and I considered the *saṅkīrtana* more important than the Vedic ritualistic ceremonies. Both the ceremonies and the *saṅkīrtana* were going on simultaneously. The ceremonies were meant for persons interested in Vedic rituals for elevation to heavenly planets (*jaḍī-kṛta-matir madhu-puṣpitāyām*), whereas the *saṅkīrtana* was meant for pure devotees interested in pleasing the Supreme Personality of Godhead. We would simply have performed *saṅkīrtana*, but then the inhabitants of Vṛndāvana would not have taken the installation ceremony seriously. As explained here, the Vedic performances are meant for those whose intelligence has been dulled by the flowery language of the *Vedas*, which describe fruitive activities intended to elevate one to the higher planets.

Especially in this age of Kali, *saṅkīrtana* alone is sufficient. If the members of our temples in the different parts of the world simply continue *saṅkīrtana* before the Deity, especially before Śrī Caitanya Mahāprabhu, they will remain perfect. There is no need of any other performances. Nevertheless, to keep oneself clean in habits and mind, Deity worship and other regulative principles are required. Śrīla Jīva Gosvāmī says that although *saṅkīrtana* is sufficient for the perfection of life, the *arcanā*, or worship of the Deity in the temple, must continue in order that the devotees may stay clean and pure. Śrīla Bhaktisiddhānta Sarasvatī Ṭhākura therefore recommended that one follow both processes simultaneously. We strictly follow his principle of performing Deity worship and *saṅkīrtana* along parallel lines. This we should continue.

TEXT 26

एवं विमृश्य सुधियो भगवत्यनन्ते
सर्वात्मना विदधते खलु भावयोगम् ।
ते मे न दण्डमर्हन्त्यथ यद्यमीषां
स्यात् पातकं तदपि हन्त्युरुगायवादः ॥२६॥

evaṁ vimṛśya sudhiyo bhagavaty anante
sarvātmanā vidadhate khalu bhāva-yogam

te me na daṇḍam arhanty atha yady amīṣāṁ
syāt pātakaṁ tad api hanty urugāya-vādaḥ

evam—thus; *vimṛśya*—considering; *su-dhiyaḥ*—those whose intelligence is sharp; *bhagavati*—unto the Supreme Personality of Godhead; *anante*—the unlimited; *sarva-ātmanā*—with all their heart and soul; *vidadhate*—take to; *khalu*—indeed; *bhāva-yogam*—the process of devotional service; *te*—such persons; *me*—my; *na*—not; *daṇḍam*—punishment; *arhanti*—deserve; *atha*—therefore; *yadi*—if; *amīṣām*—of them; *syāt*—there is; *pātakam*—some sinful activity; *tat*—that; *api*—also; *hanti*—destroys; *urugāya-vādaḥ*—the chanting of the holy name of the Supreme Lord.

TRANSLATION

Considering all these points, therefore, intelligent men decide to solve all problems by adopting the devotional service of chanting the holy name of the Lord, who is situated in everyone's heart and who is a mine of all auspicious qualities. Such persons are not within my jurisdiction for punishment. Generally they never commit sinful activities, but even if by mistake or because of bewilderment or illusion they sometimes commit sinful acts, they are protected from sinful reactions because they always chant the Hare Kṛṣṇa mantra.

PURPORT

In this regard Śrīla Viśvanātha Cakravartī Ṭhākura quotes the following verse from the prayers of Lord Brahmā (*Bhāg.* 10.14.29):

athāpi te deva padāmbuja-dvaya-
prasāda-leśānugṛhīta eva hi
jānāti tattvaṁ bhagavan-mahimno
na cānya eko 'pi ciraṁ vicinvan

The purport is that even though one is a very learned scholar of the Vedic *śāstras,* he may be completely unaware of the existence of the Supreme Personality of Godhead and His name, fame, qualities and so forth, whereas one who is not a great scholar can understand the position of the Supreme Personality of Godhead if he somehow or other becomes a pure devotee of the Lord by engaging in devotional service. Therefore this verse spoken by Yamarāja says, *evaṁ vimṛśya sudhiyo bhagavati:* those who engage in the loving service of the Lord become *sudhiyaḥ,* intelligent, but this is not so of a Vedic scholar who does not understand Kṛṣṇa's name, fame and qualities. A pure devotee is one whose intelligence is clear; he is truly thoughtful because he engages in the service of the Lord—not as a matter of show, but with love, with his mind, words and body. Nondevotees may make a show of religion, but it is not very effective because although they ostentatiously attend a temple or church, they are thinking of something else. Such persons are neglecting their religious duty and are punishable by Yamarāja. But a devotee who commits sinful acts, which he may do unwillingly or accidentally because of his former habits, is excused. That is the value of the *saṅkīrtana* movement.

TEXT 27

ते देवसिद्धपरिगीतपवित्रगाथा
ये साधवः समदृशो भगवत्प्रपन्नाः ।
तान् नोपसीदत हरेर्गदयाभिगुप्तान्
नैषां वयं न च वयः प्रभवाम दण्डे ॥२७॥

te deva-siddha-parigīta-pavitra-gāthā
ye sādhavaḥ samadṛśo bhagavat-prapannāḥ
tān nopasīdata harer gadayābhiguptān
naiṣāṁ vayaṁ na ca vayaḥ prabhavāma daṇḍe

te—they; *deva*—by the demigods; *siddha*—and the inhabitants of Siddhaloka; *parigīta*—sung; *pavitra-gāthāḥ*—whose pure narrations; *ye*—who; *sādhavaḥ*—devotees; *samadṛśaḥ*—who see everyone equally; *bhagavat-prapannāḥ*—being surrendered to the Supreme Personality of Godhead; *tān*—them; *na*—not; *upasīdata*—should go near; *hareḥ*—of the Supreme Personality of Godhead; *gadayā*—by the club; *abhiguptān*—being fully protected; *na*—not; *eṣām*—of these; *vayam*—we; *na*

His Divine Grace A.C. Bhaktivedanta Swami Prabhupāda
The Founder-Ācārya of the International Society for Krishna Consciousness and the greatest exponent of Kṛṣṇa consciousness in the modern world.

PLATE ONE: "On the way home, Ajāmila came upon a *śūdra,* a very lusty, fourth-class man, who was shamelessly embracing and kissing a prostitute." (*p.* 80)

PLATE TWO: "The order carriers of Yamarāja were snatching the soul from the core of the heart of Ajāmila, the husband of the prostitute, but with resounding voices the messengers of Lord Viṣṇu, the Viṣṇudūtas, forbade them to do so." (*p.* 46)

PLATE THREE: Accompanied by the Viṣṇudūtas, Ajāmila boarded an airplane made of gold. Passing through the airways, he went directly to the abode of Lord Viṣṇu, the husband of the goddess of fortune. (*p.* 133)

PLATE FOUR: "When the order carriers of Yamarāja were baffled and defeated by the order carriers of Viṣṇu, they approached their master, the controller of Saṁyamanī-purī and master of sinful persons, to tell him of this incident." (*p.* 144)

PLATE FIVE: The chanting of the holy name, which saved Ajāmila, was taught by Lord Caitanya Mahāprabhu as the prime religious principle of our present age, the Kali-yuga.

PLATE NINE: Prajāpati Dakṣa cursed Nārada Muni by saying that although he had the facility to travel all over the universe, he would never be able to stay in one place. (*p.* 316)

PLATE TEN: "The Supreme Personality of Godhead is beyond the creation of this material world, for He is the source of the material qualities and creation." (*p.* 221) In the beginning of the creation, the Lord expands Himself in the form of the *puruṣa* incarnation, Mahā-Viṣṇu. Lying in the Causal Ocean, the Supreme Personality of Godhead glances over His unmanifest material energy (shown here as Durgā, the personification of material nature).

PLATE ELEVEN: "Great *yogīs* meditate upon the Lord, who is situated as the Supersoul, Paramātmā, within the core of the heart." (*p.* 217)

PLATE TWELVE: "Fools deride Me when I descend in the human form. They do not know My transcendental nature and My supreme dominion over all that be." (*p.* 222)

PLATE THIRTEEN: "The Supreme Personality of Godhead, who is inconceivably opulent, who is devoid of all material names, forms and pastimes, and who is all-pervading, is especially merciful to the devotees who worship His lotus feet." (*p.* 232)

ca—and also not; *vayaḥ*—unlimited time; *prabhavāma*—are competent; *daṇḍe*—in punishing.

TRANSLATION

My dear servants, please do not approach such devotees, for they have fully surrendered to the lotus feet of the Supreme Personality of Godhead. They are equal to everyone, and their narrations are sung by the demigods and the inhabitants of Siddhaloka. Please do not even go near them. They are always protected by the club of the Supreme Personality of Godhead, and therefore Lord Brahmā and I and even the time factor are not competent to chastise them.

PURPORT

In effect, Yamarāja warned his servants, "My dear servants, despite what you may have done previously to disturb the devotees, henceforward you should stop. The actions of devotees who have surrendered unto the lotus feet of the Lord and who constantly chant the holy name of the Lord are praised by the demigods and the residents of Siddhaloka. Those devotees are so respectable and exalted that Lord Viṣṇu personally protects them with the club in His hand. Therefore, regardless of what you have done this time, henceforward you should not approach such devotees; otherwise you will be killed by the club of Lord Viṣṇu. This is my warning. Lord Viṣṇu has a club and *cakra* to punish nondevotees. Do not risk punishment by attempting to disturb the devotees. Not to speak of you, if even Lord Brahmā or I were to punish them, Lord Viṣṇu would punish us. Therefore do not disturb the devotees any further."

TEXT 28

तानानयध्वमसतो विमुखान् मुकुन्द-
पादारविन्दमकरन्दरसादजस्रम् ।
निष्किञ्चनैः परमहंसकुलैरसङ्गै-
र्जुष्टाद् गृहे निरयवर्त्मनि बद्धतृष्णान् ॥२८॥

tān ānayadhvam asato vimukhān mukunda-
pādāravinda-makaranda-rasād ajasram
niṣkiñcanaiḥ paramahaṁsa-kulair asaṅgair
juṣṭād gṛhe niraya-vartmani baddha-tṛṣṇān

tān—them; *ānayadhvam*—bring before me; *asataḥ*—nondevotees (those who have not taken to Kṛṣṇa consciousness); *vimukhān*—who have turned against; *mukunda*—of Mukunda, the Supreme Personality of Godhead; *pāda-aravinda*—of the lotus feet; *makaranda*—of the honey; *rasāt*—the taste; *ajasram*—continuously; *niṣkiñcanaiḥ*—by persons completely free from material attachment; *paramahaṁsa-kulaiḥ*—by the *paramahaṁsas*, the most exalted personalities; *asaṅgaiḥ*—who have no material attachment; *juṣṭāt*—which is enjoyed; *gṛhe*—to household life; *niraya-vartmani*—the path leading to hell; *baddha-tṛṣṇān*—whose desires are bound.

TRANSLATION

Paramahaṁsas are exalted persons who have no taste for material enjoyment and who drink the honey of the Lord's lotus feet. My dear servants, bring to me for punishment only persons who are averse to the taste of that honey, who do not associate with paramahaṁsas and who are attached to family life and worldly enjoyment, which form the path to hell.

PURPORT

After warning the Yamadūtas not to approach the devotees, Yamarāja now indicates who is to be brought before him. He specifically advises the Yamadūtas to bring him the materialistic persons who are attached to household life merely for sex. As stated in *Śrīmad-Bhāgavatam, yan maithunādi-gṛhamedhi-sukhaṁ hi tuccham:* people are attached to household life for sex only. They are always harassed in many ways by their material engagements, and their only happiness is that after working very hard all day, at night they sleep and indulge in sex. *Nidrayā hriyate naktaṁ vyavāyena ca vā vayaḥ:* at night, materialistic householders sleep or indulge in sex life. *Divā cārthehayā rājan kuṭumba-bharaṇena vā:* during the day they are busy trying to find out where money is, and if they get money they spend it to maintain their families. Yamarāja specifically advises his servants to bring these persons to him for punishment and not to bring the devotees, who always lick the honey at the lotus feet of the Lord, who are equal to everyone, and who try to preach Kṛṣṇa consciousness because of sympathy for all living entities. Devotees are not liable to punishment by Yamarāja, but persons who have no information of Kṛṣṇa consciousness cannot be protected by their material life of so-called family enjoyment. *Śrīmad-Bhāgavatam* says (2.1.4):

dehāpatya-kalatrādiṣv
ātma-sainyeṣv asatsv api
teṣāṁ pramatto nidhanaṁ
paśyann api na paśyati

Such persons complacently believe that their nations, communities or families can protect them, unaware that all such fallible soldiers will be destroyed in due course of time. In conclusion, one should try to associate with persons who engage in devotional service twenty-four hours a day.

TEXT 29

जिह्वा न वक्ति भगवद्गुणनामधेयं
चेतश्च न स्मरति तच्चरणारविन्दम् ।
कृष्णाय नो नमति यच्छिर एकदापि
तानानयध्वमसतोऽकृतविष्णुकृत्यान्॥२९॥

jihvā na vakti bhagavad-guṇa-nāmadheyaṁ
cetaś ca na smarati tac-caraṇāravindam
kṛṣṇāya no namati yac-chira ekadāpi
tān ānayadhvam asato 'kṛta-viṣṇu-kṛtyān

jihvā—the tongue; *na*—not; *vakti*—chants; *bhagavat*—of the Supreme Personality of Godhead; *guṇa*—transcendental qualities; *nāma*—and the holy name; *dheyam*—imparting; *cetaḥ*—the heart; *ca*—also; *na*—not; *smarati*—remembers; *tat*—His; *caraṇa-aravin-*

dam—lotus feet; *kṛṣṇāya*—unto Lord Kṛṣṇa through His Deity in the temple; *no*—not; *namati*—bows; *yat*—whose; *śiraḥ*—head; *ekadā api*—even once; *tān*—them; *ānayadhvam*—bring before me; *asataḥ*—the nondevotees; *akṛta*—not performing; *viṣṇu-kṛtyān*—duties toward Lord Viṣṇu.

TRANSLATION

My dear servants, please bring to me only those sinful persons who do not use their tongues to chant the holy name and qualities of Kṛṣṇa, whose hearts do not remember the lotus feet of Kṛṣṇa even once, and whose heads do not bow down even once before Lord Kṛṣṇa. Send me those who do not perform their duties toward Viṣṇu, which are the only duties in human life. Please bring me all such fools and rascals.

PURPORT

The word *viṣṇu-kṛtyān* is very important in this verse because the purpose of human life is to please Lord Viṣṇu. *Varṇāśrama-dharma* is also meant for that purpose. As stated in the *Viṣṇu Purāṇa* (3.8.9):

varṇāśramācāravatā
puruṣeṇa paraḥ pumān
viṣṇur ārādhyate panthā
nānyat tat-toṣa-kāraṇam

Human society is meant to follow strictly the *varṇāśrama-dharma*, which divides society into four social divisions (*brāhmaṇa, kṣatriya, vaiśya* and *śūdra*) and four spiritual divisions (*brahmacarya, gṛhastha, vānaprastha* and *sannyāsa*). *Varṇāśrama-dharma* easily brings one nearer to Lord Viṣṇu, who is the only true objective in human society. *Na te viduḥ svārtha-gatiṁ hi viṣṇum:* unfortunately, however, people do not know that their self-interest is to return home, back to Godhead, or to approach Lord Viṣṇu. *Durāśayā ye bahir-artha-māninaḥ:* instead, they are simply bewildered. Every human being is expected to perform duties meant for approaching Lord Viṣṇu. Therefore Yamarāja advises the Yamadūtas to bring him those persons who have forgotten their duties toward Viṣṇu (*akṛta-viṣṇu-kṛtyān*). One who does not chant the holy name of Viṣṇu (Kṛṣṇa), who does not bow down to the Deity of Viṣṇu, and who does not remember the lotus feet of Viṣṇu is punishable by Yamarāja. In summary, all *avaiṣṇavas*, persons unconcerned with Lord Viṣṇu, are punishable by Yamarāja.

TEXT 30

तत् क्षम्यतां स भगवान् पुरुषः पुराणो
नारायणः स्वपुरुषैर्यदसत्कृतं नः ।
स्वानामहो न विदुषां रचिताञ्जलीनां
क्षान्तिर्गरीयसि नमः पुरुषाय भूम्ने ॥३०॥

tat kṣamyatāṁ sa bhagavān puruṣaḥ purāṇo
nārāyaṇaḥ sva-puruṣair yad asat kṛtaṁ naḥ
svānām aho na viduṣāṁ racitāñjalīnāṁ
kṣāntir garīyasi namaḥ puruṣāya bhūmne

tat—that; *kṣamyatām*—let it be excused; *saḥ*—He; *bhagavān*—the Supreme Personality of Godhead; *puruṣaḥ*—the Supreme Person; *purāṇaḥ*—the oldest; *nārāyaṇaḥ*—Lord Nārāyaṇa; *sva-puruṣaiḥ*—by my own servants; *yat*—which; *asat*—impudence; *kṛtam*—performed; *naḥ*—of us; *svānām*—of my own men; *aho*—alas; *na viduṣām*—not knowing; *racita-añjalīnām*—folding our hands together to beg Your pardon; *kṣāntiḥ*—forgiveness; *garīyasi*—in the glorious; *namaḥ*—respectful obeisances; *puruṣāya*—unto the person; *bhūmne*—supreme and all-pervading.

TRANSLATION

[Then Yamarāja, considering himself and his servants to be offenders, spoke as follows, begging pardon from the Lord.] O my Lord, my servants have surely committed a great offense by arresting a Vaiṣṇava such as Ajāmila. O Nārāyaṇa, O supreme and oldest person, please forgive us. Because of our ignorance, we failed to recognize Ajāmila as a servant of Your Lordship, and thus we have certainly committed a great offense. Therefore with folded hands

we beg Your pardon. My Lord, since You are supremely merciful and are always full of good qualities, please pardon us. We offer our respectful obeisances unto You.

PURPORT

Lord Yamarāja took upon himself the responsibility for the offense committed by his servants. If the servant of an establishment makes a mistake, the establishment takes responsibility for it. Although Yamarāja is above offenses, his servants, practically with his permission, went to arrest Ajāmila, which was a great offense. The *nyāya-śāstra* confirms, *bhṛtyāparādhe svāmino daṇḍaḥ:* if a servant makes a mistake, the master is punishable because he is responsible for the offense. Taking this seriously, Yamarāja, along with his servants, prayed with folded hands to be excused by the Supreme Personality of Godhead, Nārāyaṇa.

TEXT 31

तस्मात् सङ्कीर्तनं विष्णोर्जगन्मङ्गलमंहसाम् ।
महतामपि कौरव्य विद्ध्यैकान्तिकनिष्कृतम् ॥३१॥

tasmāt saṅkīrtanaṁ viṣṇor
jagan-maṅgalam aṁhasām
mahatām api kauravya
viddhy aikāntika-niṣkṛtam

tasmāt—therefore; *saṅkīrtanam*—the congregational chanting of the holy name; *viṣṇoḥ*—of Lord Viṣṇu; *jagat-maṅgalam*—the most auspicious performance within this material world; *aṁhasām*—for sinful activities; *mahatām api*—even though very great; *kauravya*—O descendant of the Kuru family; *viddhi*—understand; *aikāntika*—the ultimate; *niṣkṛtam*—atonement.

TRANSLATION

Śukadeva Gosvāmī continued: My dear King; the chanting of the holy name of the Lord is able to uproot even the reactions of the greatest sins. Therefore the chanting of the saṅkīrtana movement

is the most auspicious activity in the entire universe. Please try to understand this so that others will take it seriously.

PURPORT

We should note that although Ajāmila chanted the name of Nārāyaṇa imperfectly, he was delivered from all sinful reactions. The chanting of the holy name is so auspicious that it can free everyone from the reactions of sinful activities. One should not conclude that one may continue to sin with the intention of chanting Hare Kṛṣṇa to neutralize the reactions. Rather, one should be very careful to be free from all sins and never think of counteracting sinful activities by chanting the Hare Kṛṣṇa *mantra*, for this is another offense. If by chance a devotee accidentally performs some sinful activity, the Lord will excuse him, but one should not intentionally perform sinful acts.

TEXT 32

शृण्वतां गृणतां वीर्याण्युद्दामानि हरेर्मुहुः ।
यथा सुजातया भक्त्या शुद्ध्येन्नात्मा व्रतादिभिः ॥३२॥

śṛṇvatāṁ gṛṇatāṁ vīryāṇy
uddāmāni harer muhuḥ
yathā sujātayā bhaktyā
śuddhyen nātmā vratādibhiḥ

śṛṇvatām—of those hearing; *gṛṇatām*—and chanting; *vīryāṇi*—the wonderful activities; *uddāmāni*—able to counteract sin; *hareḥ*—of the Supreme Personality of Godhead; *muhuḥ*—always; *yathā*—as; *su-jātayā*—easily brought forth; *bhaktyā*—by devotional service; *śuddhyet*—may be purified; *na*—not; *ātmā*—the heart and soul; *vrata-ādibhiḥ*—by performing ritualistic ceremonies.

TRANSLATION

One who constantly hears and chants the holy name of the Lord and hears and chants about His activities can very easily attain the platform of pure devotional service, which can cleanse the dirt

from one's heart. One cannot achieve such purification merely by observing vows and performing Vedic ritualistic ceremonies.

PURPORT

One may very easily practice chanting and hearing the holy name of the Lord and thus become ecstatic in spiritual life. *Padma Purāṇa* states:

nāmāparādha-yuktānāṁ
nāmāny eva haranty agham
aviśrānti-prayuktāni
tāny evārtha-karāṇi ca

Even if one chants the Hare Kṛṣṇa *mahā-mantra* offensively, one can avoid offenses by continuously chanting without deviation. One who becomes accustomed to this practice will always remain in a pure transcendental position, untouchable by sinful reactions. Śukadeva Gosvāmī especially requested King Parīkṣit to note this fact very carefully. There is no profit, however, in executing the Vedic ritualistic ceremonies. By performing such activities one may go to the higher planetary systems, but as stated in *Bhagavad-gītā* (9.21), *kṣīṇe puṇye martya-lokaṁ viśanti:* when the period of one's enjoyment in the heavenly planets is terminated because of the limited extent of the results of one's pious activities, one must return to earth. Thus there is no use in endeavoring to travel up and down in the universe. It is better to chant the holy name of the Lord so that one may become fully purified and eligible to return home, back to Godhead. That is the aim of life, and that is the perfection of life.

TEXT 33

कृष्णाङ्घ्रिपद्ममधुलिण् न पुनर्विसृष्ट-
मायागुणेषु रमते वृजिनावहेषु ।
अन्यस्तु कामहत आत्मरजः प्रमार्ष्टु-
मीहेत कर्म यत एव रजः पुनः स्यात्॥३३॥

kṛṣṇāṅghri-padma-madhu-liṇ na punar visṛṣṭa-
māyā-guṇeṣu ramate vṛjināvaheṣu

anyas tu kāma-hata ātma-rajaḥ pramārṣṭum
īheta karma yata eva rajaḥ punaḥ syāt

kṛṣṇa-aṅghri-padma—of the lotus feet of Lord Kṛṣṇa; *madhu*—the honey; *liṭ*—one who licks; *na*—not; *punaḥ*—again; *visṛṣṭa*—already renounced; *māyā-guṇeṣu*—in the material modes of nature; *ramate*—desires to enjoy; *vṛjina-avaheṣu*—which brings distress; *anyaḥ*—another; *tu*—however; *kāma-hataḥ*—being enchanted by lust; *ātma-rajaḥ*—the sinful infection of the heart; *pramārṣṭum*—to cleanse; *īheta*—may perform; *karma*—activities; *yataḥ*—after which; *eva*—indeed; *rajaḥ*—the sinful activity; *punaḥ*—again; *syāt*—appears.

TRANSLATION

Devotees who always lick the honey from the lotus feet of Lord Kṛṣṇa do not care at all for material activities, which are performed under the three modes of material nature and which bring only misery. Indeed, devotees never give up the lotus feet of Kṛṣṇa to return to material activities. Others, however, who are addicted to Vedic rituals because they have neglected the service of the Lord's lotus feet and are enchanted by lusty desires, sometimes perform acts of atonement. Nevertheless, being incompletely purified, they return to sinful activities again and again.

PURPORT

A devotee's duty is to chant the Hare Kṛṣṇa *mantra.* One may sometimes chant with offenses and sometimes without offenses, but if one seriously adopts this process, he will achieve perfection, which cannot be achieved through Vedic ritualistic ceremonies of atonement. Persons who are attached to the Vedic ritualistic ceremonies, but do not believe in devotional service, who advise atonement, but do not appreciate the chanting of the Lord's holy name, fail to achieve the highest perfection. Devotees, therefore, being completely detached from material enjoyment, never give up Kṛṣṇa consciousness for Vedic ritualistic ceremonies. Those who are attached to Vedic ritualistic ceremonies because of lusty desires are subjected to the tribulations of material existence again and again. Mahārāja Parīkṣit has compared their activities to *kuñjara-śauca,* the bathing of an elephant.

TEXT 34

इत्थं स्वभर्तृगदितं भगवन्महित्वं
संस्मृत्य विस्मितधियो यमकिङ्करास्ते ।
नैवाच्युताश्रयजनं प्रतिशङ्कमाना
द्रष्टुं च बिभ्यति ततः प्रभृति स्म राजन् ॥३४॥

ittham svabhartṛ-gaditaṁ bhagavan-mahitvaṁ
saṁsmṛtya vismita-dhiyo yama-kiṅkarās te
naivācyutāśraya-janaṁ pratiśaṅkamānā
draṣṭuṁ ca bibhyati tataḥ prabhṛti sma rājan

ittham—of such power; *sva-bhartṛ-gaditam*—explained by their master (Yamarāja); *bhagavat-mahitvam*—the extraordinary glory of the Supreme Personality of Godhead and His name, fame, form and attributes; *saṁsmṛtya*—remembering; *vismita-dhiyah*—whose minds were struck with wonder; *yama-kiṅkarāḥ*—all the servants of Yamarāja; *te*—they; *na*—not; *eva*—indeed; *acyuta-āśraya-janam*—a person sheltered by the lotus feet of Acyuta, Lord Kṛṣṇa; *pratiśaṅkamānāḥ*—always fearing; *draṣṭum*—to see; *ca*—and; *bibhyati*—they are afraid; *tataḥ prabhṛti*—beginning from then; *sma*—indeed; *rājan*—O King.

TRANSLATION

After hearing from the mouth of their master about the extraordinary glories of the Lord and His name, fame and attributes, the Yamadūtas were struck with wonder. Since then, as soon as they see a devotee, they fear him and dare not look at him again.

PURPORT

Since this incident, the Yamadūtas have given up the dangerous behavior of approaching devotees. For the Yamadūtas, a devotee is dangerous.

TEXT 35

इतिहासमिमं गुह्यं भगवान् कुम्भसम्भवः ।
कथयामास मलय आसीनो हरिमर्चयन् ॥३५॥

itihāsam imaṁ guhyaṁ
bhagavān kumbha-sambhavaḥ
kathayām āsa malaya
āsīno harim arcayan

itihāsam—history; *imam*—this; *guhyam*—very confidential; *bhagavān*—the most powerful; *kumbha-sambhavaḥ*—Agastya Muni, the son of Kumbha; *kathayām āsa*—explained; *malaye*—in the Malaya Hills; *āsīnaḥ*—residing; *harim arcayan*—worshiping the Supreme Personality of Godhead.

TRANSLATION

When the great sage Agastya, the son of Kumbha, was residing in the Malaya Hills and worshiping the Supreme Personality of Godhead, I approached him, and he explained to me this confidential history.

Thus end the Bhaktivedanta purports of the Sixth Canto, Third Chapter, of the Śrīmad-Bhāgavatam, *entitled "Yamarāja Instructs His Messengers."*

CHAPTER FOUR

The Haṁsa-guhya Prayers Offered to the Lord by Prajāpati Dakṣa

After Mahārāja Parīkṣit appealed to Śukadeva Gosvāmī to describe in further detail the creation of the living entities within this universe, Śukadeva Gosvāmī informed him that when the Pracetās, the ten sons of Prācīnabarhi, entered the sea to execute austerities, the planet earth was neglected because of the absence of a king. Naturally many weeds and unnecessary trees grew, and no food grains were produced. Indeed, all the land became like a forest. When the ten Pracetās came out of the sea and saw the entire world full of trees, they were very angry with the trees and decided to destroy them all to rectify the situation. Thus the Pracetās created wind and fire to burn the trees to ashes. Soma, however, the king of the moon and the king of all vegetation, forbade the Pracetās to destroy the trees, since the trees are the source of fruit and flowers for all living beings. Just to satisfy the Pracetās, Soma gave them a beautiful girl born of Pramlocā Apsarā. By the semen of all the Pracetās, Dakṣa was born of that girl.

In the beginning, Dakṣa created all the demigods, demons and human beings, but when he found the population not increasing properly, he took *sannyāsa* and went to Vindhya Mountain, where he underwent severe austerities and offered Lord Viṣṇu a particular prayer known as *Haṁsa-guhya,* by which Lord Viṣṇu became very pleased with him. The contents of the prayer were as follows.

"The Supreme Personality of Godhead, the Supersoul, Lord Hari, is the controller of both the living entities and the material nature. He is self-sufficient and self-effulgent. As the subject matter of perception is not the cause of our perceiving senses, so the living entity, although within his body, does not cause his eternal friend the Supersoul, who is the cause of creation of all the senses. Because of the living entity's ignorance, his senses are engaged with material objects. Since the living entity is alive, he can understand the creation of this material world to some extent, but he cannot understand the Supreme Personality of Godhead, who is beyond the conception of the body, mind and intelligence. Nevertheless, great sages who are always in meditation can see the personal form of the Lord within their hearts.

"Since an ordinary living being is materially contaminated, his words and intelligence are also material. Therefore he cannot ascertain the Supreme Personality of Godhead by manipulating his material senses. The conception of God derived through the material senses is inaccurate because the Supreme Lord is beyond the material senses, but when one engages his senses in devotional service, the eternal Supreme Personality of Godhead is revealed on the platform of the soul. When that Supreme Godhead becomes the aim of one's life, one is said to have attained spiritual knowledge.

"The Supreme Brahman is the cause of all causes because He originally existed before the creation. He is the original cause of everything, both material and spiritual, and His existence is independent. However, the Lord has a potency called *avidyā*, the illusory energy, which induces the false arguer to think himself perfect and which induces the illusory energy to bewilder the conditioned soul. That Supreme Brahman, the Supersoul, is very affectionate to His devotees. To bestow mercy upon them, He discloses His form, name, attributes and qualities to be worshiped within this material world.

"Unfortunately, however, those who are materially absorbed worship various demigods. As the air passes over a lotus flower and carries the scent of the flower with it, or as the air sometimes carries dust and therefore assumes colors, the Supreme Personality of Godhead appears as the various demigods according to the desires of His various foolish worshipers, but actually He is the supreme truth, Lord Viṣṇu. To fulfill the desires of His devotees, He appears in various incarnations, and therefore there is no need to worship the demigods."

Being very satisfied by the prayers of Dakṣa, Lord Viṣṇu appeared before Dakṣa with eight arms. The Lord was dressed in yellow garments and had a blackish complexion. Understanding that Dakṣa was very eager to follow the path of enjoyment, the Lord awarded him the potency to enjoy the illusory energy. The Lord offered him the daughter of Pañcajana named Asiknī, who was suitable for Mahārāja Dakṣa to enjoy in sex. Indeed, Dakṣa received his name because he was very expert in sex life. After awarding this benediction, Lord Viṣṇu disappeared.

TEXTS 1–2

श्रीराजोवाच
देवासुरनृणां सर्गो नागानां मृगपक्षिणाम् ।
सामासिकस्त्वया प्रोक्तो यस्तु स्वायम्भुवेऽन्तरे ॥ १ ॥
तस्यैव व्यासमिच्छामि ज्ञातुं ते भगवन् यथा ।
अनुसर्गं यया शक्त्या ससर्ज भगवान् परः ॥ २ ॥

śrī-rājovāca
devāsura-nṛṇāṁ sargo
nāgānāṁ mṛga-pakṣiṇām
sāmāsikas tvayā prokto
yas tu svāyambhuve 'ntare

tasyaiva vyāsam icchāmi
jñātuṁ te bhagavan yathā
anusargaṁ yayā śaktyā
sasarja bhagavān paraḥ

śrī-rājā uvāca—the King said; *deva-asura-nṛṇām*—of the demigods, the demons and the human beings; *sargaḥ*—the creation; *nāgānām*—of the Nāgas (serpentine living entities); *mṛga-pakṣiṇām*—of the beasts and birds; *sāmāsikaḥ*—briefly; *tvayā*—by you; *proktaḥ*—described; *yaḥ*—which; *tu*—however; *svāyambhuve*—of Svāyambhuva Manu; *antare*—within the period; *tasya*—of this; *eva*—indeed; *vyāsam*—the detailed account; *icchāmi*—I wish; *jñātum*—to know; *te*—from you; *bhagavan*—O my lord; *yathā*—as well as; *anusargam*—the subsequent creation; *yayā*—by which; *śaktyā*—potency; *sasarja*—created; *bhagavān*—the Supreme Personality of Godhead; *paraḥ*—transcendental.

TRANSLATION

The blessed King said to Śukadeva Gosvāmī: My dear lord, the demigods, demons, human beings, Nāgas, beasts and birds were created during the reign of Svāyambhuva Manu. You have spoken about this creation briefly [in the Third Canto]. Now I wish to know about it elaborately. I also wish to know about the potency of

the Supreme Personality of Godhead by which He brought about the secondary creation.

TEXT 3

श्रीसूत उवाच
इति सम्प्रश्नमाकर्ण्य राजर्षेर्बादरायणिः ।
प्रतिनन्द्य महायोगी जगाद मुनिसत्तमाः ॥ ३ ॥

śrī-sūta uvāca
iti sampraśnam ākarṇya
rājarṣer bādarāyaṇiḥ
pratinandya mahā-yogī
jagāda muni-sattamāḥ

śrī-sūtaḥ uvāca—Sūta Gosvāmī said; *iti*—thus; *sampraśnam*—the inquiry; *ākarṇya*—hearing; *rājarṣeḥ*—of King Parīkṣit; *bādarāyaṇiḥ*—Śukadeva Gosvāmī; *pratinandya*—praising; *mahā-yogī*—the great *yogī; jagāda*—replied; *muni-sattamāḥ*—O best of the sages.

TRANSLATION

Sūta Gosvāmī said: O great sages [assembled at Naimiṣāraṇya], after the great yogī Śukadeva Gosvāmī heard King Parīkṣit's inquiry, he praised it and thus replied.

TEXT 4

श्रीशुक उवाच
यदा प्रचेतसः पुत्रा दश प्राचीनबर्हिषः ।
अन्तःसमुद्रादुन्मग्ना ददृशुर्गां द्रुमैर्वृताम् ॥ ४ ॥

śrī-śuka uvāca
yadā pracetasaḥ putrā
daśa prācīnabarhiṣaḥ
antaḥ-samudrād unmagnā
dadṛśur gāṁ drumair vṛtām

śrī-śukaḥ uvāca—Śukadeva Gosvāmī said; *yadā*—when; *pracetasaḥ*—the Pracetās; *putrāḥ*—the sons; *daśa*—ten; *prācīna-barhiṣaḥ*—of King Prācīnabarhi; *antaḥ-samudrāt*—from within the ocean; *unmagnāḥ*—emerged; *dadṛśuḥ*—they saw; *gām*—the entire planet; *drumaiḥ vṛtām*—covered with trees.

TRANSLATION

Śukadeva Gosvāmī said: When the ten sons of Prācīnabarhi emerged from the waters, in which they were performing austerities, they saw that the entire surface of the world was covered by trees.

PURPORT

When King Prācīnabarhi was performing Vedic rituals in which the killing of animals was recommended, Nārada Muni, out of compassion, advised him to stop. Prācīnabarhi understood Nārada properly and then left the kingdom to perform austerities in the forest. His ten sons, however, were performing austerities within the water, and therefore there was no king to see to the management of the world. When the ten sons, the Pracetās, came out of the water, they saw that the earth was overrun with trees.

When the government neglects agriculture, which is necessary for the production of food, the land becomes covered with unnecessary trees. Of course, many trees are useful because they produce fruits and flowers, but many other trees are unnecessary. They could be used as fuel and the land cleared and used for agriculture. When the government is negligent, less grain is produced. As stated in *Bhagavad-gītā* (18.44), *kṛṣi-gorakṣya-vāṇijyaṁ vaiśya-karma svabhāva-jam:* the proper engagements for *vaiśyas,* according to their nature, are to farm and to protect cows. The duty of the government and the *kṣatriyas* is to see that the members of the third class, the *vaiśyas,* who are neither *brāhmaṇas* nor *kṣatriyas,* are thus properly engaged. *Kṣatriyas* are meant to protect human beings, whereas *vaiśyas* are meant to protect useful animals, especially cows.

TEXT 5

द्रुमेभ्यः क्रुध्यमानास्ते तपोदीपितमन्यवः ।
मुखतो वायुमग्निं च ससृजुस्तद्दिधक्षया ॥ ५ ॥

drumebhyaḥ krudhyamānās te
tapo-dīpita-manyavaḥ
mukhato vāyum agniṁ ca
sasṛjus tad-didhakṣayā

drumebhyaḥ—unto the trees; *krudhyamānāḥ*—being very angry; *te*—they (the ten sons of Prācīnabarhi); *tapaḥ-dīpita-manyavaḥ*—whose anger was inflamed because of long austerities; *mukhataḥ*—from the mouth; *vāyum*—wind; *agnim*—fire; *ca*—and; *sasṛjuḥ*—they created; *tat*—those forests; *didhakṣayā*—with the desire to burn.

TRANSLATION

Because of having undergone long austerities in the water, the Pracetās were very angry at the trees. Desiring to burn them to ashes, they generated wind and fire from their mouths.

PURPORT

Here the word *tapo-dīpita-manyavaḥ* indicates that persons who have undergone severe austerity (*tapasya*) are endowed with great mystic power, as evinced by the Pracetās, who created fire and wind from their mouths. Although devotees undergo severe *tapasya*, however, they are *vimanyavaḥ, sādhavaḥ,* which means that they are never angry. They are always decorated with good qualities. *Bhāgavatam* (3.25.21) states:

titikṣavaḥ kāruṇikāḥ
suhṛdaḥ sarva-dehinām
ajāta-śatravaḥ śāntāḥ
sādhavaḥ sādhu-bhūṣaṇāḥ

A *sādhu,* a devotee, is never angry. Actually the real feature of devotees who undergo *tapasya,* austerity, is forgiveness. Although a Vaiṣṇava has sufficient power in *tapasya,* he does not become angry when put into difficulty. If one undergoes *tapasya* but does not become a Vaiṣṇava, however, one does not develop good qualities. For example,

Hiraṇyakaśipu and Rāvaṇa also performed great austerities, but they did so to demonstrate their demoniac tendencies. Vaiṣṇavas must meet many opponents while preaching the glories of the Lord, but Śrī Caitanya Mahāprabhu recommends that they not become angry while preaching. Lord Caitanya Mahāprabhu has given this formula: *tṛṇād api sunīcena taror api sahiṣṇunā/ amāninā mānadena kīrtanīyaḥ sadā hariḥ.* "One should chant the holy name of the Lord in a humble state of mind, thinking oneself lower than the straw in the street; one should be more tolerant than a tree, devoid of all sense of false prestige and should be ready to offer all respect to others. In such a state of mind one can chant the holy name of the Lord constantly." Those engaged in preaching the glories of the Lord should be humbler than grass and more tolerant than a tree; then they can preach the glories of the Lord without difficulty.

TEXT 6

ताभ्यां निर्दह्यमानांस्तानुपलभ्य कुरूद्वह ।
राजोवाच महान् सोमो मन्युं प्रशमयन्निव ॥ ६ ॥

tābhyāṁ nirdahyamānāṁs tān
upalabhya kurūdvaha
rājovāca mahān somo
manyuṁ praśamayann iva

tābhyām—by the wind and fire; *nirdahyamānān*—being burned; *tān*—them (the trees); *upalabhya*—seeing; *kurūdvaha*—O Mahārāja Parīkṣit; *rājā*—the king of the forest; *uvāca*—said; *mahān*—the great; *somaḥ*—predominating deity of the moon, Somadeva; *manyum*—the anger; *praśamayan*—pacifying; *iva*—like.

TRANSLATION

My dear King Parīkṣit, when Soma, the king of the trees and predominating deity of the moon, saw the fire and wind burning all the trees to ashes, he felt great sympathy because he is the

maintainer of all herbs and trees. To appease the anger of the Pracetās, Soma spoke as follows.

PURPORT

It is understood from this verse that the predominating deity of the moon is the maintainer of all the trees and plants throughout the universe. It is due to the moonshine that trees and plants grow very luxuriantly. Therefore how can we accept the so-called scientists whose moon expeditions have informed us that there are no trees or vegetation on the moon? Śrīla Viśvanātha Cakravartī Ṭhākura says, *somo vṛkṣādhiṣṭhātā sa eva vṛkṣāṇāṁ rājā:* Soma, the predominating deity of the moon, is the king of all vegetation. How can we believe that the maintainer of vegetation has no vegetation on his own planet?

TEXT 7

न द्रुमेभ्यो महाभागा दीनेभ्यो द्रोग्धुमर्हथ ।
विवर्धयिषवो यूयं प्रजानां पतयः स्मृताः ॥ ७ ॥

na drumebhyo mahā-bhāgā
dīnebhyo drogdhum arhatha
vivardhayiṣavo yūyaṁ
prajānāṁ patayaḥ smṛtāḥ

na—not; *drumebhyaḥ*—the trees; *mahā-bhāgāḥ*—O greatly fortunate ones; *dīnebhyaḥ*—who are very poor; *drogdhum*—to burn to ashes; *arhatha*—you deserve; *vivardhayiṣavaḥ*—desiring to bring about an increase; *yūyam*—you; *prajānām*—of all living entities who have taken shelter of you; *patayaḥ*—the masters or protectors; *smṛtāḥ*—known as.

TRANSLATION

O greatly fortunate ones, you should not kill these poor trees by burning them to ashes. Your duty is to wish the citizens [prajās] all prosperity and to act as their protectors.

PURPORT

It is indicated herein that the government or king has the duty of protecting not only the human beings, but all other living entities, including animals, trees and plants. No living entity should be killed unnecessarily.

TEXT 8

अहो प्रजापतिपतिर्भगवान् हरिरव्ययः ।
वनस्पतीनोषधीश्च ससर्जोर्जमिषं विभुः ॥ ८ ॥

aho prajāpati-patir
bhagavān harir avyayaḥ
vanaspatīn oṣadhīś ca
sasarjorjam iṣaṁ vibhuḥ

aho—alas; *prajāpati-patiḥ*—the Lord of all the lords of created beings; *bhagavān hariḥ*—the Supreme Personality of Godhead, Hari; *avyayaḥ*—indestructible; *vanaspatīn*—the trees and plants; *oṣadhīḥ*—the herbs; *ca*—and; *sasarja*—created; *ūrjam*—invigorating; *iṣam*—food; *vibhuḥ*—the Supreme Being.

TRANSLATION

The Supreme Personality of Godhead, Śrī Hari, is the master of all living entities, including all the prajāpatis, such as Lord Brahmā. Because He is the all-pervading and indestructible master, He has created all these trees and vegetables as eatables for other living entities.

PURPORT

Soma, the predominating deity of the moon, reminded the Pracetās that this vegetation had been created by the Lord of lords to provide food for everyone. If the Pracetās tried to kill them off, their own subjects would also suffer, for trees are also required for food.

TEXT 9

अन्नं चराणामचरा ह्यपदः पादचारिणाम् ।
अहस्ता हस्तयुक्तानां द्विपदां च चतुष्पदः ॥ ९ ॥

annaṁ carāṇām acarā
hy apadaḥ pāda-cāriṇām
ahastā hasta-yuktānāṁ
dvi-padāṁ ca catuṣ-padaḥ

annam—food; *carāṇām*—of those that move on wings; *acarāḥ*—the nonmoving (fruits and flowers); *hi*—indeed; *apadaḥ*—the living entities without legs, like the grass; *pāda-cāriṇām*—of the animals who move on legs, like the cows and buffalo; *ahastāḥ*—animals without hands; *hasta-yuktānām*—of the animals with hands, like the tigers; *dvi-padām*—of human beings, who have two legs; *ca*—and; *catuḥ-padaḥ*—the four-legged animals like the deer.

TRANSLATION

By nature's arrangement, fruits and flowers are considered the food of insects and birds; grass and other legless living entities are meant to be the food of four-legged animals like cows and buffalo; animals that cannot use their front legs as hands are meant to be the food of animals like tigers, which have claws; and four-legged animals like deer and goats, as well as food grains, are meant to be the food of human beings.

PURPORT

By nature's law, or the arrangement of the Supreme Personality of Godhead, one kind of living entity is eatable by other living entities. As mentioned herein, *dvi-padāṁ ca catuṣ-padaḥ:* the four-legged animals (*catuṣ-padaḥ*), as well as food grains, are eatables for human beings (*dvi-padām*). These four-legged animals are those such as deer and goats, not cows, which are meant to be protected. Generally the men of the higher classes of society—the *brāhmaṇas, kṣatriyas* and *vaiśyas*—do not eat meat. Sometimes *kṣatriyas* go to the forest to kill animals like deer because they have to learn the art of killing, and sometimes they eat the animals also. *Śūdras,* too, eat animals such as goats. Cows, however, are never meant to be killed or eaten by human beings. In every *śāstra,* cow killing is vehemently condemned. Indeed, one who kills a cow must suffer for as many years as there are hairs on the body of a cow. *Manu-saṁhitā* says, *pravṛttir eṣā bhūtānāṁ nivṛttis tu mahā-phalā:* we have many tendencies in this material world, but in human life one is meant to learn how to curb those tendencies. Those who desire to eat meat may satisfy the demands of their tongues by eating lower animals, but they should never kill cows, who are actually accepted as the mothers of human society because they supply milk. The *śāstra* especially recommends, *kṛṣi-gorakṣya:* the *vaiśya* section of humanity should arrange for the food of the entire society through agricultural activities and should give full protection to the cows, which are the most useful animals because they supply milk to human society.

TEXT 10

यूयं च पित्रान्वादिष्टा देवदेवेन चानघाः ।
प्रजासर्गाय हि कथं वृक्षान् निर्दग्धुमर्हथ ॥१०॥

yūyaṁ ca pitrānvādiṣṭā
deva-devena cānaghāḥ
prajā-sargāya hi kathaṁ
vṛkṣān nirdagdhum arhatha

yūyam—you; *ca*—also; *pitrā*—by your father; *anvādiṣṭāḥ*—ordered; *deva-devena*—by the Personality of Godhead, the master of the masters; *ca*—also; *anaghāḥ*—O sinless ones; *prajā-sargāya*—for generating the population; *hi*—indeed; *katham*—how; *vṛkṣān*—the trees; *nirdagdhum*—to burn to ashes; *arhatha*—are able.

TRANSLATION

O pure-hearted ones, your father, Prācīnabarhi, and the Supreme Personality of Godhead have ordered you to generate population. Therefore how can you burn to ashes these trees and herbs, which are needed for the maintenance of your subjects and descendants?

TEXT 11

आतिष्ठत सतां मार्गं कोपं यच्छत दीपितम् ।
पित्रा पितामहेनापि जुष्टं वः प्रपितामहैः ॥११॥

ātiṣṭhata satāṁ mārgaṁ
kopaṁ yacchata dīpitam
pitrā pitāmahenāpi
juṣṭaṁ vaḥ prapitāmahaiḥ

ātiṣṭhata—just follow; *satām mārgam*—the path of the great saintly personalities; *kopam*—the anger; *yacchata*—subdue; *dīpitam*—which is now awakened; *pitrā*—by the father; *pitāmahena api*—and by the grandfather; *juṣṭam*—executed; *vaḥ*—your; *prapitāmahaiḥ*—by the great-grandfathers.

TRANSLATION

The path of goodness traversed by your father, grandfather and great-grandfathers is that of maintaining the subjects [prajās], including the men, animals and trees. That is the path you should follow. Unnecessary anger is contrary to your duty. Therefore I request you to control your anger.

PURPORT

Here the words *pitrā pitāmahenāpi juṣṭaṁ vaḥ prapitāmahaiḥ* depict an honest royal family, consisting of the kings, their father, their grandfather and their great-grandfathers. Such a royal family has a prestigious position because it maintains the citizens, or *prajās*. The word *prajā* refers to one who has taken birth within the jurisdiction of the government. The exalted royal families were conscious that all living beings, whether human, animal or lower than animal, should be given protection. The modern democratic system cannot be exalted in this way because the leaders elected strive only for power and have no sense of responsibility. In a monarchy, a king with a prestigious position follows the great deeds of his forefathers. Thus Soma, the king of the moon, here reminds the Pracetās about the glories of their father, grandfather and great-grandfathers.

TEXT 12

तोकानां पितरौ बन्धू दृशः पक्ष्म स्त्रियाः पतिः।
पतिः प्रजानां भिक्षूणां गृह्यज्ञानां बुधः सुहृत् ॥१२॥

tokānāṁ pitarau bandhū
dṛśaḥ pakṣma striyāḥ patiḥ
patiḥ prajānāṁ bhikṣūṇāṁ
gṛhy ajñānāṁ budhaḥ suhṛt

tokānām—of children; *pitarau*—the two parents; *bandhū*—the friends; *dṛśaḥ*—of the eye; *pakṣma*—the eyelid; *striyāḥ*—of the woman; *patiḥ*—the husband; *patiḥ*—the protector; *prajānām*—of the subjects; *bhikṣūṇām*—of the beggars; *gṛhī*—the householder; *ajñānām*—of the ignorant; *budhaḥ*—the learned; *su-hṛt*—the friend.

TRANSLATION

As the father and mother are the friends and maintainers of their children, as the eyelid is the protector of the eye, as the husband is the maintainer and protector of a woman, as the householder is the maintainer and protector of beggars, and as the learned is the friend of the ignorant, so the king is the protector and giver of life to all his subjects. The trees are also subjects of the king. Therefore they should be given protection.

PURPORT

By the supreme will of the Personality of Godhead, there are various protectors and maintainers for helpless living entities. The trees are also considered *prajās*, subjects of the king, and therefore the duty of the monarch is to protect even the trees, not to speak of others. The king is duty-bound to protect the living entities in his kingdom. Thus although the parents are directly responsible for the protection and maintenance of their children, the duty of the king is to see that all parents do their duty properly. Similarly, the king is also responsible for overseeing the other protectors mentioned in this verse. It may also be noted that the beggars who should be maintained by the householders are not professional beggars, but *sannyāsīs* and *brāhmaṇas*, to whom the householders should supply food and clothing.

TEXT 13

अन्तर्देहेषु भूतानामात्मास्ते हरिरीश्वरः ।
सर्वं तद्धिष्ण्यमीक्षध्वमेवं वस्तोषितो ह्यसौ ॥१३॥

antar deheṣu bhūtānām
ātmāste harir īśvaraḥ
sarvaṁ tad-dhiṣṇyam īkṣadhvam
evaṁ vas toṣito hy asau

antaḥ deheṣu—within the bodies (in the cores of the hearts); *bhūtānām*—of all living entities; *ātmā*—the Supersoul; *āste*—resides; *hariḥ*—the Supreme Personality of Godhead; *īśvaraḥ*—the Lord or director; *sarvam*—all; *tat-dhiṣṇyam*—His place of residence; *īkṣadhvam*—try to see; *evam*—in this way; *vaḥ*—with you; *toṣitaḥ*—satisfied; *hi*—indeed; *asau*—that Supreme Personality of Godhead.

TRANSLATION

The Supreme Personality of Godhead is situated as the Supersoul within the cores of the hearts of all living entities, whether moving or nonmoving, including men, birds, animals, trees and, indeed, all living entities. Therefore you should consider every body a residence or temple of the Lord. By such vision you will satisfy the Lord. You should not angrily kill these living entities in the forms of trees.

PURPORT

As stated in *Bhagavad-gītā* and confirmed by all the Vedic scriptures, *īśvaraḥ sarva-bhūtānāṁ hṛd-deśe 'rjuna tiṣṭhati:* the Supersoul is situated within everyone's heart. Therefore, since everyone's body is the residence of the Supreme Lord, one should not destroy the body because of unnecessary envy. That will dissatisfy the Supersoul. Soma told the Pracetās that because they had tried to satisfy the Supersoul, now they should not displease Him.

TEXT 14

यः समुत्पतितं देह आकाशान्मन्युमुल्बणम् ।
आत्मजिज्ञासया यच्छेत् स गुणानतिवर्तते ॥१४॥

yaḥ samutpatitaṁ deha
ākāśān manyum ulbaṇam
ātma-jijñāsayā yacchet
sa guṇān ativartate

yaḥ—anyone who; *samutpatitam*—suddenly awakened; *dehe*—in the body; *ākāśāt*—from the sky; *manyum*—anger; *ulbaṇam*—powerful; *ātma-jijñāsayā*—by inquiry into spiritual realization or self-realization; *yacchet*—subdues; *saḥ*—that person; *guṇān*—the modes of material nature; *ativartate*—transcends.

TRANSLATION

One who inquires into self-realization and thus subdues his powerful anger—which awakens suddenly in the body as if falling from the sky—transcends the influence of the modes of material nature.

PURPORT

When one becomes angry, he forgets himself and his situation, but if one is able to consider his situation by knowledge, one transcends the influence of the modes of material nature. One is always a servant of lusty desires, anger, greed, illusion, envy and so forth, but if one obtains sufficient strength in spiritual advancement, one can control them. One who obtains such control will always be transcendentally situated, untouched by the modes of material nature. This is only possible when one fully engages in the service of the Lord. As the Lord says in *Bhagavad-gītā* (14.26):

māṁ ca yo 'vyabhicāreṇa
bhakti-yogena sevate
sa guṇān samatītyaitān
brahma-bhūyāya kalpate

"One who engages in full devotional service, who does not fall down in any circumstance, at once transcends the modes of material nature and thus comes to the spiritual platform." By engaging one in devotional service, the Kṛṣṇa consciousness movement keeps one always transcendental to anger, greed, lust, envy and so forth. One must perform devotional service because otherwise one will become victimized by the modes of material nature.

TEXT 15

अलं दग्धैर्द्रुमैर्दीनैः खिलानां शिवमस्तु वः ।
वार्क्षी ह्येषा वरा कन्या पत्नीत्वे प्रतिगृह्यताम् ॥१५॥

alaṁ dagdhair drumair dīnaiḥ
khilānāṁ śivam astu vaḥ
vārkṣī hy eṣā varā kanyā
patnītve pratigṛhyatām

alam—enough; *dagdhaiḥ*—with burning; *drumaiḥ*—the trees; *dīnaiḥ*—poor; *khilānām*—of the remainder of the trees; *śivam*—all good fortune; *astu*—let there be; *vaḥ*—of you; *vārkṣī*—raised by the trees; *hi*—indeed; *eṣā*—this; *varā*—choice; *kanyā*—daughter; *patnītve*—into wifehood; *pratigṛhyatām*—let her be accepted.

TRANSLATION

There is no need to burn these poor trees any longer. Let whatever trees still remain be happy. Indeed, you should also be happy. Now, here is a beautiful, well-qualified girl named Māriṣā, who was raised by the trees as their daughter. You may accept this beautiful girl as your wife.

TEXT 16

इत्यामन्त्र्य वरारोहां कन्यामाप्सरसीं नृप ।
सोमो राजा ययौ दत्त्वा ते धर्मेणोपयेमिरे ॥१६॥

ity āmantrya varārohāṁ
kanyām āpsarasīṁ nṛpa

somo rājā yayau dattvā
te dharmeṇopayemire

iti—thus; *āmantrya*—addressing; *vara-ārohām*—possessing high, beautiful hips; *kanyām*—the girl; *āpsarasīm*—born of an Apsarā; *nṛpa*—O King; *somaḥ*—Soma, the predominating deity of the moon; *rājā*—the king; *yayau*—returned; *dattvā*—delivering; *te*—they; *dharmeṇa*—according to religious principles; *upayemire*—married.

TRANSLATION

Śukadeva Gosvāmī continued: My dear King, after thus pacifying the Pracetās, Soma, the king of the moon, gave them the beautiful girl born of Pramlocā Apsarā. The Pracetās all received Pramlocā's daughter, who had high, very beautiful hips, and married her according to the religious system.

TEXT 17

तेभ्यस्तस्यां समभवद् दक्षः प्राचेतसः किल ।
यस्य प्रजाविसर्गेण लोका आपूरितास्त्रयः ॥१७॥

tebhyas tasyāṁ samabhavad
dakṣaḥ prācetasaḥ kila
yasya prajā-visargeṇa
lokā āpūritās trayaḥ

tebhyaḥ—from all the Pracetās; *tasyām*—in her; *samabhavat*—was generated; *dakṣaḥ*—Dakṣa, the expert in begetting children; *prācetasaḥ*—the son of the Pracetās; *kila*—indeed; *yasya*—of whom; *prajā-visargeṇa*—by the generation of living entities; *lokāḥ*—the worlds; *āpūritāḥ*—filled; *trayaḥ*—three.

TRANSLATION

In the womb of that girl the Pracetās all begot a son named Dakṣa, who filled the three worlds with living entities.

PURPORT

Dakṣa was first born during the reign of Svāyambhuva Manu, but because of offending Lord Śiva he was punished by having the head of a goat substituted for his own head. Thus insulted, he had to give up that body, and in the sixth *manvantara*, called the Cākṣuṣa *manvantara*, he was born of the womb of Māriṣā as Dakṣa. In this connection Śrīla Viśvanātha Cakravartī Ṭhākura quotes this verse:

cākṣuṣe tv antare prāpte
prāk-sarge kāla-vidrute
yaḥ sasarja prajā iṣṭāḥ
sa dakṣo daiva-coditaḥ

"His previous body had been destroyed, but he, the same Dakṣa, inspired by the supreme will, created all the desired living entities in the Cākṣuṣa *manvantara*." (*Bhāg.* 4.30.49) Thus Dakṣa regained his previous opulence and again begot thousands and millions of children to fill the three worlds.

TEXT 18

यथा ससर्ज भूतानि दक्षो दुहितृवत्सलः ।
रेतसा मनसा चैव तन्ममावहितः शृणु ॥१८॥

yathā sasarja bhūtāni
dakṣo duhitṛ-vatsalaḥ
retasā manasā caiva
tan mamāvahitaḥ śṛṇu

yathā—as; *sasarja*—created; *bhūtāni*—the living entities; *dakṣaḥ*—Dakṣa; *duhitṛ-vatsalaḥ*—who is very affectionate to his daughters; *retasā*—by semen; *manasā*—by the mind; *ca*—also; *eva*—indeed; *tat*—that; *mama*—from me; *avahitaḥ*—being attentive; *śṛṇu*—please hear.

TRANSLATION

Śukadeva Gosvāmī continued: Please hear from me with great attention how Prajāpati Dakṣa, who was very affectionate to his

daughters, created different types of living entities through his semen and through his mind.

PURPORT

The word *duhitṛ-vatsalaḥ* indicates that all the *prajās* were born from Dakṣa's daughters. Śrīla Viśvanātha Cakravartī Ṭhākura says that apparently Dakṣa had no son.

TEXT 19

मनसैवासृजत्पूर्वं प्रजापतिरिमाः प्रजाः ।
देवासुरमनुष्यादीन्नभःस्थलजलौकसः ॥१९॥

manasaivāsṛjat pūrvaṁ
prajāpatir imāḥ prajāḥ
devāsura-manuṣyādīn
nabhaḥ-sthala-jalaukasaḥ

manasā—by the mind; *eva*—indeed; *asṛjat*—created; *pūrvam*—in the beginning; *prajāpatiḥ*—the *prajāpati* (Dakṣa); *imāḥ*—these; *prajāḥ*—living entities; *deva*—the demigods; *asura*—the demons; *manuṣya-ādīn*—and other living entities, headed by the human beings; *nabhaḥ*—in the skies; *sthala*—on the land; *jala*—or within the water; *okasaḥ*—who have their abodes.

TRANSLATION

With his mind, Prajāpati Dakṣa first created all kinds of demigods, demons, human beings, birds, beasts, aquatics and so on.

TEXT 20

तमबृंहितमालोक्य प्रजासर्गं प्रजापतिः ।
विन्ध्यपादानुपव्रज्य सोऽचरद् दुष्करं तपः ॥२०॥

tam abṛṁhitam ālokya
prajā-sargaṁ prajāpatiḥ

vindhya-pādān upavrajya
so 'carad duṣkaraṁ tapaḥ

tam—that; *abṛṁhitam*—not increasing; *ālokya*—seeing; *prajā-sargam*—the creation of the living entities; *prajāpatiḥ*—Dakṣa, the generator of living entities; *vindhya-pādān*—the mountains near the Vindhya mountain range; *upavrajya*—going to; *saḥ*—he; *acarat*—executed; *duṣkaram*—very difficult; *tapaḥ*—austerities.

TRANSLATION

But when Prajāpati Dakṣa saw that he was not properly generating all kinds of living entities, he approached a mountain near the Vindhya mountain range, and there he executed very difficult austerities.

TEXT 21

तत्राघमर्षणं नाम तीर्थं पापहरं परम् ।
उपस्पृश्यानुसवनं तपसातोषयद्धरिम् ॥२१॥

tatrāghamarṣaṇaṁ nāma
tīrthaṁ pāpa-haraṁ param
upaspṛśyānusavanaṁ
tapasātoṣayad dharim

tatra—there; *aghamarṣaṇam*—Aghamarṣaṇa; *nāma*—named; *tīrtham*—the holy place; *pāpa-haram*—suitable for destroying all sinful reactions; *param*—best; *upaspṛśya*—performing *ācamana* and bathing; *anusavanam*—regularly; *tapasā*—by austerity; *atoṣayat*—caused pleasure; *harim*—to the Supreme Personality of Godhead.

TRANSLATION

Near that mountain was a very holy place named Aghamarṣaṇa. There Prajāpati Dakṣa executed ritualistic ceremonies and satisfied the Supreme Personality of Godhead, Hari, by engaging in great austerities to please Him.

TEXT 22

अस्तौषीद्धंसगुह्येन भगवन्तमधोक्षजम् ।
तुभ्यं तदभिधास्यामि कस्यातुष्यद् यथा हरिः ॥२२॥

astauṣīd dhaṁsa-guhyena
bhagavantam adhokṣajam
tubhyaṁ tad abhidhāsyāmi
kasyātuṣyad yathā hariḥ

astauṣīt—satisfied; *haṁsa-guhyena*—by the celebrated prayers known as *Haṁsa-guhya; bhagavantam*—the Supreme Personality of Godhead; *adhokṣajam*—who is beyond the reach of the senses; *tubhyam*—unto you; *tat*—that; *abhidhāsyāmi*—I shall explain; *kasya*—with Dakṣa, the *prajāpati; atuṣyat*—was satisfied; *yathā*—how; *hariḥ*—the Supreme Personality of Godhead.

TRANSLATION

My dear King, I shall fully explain to you the Haṁsa-guhya prayers, which were offered to the Supreme Personality of Godhead by Dakṣa, and I shall explain how the Lord was pleased with him for those prayers.

PURPORT

It is to be understood that the *Haṁsa-guhya* prayers were not composed by Dakṣa, but were existing in the Vedic literature.

TEXT 23

श्रीप्रजापतिरुवाच

नमः परायावितथानुभूतये
गुणत्रयाभासनिमित्तबन्धवे ।
अदृष्टधाम्ने गुणतत्त्वबुद्धिभि-
र्निवृत्तमानाय दधे स्वयम्भुवे ॥२३॥

śrī-prajāpatir uvāca
namaḥ parāyāvitathānubhūtaye
guṇa-trayābhāsa-nimitta-bandhave
adṛṣṭa-dhāmne guṇa-tattva-buddhibhir
nivṛtta-mānāya dadhe svayambhuve

śrī-prajāpatiḥ uvāca—the *prajāpati* Dakṣa said; *namaḥ*—all respectful obeisances; *parāya*—unto the Transcendence; *avitatha*—correct; *anubhūtaye*—unto Him whose spiritual potency brings about realization of Him; *guṇa-traya*—of the three material modes of nature; *ābhāsa*—of the living entities who have the appearance; *nimitta*—and of the material energy; *bandhave*—unto the controller; *adṛṣṭa-dhāmne*—who is not perceived in His abode; *guṇa-tattva-buddhibhiḥ*—by the conditioned souls whose poor intelligence dictates that real truth is found in the manifestations of the three modes of material nature; *nivṛtta-mānāya*—who has surpassed all material measurements and calculations; *dadhe*—I offer; *svayambhuve*—unto the Supreme Lord, who is manifest with no cause.

TRANSLATION

Prajāpati Dakṣa said: The Supreme Personality of Godhead is transcendental to the illusory energy and the physical categories it produces. He possesses the potency for unfailing knowledge and supreme willpower, and He is the controller of the living entities and the illusory energy. The conditioned souls who have accepted this material manifestation as everything cannot see Him, for He is above the evidence of experimental knowledge. Self-evident and self-sufficient, He is not caused by any superior cause. Let me offer my respectful obeisances unto Him.

PURPORT

The transcendental position of the Supreme Personality of Godhead is explained herewith. He is not perceivable by the conditioned souls, who are accustomed to material vision and cannot understand that the Supreme Personality of Godhead exists in His abode, which is beyond that vision. Even if a materialistic person could count all the atoms in the universe, he would still be unable to understand the Supreme Personality of Godhead. As confirmed in *Brahma-saṁhitā* (5.34):

panthās tu koṭi-śata-vatsara-sampragamyo
vāyor athāpi manaso muni-puṅgavānām
so 'py asti yat-prapada-sīmny avicintya-tattve
govindam ādi-puruṣaṁ tam ahaṁ bhajāmi

The conditioned souls may try to understand the Supreme Personality of Godhead for many billions of years through their mental speculative processes, traveling at the speed of the mind or the wind, but still the Absolute Truth will remain inconceivable to them because a materialistic person cannot measure the length and breadth of the Supreme Personality of Godhead's unlimited existence. If the Absolute Truth is beyond measurement, one may ask, how can one realize Him? The answer is given here by the word *svayambhuve:* one may understand Him or not, but nevertheless He is existing in His own spiritual potency.

TEXT 24

न यस्य सख्यं पुरुषोऽवैति सख्युः
सखा वसन् संवसतः पुरेऽस्मिन् ।
गुणो यथा गुणिनो व्यक्तदृष्टे-
स्तस्मै महेशाय नमस्करोमि ॥२४॥

na yasya sakhyaṁ puruṣo 'vaiti sakhyuḥ
sakhā vasan saṁvasataḥ pure 'smin
guṇo yathā guṇino vyakta-dṛṣṭes
tasmai maheśāya namaskaromi

na—not; *yasya*—whose; *sakhyam*—fraternity; *puruṣaḥ*—the living entity; *avaiti*—knows; *sakhyuḥ*—of the supreme friend; *sakhā*—the friend; *vasan*—living; *saṁvasataḥ*—of the one living with; *pure*—in the body; *asmin*—this; *guṇaḥ*—the object of sense perception; *yathā*—just like; *guṇinaḥ*—of its respective sense organ; *vyakta-dṛṣṭeḥ*—who oversees the material manifestation; *tasmai*—unto Him; *mahā-īśāya*—unto the supreme controller; *namaskaromi*—I offer my obeisances.

TRANSLATION

As the sense objects [form, taste, touch, smell and sound] cannot understand how the senses perceive them, so the conditioned soul, although residing in his body along with the Supersoul, cannot understand how the supreme spiritual person, the master of the material creation, directs his senses. Let me offer my respectful obeisances unto that Supreme Person, who is the supreme controller.

PURPORT

The individual soul and the Supreme Soul live together within the body. This is confirmed in the *Upaniṣads* by the analogy that two friendly birds live in one tree—one bird eating the fruit of the tree and the other simply witnessing and directing. Although the individual living being, who is compared to the bird that is eating, is sitting with his friend the Supreme Soul, the individual living being cannot see Him. Actually the Supersoul is directing the workings of his senses in the enjoyment of sense objects, but as these sense objects cannot see the senses, the conditioned soul cannot see the directing soul. The conditioned soul has desires, and the Supreme Soul fulfills them, but the conditioned soul is unable to see the Supreme Soul. Thus Prajāpati Dakṣa offers his obeisances to the Supreme Soul, the Supersoul, even though unable to see Him. Another example given is that although ordinary citizens work under the direction of the government, they cannot understand how they are being governed or what the government is. In this regard, Madhvācārya quotes the following verse from the *Skanda Purāṇa:*

yathā rājñaḥ priyatvaṁ tu
bhṛtyā vedena cātmanaḥ
tathā jīvo na yat-sakhyaṁ
vetti tasmai namo 'stu te

"As the various servants in the different departments of big establishments cannot see the supreme managing director under whom they are working, the conditioned souls cannot see the supreme friend sitting within their bodies. Let us therefore offer our respectful obeisances unto the Supreme, who is invisible to our material eyes."

TEXT 25

देहोऽसवोऽक्षा मनवो भूतमात्रा-
मात्मानमन्यं च विदुः परं यत् ।
सर्वं पुमान् वेद गुणांश्च तज्ज्ञो
न वेद सर्वज्ञमनन्तमीडे ॥२५॥

deho 'savo 'kṣā manavo bhūta-mātrām
ātmānam anyaṁ ca viduḥ paraṁ yat
sarvaṁ pumān veda guṇāṁś ca taj-jño
na veda sarva-jñam anantam īḍe

dehaḥ—this body; *asavaḥ*—the life airs; *akṣāḥ*—the different senses; *manavaḥ*—the mind, understanding, intellect and ego; *bhūta-mātrām*—the five gross material elements and the sense objects (form, taste, sound and so on); *ātmānam*—themselves; *anyam*—any other; *ca*—and; *viduḥ*—know; *param*—beyond; *yat*—that which; *sarvam*—everything; *pumān*—the living being; *veda*—knows; *guṇān*—the qualities of the material nature; *ca*—and; *tat-jñaḥ*—knowing those things; *na*—not; *veda*—knows; *sarva-jñam*—unto the omniscient; *anantam*—the unlimited; *īḍe*—I offer my respectful obeisances.

TRANSLATION

Because they are only matter, the body, the life airs, the external and internal senses, the five gross elements and the subtle sense objects [form, taste, smell, sound and touch] cannot know their own nature, the nature of the other senses or the nature of their controllers. But the living being, because of his spiritual nature, can know his body, the life airs, the senses, the elements and the sense objects, and he can also know the three qualities that form their roots. Nevertheless, although the living being is completely aware of them, he is unable to see the Supreme Being, who is

omniscient and unlimited. I therefore offer my respectful obeisances unto Him.

PURPORT

Material scientists can make an analytical study of the physical elements, the body, the senses, the sense objects and even the air that controls the vital force, but still they cannot understand that above all these is the real spirit soul. In other words, the living entity, because of his being a spirit soul, can understand all the material objects, or, when self-realized, he can understand the Paramātmā, upon whom *yogīs* meditate. Nevertheless, the living being, even if advanced, cannot understand the Supreme Being, the Personality of Godhead, for He is *ananta*, unlimited, in all six opulences.

TEXT 26

यदोपरामो मनसो नामरूप-
रूपस्य दृष्टस्मृतिसम्प्रमोषात् ।
य ईयते केवलया स्वसंस्थया
हंसाय तस्मै शुचिसद्मने नमः ॥२६॥

yadoparāmo manaso nāma-rūpa-
rūpasya dṛṣṭa-smṛti-sampramoṣāt
ya īyate kevalayā sva-saṁsthayā
haṁsāya tasmai śuci-sadmane namaḥ

yadā—when in trance; *uparāmaḥ*—complete cessation; *manasaḥ*—of the mind; *nāma-rūpa*—material names and forms; *rūpasya*—of that by which they appear; *dṛṣṭa*—of material vision; *smṛti*—and of remembrance; *sampramoṣāt*—due to the destruction; *yaḥ*—who (the Supreme Personality of Godhead); *īyate*—is perceived; *kevalayā*—with spiritual; *sva-saṁsthayā*—His own original form; *haṁsāya*—unto the supreme pure; *tasmai*—unto Him; *śuci-sadmane*—who is realized only in the pure state of spiritual existence; *namaḥ*—I offer my respectful obeisances.

TRANSLATION

When one's consciousness is completely purified of the contamination of material existence, gross and subtle, without being

agitated as in the working and dreaming states, and when the mind is not dissolved as in suṣupti, deep sleep, one comes to the platform of trance. Then one's material vision and the memories of the mind, which manifests names and forms, are vanquished. Only in such a trance is the Supreme Personality of Godhead revealed. Thus let us offer our respectful obeisances unto the Supreme Personality of Godhead, who is seen in that uncontaminated, transcendental state.

PURPORT

There are two stages of God realization. One is called *sujñeyam,* or very easily understood (generally by mental speculation), and the other is called *durjñeyam,* understood only with difficulty. Paramātmā realization and Brahman realization are considered *sujñeyam,* but realization of the Supreme Personality of Godhead is *durjñeyam.* As described here, one attains the ultimate realization of the Personality of Godhead when one gives up the activities of the mind—thinking, feeling and willing—or, in other words, when mental speculation stops. This transcendental realization is above *suṣupti,* deep sleep. In our gross conditional stage we perceive things through material experience and remembrance, and in the subtle stage we perceive the world in dreams. The process of vision also involves remembrance and also exists in a subtle form. Above gross experience and dreams is *suṣupti,* deep sleep, and when one comes to the completely spiritual platform, transcending deep sleep, he attains trance, *viśuddha-sattva,* or *vasudeva-sattva,* in which the Personality of Godhead is revealed.

Ataḥ śrī-kṛṣṇa-nāmādi na bhaved grāhyam indriyaiḥ: as long as one is situated in duality, on the sensual platform, gross or subtle, realization of the original Personality of Godhead is impossible. *Sevonmukhe hi jihvādau svayam eva sphuraty adaḥ:* but when one engages his senses in the service of the Lord—specifically, when one engages the tongue in chanting the Hare Kṛṣṇa *mantra* and tasting only Kṛṣṇa *prasāda* with a spirit of service—the Supreme Personality of Godhead is revealed. This is indicated in this verse by the word *śuci-sadmane. Śuci* means purified. By the spirit of rendering service with one's senses, one's entire existence becomes *śuci-sadma,* the platform of uncontaminated purity. Dakṣa therefore offers his respectful obeisances unto the Supreme Personality of Godhead, who is revealed on the platform of *śuci-sadma.* In this regard Śrīla Viśvanātha Cakravartī Ṭhākura quotes the following prayer by Lord Brahmā from the *Śrīmad-Bhāgavatam* (10.14.6): *tathāpi bhūman mahimāguṇasya te viboddhum arhaty amalāntar-ātmabhiḥ.* "One whose heart has become completely purified, my Lord, can understand the transcendental qualities of Your Lordship and can understand the greatness of Your activities."

TEXTS 27–28

मनीषिणोऽन्तर्हृदि संनिवेशितं
स्वशक्तिभिर्नवभिश्च त्रिवृद्भिः ।
वह्निं यथा दारुणि पाञ्चदश्यं
मनीषया निष्कर्षन्ति गूढम् ॥२७॥
स वै ममाशेषविशेषमाया-
निषेधनिर्वाणसुखानुभूतिः ।
स सर्वनामा स च विश्वरूपः
प्रसीदतामनिरुक्तात्मशक्तिः ॥२८॥

manīṣiṇo 'ntar-hṛdi sanniveśitaṁ
sva-śaktibhir navabhiś ca trivṛdbhiḥ
vahniṁ yathā dāruṇi pāñcadaśyaṁ
manīṣayā niṣkarṣanti gūḍham

sa vai mamāśeṣa-viśeṣa-māyā-
niṣedha-nirvāṇa-sukhānubhūtiḥ
sa sarva-nāmā sa ca viśva-rūpaḥ
prasīdatām aniruktātma-śaktiḥ

manīṣiṇaḥ—great learned *brāhmaṇas* performing ritualistic ceremonies and sacrifices; *antaḥ-hṛdi*—within the core of the heart; *sanniveśitam*—being situated; *sva-śaktibhiḥ*—with His own spiritual potencies; *navabhiḥ*—also with the nine different material potencies (the material nature, the total material energy, the ego, the mind and the five objects of the senses); *ca*—and (the five gross material elements and the ten acting and knowledge-gathering senses); *trivṛdbhiḥ*—by the three material modes of nature; *vahnim*—fire; *yathā*—just like; *dāruṇi*—within wood; *pāñcadaśyam*—produced by chanting the fifteen hymns known as Sāmidhenī *mantras; manīṣayā*—by purified intelligence; *niṣkarṣanti*—extract; *gūḍham*—although not manifesting; *saḥ*—that Supreme Personality of Godhead; *vai*—indeed; *mama*—toward me; *aśeṣa*—all; *viśeṣa*—varieties; *māyā*—of the illusory energy; *niṣedha*—by the process of negation; *nirvāṇa*—of liberation; *sukha-anubhūtiḥ*—who is realized by transcendental bliss; *saḥ*—that Supreme Personality of Godhead; *sarva-nāmā*—who is the source of all names; *saḥ*—that Supreme Personality of Godhead; *ca*—also; *viśva-rūpaḥ*—the gigantic form of the universe; *prasīdatām*—may He be merciful; *anirukta*—inconceivable; *ātma-śaktiḥ*—the reservoir of all spiritual potencies.

TRANSLATION

Just as great learned brāhmaṇas who are expert in performing ritualistic ceremonies and sacrifices can extract the fire dormant within wooden fuel by chanting the fifteen Sāmidhenī mantras, thus proving the efficacy of the Vedic mantras, so those who are actually advanced in consciousness—in other words, those who are Kṛṣṇa conscious—can find the Supersoul, who by His own spiritual potency is situated within the heart. The heart is covered by the three modes of material nature and the nine material elements [material nature, the total material energy, the ego, the mind and the five objects of sense gratification], and also by the five material elements and the ten senses. These twenty-seven elements constitute the external energy of the Lord. Great yogīs meditate upon the Lord, who is situated as the Supersoul, Paramātmā, within the core of the heart. May that Supersoul be pleased with me. The Supersoul is realized when one is eager for liberation from the unlimited varieties of material life. One actually attains such liberation when he engages in the transcendental loving service of the Lord and realizes the Lord because of his attitude of service. The Lord may be addressed by various spiritual names, which are inconceivable to the material senses. When will that Supreme Personality of Godhead be pleased with me?

PURPORT

In his commentary to this verse, Śrīla Viśvanātha Cakravartī Ṭhākura uses the word *durvijñeyam*, which means "very difficult to realize." The pure stage of existence is described in *Bhagavad-gītā* (7.28), wherein Kṛṣṇa says:

yeṣāṁ tv anta-gataṁ pāpaṁ
janānāṁ puṇya-karmaṇām
te dvandva-moha-nirmuktā
bhajante māṁ dṛḍha-vratāḥ

"Persons who have acted piously in previous lives and in this life, whose sinful actions are completely eradicated and who are freed from the duality of delusion, engage themselves in My service with determination."

Elsewhere in *Bhagavad-gītā* (9.14) the Lord says:

satataṁ kīrtayanto māṁ
yatantaś ca dṛḍha-vratāḥ
namasyantaś ca māṁ bhaktyā
nitya-yuktā upāsate

"Always chanting My glories, endeavoring with great determination, bowing down before Me, these great souls perpetually worship Me with devotion."

One can understand the Supreme Personality of Godhead after transcending all material impediments. Therefore Lord Kṛṣṇa also says in the *Gītā* (7.3):

manuṣyāṇāṁ sahasreṣu
kaścid yatati siddhaye
yatatām api siddhānāṁ
kaścin māṁ vetti tattvataḥ

"Out of many thousands among men, one may endeavor for perfection, and of those who have achieved perfection, hardly one knows Me in truth."

To understand Kṛṣṇa, the Supreme Personality of Godhead, one must undergo severe penances and austerities, but since the path of devotional service is perfect, by following this process one can very easily come to the spiritual platform and understand the Lord. This, too, is confirmed in *Bhagavad-gītā* (18.55), wherein Kṛṣṇa says:

bhaktyā mām abhijānāti
yāvān yaś cāsmi tattvataḥ
tato māṁ tattvato jñātvā
viśate tad-anantaram

"One can understand the Supreme Personality of Godhead as He is only by devotional service. And when one is in full consciousness of the Supreme Lord by such devotion, he can enter into the kingdom of God."

Thus although the subject matter is *durvijñeyam*, extremely difficult to understand, it becomes easy if one follows the prescribed method. Coming in touch with the Supreme Personality of Godhead is possible through pure devotional service, which begins with *śravaṇaṁ kīrtanaṁ viṣṇoḥ*. In this regard, Śrīla Viśvanātha Cakravartī Ṭhākura quotes a verse from *Śrīmad-Bhāgavatam* (2.8.5): *praviṣṭaḥ karṇa-randhreṇa svānāṁ bhāva-saroruham.* The process of hearing and chanting enters the core of the heart, and in this way one becomes a pure devotee. By continuing this process, one comes to the stage of transcendental love, and then he appreciates the transcendental name, form, qualities and pastimes of the Supreme Personality of Godhead. In other words, a pure devotee, by devotional service, is able to see the Supreme Personality of Godhead despite many material impediments, which are all various energies of the Supreme Personality of Godhead. Easily making his way through these impediments, a devotee comes directly in contact with the Supreme Personality of Godhead. After all, the material impediments described in these verses are but various energies of the Lord. When a devotee is eager to see the Supreme Personality of Godhead, he prays to the Lord:

ayi nanda-tanuja kiṅkaraṁ
patitaṁ māṁ viṣame bhavāmbudhau
kṛpayā tava pāda-paṅkaja-
sthita-dhūlī-sadṛśaṁ vicintaya

"O son of Mahārāja Nanda [Kṛṣṇa], I am Your eternal servitor, yet somehow or other I have fallen into the ocean of birth and death. Please pick me up from this ocean of death and place me as one of the atoms at Your lotus feet." Being pleased with the devotee, the Lord turns all his material impediments into spiritual service. In this connection Śrīla Viśvanātha Cakravartī Ṭhākura quotes a verse from the *Viṣṇu Purāṇa:*

hlādinī sandhinī samvit
tvayy ekā sarva-saṁsthitau
hlāda-tāpa-karī miśrā
tvayi no guṇa-varjite

In the material world, the spiritual energy of the Supreme Personality of Godhead is manifested as *tāpa-karī,* which means "causing miseries." Everyone hankers for happiness, but although happiness originally comes from the pleasure potency of the Supreme Personality of Godhead, in the material world, because of material activities, the pleasure potency of the Lord becomes a source of miseries (*hlāda-tāpa-karī*). False happiness in the material world is the source of distress, but when one's endeavors for happiness are redirected toward the satisfaction of the Supreme Personality of Godhead, this *tāpa-karī* element of misery is vanquished. An example given in this connection is that extracting fire from wood is certainly difficult, but when the fire comes out it burns the wood to ashes. In other words, experiencing the Supreme Personality of Godhead is extremely difficult for those devoid of devotional service, but everything becomes easier for a devotee, and thus he can very easily meet the Supreme Lord.

Here the prayers say that the form of the Lord is beyond the jurisdiction of material form and is therefore inconceivable. A devotee prays, however, "My dear Lord, be pleased with me so that I may very easily see Your transcendental form and potency." Nondevotees try to understand the Supreme Brahman by discussions of *neti neti. Niṣedha-nirvāṇa-sukhānubhūtiḥ:* a devotee, however, simply by chanting the holy name of the Lord, avoids such laborious speculations and realizes the existence of the Lord very easily.

TEXT 29

यद्यन्निरुक्तं वचसा निरूपितं
धियाक्षभिर्वा मनसोत यस्य ।
मा भूत् स्वरूपं गुणरूपं हि तत्तत्
स वै गुणापायविसर्गलक्षणः ॥२९॥

yad yan niruktaṁ vacasā nirūpitaṁ
dhiyākṣabhir vā manasota yasya
mā bhūt svarūpaṁ guṇa-rūpaṁ hi tat tat
sa vai guṇāpāya-visarga-lakṣaṇaḥ

yat yat—whatever; *niruktam*—expressed; *vacasā*—by words; *nirūpitam*—ascertained; *dhiyā*—by so-called meditation or intelligence; *akṣabhiḥ*—by the senses; *vā*—or; *manasā*—by the mind; *uta*—certainly; *yasya*—of whom; *mā bhūt*—may not be; *sva-rūpam*—the actual form of the Lord; *guṇa-rūpam*—consisting of the three qualities; *hi*—indeed; *tat tat*—that; *saḥ*—that Supreme Personality of Godhead; *vai*—indeed; *guṇa-apāya*—the cause of the annihilation of everything made of the material modes of nature; *visarga*—and the creation; *lakṣaṇaḥ*—appearing as.

TRANSLATION

Anything expressed by material vibrations, anything ascertained by material intelligence and anything experienced by the material senses or concocted within the material mind is but an effect of the modes of material nature and therefore has nothing to do with the real nature of the Supreme Personality of Godhead. The Supreme Lord is beyond the creation of this material world, for He is the source of the material qualities and creation. As the cause of all causes, He exists before the creation and after the creation. I wish to offer my respectful obeisances unto Him.

PURPORT

One who manufactures names, forms, qualities or paraphernalia pertaining to the Supreme Personality of Godhead cannot understand Him, since He is beyond creation. The Supreme Lord is the creator of everything, and this means that He existed when there was no creation. In other words, His name, form and qualities are not materially created entities; they are transcendental always. Therefore by our material concoctions, vibrations and thoughts we cannot ascertain the Supreme Lord. This is explained in the verse *ataḥ śrī-kṛṣṇa-nāmādi na bhaved grāhyam indriyaiḥ.*

Prācetasa, Dakṣa, herein offers prayers unto the Transcendence, not to anyone within the material creation. Only fools and rascals think God a material creation. This is confirmed by the Lord Himself in *Bhagavad-gītā* (9.11):

avajānanti māṁ mūḍhā
mānuṣīṁ tanum āśritam
paraṁ bhāvam ajānanto
mama bhūta-maheśvaram

"Fools deride Me when I descend in the human form. They do not know My transcendental nature and My supreme dominion over all that be." Therefore, one must receive knowledge from a person to whom the Lord has revealed Himself; there is no value in creating an imaginary name or form for the Lord. Śrīpāda Śaṅkarācārya was an impersonalist, but nevertheless he said, *nārāyaṇaḥ paro 'vyaktāt:* Nārāyaṇa, the Supreme Personality of Godhead, is not a person of the material world. We cannot assign Nārāyaṇa a material designation, as the foolish attempt to do when they speak of *daridra-nārāyaṇa* (poor Nārāyaṇa). Nārāyaṇa is always transcendental, beyond this material creation. How can He become *daridra-nārāyaṇa?* Poverty is found within this material world, but in the spiritual world, there is no such thing as poverty. Therefore the idea of *daridra-nārāyaṇa* is merely a concoction.

Dakṣa very carefully points out that material designations cannot be names of the worshipable Lord: *yad yan niruktaṁ vacasā nirūpitam. Nirukta* refers to the Vedic dictionary. One cannot properly understand the Supreme Personality of Godhead merely by picking up expressions from a dictionary. In praying to the Lord, Dakṣa does not wish material names and forms to be the objects of his worship; rather, he wants to worship the Lord, who existed before the creation of material dictionaries and names. As confirmed in the *Vedas*, *yato vāco nivartante/ aprāpya manasā saha:* the name, form, attributes and paraphernalia of the Lord cannot be ascertained through a material dictionary. However, if one reaches the transcendental platform of understanding the Supreme Personality of Godhead, he becomes well acquainted with everything, material and spiritual. This is confirmed in another Vedic *mantra: tam eva viditvātimṛtyum eti.* If one can somehow or other, by the grace of the Lord, understand the transcendental position of the Lord, one becomes eternal. This is further confirmed by the Lord Himself in *Bhagavad-gītā* (4.9):

janma karma ca me divyam
evaṁ yo vetti tattvataḥ
tyaktvā dehaṁ punar janma
naiti mām eti so 'rjuna

"One who knows the transcendental nature of My appearance and activities does not, upon leaving the body, take his birth again in this material world, but attains My eternal abode, O Arjuna." Simply by understanding the Supreme Lord, one goes beyond birth, death, old age and disease. Śrīla Śukadeva Gosvāmī therefore advised Mahārāja Parīkṣit in *Śrīmad-Bhāgavatam* (2.1.5):

tasmād bhārata sarvātmā
bhagavān īśvaro hariḥ
śrotavyaḥ kīrtitavyaś ca
smartavyaś cecchatābhayam

"O descendant of King Bharata, one who desires to be free from all miseries must hear, glorify and also remember the Personality of Godhead, who is the Supersoul, the controller and the savior from all miseries."

TEXT 30

यस्मिन् यतो येन च यस्य यस्मै
यद् यो यथा कुरुते कार्यते च ।

परावरेषां परमं प्राक् प्रसिद्धं
तद् ब्रह्म तद्धेतुरनन्यदेकम् ॥३०॥

yasmin yato yena ca yasya yasmai
yad yo yathā kurute kāryate ca
parāvareṣāṁ paramaṁ prāk prasiddhaṁ
tad brahma tad dhetur ananyad ekam

yasmin—in whom (the Supreme Personality of Godhead or the supreme place of repose); *yataḥ*—from whom (everything emanates); *yena*—by whom (everything is enacted); *ca*—also; *yasya*—to whom everything belongs; *yasmai*—to whom (everything is offered); *yat*—which; *yaḥ*—who; *yathā*—as; *kurute*—executes; *kāryate*—is performed; *ca*—also; *para-avareṣām*—of both, in the material and spiritual existence; *paramam*—the supreme; *prāk*—the origin; *prasiddham*—well known to everyone; *tat*—that; *brahma*—the Supreme Brahman; *tat hetuḥ*—the cause of all causes; *ananyat*—having no other cause; *ekam*—one without a second.

TRANSLATION

The Supreme Brahman, Kṛṣṇa, is the ultimate resting place and source of everything. Everything is done by Him, everything belongs to Him, and everything is offered to Him. He is the ultimate objective, and whether acting or causing others to act, He is the ultimate doer. There are many causes, high and low, but since He is the cause of all causes, He is well known as the Supreme Brahman who existed before all activities. He is one without a second and has no other cause. I therefore offer my respects unto Him.

PURPORT

The Supreme Personality of Godhead, Kṛṣṇa, is the original cause, as confirmed in *Bhagavad-gītā* (*ahaṁ sarvasya prabhavaḥ*). Even this material world, which is conducted under the modes of material nature, is caused by the Supreme Personality of Godhead, who therefore also has an intimate relationship with the material world. If the material world were not a part of His body, the Supreme Lord, the supreme cause, would be incomplete. Therefore we hear, *vāsudevaḥ sarvam iti sa mahātmā sudurlabhaḥ:* if one knows that Vāsudeva is the original cause of all causes, he becomes a perfect *mahātmā.*

The *Brahma-saṁhitā* (5.1) declares:

īśvaraḥ paramaḥ kṛṣṇaḥ
sac-cid-ānanda-vigrahaḥ
anādir ādir govindaḥ
sarva-kāraṇa-kāraṇam

"Kṛṣṇa, who is known as Govinda, is the supreme controller. He has an eternal, blissful, spiritual body. He is the origin of all. He has no other origin, for He is the prime cause of all causes." The Supreme Brahman (*tad brahma*) is the cause of all causes, but He has no cause. *Anādir ādir govindaḥ sarva-kāraṇa-kāraṇam:* Govinda, Kṛṣṇa, is the original cause of all causes, but He has no cause for His appearance as Govinda. Govinda expands in multifarious forms, but nevertheless they are one. As confirmed by Madhvācārya, *ananyaḥ sadṛśābhāvād eko rūpādy-abhedataḥ:* Kṛṣṇa has no cause nor any equal, and He is one because His various forms, as *svāṁśa* and *vibhinnāṁśa,* are nondifferent from Himself.

TEXT 31

यच्छक्तयो वदतां वादिनां वै
विवादसंवादभुवो भवन्ति ।
कुर्वन्ति चैषां मुहुरात्ममोहं
तस्मै नमोऽनन्तगुणाय भूम्ने ॥३१॥

yac-chaktayo vadatāṁ vādināṁ vai
vivāda-saṁvāda-bhuvo bhavanti
kurvanti caiṣāṁ muhur ātma-mohaṁ
tasmai namo 'nanta-guṇāya bhūmne

yat-śaktayaḥ—whose multifarious potencies; *vadatām*—speaking different philosophies; *vādinām*—of the speakers; *vai*—indeed;

vivāda—of argument; *saṁvāda*—and agreement; *bhuvaḥ*—the causes; *bhavanti*—are; *kurvanti*—create; *ca*—and; *eṣām*—of them (the theorists); *muhuḥ*—continuously; *ātma-moham*—bewilderment regarding the existence of the soul; *tasmai*—unto Him; *namaḥ*—my respectful obeisances; *ananta*—unlimited; *guṇāya*—possessing transcendental attributes; *bhūmne*—the all-pervading Godhead.

TRANSLATION

Let me offer my respectful obeisances unto the all-pervading Supreme Personality of Godhead, who possesses unlimited transcendental qualities. Acting from within the cores of the hearts of all philosophers, who propagate various views, He causes them to forget their own souls while sometimes agreeing and sometimes disagreeing among themselves. Thus He creates within this material world a situation in which they are unable to come to a conclusion. I offer my obeisances unto Him.

PURPORT

Since time immemorial or since the creation of the cosmic manifestation, the conditioned souls have formed various parties of philosophical speculation, but this is not true of the devotees. Nondevotees have different ideas of creation, maintenance and annihilation, and therefore they are called *vādīs* and *prativādīs*—proponents and counterproponents. It is understood from the statement of *Mahābhārata* that there are many *munis*, or speculators:

tarko 'pratiṣṭhaḥ śrutayo vibhinnā
nāsāv ṛṣir yasya mataṁ na bhinnam

All speculators must disagree with other speculators; otherwise, why should there be so many opposing parties concerned with ascertaining the supreme cause?

Philosophy means finding the ultimate cause. As *Vedānta-sūtra* very reasonably says, *athāto brahma-jijñāsā:* human life is meant for understanding the ultimate cause. Devotees accept that the ultimate cause is Kṛṣṇa because this conclusion is supported by all Vedic literature and also by Kṛṣṇa Himself, who says, *ahaṁ sarvasya prabhavaḥ:* "I am the source of everything." Devotees have no problem understanding the ultimate cause of everything, but nondevotees must face many opposing elements because everyone who wants to be a prominent philosopher invents his own way. In India there are many parties of philosophers, such as the *dvaita-vādīs, advaita-vādīs, vaiśeṣikas, mīmāṁsakas,* Māyāvādīs and *svabhāva-vādīs,* and each of them opposes the others. Similarly, in the Western countries there are also many philosophers with different views of creation, life, maintenance and annihilation. Thus it is undoubtedly a fact that there are countless philosophers throughout the world, each of them contradicting the others.

Now, one might ask why there are so many philosophers if the ultimate goal of philosophy is one. Undoubtedly the ultimate cause is one—the Supreme Brahman. As Arjuna told Kṛṣṇa in *Bhagavad-gītā* (10.12):

paraṁ brahma paraṁ dhāma
pavitraṁ paramaṁ bhavān
puruṣaṁ śāśvataṁ divyam
ādi-devam ajaṁ vibhum

"You are the Supreme Brahman, the ultimate, the supreme abode and purifier, the Absolute Truth and the eternal divine person. You are the primal God, transcendental and original, and You are the unborn and all-pervading beauty." Nondevotee speculators, however, do not accept an ultimate cause (*sarva-kāraṇa-kāraṇam*). Because they are ignorant and bewildered concerning the soul and its activities, even though some of them have a vague idea of the soul, many controversies arise, and the philosophical speculators can never reach a conclusion. All of these speculators are envious of the Supreme Personality of Godhead, and as Kṛṣṇa says in *Bhagavad-gītā* (16.19–20):

tān ahaṁ dviṣataḥ krūrān
saṁsāreṣu narādhamān
kṣipāmy ajasram aśubhān
āsurīṣv eva yoniṣu

āsurīṁ yonim āpannā
mūḍhā janmani janmani
mām aprāpyaiva kaunteya
tato yānty adhamāṁ gatim

"Those who are envious and mischievous, who are the lowest among men, are cast by Me into the ocean of material existence, into various demoniac species of life. Attaining repeated birth among the species of demoniac life, such persons can never approach Me. Gradually they sink down to the most abominable type of existence." Because of their envy of the Supreme Personality of Godhead, nondevotees are born in demoniac families life after life. They are great offenders, and because of their offenses the Supreme Lord keeps them always bewildered. *Kurvanti caiṣāṁ muhur ātma-moham:* the Lord, the Supreme Personality of Godhead, purposely keeps them in darkness (*ātma-moham*).

The great authority Parāśara, the father of Vyāsadeva, explains the Supreme Personality of Godhead thus:

jñāna-śakti-balaiśvarya-
vīrya-tejāṁsy aśeṣataḥ
bhagavac-chabda-vācyāni
vinā heyair guṇādibhiḥ

The demoniac speculators cannot understand the transcendental qualities, form, pastimes, strength, knowledge and opulence of the Supreme Personality of Godhead, which are all free from material contamination (*vinā heyair guṇādibhiḥ*). These speculators are envious of the existence of the Lord. *Jagad āhur anīśvaram:* their conclusion is that the entire cosmic manifestation has no controller, but is just working naturally. Thus they are kept in constant darkness, birth after birth, and cannot understand the real cause of all causes. This is the reason why there are so many schools of philosophical speculation.

TEXT 32

अस्तीति नास्तीति च वस्तुनिष्ठयो-
रेकस्थयोर्भिन्नविरुद्धधर्मणोः ।

अवेक्षितं किश्चन योगसांख्ययोः
समं परं ह्यनुकूलं बृहत्तत् ॥३२॥

astīti nāstīti ca vastu-niṣṭhayor
eka-sthayor bhinna-viruddha-dharmaṇoḥ
avekṣitaṁ kiñcana yoga-sāṅkhyayoḥ
samaṁ paraṁ hy anukūlaṁ bṛhat tat

asti—there is; *iti*—thus; *na*—not; *asti*—there is; *iti*—thus; *ca*—and; *vastu-niṣṭhayoḥ*—professing knowledge of the ultimate cause; *eka-sthayoḥ*—with one and the same subject matter, establishing Brahman; *bhinna*—demonstrating different; *viruddha-dharmaṇoḥ*—and opposing characteristics; *avekṣitam*—perceived; *kiñcana*—that something which; *yoga-sāṅkhyayoḥ*—of mystic *yoga* and the Sāṅkhya philosophy (analysis of the ways of nature); *samam*—the same; *param*—transcendental; *hi*—indeed; *anukūlam*—dwelling place; *bṛhat tat*—that ultimate cause.

TRANSLATION

There are two parties—namely, the theists and the atheists. The theist, who accepts the Supersoul, finds the spiritual cause through mystic yoga. The Sāṅkhyite, however, who merely analyzes the material elements, comes to a conclusion of impersonalism and does not accept a supreme cause—whether Bhagavān, Paramātmā or even Brahman. Instead, he is preoccupied with the superfluous, external activities of material nature. Ultimately, however, both parties demonstrate the Absolute Truth because although they offer opposing statements, their object is the same ultimate cause. They are both approaching the same Supreme Brahman, to whom I offer my respectful obeisances.

PURPORT

Actually there are two sides to this argument. Some say that the Absolute has no form (*nirākāra*), and others say that the Absolute has a form (*sākāra*). Therefore the word *form* is the common factor, although some accept it (*asti* or *astika*) whereas others try to negate it (*nāsti* or *nāstika*). Since the devotee considers the word "form" (*ākāra*) the common factor for both, he offers his respectful obeisances to the form, although others may go on arguing about whether the Absolute has a form or not.

In this verse the word *yoga-sāṅkhyayoḥ* is very important. *Yoga* means *bhakti-yoga* because *yogīs* also accept the existence of the all-pervading Supreme Soul and try to see that Supreme Soul within their hearts. As stated in *Śrīmad-Bhāgavatam* (12.13.1), *dhyānāvasthita-tad-gatena manasā paśyanti yaṁ yoginaḥ*. The devotee tries to come directly in touch with the Supreme Personality of Godhead, whereas the *yogī* tries to find the Supersoul within the heart by meditation. Thus, both directly and indirectly, *yoga* means *bhakti-yoga*. Sāṅkhya, however, means physical study of the cosmic situation through speculative knowledge. This is generally known as *jñāna-śāstra*. The Sāṅkhyites are attached to the impersonal Brahman, but the Absolute Truth is known in three ways. *Brahmeti paramātmeti bhagavān iti śabdyate:* the Absolute Truth is one, but some accept Him as impersonal Brahman, some as the Supersoul existing everywhere, and some as Bhagavān, the Supreme Personality of Godhead. The central point is the Absolute Truth.

Although the impersonalists and personalists fight with one another, they focus upon the same Parabrahman, the same Absolute Truth. In the *yoga-śāstras*, Kṛṣṇa is described as follows: *kṛṣṇaṁ piśaṅgāmbaram ambujekṣaṇaṁ catur-bhujaṁ śaṅkha-gadādy-udāyudham*. Thus the pleasing appearance of the Supreme Personality of Godhead's bodily features, His limbs and His dress are described. The *sāṅkhya-śāstra*, however, denies the existence of the Lord's transcendental form. The *sāṅkhya-śāstra* says that the Supreme Absolute Truth has no hands, no legs and no name: *hy anāma-rūpa-guṇa-pāṇi-pādam acakṣur aśrotram ekam advitīyam api nāma-rūpādikaṁ nāsti*. The Vedic *mantras* say, *apāṇi-pādo javano grahītā:* the Supreme Lord has no legs and hands, but He can accept whatever is offered to Him. Actually such statements accept that the Supreme has hands and legs, but deny that He has material hands and legs. This is why the Absolute is called *aprākṛta*. Kṛṣṇa, the Supreme Personality of Godhead, has a *sac-cid-ānanda-vigraha*, a form of eternity, knowledge and bliss, not a material form. The Sāṅkhyites, or *jñānīs*, deny the material form, and the devotees also know very well that the Absolute Truth, Bhagavān, has no material form.

īśvaraḥ paramaḥ kṛṣṇaḥ
sac-cid-ānanda-vigrahaḥ
anādir ādir govindaḥ
sarva-kāraṇa-kāraṇam

"Kṛṣṇa, who is known as Govinda, is the supreme controller. He has an eternal, blissful, spiritual body. He is the origin of all. He has no other origin, for He is the prime cause of all causes." The conception of the Absolute without hands and legs and the conception of the Absolute with hands and legs are apparently contradictory, but they both coincide with the same truth about the Supreme Absolute Person. Therefore the word *vastu-niṣṭhayoḥ*, which is used herein, indicates that both the *yogīs* and Sāṅkhyites have faith in the reality, but are arguing about it from the different viewpoints of material and spiritual identities. Parabrahman, or *bṛhat*, is the common point. The Sāṅkhyites and *yogīs* are both situated in that same Brahman, but they differ because of different angles of vision.

The directions given by the *bhakti-śāstra* point one in the perfect direction because the Supreme Personality of Godhead says in *Bhagavad-gītā, bhaktyā mām abhijānāti:* "Only by devotional service am I to be known." The *bhaktas* know that the Supreme Person has no material form, whereas the *jñānīs* simply deny the material form. One should therefore take shelter of the *bhakti-mārga*, the path of devotion; then everything will be clear. *Jñānīs* concentrate on the *virāṭ-rūpa*, the gigantic universal form of the Lord. This is a good system in the beginning for those who are extremely materialistic, but there is no need to think continuously of the *virāṭ-rūpa.* When Arjuna was shown the *virāṭ-rūpa* of Kṛṣṇa, he saw it, but he did not want to see it perpetually. He therefore requested the Lord to return to His original form as two-armed Kṛṣṇa. In conclusion, learned scholars find no contradictions in the devotees' concentration upon the spiritual form of the Lord (*īśvaraḥ paramaḥ kṛṣṇaḥ sac-cid-ānanda-vigrahaḥ*). In this regard, Śrīla Madhvācārya says that less intelligent nondevotees think that their conclusion is the ultimate, but because devotees are completely learned, they can understand that the Supreme Personality of Godhead is the ultimate goal.

TEXT 33

योऽनुग्रहार्थं भजतां पादमूल-
मनामरूपो भगवाननन्तः ।
नामानि रूपाणि च जन्मकर्मभि-
र्भेजे स मह्यं परमः प्रसीदतु ॥३३॥

yo 'nugrahārthaṁ bhajatāṁ pāda-mūlam
anāma-rūpo bhagavān anantaḥ
nāmāni rūpāṇi ca janma-karmabhir
bheje sa mahyaṁ paramaḥ prasīdatu

yaḥ—who (the Supreme Personality of Godhead); *anugraha-artham*—to show His causeless mercy; *bhajatām*—to the devotees who always render devotional service; *pāda-mūlam*—to His transcendental lotus feet; *anāma*—with no material name; *rūpaḥ*—or material form; *bhagavān*—the Supreme Personality of Godhead; *anantaḥ*—unlimited, all-pervading and eternally existing; *nāmāni*—transcendental holy names; *rūpāṇi*—His transcendental forms; *ca*—also; *janma-karmabhiḥ*—with His transcendental birth and activities; *bheje*—manifests; *saḥ*—He; *mahyam*—unto me; *paramaḥ*—the Supreme; *prasīdatu*—may He be merciful.

TRANSLATION

The Supreme Personality of Godhead, who is inconceivably opulent, who is devoid of all material names, forms and pastimes, and who is all-pervading, is especially merciful to the devotees who worship His lotus feet. Thus He exhibits transcendental forms and names with His different pastimes. May that Supreme Personality of Godhead, whose form is eternal and full of knowledge and bliss, be merciful to me.

PURPORT

In regard to the significant word *anāma-rūpaḥ*, Śrī Śrīdhara Svāmī says, *prākṛta-nāma-rūpa-rahito 'pi.* The word *anāma,* which means "having no name," indicates that the Supreme Personality of Godhead has no material name. Simply by chanting the name of Nārāyaṇa to call his son, Ajāmila attained salvation. This means that Nārāyaṇa is not an ordinary mundane name; it is nonmaterial. The word *anāma*, therefore, indicates that the names of the Supreme Lord do not belong to this material world. The vibration of the Hare Kṛṣṇa *mahā-mantra* is not a material sound, and similarly the form of the Lord and His appearance and activities are all nonmaterial. To show His causeless mercy to the devotees, as well as to the nondevotees, Kṛṣṇa, the Supreme Personality of Godhead, appears in this material world with names, forms and pastimes, all of which are transcendental. Unintelligent men who cannot understand this think that these names, forms and pastimes are material, and therefore they deny that He has a name or a form.

Considered with scrutiny, the conclusion of nondevotees, who say that God has no name, and that of devotees, who know that His name is not material, are practically the same. The Supreme Personality of Godhead has no material name, form, birth, appearance or disappearance, but nevertheless, He takes His birth (*janma*). As stated in *Bhagavad-gītā* (4.6):

ajo 'pi sann avyayātmā
bhūtānām īśvaro 'pi san
prakṛtiṁ svām adhiṣṭhāya
sambhavāmy ātma-māyayā

Although the Lord is unborn (*aja*) and His body never undergoes material changes, He nevertheless appears as an incarnation, maintaining Himself always in the transcendental stage (*śuddha-sattva*). Thus He exhibits His transcendental forms, names and activities. That is His special mercy toward His devotees. Others may continue merely arguing about whether the Absolute Truth has form or not, but when a devotee, by the grace of the Lord, sees the Lord personally, he becomes spiritually ecstatic.

Unintelligent persons say that the Lord does nothing. Actually He has nothing to do, but nevertheless He has to do everything, because without His sanction no one can do anything. The unintelligent, however, cannot see how He is working and how the entire material nature is working under His direction. His different potencies work perfectly.

na tasya kāryaṁ karaṇaṁ ca vidyate
na tat-samaś cābhyadhikaś ca dṛśyate
parāsya śaktir vividhaiva śrūyate
svābhāvikī jñāna-bala-kriyā ca

(*Śvetāśvatara Upaniṣad* 6.8)

He has nothing to do personally, for since His potencies are perfect, everything is immediately done by His will. Persons to whom the Supreme Personality of Godhead is not revealed cannot see how He is working, and therefore they think that even if there is God, He has nothing to do or has no particular name.

Actually the Lord's name already exists because of His transcendental activities. The Lord is sometimes called *guṇa-karma-nāma* because He is named according to His transcendental activities. For example, *Kṛṣṇa* means "all-attractive." This is the Lord's name because His transcendental qualities make Him very attractive. As a small boy He lifted Govardhana Hill, and in His childhood He killed many demons. Such activities are very attractive, and therefore He is sometimes called Giridhārī, Madhusūdana, Agha-niṣūdana and so on. Because He acted as the son of Nanda Mahārāja, He is called Nanda-tanuja. These names already exist, but since nondevotees cannot understand the names of the Lord, He is sometimes called *anāma*, or nameless. This means that He has no material names. All His activities are spiritual, and therefore He has spiritual names.

Generally, less intelligent men are under the impression that the Lord has no form. Therefore He appears in His original form as Kṛṣṇa, *sac-cid-ānanda-vigraha*, to carry out His mission of participating in the Battle of Kurukṣetra and pastimes to protect the devotees and vanquish the demons (*paritrāṇāya sādhūnāṁ vināśāya ca duṣkṛtām*). This is His mercy. For those who think that He has no form and no work to do, Kṛṣṇa comes to show that indeed He works. He works so gloriously that no one else can perform such uncommon acts. Although He appeared as a human being, He married 16,108 wives, which is impossible for a human being to do. The Lord performs such activities to show people how great He is, how affectionate He is and how merciful He is. Although His original name is Kṛṣṇa (*kṛṣṇas tu bhagavān svayam*), He acts in unlimited ways, and therefore according to His work He has many, many thousands of names.

TEXT 34

यः प्राकृतैर्ज्ञानपथैर्जनानां
यथाशयं देहगतो विभाति ।
यथानिलः पार्थिवमाश्रितो गुणं
स ईश्वरो मे कुरुतां मनोरथम् ॥३४॥

yaḥ prākṛtair jñāna-pathair janānāṁ
yathāśayaṁ deha-gato vibhāti
yathānilaḥ pārthivam āśrito guṇaṁ
sa īśvaro me kurutāṁ manoratham

yaḥ—who; *prākṛtaiḥ*—lower grade; *jñāna-pathaiḥ*—by the paths of worship; *janānām*—of all living entities; *yathā-āśayam*—according to the desire; *deha-gataḥ*—situated within the core of the heart; *vibhāti*—manifests; *yathā*—just as; *anilaḥ*—the air; *pārthivam*—earthly; *āśritaḥ*—receiving; *guṇam*—the quality (like flavor and color); *saḥ*—He; *īśvaraḥ*—the Supreme Personality of Godhead; *me*—my; *kurutām*—may He fulfill; *manoratham*—desire (for devotional service).

TRANSLATION

As the air carries various characteristics of the physical elements, like the aroma of a flower or colors resulting from a mixture of dust in the air, the Lord appears through lower systems of worship according to one's desires, although He appears as the demigods and not in His original form. What is the use of these other forms? May the original Supreme Personality of Godhead please fulfill my desires.

PURPORT

The impersonalists imagine the various demigods to be forms of the Lord. For example, the Māyāvādīs worship five demigods (*pañcopāsanā*). They do not actually believe in the form of the Lord, but for the sake of worship they imagine some form to be God. Generally they imagine a form of Viṣṇu, a form of Śiva, and forms of Gaṇeśa, the sun-god and Durgā. This is called *pañcopāsanā*. Dakṣa, however, wanted to worship not an imaginary form, but the supreme form of Lord Kṛṣṇa.

In this regard, Śrīla Viśvanātha Cakravartī Ṭhākura describes the difference between the Supreme Personality of Godhead and an ordinary living being. As pointed out in a previous verse, *sarvaṁ pumān veda guṇāṁś ca taj-jño na veda sarva-jñam anantam īḍe:* the omnipotent Supreme Lord knows everything, but the living being does not actually know the Supreme Personality of Godhead. As Kṛṣṇa says in *Bhagavad-gītā,* "I know everything, but no one knows Me." This is the difference between the Supreme Lord and an ordinary living being. In a prayer in *Śrīmad-Bhāgavatam,* Queen Kuntī says, "My dear Lord, You exist inside and outside, yet no one can see You."

The conditioned soul cannot understand the Supreme Personality of Godhead by speculative knowledge or by imagination. One must therefore know the Supreme Personality of Godhead by the grace of the Supreme Personality of Godhead. He reveals Himself, but He cannot be understood by speculation. As stated in *Śrīmad-Bhāgavatam* (10.14.29):

athāpi te deva padāmbuja-dvaya-
prasāda-leśānugṛhīta eva hi
jānāti tattvaṁ bhagavan-mahimno
na cānya eko 'pi ciraṁ vicinvan

"My Lord, if one is favored by even a slight trace of the mercy of Your lotus feet, he can understand the greatness of Your personality. But those who speculate to understand the Supreme Personality of Godhead are unable to know You, even though they continue to study the *Vedas* for many years."

This is the verdict of the *śāstra*. An ordinary man may be a great philosopher and may speculate upon what the Absolute Truth is, what His form is and where He is existing, but he cannot understand these truths. *Sevonmukhe hi jihvādau svayam eva sphuraty adaḥ:* one can understand the Supreme Personality of Godhead only through devotional service. This is also explained by the Supreme Personality of Godhead Himself in *Bhagavad-gītā* (18.55). *Bhaktyā mām abhijānāti yāvān yaś cāsmi tattvataḥ:* "One can understand the Supreme Personality of Godhead as He is only by devotional service." Unintelligent persons want to imagine or concoct a form of the Supreme Personality of Godhead, but devotees want to worship the actual Personality of Godhead. Therefore Dakṣa prays, "One may think of You as personal, impersonal or imaginary, but I wish to pray to Your Lordship that You fulfill my desires to see You as You actually are."

Śrīla Viśvanātha Cakravartī Ṭhākura comments that this verse is especially meant for the impersonalist, who thinks that he himself is the Supreme because there is no difference between the living being and God. The Māyāvādī philosopher thinks that there is only one Supreme Truth and that he is also that Supreme Truth. Actually this is not knowledge but foolishness, and this verse is especially meant for such fools, whose knowledge has been stolen by illusion (*māyayāpahṛta-jñānāḥ*). Viśvanātha Cakravartī Ṭhākura says that such persons, *jñāni-māninaḥ*, think themselves very advanced, but actually they are unintelligent.

In regard to this verse, Śrīla Madhvācārya says:

svadeha-sthaṁ hariṁ prāhur
adhamā jīvam eva tu
madhyamāś cāpy anirṇītaṁ
jīvād bhinnaṁ janārdanam

There are three classes of men—the lowest (*adhama*), those in the middle (*madhyama*), and the best (*uttama*). The lowest (*adhama*) think that there is no difference between God and the living entity except that the living entity is under designations whereas the Absolute Truth has no designations. In their opinion, as soon as the designations of the material body are dissolved, the *jīva*, the living entity, will mix with the Supreme. They give the argument of *ghaṭākāśa-paṭākāśa*, in which the body is compared to a pot with the sky within and the sky without. When the pot breaks, the sky inside becomes one with the sky outside, and so the impersonalists say that the living being becomes one with the Supreme. This is their argument, but Śrīla Madhvācārya says that such an argument is put forward by the lowest class of men. Another class of men cannot ascertain what the actual form of the Supreme is, but they agree that there is a Supreme who controls the activities of the ordinary living being. Such philosophers are accepted as mediocre. The best, however, are those who understand the Supreme Lord (*sac-cid-ānanda-vigraha*).

Pūrṇānandādi-guṇakaṁ sarva-jīva-vilakṣaṇam: His form is completely spiritual, full of bliss, and completely distinct from that of the conditioned soul or any other living entity. *Uttamās tu hariṁ prāhus tāratamyena teṣu ca:* such philosophers are the best because they know that the Supreme Personality of Godhead reveals Himself differently to worshipers in various modes of material nature. They know that there are thirty-three million demigods just to convince the conditioned soul that there is a supreme power and to induce him to agree to worship one of these demigods so that by the association of devotees he may be able to understand that Kṛṣṇa is the Supreme Personality of Godhead. As Lord Kṛṣṇa says in *Bhagavad-gītā, mattaḥ parataraṁ nānyat kiñcid asti dhanañjaya:* "There is no truth superior to Me." *Aham ādir hi devānām:* "I am the origin of all the demigods." *Ahaṁ sarvasya prabhavaḥ:* "I am superior to everyone, even Lord Brahmā, Lord Śiva and the other demigods." These are the conclusions of the *śāstra,* and one who accepts these conclusions should be considered a first-class philosopher. Such a philosopher knows that the Supreme Personality of Godhead is the Lord of the demigods (*deva-deveśvaraṁ sūtram ānandaṁ prāṇa-vedinaḥ*).

TEXTS 35–39

श्रीशुक उवाच

इति स्तुतः संस्तुवतः स तस्मिन्नघमर्षणे ।
प्रादुरासीत् कुरुश्रेष्ठ भगवान् भक्तवत्सलः ॥३५॥
कृतपादः सुपर्णांसे प्रलम्बाष्टमहाभुजः ।
चक्रशङ्खासिचर्मेषुधनुःपाशगदाधरः ॥३६॥
पीतवासा घनश्यामः प्रसन्नवदनेक्षणः ।
वनमालानिवीताङ्गो लसच्छ्रीवत्सकौस्तुभः ॥३७॥
महाकिरीटकटकः स्फुरन्मकरकुण्डलः ।
काञ्च्यङ्गुलीयवलयनूपुराङ्गदभूषितः ॥३८॥
त्रैलोक्यमोहनं रूपं बिभ्रत् त्रिभुवनेश्वरः ।
वृतो नारदनन्दाद्यैः पार्षदैः सुरयूथपैः ।
स्तूयमानोऽनुगायद्भिः सिद्धगन्धर्वचारणैः ॥३९॥

śrī-śuka uvāca
iti stutaḥ saṁstuvataḥ
sa tasminn aghamarṣaṇe
prādurāsīt kuru-śreṣṭha
bhagavān bhakta-vatsalaḥ

kṛta-pādaḥ suparṇāṁse
pralambāṣṭa-mahā-bhujaḥ
cakra-śaṅkhāsi-carmeṣu-
dhanuḥ-pāśa-gadā-dharaḥ

pīta-vāsā ghana-śyāmaḥ
prasanna-vadanekṣaṇaḥ
vana-mālā-nivītāṅgo
lasac-chrīvatsa-kaustubhaḥ

mahā-kirīṭa-kaṭakaḥ
sphuran-makara-kuṇḍalaḥ
kāñcy-aṅgulīya-valaya-
nūpurāṅgada-bhūṣitaḥ

trailokya-mohanaṁ rūpaṁ
bibhrat tribhuvaneśvaraḥ
vṛto nārada-nandādyaiḥ
pārṣadaiḥ sura-yūthapaiḥ
stūyamāno 'nugāyadbhiḥ
siddha-gandharva-cāraṇaiḥ

śrī-śukaḥ uvāca—Śrī Śukadeva Gosvāmī said; *iti*—thus; *stutaḥ*—being praised; *saṁstuvataḥ*—of Dakṣa, who was offering prayers; *saḥ*—that Supreme Personality of Godhead; *tasmin*—in that; *aghamarṣaṇe*—holy place celebrated as Aghamarṣaṇa; *prādurāsīt*—appeared; *kuru-śreṣṭha*—O best of the Kuru dynasty; *bhagavān*—the Supreme Personality of Godhead; *bhakta-vatsalaḥ*—who is very kind to His devotees; *kṛta-pādaḥ*—whose lotus feet were placed; *suparṇa-aṁse*—on the shoulders of His carrier, Garuḍa; *pralamba*—very long; *aṣṭa-mahā-bhujaḥ*—possessing eight mighty arms; *cakra*—disc; *śaṅkha*—

conchshell; *asi*—sword; *carma*—shield; *iṣu*—arrow; *dhanuḥ*—bow; *pāśa*—rope; *gadā*—club; *dharaḥ*—holding; *pīta-vāsāḥ*—with yellow garments; *ghana-śyāmaḥ*—whose bodily hue was intense blue-black; *prasanna*—very cheerful; *vadana*—whose face; *īkṣaṇaḥ*—and glance; *vana-mālā*—by a garland of forest flowers; *nivīta-aṅgaḥ*—whose body was adorned from the neck down to the feet; *lasat*—shining; *śrīvatsa-kaustubhaḥ*—the jewel known as Kaustubha and the mark of Śrīvatsa; *mahā-kirīṭa*—of a very large and gorgeous helmet; *kaṭakaḥ*—a circle; *sphurat*—glittering; *makara-kuṇḍalaḥ*—earrings resembling sharks; *kāñcī*—with a belt; *aṅgulīya*—finger rings; *valaya*—bracelets; *nūpura*—ankle bells; *aṅgada*—upper-arm bracelets; *bhūṣitaḥ*—decorated; *trai-lokya-mohanam*—captivating the three worlds; *rūpam*—His bodily features; *bibhrat*—shining; *tri-bhuvana*—of the three worlds; *īśvaraḥ*—the Supreme Lord; *vṛtaḥ*—surrounded; *nārada*—by exalted devotees, headed by Nārada; *nanda-ādyaiḥ*—and others, like Nanda; *pārṣadaiḥ*—who are all eternal associates; *sura-yūthapaiḥ*—as well as by the heads of the demigods; *stūyamānaḥ*—being glorified; *anugāyadbhiḥ*—singing after Him; *siddha-gandharva-cāraṇaiḥ*—by the Siddhas, Gandharvas and Cāraṇas.

TRANSLATION

Śrī Śukadeva Gosvāmī said: The Supreme Personality of Godhead, Hari, who is extremely affectionate to His devotees, was very pleased by the prayers offered by Dakṣa, and thus He appeared at that holy place known as Aghamarṣaṇa. O Mahārāja Parīkṣit, best of the Kuru dynasty, the Lord's lotus feet rested on the shoulders of His carrier, Garuḍa, and He appeared with eight long, mighty, very beautiful arms. In His hands He held a disc, conchshell, sword, shield, arrow, bow, rope and club—in each hand a different weapon, all brilliantly shining. His garments were yellow and His bodily hue deep bluish. His eyes and face were very cheerful, and from His neck to His feet hung a long garland of flowers. His chest was decorated with the Kaustubha jewel and the mark of Śrīvatsa. On His head was a gorgeous round helmet, and His ears were decorated with earrings resembling sharks. All these ornaments were uncommonly beautiful. The Lord wore a golden belt on His waist, bracelets on His arms, rings on His fingers, and ankle bells on His

feet. Thus decorated by various ornaments, Lord Hari, who is attractive to all the living entities of the three worlds, is known as Puruṣottama, the best personality. He was accompanied by great devotees like Nārada, Nanda and all the principal demigods, led by the heavenly king, Indra, and the residents of various upper planetary systems such as Siddhaloka, Gandharvaloka and Cāraṇaloka. Situated on both sides of the Lord and behind Him as well, these devotees offered Him prayers continuously.

TEXT 40

रूपं तन्महदाश्चर्यं विचक्ष्यागतसाध्वसः ।
ननाम दण्डवद् भूमौ प्रहृष्टात्मा प्रजापतिः ॥४०॥

rūpaṁ tan mahad-āścaryaṁ
vicakṣyāgata-sādhvasaḥ
nanāma daṇḍavad bhūmau
prahṛṣṭātmā prajāpatiḥ

rūpam—transcendental form; *tat*—that; *mahat-āścaryam*—greatly wonderful; *vicakṣya*—seeing; *āgata-sādhvasaḥ*—in the beginning becoming afraid; *nanāma*—offered obeisances; *daṇḍa-vat*—like a stick; *bhūmau*—on the ground; *prahṛṣṭa-ātmā*—being pleased in his body, mind and soul; *prajāpatiḥ*—the *prajāpati* known as Dakṣa.

TRANSLATION

Seeing that wonderful and effulgent form of the Supreme Personality of Godhead, Prajāpati Dakṣa was first somewhat afraid, but then he was very pleased to see the Lord, and he fell to the ground like a stick [daṇḍavat] to offer his respects to the Lord.

TEXT 41

न किञ्चनोदीरयितुमशकत् तीव्रया मुदा ।
आपूरितमनोद्वारैर्ह्रदिन्य इव निर्झरैः ॥४१॥

na kiñcanodīrayitum
aśakat tīvrayā mudā

āpūrita-manodvārair
hradinya iva nirjharaiḥ

na—not; *kiñcana*—anything; *udīrayitum*—to speak; *aśakat*—he was able; *tīvrayā*—by very great; *mudā*—happiness; *āpūrita*—filled; *manaḥ-dvāraiḥ*—by the senses; *hradinyaḥ*—the rivers; *iva*—like; *nirjharaiḥ*—by torrents from the mountain.

TRANSLATION

As rivers are filled by water flowing from a mountain, all of Dakṣa's senses were filled with pleasure. Because of his highly elevated happiness, Dakṣa could not say anything, but simply remained flat on the ground.

PURPORT

When one actually realizes or sees the Supreme Personality of Godhead, he is filled with complete happiness. For example, when Dhruva Mahārāja saw the Lord in his presence, he said, *svāmin kṛtārtho 'smi varaṁ na yāce:* "My dear Lord, I have nothing to ask from You. Now I am completely satisfied." Similarly, when Prajāpati Dakṣa saw the Supreme Lord in his presence, he simply fell flat, unable to speak or ask Him for anything.

TEXT 42

तं तथावनतं भक्तं प्रजाकामं प्रजापतिम् ।
चित्तज्ञः सर्वभूतानामिदमाह जनार्दनः ॥४२॥

taṁ tathāvanataṁ bhaktaṁ
prajā-kāmaṁ prajāpatim
citta-jñaḥ sarva-bhūtānām
idam āha janārdanaḥ

tam—him (Prajāpati Dakṣa); *tathā*—in that way; *avanatam*—prostrated before Him; *bhaktam*—a great devotee; *prajā-kāmam*—desiring to increase the population; *prajāpatim*—unto the *prajāpati* (Dakṣa);

citta-jñaḥ—who can understand the hearts; *sarva-bhūtānām*—of all living entities; *idam*—this; *āha*—said; *janārdanaḥ*—the Supreme Personality of Godhead, who can appease everyone's desires.

TRANSLATION

Although Prajāpati Dakṣa could not say anything, when the Lord, who knows everyone's heart, saw His devotee prostrate in that manner and desiring to increase the population, He addressed him as follows.

TEXT 43

श्रीभगवानुवाच
प्राचेतस महाभाग संसिद्धस्तपसा भवान् ।
यच्छ्रद्धया मत्परया मयि भावं परं गतः ॥४३॥

śrī-bhagavān uvāca
prācetasa mahā-bhāga
saṁsiddhas tapasā bhavān
yac chraddhayā mat-parayā
mayi bhāvaṁ paraṁ gataḥ

śrī-bhagavān uvāca—the Supreme Personality of Godhead said; *prācetasa*—O My dear Prācetasa; *mahā-bhāga*—O you who are so fortunate; *saṁsiddhaḥ*—perfected; *tapasā*—by your austerities; *bhavān*—your good self; *yat*—because; *śraddhayā*—by great faith; *mat-parayā*—whose object is Me; *mayi*—in Me; *bhāvam*—ecstasy; *param*—supreme; *gataḥ*—attained.

TRANSLATION

The Supreme Personality of Godhead said: O most fortunate Prācetasa, because of your great faith in Me, you have attained the supreme devotional ecstasy. Indeed, because of your austerities, combined with exalted devotion, your life is now successful. You have achieved complete perfection.

PURPORT

As the Lord Himself confirms in *Bhagavad-gītā* (8.15), one reaches the highest perfection when he attains the fortune of realizing the Supreme Personality of Godhead:

mām upetya punar janma
duḥkhālayam aśāśvatam
nāpnuvanti mahātmānaḥ
saṁsiddhiṁ paramāṁ gatāḥ

"After attaining Me, the great souls, who are *yogīs* in devotion, never return to this temporary world, which is full of miseries, because they have attained the highest perfection." Therefore the Kṛṣṇa consciousness movement teaches one to follow the path toward the topmost perfection simply by performing devotional service.

TEXT 44

प्रीतोऽहं ते प्रजानाथ यत्तेऽस्योद्बृंहणं तपः ।
ममैष कामो भूतानां यद् भूयासुर्विभूतयः ॥४४॥

prīto 'haṁ te prajā-nātha
yat te 'syodbṛṁhaṇaṁ tapaḥ
mamaiṣa kāmo bhūtānāṁ
yad bhūyāsur vibhūtayaḥ

prītaḥ—very much pleased; *aham*—I; *te*—with you; *prajā-nātha*—O king of population; *yat*—because; *te*—your; *asya*—of this material world; *udbṛṁhaṇam*—causing increase; *tapaḥ*—austerity; *mama*—My; *eṣaḥ*—this; *kāmaḥ*—desire; *bhūtānām*—of the living entities; *yat*—which; *bhūyāsuḥ*—may there be; *vibhūtayaḥ*—advancement in all respects.

TRANSLATION

My dear Prajāpati Dakṣa, you have performed extreme austerities for the welfare and growth of the world. My desire also is that everyone within this world be happy. I am therefore very

pleased with you because you are endeavoring to fulfill My desire for the welfare of the entire world.

PURPORT

After every dissolution of the material cosmos, all the living entities take shelter in the body of Kāraṇodakaśāyī Viṣṇu, and when creation takes place again, they come forth from His body in their various species to resume their activities. Why does the creation take place in such a way that the living entities are put into conditioned life to suffer the threefold miseries imposed upon them by the material nature? Here the Lord says to Dakṣa, "You desire to benefit all living entities, and that is also My desire." The living entities who come in contact with the material world are meant to be corrected. All the living entities within this material world have revolted against the service of the Lord, and therefore they remain within this material world as ever conditioned, *nitya-baddha*, taking birth again and again. There is a chance, of course, of their being liberated, but nevertheless the conditioned souls, not taking advantage of this opportunity, continue in a life of sense enjoyment, and thus they are punished by birth and death again and again. This is the law of nature. As the Lord says in *Bhagavad-gītā* (7.14):

daivī hy eṣā guṇamayī
mama māyā duratyayā
mām eva ye prapadyante
māyām etāṁ taranti te

"This divine energy of Mine, consisting of the three modes of material nature, is difficult to overcome. But those who have surrendered unto Me can easily cross beyond it." Elsewhere in *Bhagavad-gītā* (15.7) the Lord says:

mamaivāṁśo jīva-loke
jīva-bhūtaḥ sanātanaḥ
manaḥ ṣaṣṭhānīndriyāṇi
prakṛti-sthāni karṣati

"The living entities in this conditioned world are My eternal, fragmental parts. Due to conditioned life, they are struggling very hard with the six senses, which include the mind." The living entity's struggle for existence within the material world is due to his rebellious nature. Unless a living entity surrenders to Kṛṣṇa, he must continue this life of struggle.

The Kṛṣṇa consciousness movement is not a fad. It is a bona fide movement intended to promote the welfare of all conditioned souls by trying to elevate everyone to the platform of Kṛṣṇa consciousness. If one does not come to this platform, he must continue in material existence perpetually, sometimes in the upper planets and sometimes in the lower planets. As confirmed in *Caitanya-caritāmṛta* (*Madhya* 20.118), *kabhu svarge uṭhāya, kabhu narake ḍubāya:* the conditioned soul sometimes descends into nescience and sometimes gets some relief by being relatively freed from it. This is the life of the conditioned soul.

Prajāpati Dakṣa is trying to benefit the conditioned souls by begetting them to give them a life with a chance for liberation. Liberation means surrender to Kṛṣṇa. If one begets children with the purpose of training them to surrender to Kṛṣṇa, fatherhood is very good. Similarly, when the spiritual master trains the conditioned souls to become Kṛṣṇa conscious, his position is successful. If one gives the conditioned souls a chance to become Kṛṣṇa conscious, all his activities are approved by the Supreme Personality of Godhead, who is extremely pleased, as stated here (*prīto 'ham*). Following the examples of the previous *ācāryas*, all the members of the Kṛṣṇa consciousness movement should try to benefit the conditioned souls by inducing them to become Kṛṣṇa conscious and giving them all facilities to do so. Such activities constitute real welfare work. By such activities, a preacher or anyone who endeavors to spread Kṛṣṇa consciousness is recognized by the Supreme Personality of Godhead. As the Lord Himself confirms in *Bhagavad-gītā* (18.68–69):

ya idaṁ paramaṁ guhyaṁ
mad-bhakteṣv abhidhāsyati
bhaktiṁ mayi parāṁ kṛtvā
mām evaiṣyaty asaṁśayaḥ

na ca tasmān manuṣyeṣu
kaścin me priya-kṛttamaḥ
bhavitā na ca me tasmād
anyaḥ priyataro bhuvi

"For one who explains the supreme secret to the devotees, devotional service is guaranteed, and at the end he will come back to Me. There is no servant in this world more dear to Me than he, nor will there ever be one more dear."

TEXT 45

ब्रह्मा भवो भवन्तश्च मनवो विबुधेश्वराः ।
विभूतयो मम ह्येता भूतानां भूतिहेतवः ॥४५॥

brahmā bhavo bhavantaś ca
manavo vibudheśvarāḥ
vibhūtayo mama hy etā
bhūtānāṁ bhūti-hetavaḥ

brahmā—Lord Brahmā; *bhavaḥ*—Lord Śiva; *bhavantaḥ*—all of you *prajāpatis; ca*—and; *manavaḥ*—the Manus; *vibudha-īśvarāḥ*—all the different demigods (such as the sun, the moon, Venus, Mars and Jupiter, who are all in charge of various activities for the welfare of the world); *vibhūtayaḥ*—expansions of energy; *mama*—My; *hi*—indeed; *etāḥ*—all these; *bhūtānām*—of all the living entities; *bhūti*—of welfare; *hetavaḥ*—causes.

TRANSLATION

Lord Brahmā, Lord Śiva, the Manus, all the other demigods in the higher planetary systems, and you prajāpatis, who are increasing the population, are working for the benefit of all living entities. Thus you expansions of My marginal energy are incarnations of My various qualities.

PURPORT

There are various types of incarnations or expansions of the Supreme Personality of Godhead. The expansions of His personal self, or *viṣṇu-tattva*, are called *svāṁśa* expansions, whereas the living entities, who are not *viṣṇu-tattva* but *jīva-tattva*, are called *vibhinnāṁśa*, separated expansions. Although Prajāpati Dakṣa is not on the same level as Lord Brahmā and Lord Śiva, he is compared to them because he engages in the service of the Lord. In the service of the Personality of Godhead, it is not that Lord Brahmā is considered very great while an ordinary human being trying to preach the glories of the Lord is considered very low. There are no such distinctions. Regardless of whether materially high or materially low, anyone engaged in the service of the Lord is spiritually very dear to Him. In this regard, Śrīla Madhvācārya gives this quotation from the *Tantra-nirṇaya:*

viśeṣa-vyakti-pātratvād
brahmādyās tu vibhūtayaḥ
tad-antaryāmiṇaś caiva
matsyādyā vibhavāḥ smṛtāḥ

From Lord Brahmā down, all the living entities engaged in the service of the Lord are extraordinary and are called *vibhūti.* As the Lord says in *Bhagavad-gītā* (10.41):

yad yad vibhūtimat sattvaṁ
śrīmad ūrjitam eva vā
tat tad evāvagaccha tvaṁ
mama tejo-'ṁśa-sambhavam

"Know that all beautiful, glorious and mighty creations spring from but a spark of My splendor." A living entity especially empowered to act on behalf of the Lord is called *vibhūti,* whereas the *viṣṇu-tattva* incarnations of the Lord, such as the Matsya *avatāra* (*keśava dhṛta-mīna-śarīra jaya jagad-īśa hare*), are called *vibhava.*

TEXT 46

तपो मे हृदयं ब्रह्मंस्तनुर्विद्या क्रियाकृतिः ।
अङ्गानि क्रतवो जाता धर्म आत्मासवः सुराः ॥४६॥

tapo me hṛdayaṁ brahmaṁs
tanur vidyā kriyākṛtiḥ
aṅgāni kratavo jātā
dharma ātmāsavaḥ surāḥ

tapaḥ—austerities like mental control, mystic *yoga* and meditation; *me*—My; *hṛdayam*—heart; *brahman*—O *brāhmaṇa; tanuḥ*—the body; *vidyā*—the knowledge derived from Vedic scripture; *kriyā*—spiritual activities; *ākṛtiḥ*—form; *aṅgāni*—the limbs of the body; *kratavaḥ*—the ritualistic ceremonies and sacrifices mentioned in the Vedic literature; *jātāḥ*—completed; *dharmaḥ*—the religious principles for executing the ritualistic ceremonies; *ātmā*—My soul; *asavaḥ*—life airs; *surāḥ*—the demigods who execute My orders in different departments of the material world.

TRANSLATION

My dear brāhmaṇa, austerity in the form of meditation is My heart, Vedic knowledge in the form of hymns and mantras constitutes My body, and spiritual activities and ecstatic emotions are My actual form. The ritualistic ceremonies and sacrifices, when properly conducted, are the various limbs of My body, the unseen good fortune proceeding from pious or spiritual activities constitutes My mind, and the demigods who execute My orders in various departments are My life and soul.

PURPORT

Sometimes atheists argue that since God is invisible to their eyes, they do not believe in God. For them the Supreme Lord is describing a method by which one can see God in His impersonal form. Intelligent persons can see God in His personal form, as stated in the *śāstras*, but if one is very eager to see the Supreme Personality of Godhead immediately, face to face, he can see the Supreme Lord through this description, which portrays the various internal and external parts of His body.

To engage in *tapasya*, or denial of material activities, is the first principle of spiritual life. Then there are spiritual activities, such as the performance of Vedic ritualistic sacrifices, study of the Vedic knowledge, meditation upon the Supreme Personality of Godhead, and chanting of the Hare Kṛṣṇa *mahā-mantra*. One should also respect the demigods and understand how they are situated, how they act and how they manage the activities of the various departments of this material world. In this way one can see how God is existing and how everything is managed perfectly because of the presence of the Supreme Lord. As the Lord says in *Bhagavad-gītā* (9.10):

mayādhyakṣeṇa prakṛtiḥ
sūyate sa-carācaram
hetunānena kaunteya
jagad viparivartate

"This material nature is working under My direction, O son of Kuntī, and it is producing all moving and nonmoving beings. By its rule this manifestation is created and annihilated again and again." If one is unable to see the Supreme Lord although He is present as Kṛṣṇa in His various incarnations, one may see the Supreme Lord's impersonal feature, according to the direction of the *Vedas*, by seeing the activities of material nature.

Anything done under the direction of the Vedic injunctions is called *dharma*, as described by the order carriers of Yamarāja (*Bhāg.* 6.1.40):

veda-praṇihito dharmo
hy adharmas tad-viparyayaḥ
vedo nārāyaṇaḥ sākṣāt
svayambhūr iti śuśruma

"That which is prescribed in the *Vedas* constitutes *dharma*, the religious principles, and the opposite of that is irreligion. The *Vedas* are directly the Supreme Personality of Godhead, Nārāyaṇa, and are self-born. This we have heard from Yamarāja."

In this connection, Śrīla Madhvācārya comments:

tapo 'bhimānī rudras tu
viṣṇor hṛdayam āśritaḥ
vidyā rūpā tathaivomā
viṣṇos tanum upāśritā

śṛṅgārādy-ākṛti-gataḥ
kriyātmā pāka-śāsanaḥ

aṅgeṣu kratavaḥ sarve
madhya-dehe ca dharma-rāṭ
prāṇo vāyuś citta-gato
brahmādyāḥ sveṣu devatāḥ

The various demigods are all acting under the protection of the Supreme Personality of Godhead, and according to their various actions the demigods are differently named.

TEXT 47

अहमेवासमेवाग्रे नान्यत् किञ्चान्तरं बहिः ।
संज्ञानमात्रमव्यक्तं प्रसुप्तमिव विश्वतः ॥४७॥

aham evāsam evāgre
nānyat kiñcāntaraṁ bahiḥ
saṁjñāna-mātram avyaktaṁ
prasuptam iva viśvataḥ

aham—I, the Supreme Personality of Godhead; *eva*—only; *āsam*—was; *eva*—certainly; *agre*—in the beginning, before the creation; *na*—not; *anyat*—other; *kiñca*—anything; *antaram*—besides Me; *bahiḥ*—external (since the cosmic manifestation is external to the spiritual world, the spiritual world existed when there was no material world); *saṁjñāna-mātram*—only the consciousness of the living entities; *avyaktam*—unmanifested; *prasuptam*—sleeping; *iva*—like; *viśvataḥ*—all over.

TRANSLATION

Before the creation of this cosmic manifestation, I alone existed with My specific spiritual potencies. Consciousness was then unmanifested, just as one's consciousness is unmanifested during the time of sleep.

PURPORT

The word *aham* indicates a person. As explained in the *Vedas*, *nityo nityānāṁ cetanaś cetanānām:* the Lord is the supreme eternal among innumerable eternals and the supreme living being among the innumerable living beings. The Lord is a person who also has impersonal features. As stated in *Śrīmad-Bhāgavatam* (1.2.11):

vadanti tat tattva-vidas
tattvaṁ yaj jñānam advayam
brahmeti paramātmeti
bhagavān iti śabdyate

"Learned transcendentalists who know the Absolute Truth call this nondual substance Brahman, Paramātmā or Bhagavān." Consideration of the Paramātmā and impersonal Brahman arose after the creation; before the creation, only the Supreme Personality of Godhead existed. As firmly declared in *Bhagavad-gītā* (18.55), the Lord can be understood only by *bhakti-yoga.* The ultimate cause, the supreme cause of creation, is the Supreme Personality of Godhead, who can be understood only by *bhakti-yoga.* He cannot be understood by speculative philosophical research or by meditation, since all such processes came into existence after the material creation. The impersonal and localized conceptions of the Supreme Lord are more or less materially contaminated. The real spiritual process, therefore, is *bhakti-yoga.* As the Lord says, *bhaktyā mām abhijānāti:* "Only by devotional service can I be understood." Before the creation, the Lord existed as a person, as indicated here by the word *aham.* When Prajāpati Dakṣa saw Him as a person, who was beautifully dressed and ornamented, he actually experienced the meaning of this word *aham* through devotional service.

Each person is eternal. Because the Lord says that He existed as a person before the creation (*agre*) and will also exist after the annihilation, the Lord is a person eternally. Śrīla Viśvanātha Cakravartī Ṭhākura therefore quotes these verses from *Śrīmad-Bhāgavatam* (10.9.13–14):

na cāntar na bahir yasya
na pūrvaṁ nāpi cāparam
pūrvāparaṁ bahiś cāntar
jagato yo jagac ca yaḥ

taṁ matvātmajam avyaktaṁ
martya-liṅgam adhokṣajam
gopikolūkhale dāmnā
babandha prākṛtaṁ yathā

The Personality of Godhead appeared in Vṛndāvana as the son of mother Yaśodā, who bound the Lord with rope just as an ordinary mother binds a material child. There are actually no divisions of external and internal for the form of the Supreme Personality of Godhead (*sac-cid-ānanda-vigraha*), but when He appears in His own form the unintelligent think Him an ordinary person. *Avajānanti māṁ mūḍhā mānuṣīṁ tanum āśritam:* although He comes in His own body, which never changes, *mūḍhas*, the unintelligent, think that the impersonal Brahman has assumed a material body to come in the form of a person. Ordinary living beings assume material bodies, but the Supreme Personality of Godhead does not. Since the Supreme Personality of Godhead is the supreme consciousness, it is stated herein that *saṁjñāna-mātram*, the original consciousness, Kṛṣṇa consciousness, was unmanifested before the creation, although the consciousness of the Supreme Personality of Godhead is the origin of everything. The Lord says in *Bhagavad-gītā* (2.12), "Never was there a time when I did not exist, nor you, nor all these kings; nor in the future shall any of us cease to be." Thus the Lord's person is the Absolute Truth in the past, present and future.

In this regard, Madhvācārya quotes two verses from the *Matsya Purāṇa:*

nānā-varṇo haris tv eko
bahu-śīrṣa-bhujo rūpāt
āsīl laye tad-anyat tu
sūkṣma-rūpaṁ śriyaṁ vinā

asuptaḥ supta iva ca
mīlitākṣo 'bhavad dhariḥ
anyatrānādarād viṣṇau
śrīś ca līneva kathyate

sūkṣmatvena harau sthānāl
līnam anyad apīṣyate

After the annihilation of everything, the Supreme Lord, because of His *sac-cid-ānanda-vigraha*, remains in His original form, but since the other living entities have material bodies, the matter merges into matter, and the subtle form of the spirit soul remains within the body of the Lord. The Lord does not sleep, but the ordinary living entities remain asleep until the next creation. An unintelligent person thinks that the opulence of the Supreme Lord is nonexistent after the annihilation, but that is not a fact. The opulence of the Supreme Personality of Godhead remains as it is in the spiritual world; only in the material world is everything dissolved. *Brahma-līna*, merging into the Supreme Brahman, is not actual *līna*, or annihilation, for the subtle form remaining in the Brahman effulgence will return to the material world after the material creation and again assume a material form. This is described as *bhūtvā bhūtvā pralīyate.* When the material body is annihilated, the spirit soul remains in a subtle form, which later assumes another material body. This is true for the conditioned souls, but the Supreme Personality of Godhead remains eternally in His original consciousness and spiritual body.

TEXT 48

मय्यनन्तगुणेऽनन्ते गुणतो गुणविग्रहः ।
यदासीत् तत एवाद्यः स्वयम्भूः समभूदजः ॥४८॥

mayy ananta-guṇe 'nante
guṇato guṇa-vigrahaḥ
yadāsīt tata evādyaḥ
svayambhūḥ samabhūd ajaḥ

mayi—in Me; *ananta-guṇe*—possessing unlimited potency; *anante*—unlimited; *guṇataḥ*—from My potency known as *māyā; guṇa-vigrahaḥ*—the universe, which is a result of the modes of nature; *yadā*—when; *āsīt*—it came into existence; *tataḥ*—therein; *eva*—indeed; *ādyaḥ*—the first living being; *svayambhūḥ*—Lord Brahmā; *samabhūt*—was born; *ajaḥ*—although not from a material mother.

TRANSLATION

I am the reservoir of unlimited potency, and therefore I am known as unlimited or all-pervading. From My material energy the cosmic manifestation appeared within Me, and in this universal manifestation appeared the chief being, Lord Brahmā, who is your source and is not born of a material mother.

PURPORT

This is a description of the history of the universal creation. The first cause is the Lord Himself, the Supreme Person. From Him, Brahmā is created, and Brahmā takes charge of the affairs of the universe. The universal affairs of the material creation depend upon the material energy of the Supreme Personality of Godhead, who is therefore the cause of the material creation. The entire cosmic manifestation is described herein as *guṇa-vigrahaḥ*, the form of the Lord's qualities. From the cosmic universal form, the first creation is Lord Brahmā, who is the cause of all living entities. In this regard, Śrīla Madhvācārya describes the unlimited attributes of the Lord:

praty-ekaśo guṇānāṁ tu
niḥsīmatvam udīryate
tadānantyaṁ tu guṇatas
te cānantā hi saṅkhyayā
ato 'nanta-guṇo viṣṇur
guṇato 'nanta eva ca

Parāsya śaktir vividhaiva śrūyate: the Lord has innumerable potencies, all of which are unlimited. Therefore the Lord Himself and all His qualities, forms, pastimes and paraphernalia are also unlimited. Because Lord Viṣṇu has unlimited attributes, He is known as Ananta.

TEXTS 49–50

स वै यदा महादेवो मम वीर्योपबृंहितः ।
मेने खिलमिवात्मानमुद्यतः स्वर्गकर्मणि ॥४९॥

अथ मेऽभिहितो देवस्तपोऽतप्यत दारुणम् ।
नव विश्वसृजो युष्मान् येनादावसृजद् विभुः ॥५०॥

sa vai yadā mahādevo
mama vīryopabṛṁhitaḥ
mene khilam ivātmānam
udyataḥ svarga-karmaṇi

atha me 'bhihito devas
tapo 'tapyata dāruṇam
nava viśva-sṛjo yuṣmān
yenādāv asṛjad vibhuḥ

saḥ—that Lord Brahmā; *vai*—indeed; *yadā*—when; *mahā-devaḥ*—the chief of all the demigods; *mama*—My; *vīrya-upabṛṁhitaḥ*—being increased by the potency; *mene*—thought; *khilam*—incapable; *iva*—as if; *ātmānam*—himself; *udyataḥ*—attempting; *svarga-karmaṇi*—in the creation of the universal affairs; *atha*—at that time; *me*—by Me; *abhihitaḥ*—advised; *devaḥ*—that Lord Brahmā; *tapaḥ*—austerity; *atapyata*—performed; *dāruṇam*—extremely difficult; *nava*—nine; *viśva-sṛjaḥ*—important personalities to create the universe; *yuṣmān*—all of you; *yena*—by whom; *ādau*—in the beginning; *asṛjat*—created; *vibhuḥ*—the great.

TRANSLATION

When the chief lord of the universe, Lord Brahmā [Svayambhū], having been inspired by My energy, was attempting to create, he thought himself incapable. Therefore I gave him advice, and in accordance with My instructions he underwent extremely difficult austerities. Because of these austerities, the great Lord Brahmā was able to create nine personalities, including you, to help him in the functions of creation.

PURPORT

Nothing is possible without *tapasya.* Lord Brahmā, however, was empowered to create this entire universe because of his austerities. The more we engage in austerities, the more we become powerful by the grace of the Lord. Therefore Ṛṣabhadeva advised His sons, *tapo divyaṁ putrakā yena sattvaṁ śuddhyed:* "One should engage in penance and austerity to attain the divine position of devotional service. By such activity, one's heart is purified." (*Bhāg.* 5.5.1) In our material existence we are impure, and therefore we cannot do anything wonderful, but if we purify our existence by *tapasya*, we can do wonderful things by the grace of the Lord. Therefore *tapasya* is very important, as stressed in this verse.

TEXT 51

एषा पञ्चजनस्याङ्ग दुहिता वै प्रजापतेः ।
असिक्नी नाम पत्नीत्वे प्रजेश प्रतिगृह्यताम् ॥५१॥

eṣā pañcajanasyāṅga
duhitā vai prajāpateḥ
asiknī nāma patnītve
prajeśa pratigṛhyatām

eṣā—this; *pañcajanasya*—of Pañcajana; *aṅga*—O My dear son; *duhitā*—the daughter; *vai*—indeed; *prajāpateḥ*—another *prajāpati; asiknī nāma*—of the name Asiknī; *patnītve*—as your wife; *prajeśa*—O *prajāpati; pratigṛhyatām*—let her be accepted.

TRANSLATION

O My dear son Dakṣa, Prajāpati Pañcajana has a daughter named Asiknī, whom I offer to you so that you may accept her as your wife.

TEXT 52

मिथुनव्यवायधर्मस्त्वं प्रजासर्गमिमं पुनः ।
मिथुनव्यवायधर्मिण्यां भूरिशो भावयिष्यसि ॥५२॥

mithuna-vyavāya-dharmas tvaṁ
prajā-sargam imaṁ punaḥ
mithuna-vyavāya-dharmiṇyāṁ
bhūriśo bhāvayiṣyasi

mithuna—of man and woman; *vyavāya*—sexual activities; *dharmaḥ*—who accepts by religious performance; *tvam*—you; *prajā-sargam*—creation of living entities; *imam*—this; *punaḥ*—again; *mithuna*—of man and woman united; *vyavāya-dharmiṇyām*—in her according to the religious performance of sexual intercourse; *bhūriśaḥ*—manifold; *bhāvayiṣyasi*—you will cause to be.

TRANSLATION

Now unite in sexual life as man and woman, and in this way, by sexual intercourse, you will be able to beget hundreds of children in the womb of this girl to increase the population.

PURPORT

The Lord says in *Bhagavad-gītā* (7.11), *dharmāviruddho bhūteṣu kāmo 'smi:* "I am sex that is not contrary to religious principles." Sexual intercourse ordained by the Supreme Personality of Godhead is *dharma*, a religious principle, but it is not intended for sense enjoyment. Indulgence in sense enjoyment through sexual intercourse is not allowed by the Vedic principles. One may follow the natural tendency for sex life only to beget children. Therefore the Lord told Dakṣa in this verse, "This girl is offered to you only for sex life to beget children, not for any other purpose. She is very fertile, and therefore you will be able to have as many children as you can beget."

Śrīla Viśvanātha Cakravartī Ṭhākura remarks in this connection that Dakṣa was given the facility for unlimited sexual intercourse. In Dakṣa's previous life he was also known as Dakṣa, but in the course of performing sacrifices he offended Lord Śiva, and thus his head was replaced with that of a goat. Then Dakṣa gave up his life because of his degraded condition, but because he maintained the same unlimited sexual desires, he underwent austerities by which he satisfied the Supreme Lord, who then gave him unlimited potency for sexual intercourse.

It should be noted that although such a facility for sexual intercourse is achieved by the grace of the Supreme Personality of Godhead, this facility is not offered to advanced devotees, who are free from material desires (*anyābhilāṣitā-śūnyam*). In this connection it may be noted that if the American boys and girls engaged in the Kṛṣṇa consciousness movement want to advance in Kṛṣṇa consciousness to achieve the supreme benefit of loving service to the Lord, they should refrain from indulging in this facility for sex life. Therefore we advise that one should at least refrain from illicit sex. Even if there are opportunities for sex life, one should voluntarily accept the limitation of having sex only for progeny, not for any other purpose. Kardama Muni was also given the facility for sex life, but he had only a slight desire for it. Therefore after begetting children in the womb of Devahūti, Kardama Muni became completely renounced. The purport is that if one wants to return home, back to Godhead, one should voluntarily refrain from sex life. Sex should be accepted only as much as needed, not unlimitedly.

One should not think that Dakṣa received the favor of the Lord by receiving the facilities for unlimited sex. Later verses will reveal that Dakṣa again committed an offense, this time at the lotus feet of Nārada. Therefore although sex life is the topmost enjoyment in the material world and although one may have an opportunity for sexual enjoyment by the grace of God, this entails a risk of committing offenses. Dakṣa was open to such offenses, and therefore, strictly speaking, he was not actually favored by the Supreme Lord. One should not seek the favor of the Lord for unlimited potency in sex life.

TEXT 53

त्वत्तोऽधस्तात् प्रजाः सर्वा मिथुनीभूय मायया ।
मदीयया भविष्यन्ति हरिष्यन्ति च मे बलिम् ॥५३॥

tvatto 'dhastāt prajāḥ sarvā
mithunī-bhūya māyayā
madīyayā bhaviṣyanti
hariṣyanti ca me balim

tvattaḥ—you; *adhastāt*—after; *prajāḥ*—the living entities; *sarvāḥ*—all; *mithunī-bhūya*—having sex life; *māyayā*—because of the influence or facilities given by the illusory energy; *madīyayā*—My; *bhaviṣyanti*—they will become; *hariṣyanti*—they will offer; *ca*—also; *me*—unto Me; *balim*—presentations.

TRANSLATION

After you give birth to many hundreds and thousands of children, they will also be captivated by My illusory energy and will engage, like You, in sexual intercourse. But because of My mercy to you and them, they will also be able to give Me presentations in devotion.

TEXT 54

श्रीशुक उवाच
इत्युक्त्वा मिषतस्तस्य भगवान् विश्वभावनः ।
स्वप्नोपलब्धार्थ इव तत्रैवान्तर्दधे हरिः ॥५४॥

śrī-śuka uvāca
ity uktvā miṣatas tasya
bhagavān viśva-bhāvanaḥ
svapnopalabdhārtha iva
tatraivāntardadhe hariḥ

śrī-śukaḥ uvāca—Śukadeva Gosvāmī continued to speak; *iti*—thus; *uktvā*—saying; *miṣataḥ tasya*—while he (Dakṣa) was personally looking on; *bhagavān*—the Supreme Personality of Godhead; *viśva-bhāvanaḥ*—who creates the universal affairs; *svapna-upalabdha-arthaḥ*—an object obtained in dreaming; *iva*—like; *tatra*—there; *eva*—certainly; *antardadhe*—disappeared; *hariḥ*—the Lord, the Supreme Personality of Godhead.

TRANSLATION

Śukadeva Gosvāmī continued: After the creator of the entire universe, the Supreme Personality of Godhead, Hari, had spoken in this way in the presence of Prajāpati Dakṣa, He immediately disappeared as if He were an object experienced in a dream.

Thus end the Bhaktivedanta purports of the Sixth Canto, Fourth Chapter, of the Śrīmad-Bhāgavatam, *entitled "The* Haṁsa-guhya *Prayers Offered to the Lord by Prajāpati Dakṣa."*

CHAPTER FIVE

Nārada Muni Cursed by Prajāpati Dakṣa

This chapter relates how all the sons of Dakṣa were delivered from the clutches of the material energy by following the advice of Nārada, who was therefore cursed by Dakṣa.

Influenced by the external energy of Lord Viṣṇu, Prajāpati Dakṣa begot ten thousand sons in the womb of his wife, Pāñcajanī. These sons, who were all of the same character and mentality, were known as the Haryaśvas. Ordered by their father to create more and more population, the Haryaśvas went west to the place where the River Sindhu (now the Indus) meets the Arabian Sea. In those days this was the site of a holy lake named Nārāyaṇa-saras, where there were many saintly persons. The Haryaśvas began practicing austerities, penances and meditation, which are the engagements of the highly exalted renounced order of life. However, when Śrīla Nārada Muni saw these boys engaged in such commendable austerities simply for material creation, he thought it better to release them from this tendency. Nārada Muni described to the boys their ultimate goal of life and advised them not to become ordinary *karmīs* to beget children. Thus all the sons of Dakṣa became enlightened and left, never to return.

Prajāpati Dakṣa, who was very sad at the loss of his sons, begot one thousand more sons in the womb of his wife, Pāñcajanī, and ordered them to increase progeny. These sons, who were named the Savalāśvas, also engaged in worshiping Lord Viṣṇu to beget children, but Nārada Muni convinced them to become mendicants and not beget children. Foiled twice in his attempts to increase population, Prajāpati Dakṣa became most angry at Nārada Muni and cursed him, saying that in the future he would not be able to stay anywhere. Since Nārada Muni, being fully qualified, was fixed in tolerance, he accepted Dakṣa's curse.

TEXT 1

श्रीशुक उवाच
तस्यां स पाञ्चजन्यां वै विष्णुमायोपबृंहितः ।
हर्यश्वसंज्ञानयुतं पुत्रानजनयद् विभुः ॥ १ ॥

śrī-śuka uvāca
tasyāṁ sa pāñcajanyāṁ vai
viṣṇu-māyopabṛṁhitaḥ
haryaśva-saṁjñān ayutaṁ
putrān ajanayad vibhuḥ

śrī-śukaḥ uvāca—Śrī Śukadeva Gosvāmī said; *tasyām*—in her; *saḥ*—Prajāpati Dakṣa; *pāñcajanyām*—his wife named Pāñcajanī; *vai*—indeed; *viṣṇu-māyā-upabṛṁhitaḥ*—being made capable by the illusory energy of Lord Viṣṇu; *haryaśva-saṁjñān*—named the Haryaśvas; *ayutam*—ten thousand; *putrān*—sons; *ajanayat*—begot; *vibhuḥ*—being powerful.

TRANSLATION

Śrīla Śukadeva Gosvāmī continued: Impelled by the illusory energy of Lord Viṣṇu, Prajāpati Dakṣa begot ten thousand sons in the womb of Pāñcajanī [Asiknī]. My dear King, these sons were called the Haryaśvas.

TEXT 2

अपृथग्धर्मशीलास्ते सर्वे दाक्षायणा नृप ।
पित्रा प्रोक्ताः प्रजासर्गे प्रतीचीं प्रययुर्दिशम् ॥ २ ॥

apṛthag-dharma-śīlās te
sarve dākṣāyaṇā nṛpa
pitrā proktāḥ prajā-sarge
pratīcīṁ prayayur diśam

apṛthak—alike in; *dharma-śīlāḥ*—good character and behavior; *te*—they; *sarve*—all; *dākṣāyaṇāḥ*—the sons of Dakṣa; *nṛpa*—O King;

pitrā—by their father; *proktāḥ*—ordered; *prajā-sarge*—to increase the population; *pratīcīm*—western; *prayayuḥ*—they went to; *diśam*—the direction.

TRANSLATION

My dear King, all the sons of Prajāpati Dakṣa were alike in being very gentle and obedient to the orders of their father. When their father ordered them to beget children, they all went in the western direction.

TEXT 3

तत्र नारायणसरस्तीर्थं सिन्धुसमुद्रयोः ।
सङ्गमो यत्र सुमहन्मुनिसिद्धनिषेवितम् ॥ ३ ॥

tatra nārāyaṇa-saras
tīrthaṁ sindhu-samudrayoḥ
saṅgamo yatra sumahan
muni-siddha-niṣevitam

tatra—in that direction; *nārāyaṇa-saraḥ*—the lake named Nārāyaṇa-saras; *tīrtham*—very holy place; *sindhu-samudrayoḥ*—of the River Sindhu and the sea; *saṅgamaḥ*—confluence; *yatra*—where; *su-mahat*—very great; *muni*—by sages; *siddha*—and perfected human beings; *niṣevitam*—frequented.

TRANSLATION

In the west, where the River Sindhu meets the sea, there is a great place of pilgrimage known as Nārāyaṇa-saras. Many sages and others advanced in spiritual consciousness live there.

TEXTS 4–5

तदुपस्पर्शनादेव विनिर्धूतमलाशयाः ।
धर्मे पारमहंस्ये च प्रोत्पन्नमतयोऽप्युत ॥ ४ ॥
तेपिरे तप एवोग्रं पित्रादेशेन यन्त्रिताः ।
प्रजाविवृद्धये यत्तान् देवर्षिस्तान् ददर्श ह ॥ ५ ॥

tad-upasparśanād eva
vinirdhūta-malāśayāḥ
dharme pāramahaṁsye ca
protpanna-matayo 'py uta

tepire tapa evograṁ
pitrādeśena yantritāḥ
prajā-vivṛddhaye yattān
devarṣis tān dadarśa ha

tat—of that holy place; *upasparśanāt*—from bathing in that water or touching it; *eva*—only; *vinirdhūta*—completely washed away; *mala-āśayāḥ*—whose impure desires; *dharme*—to the practices; *pārama-haṁsye*—executed by the topmost class of *sannyāsīs; ca*—also; *protpanna*—highly inclined; *matayaḥ*—whose minds; *api uta*—although; *tepire*—they executed; *tapaḥ*—penances; *eva*—certainly; *ugram*—severe; *pitṛ-ādeśena*—by the order of their father; *yantritāḥ*—engaged; *prajā-vivṛddhaye*—for the purpose of increasing the population; *yattān*—ready; *devarṣiḥ*—the great sage Nārada; *tān*—them; *dadarśa*—visited; *ha*—indeed.

TRANSLATION

In that holy place, the Haryaśvas began regularly touching the lake's waters and bathing in them. Gradually becoming very much purified, they became inclined toward the activities of paramahaṁsas. Nevertheless, because their father had ordered them to increase the population, they performed severe austerities to fulfill his desires. One day, when the great sage Nārada saw those boys performing such fine austerities to increase the population, Nārada approached them.

TEXTS 6–8

उवाच चाथ हर्यश्वाः कथं स्रक्ष्यथ वै प्रजाः ।
अदृष्ट्वान्तं भुवो यूयं बालिशा बत पालकाः ॥ ६ ॥

तथैकपुरुषं राष्ट्रं बिलं चादृष्टनिर्गमम् ।
बहुरूपां स्त्रियं चापि पुमांसं पुंश्चलीपतिम् ॥ ७ ॥
नदीमुभयतोवाहां पञ्चपञ्चाद्भुतं गृहम् ।
क्वचिद्धंसं चित्रकथं क्षौरपव्यं स्वयं भ्रमि ॥ ८ ॥

uvāca cātha haryaśvāḥ
kathaṁ srakṣyatha vai prajāḥ
adṛṣṭvāntaṁ bhuvo yūyaṁ
bāliśā bata pālakāḥ

tathaika-puruṣaṁ rāṣṭraṁ
bilaṁ cādṛṣṭa-nirgamam
bahu-rūpāṁ striyaṁ cāpi
pumāṁsaṁ puṁścalī-patim

nadīm ubhayato vāhāṁ
pañca-pañcādbhutaṁ gṛham
kvacid dhaṁsaṁ citra-kathaṁ
kṣaura-pavyaṁ svayaṁ bhrami

uvāca—he said; *ca*—also; *atha*—thus; *haryaśvāḥ*—O Haryaśvas, sons of Prajāpati Dakṣa; *katham*—why; *srakṣyatha*—you will beget; *vai*—indeed; *prajāḥ*—progeny; *adṛṣṭvā*—having not seen; *antam*—the end; *bhuvaḥ*—of this earth; *yūyam*—all of you; *bāliśāḥ*—inexperienced; *bata*—alas; *pālakāḥ*—although ruling princes; *tathā*—so also; *eka*—one; *puruṣam*—man; *rāṣṭram*—kingdom; *bilam*—the hole; *ca*—also; *adṛṣṭa-nirgamam*—from which there is no coming out; *bahu-rūpām*—taking many forms; *striyam*—the woman; *ca*—and; *api*—even; *pumāṁsam*—the man; *puṁścalī-patim*—the husband of a prostitute; *nadīm*—a river; *ubhayataḥ*—in both ways; *vāhām*—which flows; *pañca-pañca*—of five multiplied by five (twenty-five); *adbhutam*—a wonder; *gṛham*—the house; *kvacit*—somewhere; *haṁsam*—a swan; *citra-katham*—whose story is wonderful; *kṣaura-pavyam*—made of sharp razors and thunderbolts; *svayam*—itself; *bhrami*—revolving.

TRANSLATION

The great sage Nārada said: My dear Haryaśvas, you have not seen the extremities of the earth. There is a kingdom where only one man lives and where there is a hole from which, having entered, no one emerges. A woman there who is extremely unchaste adorns herself with various attractive dresses, and the man who lives there is her husband. In that kingdom, there is a river flowing in both directions, a wonderful home made of twenty-five materials, a swan that vibrates various sounds, and an automatically revolving object made of sharp razors and thunderbolts. You have not seen all this, and therefore you are inexperienced boys without advanced knowledge. How, then, will you create progeny?

PURPORT

Nārada Muni saw that the boys known as the Haryaśvas were already purified because of living in that holy place and were practically ready for liberation. Why then should they be encouraged to become entangled in family life, which is so dark that once having entered it one cannot leave it? Through this analogy, Nārada Muni asked them to consider why they should follow their father's order to be entangled in family life. Indirectly, he asked them to find within the cores of their hearts the situation of the Supersoul, Lord Viṣṇu, for then they would truly be experienced. In other words, one who is too involved in his material environment and does not look within the core of his heart is increasingly entangled in the illusory energy. Nārada Muni's purpose was to get the sons of Prajāpati Dakṣa to divert their attention toward spiritual realization instead of involving themselves in the ordinary but complicated affairs of propagation. The same advice was given by Prahlāda Mahārāja to his father (*Bhāg.* 7.5.5):

tat sādhu manye 'sura-varya dehināṁ
sadā samudvigna-dhiyām asad-grahāt
hitvātma-pātaṁ gṛham andha-kūpaṁ
vanaṁ gato yad dharim āśrayeta

In the dark well of family life, one is always full of anxiety because of having accepted a temporary body. If one wants to free himself from this anxiety, one should immediately leave family life and take shelter of the Supreme Personality of Godhead in Vṛndāvana. Nārada Muni advised the Haryaśvas not to enter household life. Since they were already advanced in spiritual knowledge, why should they be entangled in that way?

TEXT 9

कथं स्वपितुरादेशमविद्वांसो विपश्चितः ।
अनुरूपमविज्ञाय अहो सर्गं करिष्यथ ॥ ९ ॥

kathaṁ sva-pitur ādeśam
avidvāṁso vipaścitaḥ
anurūpam avijñāya
aho sargaṁ kariṣyatha

katham—how; *sva-pituḥ*—of your own father; *ādeśam*—the order; *avidvāṁsaḥ*—ignorant; *vipaścitaḥ*—who knows everything; *anurūpam*—suitable for you; *avijñāya*—without knowing; *aho*—alas; *sargam*—the creation; *kariṣyatha*—you will perform.

TRANSLATION

Alas, your father is omniscient, but you do not know his actual order. Without knowing the actual purpose of your father, how will you create progeny?

TEXT 10

श्रीशुक उवाच
तन्निशम्याथ हर्यश्वा औत्पत्तिकमनीषया ।
वाचःकूटं तु देवर्षेः स्वयं विममृशुर्धिया ॥१०॥

śrī-śuka uvāca
tan niśamyātha haryaśvā
autpattika-manīṣayā
vācaḥ kūṭaṁ tu devarṣeḥ
svayaṁ vimamṛśur dhiyā

śrī-śukaḥ uvāca—Śrī Śukadeva Gosvāmī said; *tat*—that; *niśamya*—hearing; *atha*—thereafter; *haryaśvāḥ*—all the sons of Prajāpati Dakṣa; *autpattika*—naturally awakened; *manīṣayā*—by possessing the power to consider; *vācaḥ*—of the speech; *kūṭam*—the enigma; *tu*—but; *devarṣeḥ*—of Nārada Muni; *svayam*—themselves; *vimamṛśuḥ*—reflected upon; *dhiyā*—with full intelligence.

TRANSLATION

Śrī Śukadeva Gosvāmī said: Hearing these enigmatic words of Nārada Muni, the Haryaśvas considered them with their natural intelligence, without help from others.

TEXT 11

भूः क्षेत्रं जीवसंज्ञं यदनादि निजबन्धनम् ।
अदृष्ट्वा तस्य निर्वाणं किमसत्कर्मभिर्भवेत् ॥११॥

bhūḥ kṣetraṁ jīva-saṁjñaṁ yad
anādi nija-bandhanam
adṛṣṭvā tasya nirvāṇaṁ
kim asat-karmabhir bhavet

bhūḥ—the earth; *kṣetram*—the field of activities; *jīva-saṁjñam*—the designation of the spiritual living being who is bound by different results of activity; *yat*—which; *anādi*—existing since time immemorial; *nija-bandhanam*—causing his own bondage; *adṛṣṭvā*—without seeing; *tasya*—of this; *nirvāṇam*—the cessation; *kim*—what benefit; *asat-karmabhiḥ*—with temporary fruitive activities; *bhavet*—there can be.

TRANSLATION

[The Haryaśvas understood the meaning of Nārada's words as follows.] The word "bhūḥ" ["the earth"] refers to the field of activities. The material body, which is a result of the living being's actions, is his field of activities, and it gives him false designations. Since time immemorial, he has received various types of material bodies, which are the roots of bondage to the material world. If

one foolishly engages in temporary fruitive activities and does not look toward the cessation of this bondage, what will be the benefit of his actions?

PURPORT

Nārada Muni spoke to the Haryaśvas, the sons of Prajāpati Dakṣa, about ten allegorical subjects—the king, the kingdom, the river, the house, the physical elements and so forth. After considering these by themselves, the Haryaśvas could understand that the living entity encaged in his body seeks happiness, but takes no interest in how to become free from his encagement. This is a very important verse, since all the living entities in the material world are very active, having obtained their particular types of bodies. A man works all day and night for sense gratification, and animals like hogs and dogs also work for sense gratification all day and night. Birds, beasts and all other conditioned living entities engage in various activities without knowledge of the soul encaged within the body. Especially in the human form of body, one's duty is to act in such a way that he can release himself from his encagement, but without the instructions of Nārada or his representative in the disciplic succession, people blindly engage in bodily activities to enjoy *māyā-sukha*—flickering, temporary happiness. They do not know how to become free from their material encagement. Ṛṣabhadeva therefore said that such activity is not at all good, since it encages the soul again and again in a body subjected to the threefold miseries of the material condition.

The Haryaśvas, the sons of Prajāpati Dakṣa, could immediately understand the purport of Nārada's instructions. Our Kṛṣṇa consciousness movement is especially meant for such enlightenment. We are trying to enlighten humanity so that people may come to the understanding that they should work hard in *tapasya* for self-realization and freedom from the continuous bondage of birth, death, old age and disease in one body after another. *Māyā*, however, is very strong; she is expert in putting impediments in the way of this understanding. Therefore sometimes one comes to the Kṛṣṇa consciousness movement but again falls into the clutches of *māyā*, not understanding the importance of this movement.

TEXT 12

एक एवेश्वरस्तुर्यो भगवान् स्वाश्रयः परः ।
तमदृष्ट्वाभवं पुंसः किमसत्कर्मभिर्भवेत् ॥१२॥

eka eveśvaras turyo
bhagavān svāśrayaḥ paraḥ
tam adṛṣṭvābhavaṁ puṁsaḥ
kim asat-karmabhir bhavet

ekaḥ—one; *eva*—indeed; *īśvaraḥ*—supreme controller; *turyaḥ*—the fourth transcendental category; *bhagavān*—the Supreme Personality of Godhead; *sva-āśrayaḥ*—independent, being His own shelter; *paraḥ*—beyond this material creation; *tam*—Him; *adṛṣṭvā*—not seeing; *abhavam*—who is not born or created; *puṁsaḥ*—of a man; *kim*—what benefit; *asat-karmabhiḥ*—with temporary fruitive activities; *bhavet*—there can be.

TRANSLATION

[Nārada Muni had said that there is a kingdom where there is only one male. The Haryaśvas realized the purport of this statement.] The only enjoyer is the Supreme Personality of Godhead, who observes everything, everywhere. He is full of six opulences and fully independent of everyone else. He is never subject to the three modes of material nature, for He is always transcendental to this material creation. If the members of human society do not understand Him, the Supreme, through their advancement in knowledge and activities, but simply work very hard like cats and dogs all day and night for temporary happiness, what will be the benefit of their activities?

PURPORT

Nārada Muni had mentioned a kingdom where there is only one king with no competitor. The complete spiritual world, and specifically the cosmic manifestation, has only one proprietor or enjoyer—the Supreme Personality of Godhead, who is beyond this material manifestation. The Lord has therefore been described as *turya*, existing on the fourth platform. He has also been described as *abhava*. The word *bhava*, which means "takes birth," comes from the word *bhū*, "to be." As stated in *Bhagavad-gītā* (8.19), *bhūtvā bhūtvā pralīyate:* the living entities in the material world must be repeatedly born and destroyed. The Supreme Personality of Godhead, however, is neither *bhūtvā* nor *pralīyate;* He is eternal. In other words, He is not obliged to take birth like human beings or animals, which repeatedly take birth and die because of ignorance of the soul. The Supreme Personality of Godhead, Kṛṣṇa, is not subjected to such changes of body, and one who thinks otherwise is considered a fool (*avajānanti māṁ mūḍhā mānuṣīṁ tanum āśritam*). Nārada Muni advises that human beings not waste their time simply jumping like cats and monkeys, without real benefit. The duty of the human being is to understand the Supreme Personality of Godhead.

TEXT 13

पुमान् नैवैति यद् गत्वा बिलस्वर्गं गतो यथा ।
प्रत्यग्धामाविद इह किमसत्कर्मभिर्भवेत् ॥१३॥

pumān naivaiti yad gatvā
bila-svargaṁ gato yathā
pratyag-dhāmāvida iha
kim asat-karmabhir bhavet

pumān—a human being; *na*—not; *eva*—indeed; *eti*—comes back; *yat*—to which; *gatvā*—having gone; *bila-svargam*—to the region of the lower planetary system known as Pātāla; *gataḥ*—gone; *yathā*—like; *pratyak-dhāma*—the effulgent spiritual world; *avidaḥ*—of the unintelligent man; *iha*—in this material world; *kim*—what benefit; *asat-karmabhiḥ*—with temporary fruitive activities; *bhavet*—there can be.

TRANSLATION

[Nārada Muni had described that there is a bila, or hole, from which, having entered, one does not return. The Haryaśvas understood the meaning of this allegory.] Hardly once has a person who has entered the lower planetary system called Pātāla

been seen to return. Similarly, if one enters the Vaikuṇṭha-dhāma [pratyag-dhāma], he does not return to this material world. If there is such a place, from which, having gone, one does not return to the miserable material condition of life, what is the use of jumping like monkeys in the temporary material world and not seeing or understanding that place? What will be the profit?

PURPORT

As stated in *Bhagavad-gītā* (15.6), *yad gatvā na nivartante tad dhāma paramaṁ mama:* there is a region from which, having gone, one does not return to the material world. This region has been repeatedly described. Elsewhere in *Bhagavad-gītā* (4.9), Kṛṣṇa says:

janma karma ca me divyam
evaṁ yo vetti tattvataḥ
tyaktvā dehaṁ punar janma
naiti mām eti so 'rjuna

"One who knows the transcendental nature of My appearance and activities does not, upon leaving the body, take his birth again in this material world, but attains My eternal abode, O Arjuna."

If one can properly understand Kṛṣṇa, who has already been described as the Supreme King, he does not return here after giving up his material body. This fact has been described in this verse of *Śrīmad-Bhāgavatam. Pumān naivaiti yad gatvā:* he does not return to this material world, but returns home, back to Godhead, to live an eternally blissful life of knowledge. Why do people not care about this? What will be the benefit of taking birth again in this material world, sometimes as a human being, sometimes a demigod and sometimes a cat or dog? What is the benefit of wasting time in this way? Kṛṣṇa has very definitely asserted in *Bhagavad-gītā* (8.15):

mām upetya punar janma
duḥkhālayam aśāśvatam
nāpnuvanti mahātmānaḥ
saṁsiddhiṁ paramāṁ gatāḥ

"After attaining Me, the great souls, who are *yogīs* in devotion, never return to this temporary world, which is full of miseries, because they have attained the highest perfection." One's real concern should be to free himself from the repetition of birth and death and attain the topmost perfection of life by living with the Supreme King in the spiritual world. In these verses the sons of Dakṣa repeatedly say, *kim asat-karmabhir bhavet:* "What is the use of impermanent fruitive activities?"

TEXT 14

नानारूपात्मनो बुद्धिः स्वैरिणीव गुणान्विता ।
तन्निष्ठामगतस्येह किमसत्कर्मभिर्भवेत् ॥१४॥

nānā-rūpātmano buddhiḥ
svairiṇīva guṇānvitā
tan-niṣṭhām agatasyeha
kim asat-karmabhir bhavet

nānā—various; *rūpā*—who has forms or dresses; *ātmanaḥ*—of the living entity; *buddhiḥ*—the intelligence; *svairiṇī*—a prostitute who freely decorates herself with different types of cloths and ornaments; *iva*—like; *guṇa-anvitā*—endowed with the mode of passion, and so on; *tat-niṣṭhām*—the cessation of that; *agatasya*—of one who has not obtained; *iha*—in this material world; *kim asat-karmabhiḥ bhavet*—what is the use of performing temporary fruitive activities.

TRANSLATION

[Nārada Muni had described a woman who is a professional prostitute. The Haryaśvas understood the identity of this woman.] Mixed with the mode of passion, the unsteady intelligence of every living entity is like a prostitute who changes dresses just to attract one's attention. If one fully engages in temporary fruitive activities, not understanding how this is taking place, what does he actually gain?

PURPORT

A woman who has no husband declares herself independent, which means that she becomes a prostitute. A prostitute generally dresses herself in various fashions intended to attract a man's attention to the lower part of her body. Today it has become a much advertised fashion for a woman to go almost naked, covering the lower part of her body only slightly, in order to draw the attention of a man to her private parts for sexual enjoyment. The intelligence engaged to attract a man to the lower part of the body is the intelligence of a professional prostitute. Similarly, the intelligence of a living entity who does not turn his attention toward Kṛṣṇa or the Kṛṣṇa consciousness movement simply changes dresses like a prostitute. What is the benefit of such foolish intelligence? One should be intelligently conscious in such a way that he need no longer change from one body to another.

Karmīs change their professions at any moment, but a Kṛṣṇa conscious person does not change his profession, for his only profession is to attract the attention of Kṛṣṇa by chanting the Hare Kṛṣṇa *mantra* and living a very simple life, without following daily changes of fashion. In our Kṛṣṇa consciousness movement, fashionable persons are taught to adopt one fashion—the dress of a Vaiṣṇava with a shaved head and *tilaka.* They are taught to be always clean in mind, dress and eating in order to be fixed in Kṛṣṇa consciousness. What is the use of changing one's dress, sometimes wearing long hair and a long beard and sometimes dressing otherwise? This is not good. One should not waste his time in such frivolous activities. One should always be fixed in Kṛṣṇa consciousness and take the cure of devotional service with firm determination.

TEXT 15

तत्सङ्गभ्रंशितैश्वर्यं संसरन्तं कुभार्यवत् ।
तद्गतीरबुधस्येह किमसत्कर्मभिर्भवेत् ॥१५॥

tat-saṅga-bhraṁśitaiśvaryaṁ
saṁsarantaṁ kubhāryavat
tad-gatīr abudhasyeha
kim asat-karmabhir bhavet

tat-saṅga—by association with the prostitute of intelligence; *bhraṁśita*—taken away; *aiśvaryam*—the opulence of independence; *saṁsarantam*—undergoing the material way of life; *ku-bhārya-vat*—exactly like a person who has a polluted wife; *tat-gatīḥ*—the movements of the polluted intelligence; *abudhasya*—of one who does not know; *iha*—in this world; *kim asat-karmabhiḥ bhavet*—what can be the benefit of performing temporary fruitive activities.

TRANSLATION

[Nārada Muni had also spoken of a man who is the husband of the prostitute. The Haryaśvas understood this as follows.] If one becomes the husband of a prostitute, he loses all independence. Similarly, if a living entity has polluted intelligence, he prolongs his materialistic life. Frustrated by material nature, he must follow the movements of the intelligence, which brings various conditions of happiness and distress. If one performs fruitive activities under such conditions, what will be the benefit?

PURPORT

Polluted intelligence has been compared to a prostitute. One who has not purified his intelligence is said to be controlled by that prostitute. As stated in *Bhagavad-gītā* (2.41), *vyavasāyātmikā buddhir ekeha kuru-nandana:* those who are actually serious are conducted by one kind of intelligence, namely, intelligence in Kṛṣṇa consciousness. *Bahu-śākhā hy anantāś ca buddhayo 'vyavasāyinām:* one who is not fixed in proper intelligence discovers many modes of life. Thus involved in material activities, he is exposed to the different modes of material nature and subjected to varieties of so-called happiness and distress. If a man becomes the husband of a prostitute, he cannot be happy, and similarly one who follows the dictations of material intelligence and material consciousness will never be happy.

One must judiciously understand the activities of material nature. As stated in *Bhagavad-gītā* (3.27):

prakṛteḥ kriyamāṇāni
guṇaiḥ karmāṇi sarvaśaḥ

ahaṅkāra-vimūḍhātmā
kartāham iti manyate

"The bewildered spirit soul, under the influence of the three modes of material nature, thinks himself to be the doer of activities, which are in actuality carried out by nature." Although one follows the dictations of material nature, he happily thinks himself the master or husband of material nature. Scientists, for example, try to be the masters of material nature, life after life, not caring to understand the Supreme Person, under whose direction everything within this material world is moving. Trying to be the masters of material nature, they are imitation gods who declare to the public that scientific advancement will one day be able to avoid the so-called control of God. In fact, however, the living being, unable to control the rulings of God, is forced to associate with the prostitute of polluted intelligence and accept various material bodies. As stated in *Bhagavad-gītā* (13.22):

puruṣaḥ prakṛti-stho hi
bhuṅkte prakṛti-jān guṇān
kāraṇaṁ guṇa-saṅgo 'sya
sad-asad-yoni-janmasu

"The living entity in material nature thus follows the ways of life, enjoying the three modes of nature. This is due to his association with that material nature. Thus he meets with good and evil amongst various species." If one fully engages in temporary fruitive activities and does not solve this real problem, what profit will he gain?

TEXT 16

सृष्ट्यप्ययकरीं मायां वेलाकूलान्तवेगिताम् ।
मत्तस्य तामविज्ञस्य किमसत्कर्मभिर्भवेत् ॥१६॥

sṛṣṭy-apyaya-karīṁ māyāṁ
velā-kūlānta-vegitām
mattasya tām avijñasya
kim asat-karmabhir bhavet

sṛṣṭi—creation; *apyaya*—dissolution; *karīm*—one who causes; *māyām*—the illusory energy; *velā-kūla-anta*—near the banks; *vegitām*—being very rapid; *mattasya*—of one who is mad; *tām*—that material nature; *avijñasya*—who does not know; *kim asat-karmabhiḥ bhavet*—what benefit can there be by performing temporary fruitive activities.

TRANSLATION

[Nārada Muni had said that there is a river flowing in both directions. The Haryaśvas understood the purport of this statement.] Material nature functions in two ways—by creation and dissolution. Thus the river of material nature flows both ways. A living entity who unknowingly falls in this river is submerged in its waves, and since the current is swifter near the banks of the river, he is unable to get out. What will be the benefit of performing fruitive activities in that river of māyā?

PURPORT

One may be submerged in the waves of the river of *māyā*, but one may also get free from the waves by coming to the banks of knowledge and austerity. Near these banks, however, the waves are very strong. If one does not understand how he is being tossed by the waves, but simply engages in temporary fruitive activities, what benefit will he derive?

In the *Brahma-saṁhitā* (5.44) there is this statement:

sṛṣṭi-sthiti-pralaya-sādhana-saktir ekā
chāyeva yasya bhuvanāni bibharti durgā

The *māyā-śakti*, Durgā, is in charge of *sṛṣṭi-sthiti-pralaya*, creation and dissolution, and she acts under the direction of the Supreme Lord (*mayādhyakṣeṇa prakṛtiḥ sūyate sa-carācaram*). When one falls in the river of nescience, he is always tossed here and there by the waves, but the same *māyā* can also save him when he surrenders to Kṛṣṇa, or becomes Kṛṣṇa conscious. Kṛṣṇa consciousness is knowledge and austerity. A Kṛṣṇa conscious person takes knowledge from the Vedic literature, and at the same time he must practice austerities.

To attain freedom from material life, one must take to Kṛṣṇa consciousness. Otherwise, if one very busily engages in the so-called advancement of science, what benefit will he derive? If one is carried away by the waves of nature, what is the meaning of being a great scientist or philosopher? Mundane science and philosophy are also material creations. One must understand how *māyā* works and how one can be released from the tossing waves of the river of nescience. That is one's first duty.

TEXT 17

पञ्चविंशतितत्त्वानां पुरुषोऽद्भुतदर्पणः ।
अध्यात्ममबुधस्येह किमसत्कर्मभिर्भवेत् ॥१७॥

pañca-viṁśati-tattvānāṁ
puruṣo 'dbhuta-darpaṇaḥ
adhyātmam abudhasyeha
kim asat-karmabhir bhavet

pañca-viṁśati—twenty-five; *tattvānām*—of the elements; *puruṣaḥ*—the Supreme Personality of Godhead; *adbhuta-darpaṇaḥ*—the wonderful manifester; *adhyātmam*—the overseer of all causes and effects; *abudhasya*—of one who does not know; *iha*—in this world; *kim asat-karmabhiḥ bhavet*—what can be the benefit of engaging in temporary fruitive activities.

TRANSLATION

[Nārada Muni had said that there is a house made of twenty-five elements. The Haryaśvas understood this analogy.] The Supreme Lord is the reservoir of the twenty-five elements, and as the Supreme Being, the conductor of cause and effect, He causes their manifestation. If one engages in temporary fruitive activities, not knowing that Supreme Person, what benefit will he derive?

PURPORT

Philosophers and scientists conduct scholarly research to find the original cause, but they should do so scientifically, not whimsically or through fantastic theories. The science of the original cause is explained in various Vedic literatures. *Athāto brahma-jijñāsā / janmādy asya yataḥ.* The *Vedānta-sūtra* explains that one should inquire about the Supreme Soul. Such inquiry about the Supreme is called *brahma-jijñāsā.* The Absolute Truth, *tattva,* is explained in *Śrīmad-Bhāgavatam* (1.2.11):

vadanti tat tattva-vidas
tattvaṁ yaj jñānam advayam
brahmeti paramātmeti
bhagavān iti śabdyate

"Learned transcendentalists who know the Absolute Truth call this nondual substance Brahman, Paramātmā or Bhagavān." The Absolute Truth appears to neophytes as impersonal Brahman and to advanced mystic *yogīs* as Paramātmā, the Supersoul, but devotees, who are further advanced, understand the Absolute Truth as the Supreme Lord, Viṣṇu.

This material cosmic manifestation is an expansion of the energy of Lord Kṛṣṇa, or Lord Viṣṇu.

eka-deśa-sthitasyāgner
jyotsnā vistāriṇī yathā
parasya brahmaṇaḥ śaktis
tathedam akhilaṁ jagat

"Whatever we see in this world is but an expansion of various energies of the Supreme Personality of Godhead, who is like a fire that spreads illumination for a long distance although it is situated in one place." (*Viṣṇu Purāṇa*) The entire cosmic manifestation is an expansion of the Supreme Lord. Therefore if one does not conduct research to find the supreme cause, but instead falsely engages in frivolous, temporary activities, what is the use of demanding recognition as an important scientist or philosopher? If one does not know the ultimate cause, what is the use of his scientific and philosophical research?

The *puruṣa,* the original person—Bhagavān, Viṣṇu—can be understood only by devotional service. *Bhaktyā mām abhijānāti yāvān yaś cāsmi tattvataḥ:* only by devotional service can one understand the

Supreme Person, who is behind everything. One must try to understand that the material elements are the separated, inferior energy of the Lord and that the living entity is the Lord's spiritual energy. Whatever we experience, including matter and the spirit soul, the living force, is but a combination of two energies of Lord Viṣṇu—the inferior energy and the superior energy. One should seriously study the facts concerning creation, maintenance and devastation, as well as the permanent place from which one never need return (*yad gatvā na nivartante*). Human society should study this, but instead of culturing such knowledge, people are attracted to temporary happiness and sense gratification, culminating in bottomless, topless passion. There is no profit in such activities; one must engage himself in the Kṛṣṇa consciousness movement.

TEXT 18

ऐश्वरं शास्त्रमुत्सृज्य बन्धमोक्षानुदर्शनम् ।
विविक्तपदमज्ञाय किमसत्कर्मभिर्भवेत् ॥१८॥

aiśvaraṁ śāstram utsṛjya
bandha-mokṣānudarśanam
vivikta-padam ajñāya
kim asat-karmabhir bhavet

aiśvaram—bringing understanding of God, or Kṛṣṇa consciousness; *śāstram*—the Vedic literature; *utsṛjya*—giving up; *bandha*—of bondage; *mokṣa*—and of liberation; *anudarśanam*—informing about the ways; *vivikta-padam*—distinguishing spirit from matter; *ajñāya*—not knowing; *kim asat-karmabhiḥ bhavet*—what can be the use of temporary fruitive activities.

TRANSLATION

[Nārada Muni had spoken of a swan. That swan is explained in this verse.] The Vedic literatures [śāstras] vividly describe how to understand the Supreme Lord, the source of all material and spiritual energy. Indeed, they elaborately explain these two energies. The swan [haṁsa] is one who discriminates between matter and spirit, who accepts the essence of everything, and who

explains the means of bondage and the means of liberation. The words of scriptures consist of variegated vibrations. If a foolish rascal leaves aside the study of these śāstras to engage in temporary activities, what will be the result?

PURPORT

The Kṛṣṇa consciousness movement is very eager to present Vedic literature in modern languages, especially Western languages such as English, French and German. The leaders of the Western world, the Americans and Europeans, have become the idols of modern civilization because the Western people are very sophisticated in temporary activities for the advancement of material civilization. A sane man, however, can see that all such grand activities, although perhaps very important for temporary life, have nothing to do with eternal life. The entire world is imitating the materialistic civilization of the West, and therefore the Kṛṣṇa consciousness movement is very much interested in giving the Western people knowledge by translating the original Sanskrit Vedic literatures into Western languages.

The word *vivikta-padam* refers to the path of logical discourses concerning the aim of life. If one does not discuss that which is important in life, one is put into darkness and must struggle for existence. What, then, is the benefit of his advancement in knowledge? The people of the West are seeing their students becoming hippies, despite gorgeous arrangements for university education. The Kṛṣṇa consciousness movement, however, is trying to convert misguided, drug-addicted students to the service of Kṛṣṇa and engage them in the best welfare activities for human society.

TEXT 19

कालचक्रं भ्रमि तीक्ष्णं सर्वं निष्कर्षयज्जगत् ।
स्वतन्त्रमबुधस्येह किमसत्कर्मभिर्भवेत् ॥१९॥

kāla-cakraṁ bhrami tīkṣṇaṁ
sarvaṁ niṣkarṣayaj jagat
svatantram abudhasyeha
kim asat-karmabhir bhavet

kāla-cakram—the wheel of eternal time; *bhrami*—revolving automatically; *tīkṣṇam*—very sharp; *sarvam*—all; *niṣkarṣayat*—driving; *jagat*—the world; *sva-tantram*—independent, not caring for the so-called scientists and philosophers; *abudhasya*—of one who does not know (this principle of time); *iha*—in this material world; *kim asat-karmabhiḥ bhavet*—what is the use of engaging in temporary fruitive activities.

TRANSLATION

[Nārada Muni had spoken of a physical object made of sharp blades and thunderbolts. The Haryaśvas understood this allegory as follows.] Eternal time moves very sharply, as if made of razors and thunderbolts. Uninterrupted and fully independent, it drives the activities of the entire world. If one does not try to study the eternal element of time, what benefit can he derive from performing temporary material activities?

PURPORT

This verse explains the words *kṣaura-pavyaṁ svayaṁ bhrami*, which especially refer to the orbit of eternal time. It is said that time and tide wait for no man. According to the moral instructions of the great politician Cāṇakya Paṇḍita:

āyuṣaḥ kṣaṇa eko 'pi
na labhyaḥ svarṇa-koṭibhiḥ
na cen nirarthakaṁ nītiḥ
kā ca hānis tato 'dhikā

Even a moment of one's lifetime could not be returned in exchange for millions of dollars. Therefore one should consider how much loss one suffers if he wastes even a moment of his life for nothing. Living like an animal, not understanding the goal of life, one foolishly thinks that there is no eternity and that his life span of fifty, sixty, or, at the most, one hundred years, is everything. This is the greatest foolishness. Time is eternal, and in the material world one passes through different phases of his eternal life. Time is compared herein to a sharp razor. A razor is meant to shave the hair from one's face, but if not carefully handled, the razor will cause disaster. One is advised not to create a disaster by misusing his lifetime. One should be extremely careful to utilize the span of his life for spiritual realization, or Kṛṣṇa consciousness.

TEXT 20

शास्त्रस्य पितुरादेशं यो न वेद निवर्तकम् ।
कथं तदनुरूपाय गुणविस्रम्भ्युपक्रमेत् ॥२०॥

śāstrasya pitur ādeśaṁ
yo na veda nivartakam
kathaṁ tad-anurūpāya
guṇa-visrambhy upakramet

śāstrasya—of the scriptures; *pituḥ*—of the father; *ādeśam*—the instruction; *yaḥ*—one who; *na*—not; *veda*—understands; *nivartakam*—which brings about the cessation of the material way of life; *katham*—how; *tat-anurūpāya*—to follow the instruction of the *śāstras; guṇa-visrambhī*—a person entangled in the three modes of material nature; *upakramet*—can engage in the creation of progeny.

TRANSLATION

[Nārada Muni had asked how one could ignorantly defy one's own father. The Haryaśvas understood the meaning of this question.] One must accept the original instructions of the śāstra. According to Vedic civilization, one is offered a sacred thread as a sign of second birth. One takes his second birth by dint of having received instructions in the śāstra from a bona fide spiritual master. Therefore, śāstra, scripture, is the real father. All the śāstras instruct that one should end his material way of life. If one does not know the purpose of the father's orders, the śāstras, he is ignorant. The words of a material father who endeavors to engage his son in material activities are not the real instructions of the father.

PURPORT

Bhagavad-gītā (16.7) says, *pravṛttiṁ ca nivṛttiṁ ca janā na vidur āsurāḥ:* demons, who are less than human beings but are not called animals, do not know the meaning of *pravṛtti* and *nivṛtti,* work to be done and work not to be done. In the material world, every living entity has a desire to lord it over the material world as much as possible. This is called *pravṛtti-mārga.* All the *śāstras,* however, advise *nivṛtti-mārga,* or release from the materialistic way of life. Apart from the *śāstras* of the Vedic civilization, which is the oldest of the world, other *śāstras* agree on this point. For example, in the Buddhist *śāstras* Lord Buddha advises that one achieve *nirvāṇa* by giving up the materialistic way of life. In the Bible, which is also *śāstra,* one will find the same advice: one should cease materialistic life and return to the kingdom of God. In any *śāstra* one may examine, especially the Vedic *śāstra,* the same advice is given: one should give up his materialistic life and return to his original, spiritual life. Śaṅkarācārya also propounds the same conclusion. *Brahma satyaṁ jagan mithyā:* this material world or materialistic life is simply illusion, and therefore one should stop his illusory activities and come to the platform of Brahman.

The word *śāstra* refers to the scriptures, particularly the Vedic books of knowledge. The *Vedas—Sāma, Yajur, Ṛg* and *Atharva*—and any other books deriving knowledge from these *Vedas* are considered Vedic literatures. *Bhagavad-gītā* is the essence of all Vedic knowledge, and therefore it is the scripture whose instructions should be especially accepted. In this essence of all *śāstras,* Kṛṣṇa personally advises that one give up all other duties and surrender unto Him (*sarva-dharmān parityajya mām ekaṁ śaraṇaṁ vraja*).

One should be initiated into following the principles of *śāstra.* In offering initiation, our Kṛṣṇa consciousness movement asks one to come to the conclusion of *śāstra* by taking the advice of the supreme speaker of the *śāstra,* Kṛṣṇa, forgetting the principles of the materialistic way of life. Therefore the principles we advise are no illicit sex, no intoxication, no gambling and no meat-eating. These four types of engagement will enable an intelligent person to get free from the materialistic life and return home, back to Godhead.

In regard to the instructions of the father and mother, it may be said that every living entity, including even the insignificant cats, dogs and serpents, takes birth of a father and mother. Therefore, getting a material father and mother is not a problem. In every form of life, birth after birth, the living entity gets a father and mother. In human society, however, if one is satisfied with his material father and mother and their instructions and does not make further progress by accepting a spiritual master and being educated in the *śāstras,* he certainly remains in darkness. The material father and mother are important only if they are interested in educating their son to become free from the clutches of death. As instructed by Ṛṣabhadeva (*Bhāg.* 5.5.18): *pitā na sa syāj jananī na sā syāt/ na mocayed yaḥ samupeta-mṛtyum.* One should not strive to become a mother or father if one cannot save one's dependent son from the impending danger of death. A parent who does not know how to save his son has no value because such fathers and mothers may be had in any form of life, even among the cats, dogs and so on. Only a father and mother who can elevate their son to the spiritual platform are bona fide parents. Therefore according to the Vedic system it is said, *janmanā jāyate śūdraḥ:* one is born of a material father and mother as a *śūdra.* The purpose of life, however, is to become a *brāhmaṇa,* a first-class man.

A first-class intelligent man is called a *brāhmaṇa* because he knows the Supreme Brahman, the Absolute Truth. According to the Vedic instructions, *tad-vijñānārthaṁ sa gurum evābhigacchet:* to know this science, one must approach a bona fide *guru,* a spiritual master who will initiate the disciple with the sacred thread so that he may understand the Vedic knowledge. *Janmanā jāyate śūdraḥ saṁskārād dhi bhaved dvijaḥ.* Becoming a *brāhmaṇa* through the endeavor of a bona fide spiritual master is called *saṁskāra.* After initiation, one is engaged in study of the *śāstra,* which teaches the student how to gain release from materialistic life and return home, back to Godhead.

The Kṛṣṇa consciousness movement is teaching this higher knowledge of retiring from materialistic life to return to Godhead, but unfortunately many parents are not very satisfied with this movement. Aside from the parents of our students, many businessmen are also dissatisfied because we teach our students to abandon intoxication, meat-eating, illicit sex and gambling. If the Kṛṣṇa consciousness movement spreads, the so-called businessmen will have to close their slaughterhouses, breweries and cigarette factories. Therefore they are also very much afraid. However, we have no alternative than to teach our disciples to free themselves from materialistic life. We must instruct them in the opposite of material life to save them from the repetition of birth and death.

Nārada Muni, therefore, advised the Haryaśvas, the sons of Prajāpati Dakṣa, that instead of begetting progeny, it would be better to leave and achieve the perfection of spiritual understanding according to the instructions of the *śāstras.* The importance of the *śāstras* is mentioned in *Bhagavad-gītā* (16.23):

yaḥ śāstra-vidhim utsṛjya
vartate kāma-kārataḥ
na sa siddhim avāpnoti
na sukhaṁ na parāṁ gatim

"One who disregards the injunctions of the *śāstras* and acts whimsically, as he likes, never achieves the perfection of life, not to speak of happiness. Nor does he return home to the spiritual world."

TEXT 21

इति व्यवसिता राजन् हर्यश्वा एकचेतसः ।
प्रययुस्तं परिक्रम्य पन्थानमनिवर्तनम् ॥२१॥

iti vyavasitā rājan
haryaśvā eka-cetasaḥ
prayayus taṁ parikramya
panthānam anivartanam

iti—thus; *vyavasitāḥ*—being fully convinced by the instructions of Nārada Muni; *rājan*—O King; *haryaśvāḥ*—the sons of Prajāpati Dakṣa; *eka-cetasaḥ*—all being of the same opinion; *prayayuḥ*—left; *tam*—Nārada Muni; *parikramya*—circumambulating; *panthānam*—on the path; *anivartanam*—which does not bring one back again to this material world.

TRANSLATION

Śukadeva Gosvāmī continued: My dear King, after hearing the instructions of Nārada, the Haryaśvas, the sons of Prajāpati Dakṣa, were firmly convinced. They all believed in his instructions and reached the same conclusion. Having accepted him as their spiritual master, they circumambulated that great sage and followed the path by which one never returns to this world.

PURPORT

From this verse we can understand the meaning of initiation and the duties of a disciple and spiritual master. The spiritual master never instructs his disciple, "Take a *mantra* from me, pay me some money, and by practicing this *yoga* system you will become very expert in materialistic life." This is not the duty of a spiritual master. Rather, the spiritual master teaches the disciple how to give up materialistic life, and the disciple's duty is to assimilate his instructions and ultimately follow the path back home, back to Godhead, from whence no one returns to this material world.

After hearing the instructions of Nārada Muni, the Haryaśvas, the sons of Prajāpati Dakṣa, decided not to be entangled in materialistic life by begetting hundreds of children and having to take care of them. This would have been unnecessarily entangling. The Haryaśvas did not consider pious and impious activities. Their materialistic father had instructed them to increase the population, but because of the words of Nārada Muni, they could not heed that instruction. Nārada Muni, as their spiritual master, gave them the śāstric instructions that they should give up this material world, and as bona fide disciples they followed his instructions. One should not endeavor to wander to different planetary systems within this universe, for even if one goes to the topmost planetary system, Brahmaloka, one must return again (*kṣīṇe puṇye martya-lokaṁ viśanti*). The endeavors of *karmīs* are a useless waste of time. One should endeavor to return home, back to Godhead. This is the perfection of life. As the Lord says in *Bhagavad-gītā* (8.16):

ābrahma-bhuvanāl lokāḥ
punar āvartino 'rjuna

mām upetya tu kaunteya
punar janma na vidyate

"From the highest planet in the material world down to the lowest, all are places of misery wherein repeated birth and death take place. But one who attains to My abode, O son of Kuntī, never takes birth again."

TEXT 22

स्वरब्रह्मणि निर्भातहृषीकेशपदाम्बुजे ।
अखण्डं चित्तमावेश्य लोकाननुचरन्मुनिः ॥२२॥

svara-brahmaṇi nirbhāta-
hṛṣīkeśa-padāmbuje
akhaṇḍaṁ cittam āveśya
lokān anucaran muniḥ

svara-brahmaṇi—in spiritual sound; *nirbhāta*—placing clearly before the mind; *hṛṣīkeśa*—of the Supreme Personality of Godhead, Kṛṣṇa, the master of the senses; *padāmbuje*—the lotus feet; *akhaṇḍam*—unbroken; *cittam*—consciousness; *āveśya*—engaging; *lokān*—all the planetary systems; *anucarat*—traveled around; *muniḥ*—the great sage Nārada Muni.

TRANSLATION

The seven musical notes—ṣa, ṛ, gā, ma, pa, dha and ni—are used in musical instruments, but originally they come from the Sāma Veda. The great sage Nārada vibrates sounds describing the pastimes of the Supreme Lord. By such transcendental vibrations, such as Hare Kṛṣṇa, Hare Kṛṣṇa, Kṛṣṇa Kṛṣṇa, Hare Hare/ Hare Rāma, Hare Rāma, Rāma Rāma, Hare Hare, he fixes his mind at the lotus feet of the Lord. Thus he directly perceives Hṛṣīkeśa, the master of the senses. After delivering the Haryaśvas, Nārada Muni continued traveling throughout the planetary systems, his mind always fixed at the lotus feet of the Lord.

PURPORT

The goodness of the great sage Nārada Muni is described herewith. He always chants about the pastimes of the Lord and delivers the fallen souls back to Godhead. In this regard, Śrīla Bhaktivinoda Ṭhākura has sung:

nārada-muni, bājāya vīṇā,
'rādhikā-ramaṇa'-nāme
nāma amani, udita haya,
bhakata-gīta-sāme

amiya-dhārā, variṣe ghana,
śravaṇa-yugale giyā
bhakata-jana, saghane nāce,
bhariyā āpana hiyā

mādhurī-pūra, āsaba paśi',
mātāya jagata-jane
keha vā kāṅde, keha vā nāce,
keha māte mane mane

pañca-vadana, nārade dhari',
premera saghana rola
kamalāsana, nāciyā bale,
'bola bola hari bola'

sahasrānana, parama-sukhe,
'hari hari' bali' gāya
nāma-prabhāve, mātila viśva,
nāma-rasa sabe pāya

śrī-kṛṣṇa-nāma, rasane sphuri',
purā'la āmāra āśa
śrī-rūpa-pade, yācaye ihā,
bhakativinoda dāsa

The purport of this song is that Nārada Muni, the great soul, plays a stringed instrument called a *vīṇā*, vibrating the sound *rādhikā-ramaṇa*, which is another name for Kṛṣṇa. As soon as he strokes the strings, all the devotees begin responding, making a very beautiful vibration. Accompanied by the stringed instrument, the singing seems like a shower of nectar, and all the devotees dance in ecstasy to the fullest extent of their satisfaction. While dancing, they appear madly intoxicated with ecstasy, as if drinking the beverage called *mādhurī-pūra.* Some of them cry, some of them dance, and some of them, although unable to dance publicly, dance within their hearts. Lord Śiva embraces Nārada Muni and begins talking in an ecstatic voice, and seeing Lord Śiva dancing with Nārada, Lord Brahmā also joins, saying, "All of you kindly chant 'Hari bol! Hari bol!' " The King of heaven, Indra, also gradually joins with great satisfaction and begins dancing and chanting "Hari bol! Hari bol!" In this way, by the influence of the transcendental vibration of the holy name of God, the whole universe becomes ecstatic. Bhaktivinoda Ṭhākura says, "When the universe becomes ecstatic, my desire is satisfied. I therefore pray unto the lotus feet of Rūpa Gosvāmī that this chanting of *harer nāma* may go on nicely like this."

Lord Brahmā is the *guru* of Nārada Muni, who is the *guru* of Vyāsadeva, and Vyāsadeva is the *guru* of Madhvācārya. Thus the Gauḍīya-Mādhva-sampradāya is in the disciplic succession from Nārada Muni. The members of this disciplic succession—in other words, the members of the Kṛṣṇa consciousness movement—should follow in the footsteps of Nārada Muni by chanting the transcendental vibration Hare Kṛṣṇa, Hare Kṛṣṇa, Kṛṣṇa Kṛṣṇa, Hare Hare/ Hare Rāma, Hare Rāma, Rāma Rāma, Hare Hare. They should go everywhere to deliver the fallen souls by vibrating the Hare Kṛṣṇa *mantra* and the instructions of *Bhagavad-gītā, Śrīmad-Bhāgavatam* and *Caitanya-caritāmṛta.* That will please the Supreme Personality of Godhead. One can spiritually advance if one actually follows the instructions of Nārada Muni. If one pleases Nārada Muni, then the Supreme Personality of Godhead, Hṛṣīkeśa, is also pleased (*yasya prasādād bhagavat-prasādaḥ*). The immediate spiritual master is the representative of Nārada Muni; there is no difference between the instructions of Nārada Muni and those of the present spiritual master. Both Nārada Muni and the present spiritual master speak the same teachings of Kṛṣṇa, who says in *Bhagavad-gītā* (18.65–66):

man-manā bhava mad-bhakto
mad-yājī māṁ namaskuru
mām evaiṣyasi satyaṁ te
pratijāne priyo 'si me

sarva-dharmān parityajya
mām ekaṁ śaraṇaṁ vraja
ahaṁ tvāṁ sarva-pāpebhyo
mokṣayiṣyāmi mā śucaḥ

"Always think of Me and become My devotee. Worship Me and offer your homage unto Me. Thus you will come to Me without fail. I promise you this because you are My very dear friend. Abandon all varieties of religion and just surrender unto Me. I shall deliver you from all sinful reaction. Do not fear."

TEXT 23

नाशं निशम्य पुत्राणां नारदाच्छीलशालिनाम् ।
अन्वतप्यत कः शोचन् सुप्रजस्त्वं शुचां पदम् ॥२३॥

nāśaṁ niśamya putrāṇāṁ
nāradāc chīla-śālinām
anvatapyata kaḥ śocan
suprajastvaṁ śucāṁ padam

nāśam—the loss; *niśamya*—hearing of; *putrāṇām*—of his sons; *nāradāt*—from Nārada; *śīla-śālinām*—who were the best of well-behaved persons; *anvatapyata*—suffered; *kaḥ*—Prajāpati Dakṣa; *śocan*—lamenting; *su-prajastvam*—having ten thousand well-behaved sons; *śucām*—of lamentation; *padam*—position.

TRANSLATION

The Haryaśvas, the sons of Prajāpati Dakṣa, were very well behaved, cultured sons, but unfortunately, because of the instructions of Nārada Muni, they deviated from the order of their

father. When Dakṣa heard this news, which was brought to him by Nārada Muni, he began to lament. Although he was the father of such good sons, he had lost them all. Certainly this was lamentable.

PURPORT

The Haryaśvas, the sons of Prajāpati Dakṣa, were certainly well behaved, learned and advanced, and in accordance with the order of their father they went to perform austerities to beget good sons for their family. But Nārada Muni took advantage of their good behavior and culture to properly direct them not to be involved with this material world, but to use their culture and knowledge to end their material affairs. The Haryaśvas abided by the order of Nārada Muni, but when news of this was brought to Prajāpati Dakṣa, the *prajāpati,* instead of being happy with the actions of Nārada Muni, was extremely sorrowful. Similarly, we are trying to bring as many young men as possible to the Kṛṣṇa consciousness movement for their ultimate benefit, but the parents of the young men joining this movement, being very sorry, are lamenting and making counterpropaganda. Of course, Prajāpati Dakṣa did not make propaganda against Nārada Muni, but later, as we shall see, Dakṣa cursed Nārada Muni for his benevolent activities. This is the way of materialistic life. A materialistic father and mother want to engage their sons in begetting children, striving for improved economic conditions and rotting in materialistic life. They are not unhappy when their children become spoiled, useless citizens, but they lament when they join the Kṛṣṇa consciousness movement to achieve the ultimate goal of life. This animosity between parents and the Kṛṣṇa consciousness movement has existed since time immemorial. Even Nārada Muni was condemned, not to speak of others. Nevertheless, Nārada Muni never gives up his mission. To deliver as many fallen souls as possible, he continues playing his musical instrument and vibrating the transcendental sound Hare Kṛṣṇa, Hare Kṛṣṇa, Kṛṣṇa Kṛṣṇa, Hare Hare/ Hare Rāma, Hare Rāma, Rāma Rāma, Hare Hare.

TEXT 24

स भूयः पाञ्चजन्यायामजेन परिसान्त्वितः ।
पुत्रानजनयद् दक्षः सवलाश्वान् सहस्रिणः ।।२४।।

sa bhūyaḥ pāñcajanyāyām
ajena parisāntvitaḥ
putrān ajanayad dakṣaḥ
savalāśvān sahasriṇaḥ

saḥ—Prajāpati Dakṣa; *bhūyaḥ*—again; *pāñcajanyāyām*—in the womb of his wife Asiknī, or Pāñcajanī; *ajena*—by Lord Brahmā; *parisāntvitaḥ*—being pacified; *putrān*—sons; *ajanayat*—begot; *dakṣaḥ*—Prajāpati Dakṣa; *savalāśvān*—named the Savalāśvas; *sahasriṇaḥ*—numbering one thousand.

TRANSLATION

When Prajāpati Dakṣa was lamenting for his lost children, Lord Brahmā pacified him with instructions, and thereafter Dakṣa begot one thousand more children in the womb of his wife, Pāñcajanī. This time his sons were known as the Savalāśvas.

PURPORT

Prajāpati Dakṣa was so named because he was very expert in begetting children. (The word *dakṣa* means "expert.") First he begot ten thousand children in the womb of his wife, and when the children were lost—when they returned home, back to Godhead—he begot another set of children, known as the Savalāśvas. Prajāpati Dakṣa is very expert in begetting children, and Nārada Muni is very expert in delivering all the conditioned souls back home, back to Godhead. Therefore the materialistic experts do not agree with the spiritual expert Nārada Muni, but this does not mean that Nārada Muni will give up his engagement of chanting the Hare Kṛṣṇa *mantra.*

TEXT 25

ते च पित्रा समादिष्टाः प्रजासर्गे धृतव्रताः ।
नारायणसरो जग्मुर्यत्र सिद्धाः स्वपूर्वजाः ॥२५॥

te ca pitrā samādiṣṭāḥ
prajā-sarge dhṛta-vratāḥ

nārāyaṇa-saro jagmur
yatra siddhāḥ sva-pūrvajāḥ

te—these sons (the Savalāśvas); *ca*—and; *pitrā*—by their father; *samādiṣṭāḥ*—being ordered; *prajā-sarge*—in increasing progeny or population; *dhṛta-vratāḥ*—accepted vows; *nārāyaṇa-saraḥ*—the holy lake named Nārāyaṇa-saras; *jagmuḥ*—went to; *yatra*—where; *siddhāḥ*—perfected; *sva-pūrva-jāḥ*—their older brothers, who had previously gone there.

TRANSLATION

In accordance with their father's order to beget children, the second group of sons also went to Nārāyaṇa-saras, the same place where their brothers had previously attained perfection by following the instructions of Nārada. Undertaking great vows of austerity, the Savalāśvas remained at that holy place.

PURPORT

Prajāpati Dakṣa sent his second group of sons to the same place where his previous sons had attained perfection. He did not hesitate to send his second group of sons to the same place, although they too might become victims of Nārada's instructions. According to the Vedic culture, one should be trained in spiritual understanding as a *brahmacārī* before entering household life to beget children. This is the Vedic system. Thus Prajāpati Dakṣa sent his second group of sons for cultural improvement, despite the risk that because of the instructions of Nārada they might become as intelligent as their older brothers. As a dutiful father, he did not hesitate to allow his sons to receive cultural instructions concerning the perfection of life; he depended upon them to choose whether to return home, back to Godhead, or to rot in this material world in various species of life. In all circumstances, the duty of the father is to give cultural education to his sons, who must later decide which way to go. Responsible fathers should not hinder their sons who are making cultural advancement in association with the Kṛṣṇa consciousness movement. This is not a father's duty. The duty of a father is to give his son complete freedom to make his choice after becoming spiritually advanced by following the instructions of the spiritual master.

TEXT 26

तदुपस्पर्शनादेव विनिर्धूतमलाशयाः ।
जपन्तो ब्रह्म परमं तेपुस्तत्र महत् तपः ॥२६॥

tad-upasparśanād eva
vinirdhūta-malāśayāḥ
japanto brahma paramaṁ
tepus tatra mahat tapaḥ

tat—of that holy place; *upasparśanāt*—by bathing regularly in the water; *eva*—indeed; *vinirdhūta*—completely purified; *mala-āśayāḥ*—of all the dirt within the heart; *japantaḥ*—chanting or murmuring; *brahma*—*mantras* beginning with *oṁ* (such as *oṁ tad viṣṇoḥ paramaṁ padaṁ sadā paśyanti sūrayaḥ*); *paramam*—the ultimate goal; *tepuḥ*—performed; *tatra*—there; *mahat*—great; *tapaḥ*—penances.

TRANSLATION

At Nārāyaṇa-saras, the second group of sons performed penances in the same way as the first. They bathed in the holy water, and by its touch all the dirty material desires in their hearts were cleansed away. They murmured mantras beginning with oṁkāra and underwent a severe course of austerities.

PURPORT

Every Vedic *mantra* is called *brahma* because each *mantra* is preceded by the *brahmākṣara* (*aum* or *oṁkāra*). For example, *oṁ namo bhagavate vāsudevāya.* Lord Kṛṣṇa says in *Bhagavad-gītā* (7.8), *praṇavaḥ sarva-vedeṣu:* "In all the Vedic *mantras,* I am represented by *praṇava,* or *oṁkāra.*" Thus chanting of the Vedic *mantras* beginning with *oṁkāra* is directly chanting of Kṛṣṇa's name. There is no difference. Whether one *chants oṁkāra* or addresses the Lord as "Kṛṣṇa," the meaning is the same, but Śrī Caitanya Mahāprabhu has recommended that in this age one chant the Hare Kṛṣṇa *mantra* (*harer nāma eva kevalam*). Although there is no difference between Hare Kṛṣṇa and the Vedic *mantras* beginning with *oṁkāra,* Śrī Caitanya Mahāprabhu, the leader of the spiritual movement for this age, has recommended that one chant Hare Kṛṣṇa, Hare Kṛṣṇa, Kṛṣṇa Kṛṣṇa, Hare Hare/ Hare Rāma, Hare Rāma, Rāma Rāma, Hare Hare.

TEXTS 27–28

अब्भक्षाः कतिचिन्मासान् कतिचिद् वायुभोजनाः ।
आराधयन् मन्त्रमिममभ्यस्यन्त इडस्पतिम् ॥२७॥
ॐ नमो नारायणाय पुरुषाय महात्मने ।
विशुद्धसत्त्वधिष्ण्याय महाहंसाय धीमहि ॥२८॥

ab-bhakṣāḥ katicin māsān
katicid vāyu-bhojanāḥ
ārādhayan mantram imam
abhyasyanta iḍaspatim

oṁ namo nārāyaṇāya
puruṣāya mahātmane
viśuddha-sattva-dhiṣṇyāya
mahā-haṁsāya dhīmahi

ap-bhakṣāḥ—drinking only water; *katicit māsān*—for some months; *katicit*—for some; *vāyu-bhojanāḥ*—merely breathing, or eating air; *ārādhayan*—worshiped; *mantram imam*—this *mantra,* which is nondifferent from Nārāyaṇa; *abhyasyantaḥ*—practicing; *iḍaḥ-patim*—the master of all *mantras,* Lord Viṣṇu; *oṁ*—O Lord; *namaḥ*—respectful obeisances; *nārāyaṇāya*—unto Lord Nārāyaṇa; *puruṣāya*—the Supreme Person; *mahā-ātmane*—the exalted Supersoul; *viśuddha-sattva-dhiṣṇyāya*—who is always situated in the transcendental abode; *mahā-haṁsāya*—the great swanlike Personality of Godhead; *dhīmahi*—we always offer.

TRANSLATION

For a few months the sons of Prajāpati Dakṣa drank only water and ate only air. Thus undergoing great austerities, they recited this mantra: "Let us offer our respectful obeisances unto

Nārāyaṇa, the Supreme Personality of Godhead, who is always situated in His transcendental abode. Since He is the Supreme Person [paramahaṁsa], let us offer our respectful obeisances unto Him."

PURPORT

From these verses it is apparent that the chanting of the *mahā-mantra* or the Vedic *mantras* must be accompanied by severe austerities. In Kali-yuga, people cannot undergo severe austerities like those mentioned herein—drinking only water and eating only air for many months. One cannot imitate such a process. But at least one must undergo some austerity by giving up four unwanted principles, namely illicit sex, meat-eating, intoxication and gambling. Anyone can easily practice this *tapasya,* and then the chanting of the Hare Kṛṣṇa *mantra* will be effective without delay. One should not give up the process of austerity. If possible, one should bathe in the waters of the Ganges or Yamunā, or in the absence of the Ganges and Yamunā one may bathe in the water of the sea. This is an item of austerity. Our Kṛṣṇa consciousness movement has therefore established two very large centers, one in Vṛndāvana and another in Māyāpur, Navadvīpa. There one may bathe in the Ganges or Yamunā, chant the Hare Kṛṣṇa *mantra* and thus become perfect and return home, back to Godhead.

TEXT 29

इति तानपि राजेन्द्र प्रजासर्गधियो मुनिः ।
उपेत्य नारदः प्राह वाचःकूटानि पूर्ववत् ॥२९॥

iti tān api rājendra
prajā-sarga-dhiyo muniḥ
upetya nāradaḥ prāha
vācaḥ kūṭāni pūrvavat

iti—thus; *tān*—them (the sons of Prajāpati Dakṣa known as the Savalāśvas); *api*—also; *rājendra*—O King Parīkṣit; *prajā-sarga-dhiyaḥ*—who were under the impression that begetting children was the most important duty; *muniḥ*—the great sage; *upetya*—approaching;

nāradaḥ—Nārada; *prāha*—said; *vācaḥ*—words; *kūṭāni*—enigmatic; *pūrva-vat*—as he had done previously.

TRANSLATION

O King Parīkṣit, Nārada Muni approached these sons of Prajāpati Dakṣa, who were engaged in tapasya to beget children, and spoke enigmatic words to them just as he had spoken to their elder brothers.

TEXT 30

दाक्षायणाः संशृणुत गदतो निगमं मम ।
अन्विच्छतानुपदवीं भ्रातॄणां भ्रातृवत्सलाः ॥३०॥

dākṣāyaṇāḥ saṁśṛṇuta
gadato nigamaṁ mama
anvicchatānupadavīṁ
bhrātṝṇāṁ bhrātṛ-vatsalāḥ

dākṣāyaṇāḥ—O sons of Prajāpati Dakṣa; *saṁśṛṇuta*—please hear with attention; *gadataḥ*—who am speaking; *nigamam*—instruction; *mama*—my; *anvicchata*—follow; *anupadavīm*—the path; *bhrātṝṇām*—of your brothers; *bhrātṛ-vatsalāḥ*—O you who are very much affectionate to your brothers.

TRANSLATION

O sons of Dakṣa, please hear my words of instruction attentively. You are all very affectionate to your elder brothers, the Haryaśvas. Therefore you should follow their path.

PURPORT

Nārada Muni encouraged Prajāpati Dakṣa's second group of sons by awakening their natural affinity for their brothers. He urged them to follow their older brothers if they were at all affectionate toward them. Family affection is very strong, and therefore Nārada Muni followed this tactic of reminding them of their family relationship with the Haryaśvas.

Generally the word *nigama* refers to the *Vedas*, but here *nigama* refers to the instructions contained in the *Vedas. Śrīmad-Bhāgavatam* says, *nigama-kalpa-taror galitaṁ phalam:* the Vedic instructions are like a tree, of which *Śrīmad-Bhāgavatam* is the ripened fruit. Nārada Muni is engaged in distributing this fruit, and therefore he instructed Vyāsadeva to write this *Mahā-purāṇa, Śrīmad-Bhāgavatam,* for the benefit of ignorant human society.

anarthopaśamaṁ sākṣād
bhakti-yogam adhokṣaje
lokasyājānato vidvāṁś
cakre sātvata-saṁhitām

"The material miseries of the living entity, which are superfluous to him, can be directly mitigated by the linking process of devotional service. But the mass of people do not know this, and therefore the learned Vyāsadeva compiled this Vedic literature, which is in relation to the Supreme Truth." (*Bhāg.* 1.7.6) People are suffering because of ignorance and are following a wrong path for happiness. This is called *anartha.* These material activities will never make them happy, and therefore Nārada instructed Vyāsadeva to record the instructions of *Śrīmad-Bhāgavatam.* Vyāsadeva actually followed Nārada and did this. *Śrīmad-Bhāgavatam* is the supreme instruction of the *Vedas. Galitaṁ phalam:* the ripened fruit of the *Vedas* is *Śrīmad-Bhāgavatam.*

TEXT 31

भ्रातॄणां प्रायणं भ्राता योऽनुतिष्ठति धर्मवित् ।
स पुण्यबन्धुः पुरुषो मरुद्भिः सह मोदते ॥३१॥

bhrātṝṇāṁ prāyaṇaṁ bhrātā
yo 'nutiṣṭhati dharmavit
sa puṇya-bandhuḥ puruṣo
marudbhiḥ saha modate

bhrātṝṇām—of elder brothers; *prāyaṇam*—the path; *bhrātā*—a faithful brother; *yaḥ*—one who; *anutiṣṭhati*—follows; *dharma-vit*—

knowing the religious principles; *saḥ*—that; *puṇya-bandhuḥ*—highly pious; *puruṣaḥ*—person; *marudbhiḥ*—the demigods of the winds; *saha*—with; *modate*—enjoys life.

TRANSLATION

A brother aware of the principles of religion follows in the footsteps of his elder brothers. Because of being highly elevated, such a pious brother gets the opportunity to associate and enjoy with demigods like the Maruts, who are all affectionate to their brothers.

PURPORT

According to their belief in various material relationships, people are promoted to various planets. Here it is said that one who is very faithful to his brothers should follow a path similar to theirs and get the opportunity for promotion to Marudloka. Nārada Muni advised Prajāpati Dakṣa's second group of sons to follow their elder brothers and be promoted to the spiritual world.

TEXT 32

एतावदुक्त्वा प्रययौ नारदोऽमोघदर्शनः ।
तेऽपि चान्वगमन् मार्गं भ्रातॄणामेव मारिष ॥३२॥

etāvad uktvā prayayau
nārado 'mogha-darśanaḥ
te 'pi cānvagaman mārgaṁ
bhrātṝṇām eva māriṣa

etāvat—this much; *uktvā*—speaking; *prayayau*—departed from that place; *nāradaḥ*—the great sage Nārada; *amogha-darśanaḥ*—whose glance is all-auspicious; *te*—they; *api*—also; *ca*—and; *anvagaman*—followed; *mārgam*—the path; *bhrātṝṇām*—of their previous brothers; *eva*—indeed; *māriṣa*—O great Āryan king.

TRANSLATION

Śukadeva Gosvāmī continued: O best of the advanced Āryans, after saying this much to the sons of Prajāpati Dakṣa, Nārada

Muni, whose merciful glance never goes in vain, left as he had planned. The sons of Dakṣa followed their elder brothers. Not attempting to produce children, they engaged themselves in Kṛṣṇa consciousness.

TEXT 33

सध्रीचीनं प्रतीचीनं परस्यानुपथं गताः ।
नाद्यापि ते निवर्तन्ते पश्चिमा यामिनीरिव ॥३३॥

sadhrīcīnaṁ pratīcīnaṁ
parasyānupathaṁ gatāḥ
nādyāpi te nivartante
paścimā yāminīr iva

sadhrīcīnam—completely correct; *pratīcīnam*—obtainable by adopting a mode of life aimed at the highest goal, devotional service; *parasya*—of the Supreme Lord; *anupatham*—the pathway; *gatāḥ*—taking to; *na*—not; *adya api*—even until today; *te*—they (the sons of Prajāpati Dakṣa); *nivartante*—have come back; *paścimāḥ*—western (those that have past); *yāminīḥ*—nights; *iva*—like.

TRANSLATION

The Savalāśvas took to the correct path, which is obtainable by a mode of life meant to achieve devotional service, or the mercy of the Supreme Personality of Godhead. Like nights that have gone to the west, they have not returned even until now.

TEXT 34

एतस्मिन् काल उत्पातान् बहून् पश्यन् प्रजापतिः ।
पूर्ववन्नारदकृतं पुत्रनाशमुपाशृणोत् ॥३४॥

etasmin kāla utpātān
bahūn paśyan prajāpatiḥ
pūrvavan nārada-kṛtaṁ
putra-nāśam upāśṛṇot

etasmin—at this; *kāle*—time; *utpātān*—disturbances; *bahūn*—many; *paśyan*—seeing; *prajāpatiḥ*—Prajāpati Dakṣa; *pūrva-vat*—like before; *nārada*—by the great sage Nārada Muni; *kṛtam*—done; *putra-nāśam*—the loss of his children; *upāśṛṇot*—he heard of.

TRANSLATION

At this time, Prajāpati Dakṣa observed many inauspicious signs, and he heard from various sources that his second group of sons, the Savalāśvas, had followed the path of their elder brothers in accordance with the instructions of Nārada.

TEXT 35

चुक्रोध नारदायासौ पुत्रशोकविमूर्च्छितः ।
देवर्षिमुपलभ्याह रोषाद्विस्फुरिताधरः ॥३५॥

cukrodha nāradāyāsau
putra-śoka-vimūrcchitaḥ
devarṣim upalabhyāha
roṣād visphuritādharaḥ

cukrodha—became very angry; *nāradāya*—at the great sage Nārada Muni; *asau*—that one (Dakṣa); *putra-śoka*—due to lamentation for the loss of his children; *vimūrcchitaḥ*—almost fainting; *devarṣim*—the great sage Devarṣi Nārada; *upalabhya*—seeing; *āha*—he said; *roṣāt*—out of great anger; *visphurita*—trembling; *adharaḥ*—whose lips.

TRANSLATION

When he heard that the Savalāśvas had also left this world to engage in devotional service, Dakṣa was angry at Nārada, and he almost fainted due to lamentation. When Dakṣa met Nārada, Dakṣa's lips began trembling in anger, and he spoke as follows.

PURPORT

Śrīla Viśvanātha Cakravartī Ṭhākura comments that Nārada Muni had delivered the entire family of Svāyambhuva Manu, beginning with

Priyavrata and Uttānapāda. He had delivered Uttānapāda's son Dhruva and had even delivered Prācīnabarhi, who was engaged in fruitive activities. Nevertheless, he could not deliver Prajāpati Dakṣa. Prajāpati Dakṣa saw Nārada before him because Nārada had personally come to deliver him. Nārada Muni took the opportunity to approach Prajāpati Dakṣa in his bereavement because the time of bereavement is a suitable time for appreciating *bhakti-yoga.* As stated in *Bhagavad-gītā* (7.16), four kinds of men—*ārta* (one who is distressed), *arthārthī* (one in need of money), *jijñāsu* (one who is inquisitive) and *jñānī* (a person in knowledge)—try to understand devotional service. Prajāpati Dakṣa was in great distress because of the loss of his sons, and therefore Nārada took the opportunity to instruct him regarding liberation from material bondage.

TEXT 36

श्रीदक्ष उवाच
अहो असाधो साधूनां साधुलिङ्गेन नस्त्वया ।
असाध्वकार्यर्भकाणां भिक्षोर्मार्गः प्रदर्शितः ॥३६॥

śrī-dakṣa uvāca
aho asādho sādhūnāṁ
sādhu-liṅgena nas tvayā
asādhv akāry arbhakāṇāṁ
bhikṣor mārgaḥ pradarśitaḥ

śrī-dakṣaḥ uvāca—Prajāpati Dakṣa said; *aho asādho*—O greatly dishonest nondevotee; *sādhūnām*—of the society of devotees and great sages; *sādhu-liṅgena*—wearing the dress of a saintly person; *naḥ*—unto us; *tvayā*—by you; *asādhu*—a dishonesty; *akāri*—has been done; *arbhakāṇām*—of poor boys who were very inexperienced; *bhikṣoḥ mārgaḥ*—the path of a beggar or mendicant *sannyāsī; pradarśitaḥ*—shown.

TRANSLATION

Prajāpati Dakṣa said: Alas, Nārada Muni, you wear the dress of a saintly person, but you are not actually a saint. Indeed, although I

am now in gṛhastha life, I am a saintly person. By showing my sons the path of renunciation, you have done me an abominable injustice.

PURPORT

Śrī Caitanya Mahāprabhu said, *sannyāsīra alpa chidra sarva-loke gāya* (Cc. *Madhya* 12.51). In society one will find many *sannyāsīs, vānaprasthas, gṛhasthas* and *brahmacārīs*, but if all of them properly live in accordance with their duties, they are understood to be *sādhus.* Prajāpati Dakṣa was certainly a *sādhu* because he had executed such great austerities that the Supreme Personality of Godhead, Lord Viṣṇu, had appeared before him. Nevertheless, he had a fault-finding mentality. He improperly thought Nārada Muni to be *asādhu,* or nonsaintly, because Nārada had foiled his intentions. Desiring to train his sons to become *gṛhasthas* fully equipped with knowledge, Dakṣa had sent them to execute austerities by Nārāyaṇa-saras. Nārada Muni, however, taking advantage of their highly elevated position in austerity, instructed them to become Vaiṣṇavas in the renounced order. This is the duty of Nārada Muni and his followers. They must show everyone the path of renouncing this material world and returning home, back to Godhead. Prajāpati Dakṣa, however, could not see the exaltedness of the duties Nārada Muni performed in relation to his sons. Unable to appreciate Nārada Muni's behavior, Dakṣa accused Nārada of being *asādhu.*

The words *bhikṣor mārga,* "the path of the renounced order," are very significant in this regard. A *sannyāsī* is called *tridaṇḍi-bhikṣu* because his duty is to beg alms from the homes of *gṛhasthas* and to give the *gṛhasthas* spiritual instructions. A *sannyāsī* is allowed to beg from door to door, but a *gṛhastha* cannot do so. *Gṛhasthas* may earn their living according to the four divisions of spiritual life. A *brāhmaṇa gṛhastha* may earn his livelihood by becoming a learned scholar and teaching people in general how to worship the Supreme Personality of Godhead. He may also assume the duty of worship himself. Therefore it is said that only *brāhmaṇas* may engage in Deity worship, and they may accept as *prasāda* whatever people offer the Deity. Although a *brāhmaṇa* may sometimes accept charity, it is not for his personal maintenance but for the worship of the Deity. Thus a *brāhmaṇa* does not stock anything for his future use. Similarly, *kṣatriyas* may collect taxes from the citizens, and they must also protect the citizens, enforce rules and regulations, and maintain law and order. *Vaiśyas* should earn their livelihood through agriculture and cow protection, and *śūdras* should maintain their livelihood by serving the three higher classes. Unless one becomes a *brāhmaṇa,* one cannot take *sannyāsa. Sannyāsīs* and *brahmacārīs* may beg alms door to door, but a *gṛhastha* cannot.

Prajāpati Dakṣa condemned Nārada Muni because Nārada, a *brahmacārī* who could beg from door to door, had made *sannyāsīs* of Dakṣa's sons, who were being trained to be *gṛhasthas.* Dakṣa was extremely angry at Nārada because he thought that Nārada had done him a great injustice. According to Dakṣa's opinion, Nārada Muni had misled Dakṣa's inexperienced sons (*asādhv akāry arbhakāṇām*). Dakṣa regarded his sons as innocent boys who had been misled when Nārada showed them the renounced order of life. Because of all these considerations, Prajāpati Dakṣa charged that Nārada Muni was *asādhu* and should not have adopted the dress of a *sādhu.*

Sometimes a saintly person is misunderstood by *gṛhasthas,* especially when he instructs their young sons to accept Kṛṣṇa consciousness. Generally a *gṛhastha* thinks that unless one enters *gṛhastha* life he cannot properly enter the renounced order. If a young man immediately adopts the path of the renounced order in accordance with the instructions of Nārada or a member of his disciplic succession, his parents become very angry. This same phenomenon is occurring in our Kṛṣṇa consciousness movement because we are instructing all the young boys in the Western countries to follow the path of renunciation. We allow *gṛhastha* life, but a *gṛhastha* also follows the path of renunciation. Even a *gṛhastha* has to give up so many bad habits that his parents think his life has been practically destroyed. We allow no meat-eating, no illicit sex, no gambling and no intoxication, and consequently the parents wonder how, if there are so many no's, one's life can be positive. In the Western countries especially, these four prohibited activities practically constitute the life and soul of the modern population. Therefore parents sometimes dislike our movement, just as Prajāpati Dakṣa disliked the activities of Nārada and accused Nārada of dishonesty. Nevertheless, although parents may be angry at us, we must perform our duty without hesitation because we are in the disciplic succession from Nārada Muni.

People addicted to householder life wonder how one can give up the enjoyment of *gṛhastha* life, which is a concession for sex enjoyment, simply to become a mendicant in Kṛṣṇa consciousness. They do not know that the householder's concession for sex life cannot be regulated unless one accepts the life of a mendicant. The Vedic civilization therefore enjoins that at the end of one's fiftieth year one must give up household life. This is compulsory. However, because modern civilization is misled, householders want to remain in family life until death, and therefore they are suffering. In such cases, the disciples of Nārada Muni advise all the members of the younger generation to join the Kṛṣṇa consciousness movement immediately. There is nothing wrong in this.

TEXT 37

ऋणैस्त्रिभिरमुक्तानाममीमांसितकर्मणाम् ।
विघातः श्रेयसः पाप लोकयोरुभयोः कृतः ॥३७॥

ṛṇais tribhir amuktānām
amīmāṁsita-karmaṇām
vighātaḥ śreyasaḥ pāpa
lokayor ubhayoḥ kṛtaḥ

ṛṇaiḥ—from the debts; *tribhiḥ*—three; *amuktānām*—of persons not freed; *amīmāṁsita*—not considering; *karmaṇām*—the path of duty; *vighātaḥ*—ruin; *śreyasaḥ*—of the path of good fortune; *pāpa*—O most sinful (Nārada Muni); *lokayoḥ*—of the worlds; *ubhayoḥ*—both; *kṛtaḥ*—done.

TRANSLATION

Prajāpati Dakṣa said: My sons were not at all freed from their three debts. Indeed, they did not properly consider their obligations. O Nārada Muni, O personality of sinful action, you have obstructed their progress toward good fortune in this world and the next because they are still indebted to the saintly persons, the demigods and their father.

PURPORT

As soon as a *brāhmaṇa* takes birth, he assumes three kinds of debts—debts to great saints, debts to the demigods and debts to his father. The son of a *brāhmaṇa* must undergo celibacy (*brahmacarya*) to clear his debts to the saintly persons, he must perform ritualistic ceremonies to clear his debts to the demigods, and he must beget children to become free from his debts to his father. Prajāpati Dakṣa argued that although the renounced order is recommended for liberation, one cannot attain liberation unless one fulfills his obligations to the demigods, the saints and his father. Since Dakṣa's sons had not liberated themselves from these three debts, how could Nārada Muni have led them to the renounced order of life? Apparently, Prajāpati Dakṣa did not know the final decision of the *śāstras*. As stated in *Śrīmad-Bhāgavatam* (11.5.41):

devarṣi-bhūtāpta-nṛṇāṁ pitṝṇāṁ
na kiṅkaro nāyam ṛṇī ca rājan
sarvātmanā yaḥ śaraṇaṁ śaraṇyaṁ
gato mukundaṁ parihṛtya kartam

Everyone is indebted to the demigods, to living entities in general, to his family, to the *pitās* and so on, but if one fully surrenders to Kṛṣṇa, Mukunda, who can give one liberation, even if one performs no *yajñas*, one is freed from all debts. Even if one does not repay his debts, he is freed from all debts if he renounces the material world for the sake of the Supreme Personality of Godhead, whose lotus feet are the shelter of everyone. This is the verdict of the *śāstra*. Therefore Nārada Muni was completely right in instructing the sons of Prajāpati Dakṣa to renounce this material world immediately and take shelter of the Supreme Personality of Godhead. Unfortunately, Prajāpati Dakṣa, the father of the Haryaśvas and Savalāśvas, did not understand the great service rendered by Nārada Muni. Dakṣa therefore addressed him as *pāpa* (the personality of sinful activities) and *asādhu* (a nonsaintly person). Since Nārada Muni was a great saint and Vaiṣṇava, he tolerated all such accusations from Prajāpati Dakṣa. He merely performed his duty as a Vaiṣṇava by delivering all the sons of Prajāpati Dakṣa, enabling them to return home, back to Godhead.

TEXT 38

एवं त्वं निरनुक्रोशो बालानां मतिभिद्धरेः ।
पार्षदमध्ये चरसि यशोहा निरपत्रपः ॥३८॥

evaṁ tvaṁ niranukrośo
bālānāṁ mati-bhid dhareḥ
pārṣada-madhye carasi
yaśo-hā nirapatrapaḥ

evam—thus; *tvam*—you (Nārada); *niranukrośaḥ*—without compassion; *bālānām*—of innocent, inexperienced boys; *mati-bhit*—contaminating the consciousness; *hareḥ*—of the Supreme Personality of Godhead; *pārṣada-madhye*—among the personal associates; *carasi*—travel; *yaśaḥ-hā*—defaming the Supreme Personality of Godhead; *nirapatrapaḥ*—(although you do not know what you are doing, you are executing sinful activities) without shame.

TRANSLATION

Prajāpati Dakṣa continued: Thus committing violence against other living entities and yet claiming to be an associate of Lord Viṣṇu, you are defaming the Supreme Personality of Godhead. You needlessly created a mentality of renunciation in innocent boys, and therefore you are shameless and devoid of compassion. How could you travel with the personal associates of the Supreme Lord?

PURPORT

This mentality of Prajāpati Dakṣa still continues even today. When young boys join the Kṛṣṇa consciousness movement, their fathers and so-called guardians are very angry at the propounder of the Kṛṣṇa consciousness movement because they think that their sons have been unnecessarily induced to deprive themselves of the material enjoyments of eating, drinking and merrymaking. *Karmīs*, fruitive workers, think that one should fully enjoy his present life in this material world and also perform some pious activities to be promoted to higher planetary systems for further enjoyment in the next life. A *yogī*, however, especially a *bhakti-yogī*, is callous to the opinions of this material world. He is not interested in traveling to the higher planetary systems of the demigods to enjoy a long life in an advanced materialistic civilization. As stated by Prabodhānanda Sarasvatī, *kaivalyaṁ narakāyate tridaśa-pūr ākāśa-puṣpāyate:* for a devotee, merging into the Brahman existence is hellish, and life in the higher planetary systems of the demigods is a will-o'-the-wisp, a phantasmagoria with no real existence at all. A pure devotee is not interested in yogic perfection, travel to higher planetary systems, or oneness with Brahman. He is interested only in rendering service to the Personality of Godhead. Since Prajāpati Dakṣa was a *karmī,* he could not appreciate the great service Nārada Muni had rendered his eleven thousand sons. Instead, he accused Nārada Muni of being sinful and charged that because Nārada Muni was associated with the Supreme Personality of Godhead, the Lord would also be defamed. Thus Dakṣa criticized that Nārada Muni was an offender to the Lord although he was known as an associate of the Lord.

TEXT 39

ननु भागवता नित्यं भूतानुग्रहकातराः ।
ऋते त्वां सौहृदघ्नं वै वैरङ्करमवैरिणाम् ॥३९॥

nanu bhāgavatā nityaṁ
bhūtānugraha-kātarāḥ
ṛte tvāṁ sauhṛda-ghnaṁ vai
vairaṅ-karam avairiṇām

nanu—now; *bhāgavatāḥ*—devotees of the Supreme Personality of Godhead; *nityam*—eternally; *bhūta-anugraha-kātarāḥ*—very much anxious to bestow benedictions upon the fallen conditioned souls; *ṛte*—except; *tvām*—yourself; *sauhṛda-ghnam*—a breaker of friendship (therefore not countable among the *bhāgavatas,* or devotees of the Lord); *vai*—indeed; *vairam-karam*—you create enmity; *avairiṇām*—toward persons who are not enemies.

TRANSLATION

All the devotees of the Lord but you are very kind to the conditioned souls and are eager to benefit others. Although you

wear the dress of a devotee, you create enmity with people who are not your enemies, or you break friendship and create enmity between friends. Are you not ashamed of posing as a devotee while performing these abominable actions?

PURPORT

Such are the criticisms that must be borne by the servants of Nārada Muni in the disciplic succession. Through the Kṛṣṇa consciousness movement, we are trying to train young people to become devotees and return home, back to Godhead, by following rigid regulative principles, but our service is appreciated neither in India nor abroad in the Western countries where we are endeavoring to spread this Kṛṣṇa consciousness movement. In India the caste *brāhmaṇas* have become enemies of the Kṛṣṇa consciousness movement because we elevate foreigners, who are supposed to be *mlecchas* and *yavanas*, to the position of *brāhmaṇas*. We train them in austerities and penances and recognize them as *brāhmaṇas* by awarding them sacred threads. Thus the caste *brāhmaṇas* of India are very displeased by our activities in the Western world. In the West also, the parents of the young people who join this movement have also become enemies. We have no business creating enemies, but the process is such that nondevotees will always be inimical toward us. Nevertheless, as stated in the *śāstras*, a devotee should be both tolerant and merciful. Devotees engaged in preaching should be prepared to be accused by ignorant persons, and yet they must be very merciful to the fallen conditioned souls. If one can execute his duty in the disciplic succession of Nārada Muni, his service will surely be recognized. As the Lord says in *Bhagavad-gītā* (18.68–69):

ya idaṁ paramaṁ guhyaṁ
mad-bhakteṣv abhidhāsyati
bhaktiṁ mayi parāṁ kṛtvā
mām evaiṣyaty asaṁśayaḥ

na ca tasmān manuṣyeṣu
kaścin me priya-kṛttamaḥ
bhavitā na ca me tasmād
anyaḥ priyataro bhuvi

"For one who explains the supreme secret to the devotees, devotional service is guaranteed, and at the end he will come back to Me. There is no servant in this world more dear to Me than he, nor will there ever be one more dear." Let us continue preaching the message of Lord Kṛṣṇa and not be afraid of enemies. Our only duty is to satisfy the Lord by this preaching, which will be accepted as service by Lord Caitanya and Lord Kṛṣṇa. We must sincerely serve the Lord and not be deterred by so-called enemies.

In this verse the word *sauhṛda-ghnam* ("a breaker of friendship") is used. Because Nārada Muni and the members of his disciplic succession disrupt friendships and family life, they are sometimes accused of being *sauhṛda-ghnam*, creators of enmity between relatives. Actually such devotees are friends of every living entity (*suhṛdaṁ sarva-bhūtānām*), but they are misunderstood to be enemies. Preaching can be a difficult, thankless task, but a preacher must follow the orders of the Supreme Lord and be unafraid of materialistic persons.

TEXT 40

नेत्थं पुंसां विरागः स्यात् त्वया केवलिना मृषा ।
मन्यसे यद्युपशमं स्नेहपाशनिकृन्तनम् ॥४०॥

nettham puṁsāṁ virāgaḥ syāt
tvayā kevalinā mṛṣā
manyase yady upaśamaṁ
sneha-pāśa-nikṛntanam

na—not; *ittham*—in this way; *puṁsām*—of persons; *virāgaḥ*—renunciation; *syāt*—is possible; *tvayā*—by you; *kevalinā mṛṣā*—possessing knowledge falsely; *manyase*—you think; *yadi*—if; *upaśamam*—renunciation of material enjoyment; *sneha-pāśa*—the bonds of affection; *nikṛntanam*—cutting.

TRANSLATION

Prajāpati Dakṣa continued: If you think that simply awakening the sense of renunciation will detach one from the material world, I must say that unless full knowledge is awakened, simply

changing dresses as you have done cannot possibly bring detachment.

PURPORT

Prajāpati Dakṣa was correct in stating that changing one's dress cannot detach one from this material world. The *sannyāsīs* of Kali-yuga who change their robes from white to saffron and then think they can do whatever they like are more abominable than materialistic *gṛhasthas.* This is not recommended anywhere. Prajāpati Dakṣa was right in pointing out this defect, but he did not know that Nārada Muni had aroused the spirit of renunciation in the Haryaśvas and Savalāśvas through full knowledge. Such enlightened renunciation is desirable. One should enter the renounced order with full knowledge (*jñāna-vairāgya*), for the perfection of life is possible for one who renounces this material world in that way. This elevated stage can be reached very easily, as supported by the statements of *Śrīmad-Bhāgavatam* (1.2.7):

vāsudeve bhagavati
bhakti-yogaḥ prayojitaḥ
janayaty āśu vairāgyaṁ
jñānaṁ ca yad ahaitukam

"By rendering devotional service unto the Personality of Godhead, Śrī Kṛṣṇa, one immediately acquires causeless knowledge and detachment from the world." If one seriously engages in devotional service to Lord Vāsudeva, *jñāna* and *vairāgya* are automatically manifest in one's person. There is no doubt of this. Prajāpati Dakṣa's accusation that Nārada had not actually elevated his sons to the platform of knowledge was not factual. All the sons of Prajāpati Dakṣa had first been raised to the platform of *jñāna* and had then automatically renounced this world. In summary, unless one's knowledge is awakened, renunciation cannot take place, for without elevated knowledge one cannot give up attachment for material enjoyment.

TEXT 41

नानुभूय न जानाति पुमान् विषयतीक्ष्णताम् ।
निर्विद्यते स्वयं तस्मान्न तथा भिन्नधीः परैः ॥४१॥

nānubhūya na jānāti
pumān viṣaya-tīkṣṇatām
nirvidyate svayaṁ tasmān
na tathā bhinna-dhīḥ paraiḥ

na—not; *anubhūya*—experiencing; *na*—not; *jānāti*—knows; *pumān*—a person; *viṣaya-tīkṣṇatām*—the sharpness of material enjoyment; *nirvidyate*—becomes aloof; *svayam*—himself; *tasmāt*—from that; *na tathā*—not like that; *bhinna-dhīḥ*—whose intelligence is changed; *paraiḥ*—by others.

TRANSLATION

Material enjoyment is indeed the cause of all unhappiness, but one cannot give it up unless one has personally experienced how much suffering it is. Therefore one should be allowed to remain in so-called material enjoyment while simultaneously advancing in knowledge to experience the misery of this false material happiness. Then, without help from others, one will find material enjoyment detestful. Those whose minds are changed by others do not become as renounced as those who have personal experience.

PURPORT

It is said that unless a woman becomes pregnant, she cannot understand the trouble of giving birth to a child. *Bandhyā ki bujhibe prasava-vedanā.* The word *bandhyā* means a sterile woman. Such a woman cannot give birth to a child. How, then, can she perceive the pain of delivery? According to the philosophy of Prajāpati Dakṣa, a woman should first become pregnant and then experience the pain of childbirth. Then, if she is intelligent, she will not want to be pregnant again. Actually, however, this is not a fact. Sex enjoyment is so strong that a woman becomes pregnant and suffers at the time of childbirth, but she becomes pregnant again, despite her experience. According to Dakṣa's philosophy, one should become implicated in material enjoyment so that after experiencing the distress of such enjoyment, one will automatically renounce. Material nature, however, is so strong that although a man suffers at every step, he will not cease his attempts to enjoy (*tṛpyanti neha kṛpaṇā bahu-duḥkha-bhājaḥ*). Under the circumstances, unless one gets the association of a devotee like Nārada Muni or his servant in the disciplic succession, one's dormant spirit of renunciation cannot be awakened. It is not a fact that because material enjoyment involves so many painful conditions one will automatically become detached. One needs the blessings of a devotee like Nārada Muni. Then one can renounce his attachment for the material world. The young boys and girls of the Kṛṣṇa consciousness movement have given up the spirit of material enjoyment not because of practice but by the mercy of Lord Śrī Caitanya Mahāprabhu and His servants.

TEXT 42

यन्नस्त्वं कर्मसन्धानां साधूनां गृहमेधिनाम् ।
कृतवानसि दुर्मर्षं विप्रियं तव मर्षितम् ॥४२॥

yan nas tvaṁ karma-sandhānāṁ
sādhūnāṁ gṛhamedhinām
kṛtavān asi durmarṣaṁ
vipriyaṁ tava marṣitam

yat—which; *naḥ*—unto us; *tvam*—you; *karma-sandhānām*—who strictly follow the fruitive ritualistic ceremonies according to Vedic injunctions; *sādhūnām*—who are honest (because we honestly seek elevated social standards and bodily comfort); *gṛha-medhinām*—although situated with a wife and children; *kṛtavān asi*—have created; *durmarṣam*—unbearable; *vipriyam*—wrong; *tava*—your; *marṣitam*—forgiven.

TRANSLATION

Although I live in household life with my wife and children, I honestly follow the Vedic injunctions by engaging in fruitive activities to enjoy life without sinful reactions. I have performed all kinds of yajñas, including the deva-yajña, ṛṣi-yajña, pitṛ-yajña and nṛ-yajña. Because these yajñas are called vratas [vows], I am

known as a gṛhavrata. Unfortunately, you have given me great displeasure by misguiding my sons, for no reason, to the path of renunciation. This can be tolerated once.

PURPORT

Prajāpati Dakṣa wanted to prove that he had been most tolerant in not having said anything when Nārada Muni, for no reason, induced his ten thousand innocent sons to adopt the path of renunciation. Sometimes householders are accused of being *gṛhamedhīs,* for *gṛhamedhīs* are satisfied with family life without spiritual advancement. *Gṛhasthas,* however, are different because although *gṛhasthas* live in householder life with their wives and children, they are eager for spiritual advancement. Wanting to prove that he had been magnanimous to Nārada Muni, Prajāpati Dakṣa stressed that when Nārada had misled his first sons, Dakṣa had taken no action; he had been kind and tolerant. He was aggrieved, however, because Nārada Muni had misled his sons for a second time. Therefore he wanted to prove that Nārada Muni, although dressed like a *sādhu,* was not actually a *sādhu;* he himself, although a householder, was a greater *sādhu* than Nārada Muni.

TEXT 43

तन्तुकृन्तन यन्नस्त्वमभद्रमचरः पुनः ।
तस्माल्लोकेषु ते मूढ न भवेद्भ्रमतः पदम् ॥४३॥

tantu-kṛntana yan nas tvam
abhadram acaraḥ punaḥ
tasmāl lokeṣu te mūḍha
na bhaved bhramataḥ padam

tantu-kṛntana—O mischiefmonger who have mercilessly separated my sons from me; *yat*—which; *naḥ*—unto us; *tvam*—you; *abhadram*—an inauspicious thing; *acaraḥ*—have done; *punaḥ*—again; *tasmāt*—therefore; *lokeṣu*—in all the planetary systems within the universe; *te*—of you; *mūḍha*—O rascal not knowing how to act; *na*—not; *bhavet*—there may be; *bhramataḥ*—who are wandering; *padam*—an abode.

TRANSLATION

You have made me lose my sons once, and now you have again done the same inauspicious thing. Therefore you are a rascal who does not know how to behave toward others. You may travel all over the universe, but I curse you to have no residence anywhere.

PURPORT

Because Prajāpati Dakṣa was a *gṛhamedhī* who wanted to remain in household life, he thought that if Nārada Muni could not remain in one place, but had to travel all over the world, that would be a great punishment for him. Actually, however, such a punishment is a boon for a preacher. A preacher is known as *parivrājakācārya*—an *ācārya*, or teacher, who always travels for the benefit of human society. Prajāpati Dakṣa cursed Nārada Muni by saying that although he had the facility to travel all over the universe, he would never be able to stay in one place. In the *paramparā* system from Nārada Muni, I have also been cursed. Although I have many centers that would be suitable places of residence, I cannot stay anywhere, for I have been cursed by the parents of my young disciples. Since the Kṛṣṇa consciousness movement was started, I have traveled all over the world two or three times a year, and although I am provided comfortable places to stay wherever I go, I cannot stay anywhere for more than three days or a week. I do not mind this curse by the parents of my disciples, but now it is necessary that I stay in one place to finish another task—this translation of *Śrīmad-Bhāgavatam.* If my young disciples, especially those who have taken *sannyāsa,* take charge of traveling all over the world, it may be possible for me to transfer the curse of the parents to these young preachers. Then I may sit down conveniently in one place for the work of translation.

TEXT 44

श्रीशुक उवाच

प्रतिजग्राह तद् बाढं नारदः साधुसम्मतः ।
एतावान् साधुवादो हि तितिक्षेतेश्वरः स्वयम् ॥४४॥

śrī-śuka uvāca
pratijagrāha tad bāḍhaṁ
nāradaḥ sādhu-sammataḥ
etāvān sādhu-vādo hi
titikṣeteśvaraḥ svayam

śrī-śukaḥ uvāca—Śrī Śukadeva Gosvāmī said; *pratijagrāha*—accepted; *tat*—that; *bāḍham*—so be it; *nāradaḥ*—Nārada Muni; *sādhu-sammataḥ*—who is an approved *sādhu; etāvān*—this much; *sādhu-vādaḥ*—appropriate for a saintly person; *hi*—indeed; *titikṣeta*—he may tolerate; *īśvaraḥ*—although able to curse Prajāpati Dakṣa; *svayam*—himself.

TRANSLATION

Śrī Śukadeva Gosvāmī continued: My dear King, since Nārada Muni is an approved saintly person, when cursed by Prajāpati Dakṣa he replied, tad bāḍham: "Yes, what you have said is good. I accept this curse." He could have cursed Prajāpati Dakṣa in return, but because he is a tolerant and merciful sādhu, he took no action.

PURPORT

As stated in *Śrīmad-Bhāgavatam* (3.25.21):

titikṣavaḥ kāruṇikāḥ
suhṛdaḥ sarva-dehinām
ajāta-śatravaḥ śāntāḥ
sādhavaḥ sādhu-bhūṣaṇāḥ

"The symptoms of a *sādhu* are that he is tolerant, merciful and friendly to all living entities. He has no enemies, he is peaceful, he abides by the scriptures, and all his characteristics are sublime." Because Nārada Muni is the most elevated of *sādhus*, devotees, to deliver Prajāpati Dakṣa he silently tolerated the curse. Śrī Caitanya Mahāprabhu has taught this principle to all His devotees:

tṛṇād api sunīcena
taror api sahiṣṇunā

amāninā mānadena
kīrtanīyaḥ sadā hariḥ

"One should chant the holy name of the Lord in a humble state of mind, thinking oneself lower than the straw in the street; one should be more tolerant than a tree, devoid of all sense of false prestige and should be ready to offer all respects to others. In such a state of mind one can chant the holy name of the Lord constantly." Following the orders of Śrī Caitanya Mahāprabhu, one who preaches the glories of the Lord all over the world or all over the universe should be humbler than grass and more tolerant than a tree because a preacher cannot live an easygoing life. Indeed, a preacher must face many impediments. Not only is he sometimes cursed, but sometimes he must also suffer personal injury. For example, when Nityānanda Prabhu went to preach Kṛṣṇa consciousness to the two roguish brothers Jagāi and Mādhāi, they injured Him and made His head bleed, but nevertheless, He tolerantly delivered the two rogues, who became perfect Vaiṣṇavas. This is the duty of a preacher. Lord Jesus Christ even tolerated crucifixion. Therefore the curse against Nārada was not very astonishing, and he tolerated it.

Now, it may be asked why Nārada Muni stayed in the presence of Prajāpati Dakṣa and tolerated all his accusations and curses. Was that for Dakṣa's deliverance? The answer is yes. Śrīla Viśvanātha Cakravartī Ṭhākura says that after being insulted by Prajāpati Dakṣa, Nārada Muni should have left immediately, but he purposely stayed to hear all Dakṣa's strong words so that Dakṣa might be relieved of his anger. Prajāpati Dakṣa was not an ordinary man; he had accumulated the results of many pious activities. Therefore Nārada Muni expected that after delivering his curse, Dakṣa, satisfied and freed from anger, would repent his misbehavior and thus get a chance to become a Vaiṣṇava and be delivered. When Jagāi and Mādhāi offended Lord Nityānanda, Lord Nityānanda stood tolerantly, and therefore both brothers fell at His lotus feet and repented. Consequently they later became perfect Vaiṣṇavas.

Thus end the Bhaktivedanta purports of the Sixth Canto, Fifth Chapter, of the Śrīmad-Bhāgavatam, *entitled "Nārada Muni Cursed by Prajāpati Dakṣa."*

Appendixes

The Author

His Divine Grace A.C. Bhaktivedanta Swami Prabhupāda appeared in this world in 1896 in Calcutta, India. He first met his spiritual master, Śrīla Bhaktisiddhānta Sarasvatī Gosvāmī, in Calcutta in 1922. Bhaktisiddhānta Sarasvatī was a prominent religious scholar and the founder of the Gauḍīya Maṭha (a *Vaiṣṇava* movement with sixty-four centres) in India. He liked this educated young man and convinced him to dedicate his life to teaching Vedic knowledge. Śrīla Prabhupāda became his student and, in 1933, received initiation as his disciple.

At their first meeting Śrīla Bhaktisiddhānta Sarasvatī requested Śrīla Prabhupāda to broadcast Vedic knowledge in English. In the years that followed, Śrīla Prabhupāda wrote a commentary on the *Bhagavad-gītā* and assisted the Gauḍīya Maṭha in its work. In 1944, he started *Back to Godhead,* a fortnightly magazine in English. Singlehandedly, Śrīla Prabhupāda edited it, typed the manuscripts, checked the galley proofs, and even distributed the individual copies. The magazine now continues to be published by his disciples throughout the world in different languages.

In 1950 Śrīla Prabhupāda retired from domestic life to devote more time to his studies and writing. He travelled to the holy town of Vṛndāvana, where he lived in humble circumstances in the historic temple of Rādhā-Dāmodara. There, for several years, he engaged in deep study and writing. He accepted the renounced order of life (*sannyāsa*) in 1959. It was at the Rādhā-Dāmodara temple that Śrīla Prabhupāda began to work on his life's masterpiece: a multivolume translation of the eighteen-thousand verse *Śrīmad-Bhāgavatam* (*Bhāgavata Purāṇa*) with full commentary. After publishing three volumes of the *Bhāgavatam,* Śrīla Prabhupāda travelled by freighter to New York City. He was practically penniless, but had faith that the mission of his spiritual master could be successful. On the day he landed in America and saw the grey mists hanging over the towering skyscrapers, he penned these words in his diary: "My dear Lord Kṛṣṇa, I am sure that when this transcendental message penetrates their hearts, they will certainly feel gladdened and thus become liberated from all unhappy conditions of life." He was sixty-nine years old, alone and with few resources, but the wealth of spiritual knowledge and devotion he possessed was an unwavering source of strength and inspiration.

"At a very advanced age, when most people would be resting on their laurels," writes Harvey Cox, Harvard University theologian and author, "Śrīla Prabhupāda harkened to the mandate of his own spiritual teacher and set out on the difficult and demanding voyage to America. Śrīla Prabhupāda is, of course, only one of thousands of teachers. But in another sense, he is one in a thousand, maybe one in a million."

In 1966, Śrīla Prabhupāda founded the International Society for Krishna Consciousness, which became the formal name for the Hare Kṛṣṇa Movement.

In the years that followed, Śrīla Prabhupāda gradually attracted tens of thousands of followers, started more than a hundred temples and *āśramas,* and published scores of books. His achievement is remarkable in that he transplanted India's ancient spiritual culture to the twentieth-century Western world.

In 1968, Śrīla Prabhupāda sent 3 devotee couples to bring Kṛṣṇa consciousness to the U.K. At first, these devotees were cared for by Hindu families who appreciated their mission, but soon they became well-known in London for the street chanting in Oxford Street. A headline in the Times announced, "Kṛṣṇa Chant Startles London." But the *mahā-mantra* soon became popular. Former-Beatle, George Harrison, who had known Śrīla Prabhupāda and the chanting before the devotees came to England, wanted to help. He arranged to produce a recording of the *mantra* on the Beatles' Apple label. It reached the Top Ten in Britain and number one in some other countries.

When Śrīla Prabhupāda arrived in England, he was the guest of John Lennon at his estate in Tittenhurst, while work was progressing on the temple in Bloomsbury, near the British Museum. In November 1969, Śrīla Prabhupāda opened the temple — the first Rādhā-Kṛṣṇa temple in Europe. The movement grew from strength to strength. Once again, George Harrison offered to help by donating a beautiful mock-Tudor manor house and estate in Hertfordshire. Now named Bhaktivedanta Manor, it is the Society's main training centre in Britain.

New devotees of Kṛṣṇa soon became highly visible in all the major cities around the world by their public chanting and their distribution of Śrīla Prabhupāda's books of Vedic knowledge. They began staging joyous cultural festivals throughout the year and serving millions of plates of delicious food offered to Kṛṣṇa (known as *prasādam*) throughout the world.

As a result, ISKCON has significantly influenced the lives of hundreds of thousands of people. The late A.L. Basham, one of the world's leading authorities on Indian history and culture, wrote, "The Hare Kṛṣṇa movement arose out of next to nothing in less than twenty years and has become known all over the West. This is an important fact in the history of the Western world."

In just twelve years, despite his advanced age, Śrīla Prabhupāda circled the globe fourteen times on lecture tours that took him to six continents. Yet this vigorous schedule did not slow his prolific literary output. His writings consititute a veritable library of Vedic philosophy, religion, literature, and culture.

Indeed, Śrīla Prabhupāda's most significant contribution is his books. Highly respected by academics for their authority, depth and clarity, they are used as textbooks in numerous university courses.

Garry Gelade, a professor at Oxford University's Department of Philosophy, wrote of them: "These texts are to be treasured. No one of whatever faith or philosophical persuasion who reads these books with an open mind can fail to be moved and impressed." And Dr. Larry Shinn, Dean of the College of Arts and Sciences at Bucknell University, wrote, "Prabhupāda's personal piety gave him real authority. He exhibited complete command of the scriptures, and unusual depth of realization, and an outstanding personal example, because he actually lived what he taught."

His writings have been translated into over 50 languages. The Bhaktivedanta Book Trust, established in 1972 to publish the works of His Divine Grace, has thus become the world's largest publisher of books in the field of Indian religion and philosophy. 450 million copies in over 50 languages had been sold by the end of 1991.

Before he passed away on the 14th of November 1977 he had guided that Society and seen it grow to a world-wide confederation of more than one hundred *āśramas,* schools, temples, institutes, and farm communities.

Glossary

A

Ācārya—a spiritual master who teaches by example.
Adharma—irreligion.
Adhibhautika—material suffering caused by other living entities.
Adhidaivika—material suffering caused by natural occurrences.
Adhyātmika—material suffering caused by one's own body and mind.
Advaita-vādīs—atheistic philosophers who say that any distinction must be material.
Ajñāta-sukṛti—pious deeds performed accidentally, without knowledge of their effect.
Ārati—a ceremony for greeting the Lord with offerings of food, lamps, fans, flowers and incense.
Arcanā—the devotional process of regulated Deity worship.
Āśrama—an order of spiritual life.

B

Balarāma, Lord—Kṛṣṇa's first expansion and elder brother.
Bhagavad-gītā—the basic directions for spiritual life spoken by the Lord Himself.
Bhāgavata-dharma—the eternal religion or occupational duty of service to the Supreme Personality of Godhead.
Bhakta—a devotee.
Bhakti-yoga—devotional service.
Bhoga—sense gratification; food not offered to the Lord.
Brahmacarya—celibate student life; the first order of Vedic spiritual life.
Brahmaloka—the abode of Lord Brahmā; the highest planetary system.
Brahman—the Absolute Truth; especially, the impersonal aspect of the Absolute.
Brāhmaṇa—a person in the mode of goodness; first Vedic social order.

C

Caitanya-caritāmṛta—Śrīla Kṛṣṇadāsa Kavirāja's authorized biography of

Lord Caitanya Mahāprabhu, presenting the Lord's pastimes and teachings.

Cakra—the Lord's personal disc weapon.

D

Daivī māyā—the Lord's divine deluding potency, the material energy.

Daridra-nārāyaṇa—(lit., poor Nārāyaṇa), the false conception that the Supreme Lord can fall to the status of an ordinary conditioned soul.

Dharma—one's innate eternal activity.

Dharma-śāstras—religious scriptures that prescribe regulations of social organization and religion.

Dharmī—one who abides by Vedic law.

Dhīra—one who is undisturbed in all circumstances.

G

Gauḍīya-Mādhva-sampradāya—the authorized disciplic succession from Madhvācārya through Śrī Caitanya Mahāprabhu.

Goloka Vṛndāvana—the highest spiritual planet, the personal abode of Lord Kṛṣṇa.

Gṛhamedhī—a person who is envious because of too much attachment to family life.

Gṛhastha—one who follows regulated householder life according to Vedic principles.

Guru—a spiritual master.

H

Hari—the Supreme Lord, Viṣṇu.

J

Jīva-tattva—the living entities, who are small parts of the Lord.

Jñāna—speculative knowledge.

Jñāna-yoga—the process of approaching the Supreme by the cultivation of knowledge.

K

Kali-yuga—the present age of quarrel, which began 5,000 years ago.
Karma—fruitive work, for which there is always reaction, good or bad.
Karma-kāṇḍa—the parts of the *Vedas* that describe fruitive activities for improving one's material standard of life.
Karma-yoga—the process of linking with the Supreme by offering all the fruits of one's work.
Karmī—one who is satisfied with working hard for material results.
Kṛṣṇaloka—*See:* Goloka Vṛndāvana.
Kṣatriya—a warrior or administrator; the second Vedic social order.

L

Liṅga—the subtle body: mind, intelligence and false ego.

M

Mahājanas—great souls who have established the science of devotional service.
Mahā-mantra—the great chanting for deliverance: Hare Kṛṣṇa, Hare Kṛṣṇa, Kṛṣṇa Kṛṣṇa, Hare Hare/ Hare Rāma, Hare Rāma, Rāma Rāma, Hare Hare.
Mahātmā—a great liberated personality.
Mantra—a sound vibration for liberating the mind.
Manu-saṁhitā—the original lawbook written by Svāyambhuva Manu for humanity.
Manvantara—the duration of the life of each Manu (progenitor of mankind); standard unit of measurement for universal time.
Marudloka—the planet of the Maruts, associates of King Indra.
Māyā—the external, illusory energy of the Lord, comprising this material world.
Māyā-sukha—illusory, temporary happiness.

Māyāvādīs—impersonal philosophers who say that the Lord cannot have a transcendental body.
Mīmāṁsakas—atheistic philosophers who say that even if God exists, He is obliged to reward us the fruits of our work.
Mlecchas—meat-eaters, who are outside Vedic society.
Mṛdaṅga—a clay drum used for congregational chanting.
Mukti—liberation.

N

Nāma-aparādha—offense against the holy name of the Lord.
Nārāyaṇa—the Supreme Lord in His majestic four-armed form, an expansion of Kṛṣṇa.
Nitya-muktas—eternally liberated souls.
Nivṛtti-mārga—the path of liberation.
Nyāya-śāstras—Vedic textbooks of logic.

O

Oṁkāra—the sound incarnation of Kṛṣṇa.

P

Pañcopāsanā—worship by impersonalists of five deities (Viṣṇu, Durgā, Brahmā, Gaṇeśa and Vivasvān) that is motivated by the desire to ultimately abandon all conceptions of a personal Absolute.
Parabrahman—Kṛṣṇa, who is the Supreme Absolute Truth.
Paramātmā—the Supersoul, Lord Viṣṇu, in the heart of all living entities.
Paramparā—the chain of spiritual masters in disciplic succession.
Prajāpatis—the progenitors of the universal population.
Prajās—citizens (including all species of life).
Prakṛti—nature, the Lord's energy.
Prasāda—food spiritualized by being offered to the Lord.
Pravṛtti-mārga—the path of material enjoyment.
Prāyaścitta—atonement to counteract sinful acts.
Purāṇas—Vedic histories of the universe.
Puruṣa—the supreme enjoyer; the Lord of the universe.

R

Rajo-guṇa—the material mode of passion.
Ṛṣis—great sages.

S

Sac-cid-ānanda-vigraha—the Lord's transcendental form, which is eternal, full of knowledge and bliss.
Sādhu—a saintly person.
Sampradāya—a disciplic succession.
Saṁsṛti—the cycle of repeated birth and death.
Sanātana-dharma—eternal religion.
Sāṅkhya—analytical study of the material world.
Saṅkīrtana—public chanting of the names of God, the approved *yoga* process for this age.
Sannyāsa—the renounced order of spiritual life.
Śāstra—revealed scripture.
Sattva-guṇa—the material mode of goodness.
Siddha—a perfected living being.
Siddhaloka—the heavenly planet whose inhabitants possess all mystic powers.
Smārta-brāhmaṇas—nondevotees who strictly follow the *Vedas* for material benefit.
Smṛti-śāstra—Vedic scriptures other than the original *Vedas, Upaniṣads* and *Vedānta-sūtra.*
Śravaṇaṁ kīrtanaṁ viṣṇoḥ—hearing and chanting about Lord Viṣṇu.
Śuddha-sattva—See: Viśuddha-sattva.
Śūdra—a laborer; the fourth of the Vedic social orders.
Suṣupti—deep sleep, one of the levels of material consciousness.
Svāṁśa—Godhead in one of His personal expansions.
Svargaloka—the heavenly planets of the material world.

T

Tamo-guṇa—the material mode of ignorance.
Tapasya—austerity; accepting some voluntary inconvenience for a higher purpose.

Tilaka—auspicious clay marks that sanctify a devotee's body as a temple of the Lord.

Trayī—one who follows the three *Vedas* (*Ṛg*, *Sāma* and *Yajur*), which explain fruitive activities for material benefits.

U

Upaniṣads—the most significant philosophical sections of the *Vedas.*

V

Vaikuṇṭha—the planets of the spiritual sky, where there is no anxiety.

Vairāgya—renunciation of material pleasure.

Vaiṣṇava—a devotee of Lord Viṣṇu, or Kṛṣṇa.

Vaiśyas—farmers and merchants; the third Vedic social order.

Vānaprastha—one who has retired from family life; the third order of Vedic spiritual life.

Varṇāśrama—the Vedic social system of four social and four spiritual orders.

Vāsudeva-parāyaṇa—one whose desire is fixed on the Supreme Lord.

Vedānta—the philosophy that describes the end of all knowledge, pure devotional service to the Supreme Lord, Śrī Kṛṣṇa.

Vedas—the original revealed scriptures, first spoken by the Lord Himself.

Vibhinnāṁśa—the separated expansions of the Lord, the minute living entities.

Vibhūti—the Lord's glory and opulence.

Vipra—*See: Brāhmaṇa.*

Virāṭa-rūpa—Lord Viṣṇu's universal form.

Viṣṇudūtas—the order carriers of Lord Viṣṇu.

Viśuddha-sattva—the spiritual platform of pure goodness.

Y

Yajña—sacrifice; work done for the satisfaction of Viṣṇu.

Yamadūtas—the messengers of Yamarāja, the lord of death.

Yavanas—those outside the Vedic social system.

Yogī—a transcendentalist who is striving to reestablish his link with the Supreme.

Sanskrit Pronunciation Guide

Vowels

अ a आ ā इ i ई ī उ u ऊ ū ऋ ṛ ॠ ṝ

ऌ ḷ ए e ऐ ai ओ o औ au

ं ṁ *(anusvāra)* ः ḥ *(visarga)*

Consonants

Gutturals:	क ka	ख kha	ग ga	घ gha	ङ ṅa
Palatals:	च ca	छ cha	ज ja	झ jha	ञ ña
Cerebrals:	ट ṭa	ठ ṭha	ड ḍa	ढ ḍha	ण ṇa
Dentals:	त ta	थ tha	द da	ध dha	न na
Labials:	प pa	फ pha	ब ba	भ bha	म ma
Semivowels:	य ya	र ra	ल la	व va	
Sibilants:	श śa	ष ṣa	स sa		
Aspirate:	ह ha	ऽ ' *(avagraha)* – the apostrophe			

The vowels above should be pronounced as follows:

a – like the *a* in org*a*n or the *u* in b*u*t.
ā – like the *a* in f*a*r but held twice as long as short *a*.
i – like the *i* in p*i*n.
ī – like the *i* in p*i*que but held twice as long as short *i*.
u – like the *u* in p*u*sh.
ū – like the *u* in r*u*le but held twice as long as short *u*.

ṛ – like the *ri* in *ri*m.
ṝ – like *ree* in *ree*d.
ḷ – like *l* followed by *ṛ* (*lṛ*).
e – like the *e* in th*ey*.
ai – like the *ai* in *ai*sle.
o – like the *o* in g*o*.
au – like the *ow* in h*ow*.
ṁ (*anusvāra*) – a resonant nasal like the *n* in the French word *bon*.
ḥ (*visarga*) – a final *h*-sound: *aḥ* is pronounced like *aha; iḥ* like *ihi*.

The consonants are pronounced as follows:

k – as in *k*ite
kh – as in Ec*kh*art
g – as in *g*ive
gh – as in di*g-h*ard
ṅ – as in si*ng*
c – as in *ch*air
ch – as in staun*ch-h*eart
j – as in *j*oy
jh – as in he*dgeh*og
ñ – as in ca*ny*on
ṭ – as in *t*ub
ṭh – as in ligh*t-h*eart
ḍ – as in *d*ove
ḍha- as in re*d-h*ot
ṇ – as r*na* (prepare to say the *r* and say *na*).

Cerebrals are pronounced with tongue to roof of mouth, but the following dentals are pronounced with tongue against teeth:

t – as in *t*ub but with tongue against teeth.
th – as in ligh*t-h*eart but with tongue against teeth.
d – as in *d*ove but with tongue against teeth.
dh – as in re*d-h*ot but with tongue against teeth.
n – as in *n*ut but with tongue between teeth.
p – as in *p*ine
ph – as in u*ph*ill (not *f*)
b – as in *b*ird
bh – as in ru*b-h*ard
m – as in *m*other
y – as in *y*es
r – as in *r*un
l – as in *l*ight
v – as in *v*ine
ś (palatal) – as in the *s* in the German word *sprechen*
ṣ (cerebral) – as the *sh* in *sh*ine
s – as in *s*un
h – as in *h*ome

There is no strong accentuation of syllables in Sanskrit, only a flowing of short and long (twice as long as the short) syllables.

References

The purports of *Śrīmad-Bhāgavatam* are all confirmed by standard Vedic authorities. The following authentic scriptures are specifically cited in this volume.

Amara-kośa dictionary, 170

Bhagavad-gītā, 4, 5, 8, 9, 12, 17, 21, 23, 27, 31, 32, 33, 47, 49, 54, 56, 57, 59, 63, 64, 72, 75, 77, 84, 104, 106, 114, 116, 122, 130, 132, 153, 154, 158, 159, 163, 167, 173, 184, 193, 202, 203, 218, 219 222, 223, 224, 227, 231, 233, 236, 238, 244, 245, 246, 248, 250, 253, 258, 271, 272, 275, 276, 284, 286, 287, 291, 295, 303, 310

Bhakti-rasāmṛta-sindhu (Rūpa Gosvāmī), 24, 34

Brahma-saṁhitā, 59, 211, 225, 231, 277

Brahma-yāmala, 34

Bṛhad-viṣṇu Purāṇa, 97

Caitanya-caritāmṛta (Kṛṣṇadāsa Kavirāja), 6, 122, 246, 304

Garuḍa Purāṇa, 97

Mahābhārata, 226

Matsya Purāṇa, 253

Padma Purāṇa, 171, 184

Skanda Purāṇa, 98, 153, 212

Centres of the International Society for Krishna Consciousness

Founder-*Ācārya:* His Divine Grace
A.C. Bhaktivedanta Swami Prabhupāda

August 1993

"For further information of classes, programmes, festivals or residential courses, please contact your local centre. There may be other meetings held locally. Please contact the centre nearest you."

UNITED KINGDOM AND IRELAND

Belfast, Northern Ireland – Brookland, 140 Upper Dunmurray Lane, BT17 OHE/ Tel. +44 (0232) 620530
Birmingham, West Midlands – 84 Stanmore Rd., Edgbaston, B16 9TB/ Tel. +44 (021) 420-4999
Dublin, Ireland – Hare Krishna Centre, 56 Dame St., Dublin 2/ Tel. +353 (1) 6791306
Leicester, England – 21 Thoresby St., North Evington, Leicester LE5 4GU/ Tel. +44 (0533) 762587
Liverpool, England – 114 Bold Street, L1 4HY/ Tel. +44 (051) 708-9400
London, England (city) – Sri Sri Radha Krishna Temple, 10 Soho St., London W1V 5DA/ Tel. +44 (071) 4373662
London, England (country) – Bhaktivedanta Manor, Letchmore Heath, Watford, Hertfordshire WD2 8EP/ Tel. +44 (0923) 857244
Manchester, England – 20 Mayfield Rd., Whalley Range, Manchester M16 8FT/ Tel. +44 (061) 2264416
Newcastle upon Tyne, England – Hare Krishna Centre, 21 Leazes Park Rd., NE1 4PF/ Tel. +44 (091) 2220150
Scotland – Karuna Bhavan, Bankhouse Road, Lesmahagow, Lanarkshire ML11 9PT/ Tel. +44 (0555) 894790

FARM COMMUNITIES

Lisnaskea, North Ireland – Lake Island of Inis Rath, Lisnaskea Co. Fermanagh/ Tel. +44 (03657) 21512
London, England – (contact Bhaktivedanta Manor)

RESTAURANT

London, England – Govinda's, 10 Soho St./ Tel. +44 (071) 4373662
Manchester, England – Govinda's, 244 Deansgate/ Tel. +44 (061) 834- 9197

Kṛṣṇa conscious programmes are held regularly in more than twenty other cities in the U.K. For information, contact Bhaktivedanta Books Ltd., Reader Services Dept., P.O. Box 324, Borehamwood, Herts WD6 1NB/ Tel. (081) 9051244.

NORTH AMERICA

CANADA

Montreal, Quebec – 1626 Pie IX Boulevard, H1V 2C5/ Tel. +1 (514) 521-1301
Ottawa, Ontario – 212 Somerset St. E., K1N 6V4/ Tel. +1 (613) 565-6544
Regina, Saskatchewan – 1279 Retallack St., S4T 2H8/ Tel. +1 (306) 525-1640
Toronto, Ontario – 243 Avenue Rd., M5R 2J6/ Tel. +1 (416) 922-5415
Vancouver, B.C. – 5462 S.E. Marine Dr., Burnaby V5J 3G8/ Tel. +1 (604) 433-9728

FARM COMMUNITY

Ashcroft, B.C. – Saranagati Dhama, Box 99, Ashcroft, B.C. V0K 1A0

RESTAURANTS

Hamilton, Ontario – Govinda's, 195 Locke St. South, L8T 4B5/ Tel. +1 (416) 523-6209
Ottawa – (at ISKCON Ottawa)
Toronto – Hare Krishna Dining Room (at ISKCON Toronto)
Vancouver – Hare Krishna Buffet (at ISKCON Vancouver)
Vancouver – The Hare Krishna Place, 46 Begbie St., New Westminster

U.S.A.

Atlanta, Georgia – 1287 South Ponce de Leon Ave. N.E., 30306/ Tel. +1 (404) 378-9234
Baltimore, Maryland – 200 Bloomsbury Ave., Catonsville, 21228/ Tel. +1 (410) 744-1624 or 4069
Boise, Idaho – 1615 Martha St., 83706/ Tel. +1 (208) 344-4274
Boston, Massachusetts – 72 Commonwealth Ave., 02116/ Tel. +1 (617) 247-8611
Boulder, Colorado – 917 Pleasant St., 80302/ Tel. +1 (303) 444-7005
Chicago, Illinois – 1716 W. Lunt Ave., 60626/ Tel. +1 (312) 973-0900
Cleveland, Ohio – 11206 Clifton Blvd., 44102/ Tel. +1 (216) 651-6670
Dallas, Texas – 5430 Gurley Ave. 75223/ Tel. +1 (214) 827-6330
Denver, Colorado – 1400 Cherry St., 80220/ Tel. +1 (303) 333-5461
Detroit, Michigan – 383 Lenox Ave., 48215/ Tel. +1 (313) 824-6000
Gainesville, Florida – 214 N.W. 14th St., 32603/ Tel. +1 (904) 336-4183
Gurabo, Puerto Rico – Route 181, P.O. Box 8440 HC-01, 00778-9763/ Tel. (809) 737-5222
Hartford, Connecticut – 1683 Main St., E. Hartford, 06108/ Tel. +1 (203) 289-7252
Honolulu, Hawaii – 51 Coelho Way, 96817/ Tel. +1 (808) 595-3947
Houston, Texas – 1320 W. 34th St., 77018/ Tel. +1 (713) 686-4482
Laguna Beach, California – 285 Legion St. 92651/ Tel. +1 (714) 494-7029
Lansing, Michigan – 1914 E. Michigan Ave. 48912/ Tel. +1 (517) 484-2209
Long Island, New York – 197 S. Ocean Ave., Freeport, 11520/ Tel. +1 (516) 867-9045
Los Angeles, California – 3764 Watseka Ave., 90034/ Tel. +1 (310) 836-2676
Miami, Florida – 3220 Virginia St., 33133/ Tel. +1 (305) 442-7218
New Orleans, Louisiana – 2936 Esplanade Ave., 70119/ Tel. +1 (504) 484-6084
New York, New York – 305 Schermerhorn St., Brooklyn, 11217/ Tel. +1 (718) 855-6714
New York, New York – 26 Second Avenue, 10003/ Tel. +1 (212) 420-8803
Philadelphia, Pennsylvania – 51 West Allens Lane, 19119/ Tel. +1 (215) 247-4600
Philadelphia, Pennsylvania – 529 South St., 19147/ Tel. +1 (215) 829-0077
St. Louis, Missouri – 3926 Lindell Blvd., 63108/ Tel. +1 (314) 535-8085
San Diego, California – 1030 Grand Ave., Pacific Beach, 92109/ Tel. +1 (619) 483-2500
San Francisco, California – 84 Carl St., 94117/ Tel. +1 (415) 661-7320
San Francisco, California – 2334 Stuart St., Berkeley, 94705/ Tel. +1 (510) 644-1113
Seattle, Washington – 1420 228th Ave. S.E., Issaquah, 98027/ Tel. +1 (206) 391-3293
Tallahassee, Florida – 1323 Nylic St. (mail: P.O. Box 20224, 32304)/ Tel. +1 (904) 681-9258

Topanga, California – 20395 Callon Dr. 90290/ Tel. +1 (213) 455-1658
Towaco, New Jersey – (mail: P.O. Box 109, 07082)/ Tel. +1 (201) 299-0970
Tucson, Arizona – 711 E. Blacklidge Dr., 85719/ Tel. +1 (602) 792-0630
Walla Walla, Washington – 314 E. Poplar, 99362/ Tel. +1 (509) 525-7133
Washington, D.C. – 10310 Oaklyn Dr., Potomac, Maryland 20854/ Tel. +1 (301) 299-2100

FARM COMMUNITIES

Alachua, Florida (New Ramana-reti) – Box 819, Alachua, 32615/ Tel. +1 (904) 462-2017
Carriere, Mississippi (New Talavan) – 31492 Anner Road, 39426/ Tel. +1 (601) 798-6623
Gurabo, Puerto Rico (New Govardhana Hill) – (contact ISKCON Gurabo)
Hillsborough, North Carolina (New Goloka) – Rt. 6, Box 701, 27278/ Tel. (919) 732-6492
Mulberry, Tennessee (Murari-sevaka) – Rt. No. 1, Box 146-A, 37359/ Tel. (615) 759-6888
Port Royal, Pennsylvania (Gita Nagari) – R.D. No. 1, Box 839, 17082/ Tel. (717) 527-4101

RESTAURANTS AND DINING

Atlanta – The Hare Krishna Dinner Club (at ISKCON Atlanta)
Boise – Govinda's, 500 W. Main St./ Tel. +1 (208) 338-9710
Chicago – Govinda's Buffet (at ISKCON Chicago)
Dallas – Kalachandji's (at ISKCON Dallas)
Denver – Govinda's (at ISKCON Denver)
Detroit – Govinda's (at ISKCON Detroit)/ Tel. +1 (313) 331-6740
Eugene, Oregon – Govinda's Vegetarian Buffet, 270 W. 8th St., 97401/ Tel. +1 (503) 686-3531
Honolulu – Gauranga's Vegetarian Dining (at ISKCON Honolulu)
Laguna Beach, California – Gauranga's (at ISKCON Laguna Beach)
Lansing, Michigan – Govinda's Diners' Club (at ISKCON Lansing)
Los Angeles – Govinda's, 9624 Venice Blvd., Culver City, 90230/ Tel. +1 (310) 836-1269
Miami – (at ISKCON Miami)
Ojai, California – Govinda's Veggie Buffet, 1002 E. Ojai Ave., 93023/ Tel. +1 (805) 646-1133
Philadelphia – Govinda's, 521 South Street, 19147/ Tel. +1 (215) 829-0077
Provo, Utah – Govinda's Buffet, 260 North University, 84601/ Tel. +1 (801) 375-0404
St. Louis, Missouri – Govinda's (at ISCKON St. Louis)
San Diego – Govinda's at the Beach (at ISKCON San Diego)/ Tel. +1 (619) 483-5266
San Francisco – Govinda's (at ISKCON Berkeley)/ Tel. +1 (510) 644- 2777

AUSTRALASIA

AUSTRALIA

Adelaide – 74 Semaphore Rd., Semaphore, S.A. 5019/ Tel. +61 (08) 493 200
Brisbane – 95 Bank Rd., Graceville, Q.L.D. (mail: P.O. Box 83, Indooroopilly 4068)/ Tel. +61 (07) 379-5455
Canberra – P.O. Box 1411, Canberra ACT 2060/ Tel. +61 (06) 290-1869
Melbourne – 197 Danks St., Albert Park, Victoria 3206 (mail: P.O. Box 125)/ Tel. +61 (03) 699-5122
Perth – 144 Railway Parade (cnr. The Strand), Bayswater (mail: P.O. Box 102, Bayswater, W.A. 6053)/ Tel. +61 (09) 370-1552
Sydney – 180 Falcon St., North Sydney, N.S.W. 2060 (mail: P. O. Box 459, Cammeray, N.S.W. 2062)/ Tel. +61 (02) 959-4558

FARM COMMUNITIES

Bambra (New Nandagram) – Oak Hill, Dean's Marsh Road, Bambra, VIC 3241/ Tel. +61 (052) 88-7383
Millfield, N.S.W. – New Gokula Farm, Lewis Lane (off Mt. View Rd. Millfield near Cessnock), N.S.W. (mail: P.O. Box 399, Cesnock 2325, N.S.W., Australia)/ Tel. +61 (049) 98-1800

Murwillumbah (New Govardhana) – Tyalgum Rd., Eungella, via Murwillumbah N.S.W. 2484 (mail: P.O. Box 687)/ Tel. +61 (066) 72-1903

RESTAURANTS

Brisbane – Govinda's, 1st floor, 99 Elizabeth St./ Tel. +61 (07) 210-0255

Melbourne – Crossways, 1st floor, 123 Swanston St., Melbourne, Victoria 3000/ Tel. +61 (03) 650 2939

Melbourne – Gopal's, 139 Swanston St., Melbourne, Victoria 3000/ Tel. +61 (03) 650-1578

Perth – Perth - Hare Krishna Food for Life, 200 William St., Northbridge, WA 6003/ Tel. +61 (09) 22716

Sydney – Govinda's Upstairs and Govinda's Take-Away, 112 Darlinghurst Rd., Darlinghurst, N.S.W. 2010/ Tel. +61 (02) 380- 5162

Sydney – Gopal's (at ISKCON Sydney)

NEW ZEALAND AND FIJI

Christchurch, New Zealand – 83 Bealey Ave. (mail: P.O. Box 25-190 Christchurch/ Tel. +64 (03) 3665-174

Labasa, Fiji – Delailabasa (mail: Box 133)/ Tel. +679 822912

Lautoka, Fiji – 5 Tavewa Ave. (mail: P.O. Box 125)/ Tel. +679 64112

Rakiraki, Fiji – Rewasa, Rakiraki (mail: P.O. Box 94243)

Suva, Fiji – Nasinu 7½ miles (P.O. Box 6376)/ Tel. +679 391-282

Wellington, New Zealand – 6 Shotter St., Karori (mail: P.O. Box 2753, Wellington)/ Tel. +64 (04) 764445

RESTAURANTS

Auckland, New Zealand – Gopal's, 1st floor, Civic House, 291 Queen St./ Tel. +64 (09) 3034885

Christchurch, New Zealand – Gopal's, 143 Worcester St./ Tel. +64 (03) 3667-035

Labasa, Fiji – Govinda's, Naseakula Road/ Tel. +679 811364

Lautoka, Fiji – Gopal's, Corner of Yasawa St. and Naviti St./ Tel. +679 62990

Suva, Fiji – Gopal's, 18 Pratt St./ Tel. +679 62990

Suva, Fiji – Gopal's, 37 Cumming St./ Tel. +679 312259

FARM COMMUNITY

Auckland, New Zealand (New Varshan) – Hwy. 18, Riverhead, next to Huapai Golf Course (mail: R.D. 2, Kumeu, Auckland)/ Tel. +64 (09) 4128075

EUROPE

GERMANY

Berlin – Bhakti-Yoga-Zentrum, Muskauerstr. 27, 10997 Berlin/ Tel. +49 (030) 6189112

Hamburg – Mühlenstr. 93, 25421 Pinneberg/ Tel. +49 (04101) 23931

Heidelberg – Center for Vedic Studies, Kurfürsten-Anlage 5, 69115 Heidelberg/ Tel. +49 (06221) 165101

Hörup – Neuhörup 1, 24980 Hörup/ Tel. +49 (04639) 7336

Cologne – Taunusstr. 40, 51105 Köln-Gremberg/ Tel. +49 (0221) 8303778

Leipzig – Hare-Krishna-Kulturzentrum, Peterssteinweg 10b, 04107 Leipzig/ Tel. +49 (0341) 2513302

Munich – Bhakti-Yoga-Zentrum, c/o Braukmann, Theresienhöhe 6c, 80339 München/ Tel. +49 (089) 501624

Nürnberg – Bhakti-Yoga-Zentrum, Kopernikusplatz 12, 90459 Nürnberg/ Tel. +49 (0911) 453286

Weil der Stadt – Dr. Dietter-Str. 12, 71263 Weil der Stadt 2/ Tel. +49 (07033) 3592

Weimar – Rothäuserbergweg 6, 99425 Weimar/ Tel. +49 (03643) 59548

Wiesbaden – Center für Vedische Studien, Schiersteinerstraße 6, 65187 Wiesbaden/ Tel. +49 (0611) 373312

FARM COMMUNITY

Jandelsbrunn – Nava-Jiyada-Nrsimha-Ksetra, Zielberg 20, 94118 Jandelsbrunn/ Tel. +49 (08583) 316

RESTAURANTS

Berlin – Higher Taste, Kurfürstendamm 157/158, 10709 Berlin 31/ Tel. +49 (030) 8929917
Flensburg – Goloka, Heiligengeistgang 9, 24937 Flensburg/ Tel. +49 (0461) 13878
Cologne – Govinda, Taunusstr. 40, 51105 Köln-Gremberg/ Tel. +49 (0221) 8301241

ITALY

Bergamo – Villaggio Hare Krishna, Via Galileo Galilei 41, 24040 Chignolo D'isola (BG)/ Tel. +39 (035) 490706
Bologna – Via Ramo Barchetta 2, 40010 Bentivoglio (BO)/ Tel. +39 (051) 863924
Catania – Via San Nicolo al Borgo 28, 95128 Catania, Sicily/ Tel. +39 (095) 522-252
Naples – Via Vesuvio, N33, Ercolano LNA7/ Tel. +39 (081) 739-0398
Rome – Via di Tor Tre Teste 142, 00169 Roma/ Tel. +39 (06) 262913
Vicenza – Via Roma 9, 36020 Albettone (Vicenza) / Tel. +39 (0444) 790573 or 790566

FARM COMMUNITY

Florence (Villa Vrindavan) – Via Communale degli Scopeti 108, S. Andrea in Percussina, San Casciano, Val di Pesa (FI) 5002/ Tel. +39 (055) 820-054

RESTAURANTS

Catania – Govinda's (at ISKCON Catania)
Milan – Govinda's, Via Valpetrosa 3/5, 20123 Milano/ Tel. +39 (02) 862-417
Rome – Govinda's, Via di San Simone 73/A, 00186 Roma/ Tel. +39 (06) 654-1973

SWEDEN

Gothenburg – Lagmansgatan 11, S-41653 Göteborg/ Tel. +46 (031) 192319
Grödinge – Korsnäs Gård, S-14792 Grödinge/ Tel. +46 (08) 53029151
Malmö – Hare Krishna Temple, Gustav Adolfs Torg 10A, S-21139 Malmö/ Tel. +46 (040) 127181
Stockholm – Fridhemsgatan 22, S-11240 Stockholm/ Tel. +46 (08) 6549 002
Uppsala – Nannaskolan sal F 3, Kungsgatan 22, 75332 Uppsala/ Tel. +46 (018) 102924 (mail: Box 833, 75108 Uppsala)

FARM COMMUNITY

Järna – Almviks Gård, S-15300 Järna/ Tel. +46 (08) 551-52050; 551-52073

RESTAURANTS

Malmo – Higher Taste, Amiralsgatan 6, S-21155 Malmö/ Tel. +46 (040) 970600
Stockholm – Govinda's (at ISKCON Stockholm)
Stockholm – Gopal, Timmermansgatan 13/ Tel. +46 (08) 6441035
Uppsala – Govinda's (at ISKCON Uppsala)

OTHER COUNTRIES

Amsterdam, The Netherlands – Van Hilligaertstr. 17, 1072 JX/ Tel. +31 (020) 6751404
Antwerp, Belgium – Amerikalei 184, B-2000 Antwerpen/ Tel. +32 (03) 2370037
Athens, Greece – Methimnis 18, Kypseli, 11257 Athens/ Tel. +30 (01) 993-7080
Barcelona, Spain – c/de L'Oblit 67, 08026 Barcelona/ Tel. +34 (93) 347-9933
Belgrade, Yugoslavia – VVZ-Veda, Custendilska 17, 11000 Beograd/ Tel. +38 (11) 781-695
Bellinzona, Switzerland – New Nandagram, al Chiossacio, CH-6594 Contone TI/ Tel. +41 (092) 622747
Bern, Switzerland – Govinda Kulturtreff, Weihergasse 7, CH-3005 Bern/ Tel. +41 (31) 213825

Budapest, Hungary – Hare Krishna Temple, Dimitrov u. 77, Budapest 1028 II
Debrecen, Hungary – L. Hegyi Mihalyne u.62, Debrecen 4030
Gdynia, Poland – ul. Kapitanska 9a, 81-331 Gdynia/ Tel./Fax +48 (58) 202865
Helsinki, Finland – Eljaksentie 9, SF-00370 Helsinki/ Tel. +358 (0) 5062108
Helsinki, Finland – Ruoholahdenkatu 24d, 00180, Helsinki/ Tel. +358 06949879
Hillerød, Denmark – Bauneholm Baunevey 23, Bendstrup, DK-3400 Hillerød/ Tel. +45 42286446 Fax: 42287331
Kaunas, Lithuania – Savanoryu 37, 233 000 Kaunas/ Tel. +7 (0127) 22-25-74
Kracow, Poland – ISKCON, ul. Ehrenberga 15, 31-309 Krakow/ Tel. +48 (12) 36 28 85
Lisbon, Portugal – Rua Fernao Lopes 6, Cascais 2750 (mail: Apartado 2489, Lisbo 1112)/ Tel. +351 (011) 286 713
Ljubljana, Slovenia – ISKCON Slovenia, Zibertova 27, 61000 Ljubljana, Slovenia
Malaga, Spain – Ctra. Alora, 3 int., 29140 Churriana/ Tel. +34 (952) 621038
Oslo, Norway – Center for Krishnabevidsthed, Skolestien 11, N-0373 Oslo 3/ Tel. +47 (02) 494790
Paris, France – 31 Rue Jean Vacquier, 93160 Noisy le Grand/ Tel. +33 (01) 43043263 or 43043115
Plovdiv, Bulgaria – ul. Sasho Dimitrov 80, 4000 Plovdiv, Bulgaria/ Tel. +359 (32) 453987
Porto, Portugal – Rua S. Miguel, 19 C.P. 4000 (mail: Apartado 4108, 4002 Porto Codex)/ Tel. +351 (02) 2005469
Poznan, Poland – ul. Nizinna 26, 61-424 Poznan/ Tel./Fax +48 61 323838
Prague, Czechoslovakia – Hare Krishna, Na Hrazi 5, 18000 Praha 8/ Tel. +42 (02) 6837226
Riga, Latvia – Krishyana Barona 56/ Tel. +7 (0132) 272490
Rijeka, Croatia – Centar za Vedske Studije, Boze Starca Jurica 5, 51000 Rijeka/ Tel. +38 (051) 611-589
Rotterdam, The Netherlands – Braamberg 45, 2905 BK Capelle a/d Yssel/ Tel. +31 (010) 4580873
Sarajevo, Bosnia-Herzegovina – Krajiska 5, 71000 Sarajevo/ Tel. +38 (071) 22-663
Septon-Durbuy, Belgium – Château de Petite Somme, 6940 Septon-Durbuy/ Tel. +32 (086) 322926
Sofia, Bulgaria – Angel Kanchev 34, 1st Floor, Sofia 1000, Bulgaria/ Tel. +359 (02) 878948
Timisoara, Romania – ISKCON, Porumbescu 92, 1900 Timisoara, Romania/ Tel. +40 (961) 54776
Turku, Finland – Kaurakatu 39, 20740 Turku 74/ Tel. +358 (9) 21 364 055
Vienna, Austria – Center for Vedic Studies, Rosenackerstraße 26, A-1170 Wien/ Tel. +43 (0222) 455830
Vilnius, Lithuania – Raugyklos G. 23-1, 2056 Vilnius/ Tel. +7 (0122) 661218
Warsaw, Poland – Mysiadlo k. Warszawy, ul. Zakret 11, 05-500 Piaseczno/ Tel. +48 (22) 562-711
Wroclaw, Poland – ul. Nowowiejska 87/8, 50-340 Wroclaw/ Tel./Fax +48 (71) 225704
Zagreb, Croatia – Centar za Vedske Studije, 1 Bizek 5, 41090 Zagreb/ Tel. +38 (41) 190548
Zurich, Switzerland – Bergstrasse 54, CH-8030 Zürich/ Tel. +41 (01) 2623388
Zurich, Switzerland – Preyergrasse 16, CH-8001 Zürich/ Tel. +41 (01) 2518859

FARM COMMUNITIES

Czechoslovakia – Krsnův Dvůr c. 1, 257 28 Chotysany
Denmark – Gl. Kirkevej 3, DK-6650 Brørup/ Tel. +45 (075) 392921
France (La Nouvelle Mayapura) – Domaine d'Oublaisse, 36360, Lucay le Mâle/ Tel. +33 (054) 402481
Poland (New Santipura) – Czarnow 21, k. Kamiennej gory, woj. Jelenia Gora/ Tel. +48 (8745) 1892
Spain (New Vraja Mandala) – (Santa Clara) Brihuega, Guadalajara/ Tel. +34 (911) 280018
Switzerland – Gokula Project, Vacherie Dessous, CH-2913 Roche d'Or/ Tel. +41 (066) 766160

RESTAURANTS

Barcelona, Spain – Restaurante Govinda, Plaza de la Villa de Madrid 4-5, 08002 Barcelona
Bern, Switzerland – Weihergasse 7 (Marzili), 3005 Bern/ Tel. +41 (031) 21 38 25
Biel, Switzerland – Govinda, Untergasse 29 (Alstadt), 2502 Biel/ Tel. +41 (032) 23 12 91
Copenhagen, Denmark – Govinda's Vegetarisk Restaurant, Noerre Farimagsgade 82, Copenhagen/ Tel. +45 33337444
Septon-Durbuy, Belgium – Gopinatha's Garden (at ISKCON Septon-Durbuy)
Zurich, Switzerland – Govinda's Restaurant, Preyergasse 16, 8001 Zürich/ Tel. +41 (01) 251-8859

COMMONWEALTH OF INDEPENDENT STATES

RUSSIA

Moscow – Khoroshevskoye shosse d.8, korp.3, 125 284, Moscow/ Tel. +7 (095) 945-4755
Moscow – Prospekt Mira d.5, kv. 8, Moscow/ Tel. +7 (095) 207-07-38
Novosibirsk – ul. Leningradskaya 111-20, Novosibirsk
St. Petersburg – ul. Burtseva 20-147, 198 261 St. Petersburg/ Tel. +7 (0812) 150-28-80
Vladivostok – ul. Sakhalinskaya 48-12, 690 080 Vladivostok

UKRAINE

Chernigov – ul. Krasnogvardeyskaya, 10-56, 250033 Chernigov/ Tel. +7 (865571) 54263
Dnepropetrovsk – ul. Ispolkomovskaya, 56A, Dnepropetrovsk
Donetsk – ul. Treneva, 3 Flat N44, Donetsk
Kharkov – ul. Verhne-Gievskaya, 43, 310015 Kharkov
Kiev – Kotovskogo 3-39, 252 060 Kiev/ Tel. +7 (044) 440-7309
Lvov – 292066 Lvivska obl. Buski rajon. S. Zbolotni Chuchmani
Odessa – ul. desi Ukrainki, 47-57, Odessa

OTHER COUNTRIES

Baku, Azerbaijan – ul. Mikrorayon 123-72, Baku 9
Kishinev, Moldova – ul. George Asaki, 68/1 Flat 105, 277028 Kishinev/ Tel. +7 (0127) 737024
Minsk, Belarus – ul. Pavlova 11, 220 053 Minsk
Sukhumi, Georgia – Pr. Mira 274, Sukhumi
Tashkent, Uzbekistan – ul. Babadjanova 36-34
Yerevan, Armenia – St. Krupskaya 18, 375019 Yerevan/ Tel. +7 (8852) 275106

AFRICA

Abeokuta, Nigeria – Ibadan Rd., Obantoko, behind NET (mail: P.O. Box 5177)
Abidjan, Ivory Coast – 01 BP 8366, Abidjan
Accra, Ghana – 582 Blk. 20, Odokor, Official Town (mail: P.O. Box 01568, Osu)
Buea, Cameroon – Southwest Province (mail: c/o Yuh Laban Nkesah, P and T, VHS)
Cape Town, South Africa – 17 St. Andrews Rd., Rondebosch 7700/ Tel. +27 (21) 689 1529
Durban (Natal), S. Africa – Chatsworth Centre, Chatsworth 4030 (mail: P.O. Box 56003)/ Tel. +27 (31) 435-815
Freetown, Sierra Leone – 13 Bright St., Brookfields (mail: P.O. Box 812, Freetown)
Johannesburg, South Africa – 14 Goldreich St., Hillbrow, 2001 (mail: P.O. Box 10667, Johannesburg 2000)/ Tel. +27 (11) 484-3273
Kampala, Uganda – Bombo Rd., near Makerere University (mail: P.O. Box 1647, Kampala)

Kisumu, Kenya – P.O. Box 547/ Tel. +254 (035) 42546

Lagos, Nigeria – No. 2 Murtala Mohammed International Airport Expressway, Mafaluku (mail: P.O. Box 8793, Lagos)/ Tel. +234 (01) 966613

Marondera, Zimbabwe – 6 Pine Street (mail: P.O. Box 339)/ Tel. +263 (028) 8877801

Mombasa, Kenya – Hare Krishna House, Sauti Ya Kenya and Kisumu Rds. (mail: P.O. Box 82224, Mombasa)/ Tel. +254 (011) 312248

Nairobi, Kenya – Muhuroni Close, off West Nagara Rd. (mail: P.O. Box 28946, Nairobi)/ Tel. +254 (05) 744365

Nkawkaw, Ghana – ISKCON Nkawkaw, P.O. Box 366, Nkawkaw, Ghana

Phoenix, Mauritius – Hare Krishna Land, Pont Fer, Phoenix (mail: P.O. Box 108, Quartre Bornes, Mauritius)/ Tel. +230 696-5804

Port Elizabeth, South Africa – 10 Skegnes Rd., Summerstrand/ Tel. +27 (41) 153-3353

Port Harcourt, Nigeria – 2 Eligbam Rd. (corner of Obana Obhan St.), G.R.A. II (mail: P.O. Box 4429, Trans Amadi)/ Tel. +234 (084) 330-020

Tokoradi, Ghana – 64 Windy Ridge (mail: P.O. Box 328)

Warri, Nigeria – 48 Warri-Sapele Rd. (P.O. Box 1922, Warri)/ Tel. +234 (053) 231-859

FARM COMMUNITY

Mauritius (ISKCON Vedic Farm) – Hare Krishna Rd., Vrindaban, Bon Acceuil/ Tel. +230 418-3955

RESTAURANT

Durban, South Africa – Govinda's (contact ISKCON Durban)

ASIA

INDIA

Agartala, Tripura – Assam-Agartala Rd., Banamalipur, 799001

Ahmedabad, Gujarat – Sattelite Rd., Gandhinagar Highway Crossing, Ahmedabad 380 054/ Tel. +91 (0272) 449945

Bamanbore, Gujarat – N.H. 8A, Surendranagar District

Bangalore, Karnataka – Hare Krishna Hill, 1 R' Block, Chord Road, Rajaji Nagar 560 010/ Tel. +91 (0812) 321 956 or 342 818 or 322 346

Baroda, Gujarat – Hare Krishna Land, Gotri Rd., 390 021/ Tel. +91 (0265) 326299

Bhayandar, Maharashtra – Shivaji Chowk, Station Road, Bhayandar (West), Thane 401101/ Tel. +91 (022) 8191920

Bhubaneswar, Orissa – National Highway No. 5, Nayapali, 751 001/ Tel. +91 (0674) 53125

Bombay, Maharashtra – Hare Krishna Land, Juhu 400 049/ Tel. +91 (022) 6206860

Calcutta, W. Bengal – 3C Albert Rd., 700 017/ Tel. +91 (033) 2473757, 2476075

Chandigarh, Punjab – Hare Krishna Land, Dakshin Marg, Sector 36-B, 160 036/ Tel. +91 (0172) 44634

Coimbatore, Tamil Nadu – Padmam 387, VGR Puram, Alagesan Road 1, 641-011/ Tel. +91 (0422) 45978

Gauhati, Assam – Ulubari Charali, Gauhati 781 001/ Tel. +91 (0361) 31208

Guntur, A.P. – Opp. Sivalayam, Peda Kakani 522 509

Hyderabad, A.P. – Hare Krishna Land, Nampally Station Rd., 500 001/ Tel. +91 (0842) 551018, 552924

Imphal, Manipur – Hare Krishna Land, Airport Road, 795 001/ Tel. +91 (0385) 21587

Jagannatha Puri, Orissa – Bhakti Kuthi, Swargadwar, Puri

Kurukshetra, Haryana – Hare Krishna Dham, 805, Sector 13, Kurukshetra/ Tel. 1408

Madras, Tamil Nadu – 59, Burkit Rd., T. Nagar, 600 017/ Tel. +91 443266

Mayapur, W. Bengal – Shree Mayapur Chandrodaya Mandir, P.O Shree Mayapur Dham, Dist. Nadia/ Tel. +91 (034) 762218 or 762213

Moirang, Manipur–Nongban Ingkhon, Tidim Rd./ Tel. +91 795133
Nagpur, Maharashtra–70 Hill Road, Ramnagar, 440 010/ Tel. +91 (0712) 533513
New Delhi–Sant Nagar Main Road (Garhi), behind Nehru Place Complex (mail: P.O. Box 7061, New Delhi 110 065/ Tel. +91 (011) 6419701 or 6412058
New Delhi–14/63, Punjabi Bagh, 110 026/ Tel. +91 (011) 5410782
Pandharpur, Maharashtra–Hare Krishna Ashram, across Chandrabhaga River, Dist. Sholapur, 413 304
Patna, Bihar–Rajendra Nagar Road No. 12, 800 016/ Tel. +91 (0612) 50765
Pune, Maharashtra–4 Tarapoor Rd. Camp, 411 001/ Tel. +91 (0212) 60124 and 64003
Secunderabad, A.P.–9-1-1 St. John's Road, 500 026/ Tel. +91 (0842) 825232
Silchar, Assam–Ambikapatti, Silchar, Cachar Dist., 788004
Siliguri, W. Bengal–Gitalpara 734 401/ Tel. +91 (0353) 26619
Surat, Gujarat–Rander Rd., Jahangirpura, 395 005/ Tel. +91 (0261) 84215
Tirupati, A.P.–K.T. Road, Vinayaka Nagar 517 507/ Tel. +91 (08574) 20114
Trivandrum, Kerala–T.C. 224/1485, WC Hospital Rd., Thycaud, 695 014/ Tel. +91 (0471) 68197
Udhampur, Jammu and Kashmir–Srila Prahbupada Ashram, Prabhupada Marg, Prabhupada Nagar, Udhampur 182 101/ Tel. +91 (0199) 298
Vallabh Vidyanagar, Gujarat–ISKCON Hare Krishna Land, Vallabh Vidyanagar 338 120/ Tel. +91 (02692) 30796
Vrindavana, U.P.–Krishna-Balaram Mandir, Bhaktivedanta Swami Marg, Raman Reti, Mathur Dist. 281 124/ Tel. +91 (05664) 82478

FARM COMMUNITIES

Ahmedabad District, Gujarat–Hare Krishna Farm, Katwada (contact ISKCON Ahmedabad)
Assam–Karnamadhu, Dist. Karimganj
Chamorshi, Maharashtra–78 Krishnanagar Dham, District Gadhachiroli, 442 603
Hyderabad, A.P.–P.O. Dabilpur Village, Medchal Tq., R.R. District, 501 401/ Tel. +91 552924
Mayapur, W. Bengal–(contact ISKCON Mayapur)

RESTAURANTS

Bombay–Govinda's (at Hare Krishna Land)
Calcutta–Hare Krishna Karma-Free Confectionary, 6 Russel Street, Calcutta 700 071
Mayapur–Govinda's (at ISKCON Mayapur)
Vrindavana–Krishna-Balaram Mandir Guesthouse

OTHER COUNTRIES

Bali, Indonesia–(Contact ISKCON Jakarta)
Bangkok, Thailand–139 Soi Puttha Osotha, New Road (near GPO), Bangkok 10500
Cagayan de Oro, Philippines–30 Dahlia St., Ilaya Carmen, 900 Cagayan de Oro (c/o Sepulveda's Compound)
Chittagong, Bangladesh–Caitanya Cultural Society, Sri Pundarik Dham, Mekhala, Hathazari (city office and mail: 23 Nandan Kanan, Chittagong)/ Tel. +880 (031) 202219
Colombo, Sri Lanka–188 New Chetty St., Colombo 13/ Tel. +94 (01) 433325
Dhaka, Bangladesh–5 Chandra Mohon Basak St., Banagram, Dhaka 1203
Hong Kong–27 Chatam Road South, 6/F, Kowloon/ Tel. +852 7396818
Iloilo City, Philippines–13-1-1 Tereos St., La Paz, Iloilo City, Iloilo/ Tel. +63 (033) 73391
Jakarta, Indonesia–P.O. Box 2694, Jakarta Pusat 10001/ Tel. +62 (021) 4899646
Jessore, Bangladesh–Nitai Gaur Mandir, Kathakhali Bazaar, P.O. Panjia, Dist. Jessore
Jessore, Bangladesh–Rupa-Sanatana Smriti Tirtha, Ramsara, P.O. Magura Hat, Dist. Jessore
Kathmandu, Nepal–Vishnu Gaun Panchayat Ward No. 2, Budhanilkantha/ Tel. +977 4-10368
Kuala Lumpur, Malaysia–Lot 9901, Jalan Awan Jawa, Taman Yarl, off 5½ Mile, Jalan Kelang Lama, Petaling/ Tel. +60 (03) 7830172
Manila, Philippines–170 R. Fernandez, San Juan, Metro Manila/ Tel. +63 (02) 707410

Tel Aviv, Israel – (mail: P.O.B. 48163, Tel Aviv 61480)/ Tel. +972 (04) 390342
Singapore – Govinda's Gifts, 763 Mountbatten Road, Singapore 1543/ Tel. +65 440-9092
Taipei, Taiwan – (mail: c/o ISKCON Hong Kong)
Tehran, Iran – Keshavarz-Dehkedeh Ave., Kamran St. No. 58/ Tel. +98 (021) 658870
Tokyo, Japan – 1-29-2-202 Izumi, Suginami-ku, Tokyo 168/ Tel. +81 (03) 3327-1541
Yogyakarta, Indonesia – P.O. Box 25, Babarsari YK, DIY

FARM COMMUNITIES

Indonesia – Govinda Kunja (contact ISKCON Jakarta)
Malaysia – Jalan Sungai Manik, 36000 Teluk Intan, Perak
Philippines (Hare Krishna Paradise) – 231 Pagsabungan Rd., Basak, Mandaue City/ Tel. +63 (032) 83254

RESTAURANTS

Cebu, Philippines – Govinda's, 26 Sanchiangko St.
Hong Kong – The Higher Taste Vegetarian Dining Club (at ISKCON Hong Kong)
Kuala Lumpur, Malaysia – Govinda's, 16-1 Jalan Bunus Enam Masjid, India/ Tel. +60 (03) 2986785

LATIN AMERICA

BRAZIL

Belém, PA – Rua Lindolpho Collor, 42, Marco, CEP 66095-310
Belo Horizonte, MG – Rua St. Antonio, 45, Venda Nova, CEP 31515-100
Brazilia, DF – HIGS 706, Bloco C, Casa 29, CEP 70350-752/ Tel. +55 (061) 242-7579
Caxias Do Sul, RS – Rua Italia Travi, 601, Rio Branco, CEP 95097- 710
Curitiba, PR - Comunidade Nova Goloka, Pinhais (Mail: R. Cel Anibal dos Santos 67, Vila Fanny, Curitiba, CEP 81030-210)
Florianopolis, SC - Rua Joao de Souza, 200, Praia do Santinho, CEP 88056-678
Guarulhos, SP - Rua Dom Pedro II, 195, Centro, 3rd floor, CEP 07131-418/ Tel. +55 (011) 209-6669
Fortaleza, CE - Rua Jose Lourenţo, 2114, Aldeota, CEP 60115- 288/ Tel. +55 (085) 266-1273
Manaus, AM - Av. 7 de Setembro, 1559, Centro, CEP 69005-141/ Tel. +55 (092) 232-0202
Natal, RN - Av. Praia do Timbau, 2133, Ponta Negra, CEP 59894- 588
Pirajui, SP - Estr. Pirajui-Estiva, Km 2, CEP 16600-000/ Tel. +55 (0142) 72-2309
Porto Alegre, RS - Rua Tomas Flores, 331, Bonfim, CEP 90035- 201
Recife, PE - Rua Zenobio Lins, 70, Cordeiro, CEP 50711-300
Ribeirao, Preto - Rua dos Aliados, 155, Campos Eliseos, CEP 14080-570
Rio de Janeiro, RJ - Rua Armando C. de Freitas, 108, B. Tijuca, CEP 22628-098/ Tel. +55 (021) 399-4493
Salvador, BA - Rua Alvaro Adrono, 17, Brotas, CEP 40255-460/ Tel. +55 (071) 244-0418
Santos, SP - Rua Nabuco de Araujo, 151, Embare, CEP 11025-011/ Tel. +55 (0132) 38-4655
Sao Paulo, SP - Av. Angelica, 2583, Centro, CEP 01227-200/ Tel. +55 (011) 259-7352
Teresopolis, RJ - Comunidade Vrajabhumi (contact ISKCON Rio)

FARM COMMUNITIES

Caruaru, PE - Nova Vrajadhama, Distrito de Murici (mail: C.P. 283, CEP 55000-000)
Parati, RJ - Goura Vrindavana, Sertao Indaituba (mail: 62 Parati, CEP 23970-000
Pindamonhangaba, SP - Nova Gokula, Bairro de Ribeirao Grande (mail: C.P. 108, CEP 12400-000)/ Tel. +55 (0122) 42-5002

RESTAURANTS

Brasilia - (at ISKCON Brasilia)
Caxias do Sul, RS - Av. Julio de Castilhos, 1095, Centro
Fortaleza, CE - (at ISKCON Fortaleza)

Porto Alegre, RS - (at ISKCON Porto Alegre)

MEXICO

Guadalajara – Pedro Moreno No. 1791, Sector Juarez/ Tel. +52 (36) 26-58-69
Mexico City – Gob. Tiburcio Montiel No. 45, 11850 Mexico, D.F./ Tel. +52 (5) 271-22-23
Monterrey – Via Pamplona 2916, Col. Mas Palomas/ Tel. +52 (83) 57-09-39
Saltillo – Blvd. Saltillo No. 520, Col. Buenos Aires
Veracruz – Heroes de Puebla No. 85, E/ Tuero Molina y Orizaba, 91910 Veracruz, Ver./ Tel. +52 (29) 37-63-1

FARM COMMUNITY

Guadalajara – Contact ISKCON Guadalajara

RESTAURANTS

Orizaba – Restaurante Radhe, Sur 5 No. 50, Orizaba, Ber./ Tel. +52 (272) 5-75-25
Tulancingo – Restaurante Govinda, Calle Juarez 213, Tulancingo, Hgo./ Tel. +52 (775) 3-51-53

PERU

Arequipa – Jerusalen 402/ Tel. +51 (054) 229523
Cuzco – San Juan de Dios 285
Lima – Pasaje Solea 101, Santa Maria-Chosica/ Tel. +51 (014) 910891
Lima – Schell 634 Miraflores
Lima – Av. Garcilazo de la Vega 1670-1680/ Tel. +51 (014) 259523

FARM COMMUNITY

Hare Krishna-Correo De Bella Vista – DPTO De San Martin

RESTAURANTS

Arequipa – (at ISKCON Arequipa)
Cuzco – Espaderos 128
Lima – Schell 634 Miraflores

OTHER COUNTRIES

Asunción, Paraguay – Centro Bhaktivedanta, Paraguari 469, Asunción/ Tel. +595 (021) 492-800
Bahia Blanca, Argentina – Centro de Estudios Vedicos, Rondeau 473, (8000) Bahia Blanca
Bogotá, Colombia – Calle 63A, #10-62, Chapinero/ Tel. +57 (01) 249-5797
Buenos Aires, Argentina – Centro Bhaktivedanta, Andonaegui 2054, (1431)/ Tel. +54 (01) 515567
Cali, Colombia – Avenida 2 EN, #24N-39/ Tel. +57 (023) 68-88-53
Caracas, Venezuela – Avenida Berlin, Quinta Tia Lola, La California Norte/ Tel. +58 (02) 225463
Cochabamba, Bolivia – Av. Heroinas E-0435 Apt. 3 (mail: P.O. Box 2070, Cochabamba)/ Tel. +591 (042) 50907
Cuenca, Ecuador – Entrada de Las Pencas 1, Avenida de Las Americas/ Tel. +593 (07) 825211
Essequibo Coast, Guyana – New Navadvipa Dham, Mainstay, Essequibo Coast
Georgetown, Guyana – 24 Uitvlugt Front, West Coast Demerara
Guatemala, Guatemala – Apartado Postal 1534
Guayaquil, Ecuador – 6 de Marzo 226 y. V.M. Rendon/ Tel. +593 (04) 308412 or 309420
Mendoza, Argentina – Espejo 633, (5000) Mendoza/ Tel. +54 (061) 257193
Montevideo, Uruguay – Centro de Bhakti-Yoga, Pablo de Maria 1427, Montevideo/ Tel. +598 (02) 2484551
Panama, Republic of Panama – Via las Cumbres, entrada Villa Zaita, frente a INPSA No. 1 (mail: P.O. Box 6-29-54, Panama)
Pereira, Colombia – Carrera 5a, #19-36

Quito, Ecuador – Inglaterra y Amazonas

Rosario, Argentina – Centro de Bhakti-Yoga, Paraguay 556, (2000) Rosario/ Tel. +54 (041) 252630

San José, Costa Rica – Centro Cultural Govinda, Av. 7, Calles 1 y 3, 235 mtrs. norte del Banco Anglo, San Pedro (mail: Apdo. 166, 1002)/ Tel. +506 23-5238

San Salvador, El Salvador – Avenida Universitaria 1132, Media Quadra al sur de la Embajada Americana, San Salvador (mail: P.O. box 1506)/ Tel. +503 25-96-17

Santiago, Chile – Carrera 330/ Tel. +56 (02) 698-8044

Santa Domingo, Dominican Republic – Calle Cayetano Rodriquez No. 254

Trinidad and Tobago, West Indies – Orion Drive, Debe/ Tel. +1 (809) 647-3165

Trinidad and Tobago, West Indies – Prabhupada Ave. Longdenville, Chaguanas

FARM COMMUNITIES

Argentina (Bhaktilata Puri) – Casilla de Correo No. 77, 1727 Marcos Paz, Pcia. Bs. As., Republica Argentina

Bolivia – Contact ISKCON Cochabamba

Colombia (Nueva Mathura) – Cruzero del Guali, Municipio de Caloto, Valle del Cauca/ Tel. +57 (023) 61-26-88 en cali

Costa Rica – Granja Nueva Goloka Vrindavana, Carretera a Paraiso, de la entrada del Jardin Lancaster (por Calle Concava), 200 metros as sur (mano derecha) Cartago (mail: Apdo. 166, 1002)/ Tel. +506 51-6752

Ecuador (Nueva Mayapur) – Ayampe (near Guayaquil)

El Salvador – Carretera a Santa Ana, Km. 34, Canton Los Indios, Zapotitan, Dpto. de La Libertad

Guyana – Seawell Village, Corentyne, East Berbice

RESTAURANTS

Cochabamba, Bolivia – Gopal Restaurant, calle Espana N-0250 (Galeria Olimpia), Cochabamba (mail: P.O. Box 2070, Cochabamba)/ Tel. +591 (042) 26626

Guatemala, Guatemala – Callejor Santandes a una cuadra abajo de Guatel, Panajachel Solola

Quito, Ecuador – (contact ISKCON Quito)

San Salvador, El Salvador – 25 Avenida Norte 1132

Santa Cruz, Bolivia – Snack Govinda, Av. Argomosa (1ero anillo), esq. Bolivar/ Tel. +591 (03) 345189

An Introduction to ISKCON and Devotee Lifestyle

What is the International Society for Krishna Consciousness?

The International Society for Krishna Consciousness (ISKCON), popularly known as the Hare Kṛṣṇa movement, is a world-wide association of devotees of Kṛṣṇa, the Supreme Personality of Godhead. The same God is known by many names in the various scriptures of the world. In the Bible He is known as Jehovah ("the almighty one"), in the Koran as Allah ("the great one"), and in the *Bhagavad-gītā* as Kṛṣṇa, a Sanskrit name meaning "the all-attractive one."

The movement's main purpose is to promote the well-being of human society by teaching the science of God consciousness (Kṛṣṇa consciousness) according to the timeless Vedic scriptures of India.

The best known of the Vedic texts is the *Bhagavad-gītā* ("Song of God"). It is said to date back 5,000 years to the time when Kṛṣṇa incarnated on earth to teach this sacred message. It is the philosophical basis for the Hare Kṛṣṇa movement and is revered by more than 700 million people today.

This exalted work has been praised by scholars and leaders the world over. M.K. Gandhi said, "When doubts haunt me, when disappointments stare me in the face and I see not one ray of hope, I turn to the *Bhagavad-gītā* and find a verse to comfort me." Ralph Waldo Emerson wrote, "It was the first of books; it was as if an empire spoke to us, nothing small or unworthy, but large, serene, consistent, the voice of an old intelligence which in another age and climate had pondered and thus disposed of the same questions which exercise us." And Henry David Thoreau said, "In the morning I bathe my intellect in the stupendous and cosmogonal philosophy of the *Bhagavad-gītā*."

Lord Kṛṣṇa teaches in the *Bhagavad-gītā* that we are not these temporary material bodies but are spirit souls, or conscious entities, and that we can find genuine peace and happiness only in spiritual devotion to God. The *Gītā* and other world scriptures recommend that people joyfully chant the holy name of God. Whether one chants His name as Kṛṣṇa, Allah, or Jehovah, one may become blessed with pure love of God.

A Sixteenth-Century Incarnation of Kṛṣṇa

Kṛṣṇa incarnated again in the sixteenth century as Śrī Caitanya Mahāprabhu and popularized the chanting of God's names all over India. He constantly sang these names of God, as prescribed in the Vedic literatures: Hare Kṛṣṇa, Hare Kṛṣṇa, Kṛṣṇa Kṛṣṇa, Hare Hare/ Hare Rāma, Hare Rāma, Rāma Rāma, Hare Hare. The Hare Kṛṣṇa *mantra* is a transcendental sound vibration. It purifies the mind and awakens the dormant love of God in the hearts of all living beings. Lord Caitanya requested His followers to spread this chanting to every town and village of the world.

Anyone can take part in the chanting of Hare Kṛṣṇa and learn the science of spiritual devotion by studying the *Bhagavad-gītā.* This easy and practical process of self-realization will awaken our natural state of peace and happiness.

Many academics and religious leaders who understand the roots of the modern day Hare Kṛṣṇa movement have affirmed the movement's authenticity. Diana L. Eck, professor of comparative religion and Indian studies at Harvard University, describes the movement as a "tradition that commands a respected place in the religious life of humankind."

Hare Kṛṣṇa Lifestyles

The devotees seen dancing and chanting in the streets, dressed in traditional Indian robes, are, for the most part, full-time students of the Hare Kṛṣṇa movement. The vast majority of followers, however, live and work in the general community, practising Kṛṣṇa consciousness in their homes and attending temples on a regular basis.

There are about 5,000 full-time devotees throughout the world and 200,000 congregational members outside of India. The movement is presently comprised of 267 temples, 40 rural communities, 26 schools, and 45 restaurants in 71 countries. The basic principle of the Hare Kṛṣṇa lifestyle is "simple living and high thinking." A devotee of Kṛṣṇa is encouraged to use his time, energy, talents, and resources in devotional service to God, and not to hanker for selfish ambitions or pleasures which result in frustration and anxiety.

Devotees try to cultivate humanity's inherent spiritual qualities of compassion, truthfulness, cleanliness and austerity. There are four regulative principles which devotees adopt to assist them to develop those qualities and also to help control the insatiable urges of the mind and senses. These are:

1. No eating of meat, fish or eggs.
2. No gambling.
3. No sex other than for procreation within marriage.
4. No intoxication, including all recreational drugs, alcohol, tobacco, tea and coffee.

According to the *Bhagavad-gītā,* indulgence in the above activities disrupts our physical, mental, and spiritual well-being and increases anxiety and conflict in society.

A Philosophy for Everyone

The philosophy of the Hare Kṛṣṇa movement is a non-sectarian monotheistic tradition. It may be summarized in the following eight points:

1. By sincerely cultivating an authentic spiritual science, we can become free from anxiety and achieve a state of pure, unending, blissful consciousness.
2. Each one of us is not the material body but an eternal spirit soul, part and parcel of God (Kṛṣṇa). As such, we are all interrelated through Kṛṣṇa, our common father.
3. Kṛṣṇa is eternal, all-knowing, omnipresent, all-powerful, and all-attractive. He is the seed-giving father of all living beings and the sustaining energy of the universe. He is the source of all incarnations of God.
4. The *Vedas* are the oldest scriptures in the world. The essence of the *Vedas* is found in the *Bhagavad-gītā,* a literal record of Kṛṣṇa's words spoken 5,000 years ago in India. The goal of Vedic knowledge — and of all theistic religions — is to achieve love of God.
5. We can perfectly understand the knowledge of self-realization through the instructions of a genuine spiritual master — one who is free from selfish motives and whose mind is firmly fixed in meditation on Kṛṣṇa.
6. All that we eat should first be offered to Kṛṣṇa with a prayer. In this way Kṛṣṇa accepts the offering and blesses it for our purification.
7. Rather than living in a self-centred way, we should act for the pleasure of Kṛṣṇa. This is known as *bhakti-yoga,* the science of devotional service.

8. The most effective means for achieving God consciousness in this age is to chant the holy names of the Lord: Hare Kṛṣṇa, Hare Kṛṣṇa, Kṛṣṇa Kṛṣṇa, Hare Hare, Hare Rāma, Hare Rāma, Rāma Rāma, Hare Hare.

Kṛṣṇa Consciousness at Home

From what we've read in this book, it is clear how important it is for everyone to practise Kṛṣṇa consciousness, devotional service to Lord Kṛṣṇa. Of course, living in the association of Kṛṣṇa's devotees in a temple or *aśrama* makes it easier to perform devotional service. But if you're determined, you can follow the teachings of Kṛṣṇa consciousness at home and thus convert your home into a temple.

Spiritual life, like material life, means practical activity. The difference is that, whereas we perform material activities for the benefit of ourselves or those we consider ours, we perform spiritual activities for the benefit of Lord Kṛṣṇa, under the guidance of the scriptures and the spiritual master. Kṛṣṇa declares in the *Bhagavad-gītā* that a person can achieve neither happiness nor the supreme destination of life — going back to Godhead, back to Lord Kṛṣṇa — if he or she does not follow the injunctions of the scriptures. How to follow the scriptural rules by engaging in practical service to the Lord is explained by a bona fide spiritual master who is in an authorized chain of disciplic succession coming from Kṛṣṇa Himself.

These timeless practices which are outlined in this book have been taught to us by His Divine Grace A.C. Bhaktivedanta Swami Prabhupāda, the foremost exponent of Kṛṣṇa consciousness in our time.

The purpose of spiritual knowledge is to bring us closer to God, or Kṛṣṇa. Kṛṣṇa says in the *Bhagavad-gītā* (18.55), *bhaktyā mām abhijānāti:* "I can be known only by devotional service." Spiritual knowledge guides us in proper action to satisfy the desires of Kṛṣṇa through practical engagements in His loving service. Without practical application, theoretical knowledge is of little value.

Spiritual knowledge offers direction in all aspects of life. We should endeavour, therefore, to organize our lives in such a way as to follow Kṛṣṇa's teachings as far as possible. We should try to do our best, to do more than is simply convenient. Then it will be possible for us to rise to the transcendental plane of Kṛṣṇa consciousness, even while living far from a temple.

Chanting Hare Kṛṣṇa

The first principle in devotional service is to chant the Hare Kṛṣṇa *mahā-mantra* (*mahā* means "great"; *mantra* means "sound that liberates the mind from ignorance"):

Hare Kṛṣṇa, Hare Kṛṣṇa, Kṛṣṇa Kṛṣṇa, Hare Hare
Hare Rāma, Hare Rāma, Rāma Rāma, Hare Hare

You can chant these holy names of the Lord anywhere and at any time, but it is best to do it at a specific time of the day. Early morning hours are ideal.

The chanting can be done in two ways: singing the *mantra,* called *kīrtana* (usually done in a group), and saying the *mantra* to oneself, called *japa* (which literally means "to speak softly"). Concentrate on hearing the sound of the holy names. As you chant, pronounce the names clearly and distinctly, addressing Kṛṣṇa in a prayerful mood. When your mind wanders, bring it back to the sound of the Lord's name. Chanting is a prayer to Kṛṣṇa that means "O energy of the Lord (Hare), O all-attractive Lord (Kṛṣṇa), O supreme enjoyer (Rāma), please engage me in Your service." The more attentively and sincerely you chant these names of God, the more spiritual progress you will make.

Since God is all-powerful and all-merciful, He has kindly made it very easy for us to chant His names, and He has also invested all His powers in them. Therefore the names of God and God Himself are identical. This means that when we chant the holy names of Kṛṣṇa and Rāma we are directly associating with God and being purified by such communion. Therefore we should always try to chant with devotion and reverence. The Vedic literature states that Lord Kṛṣṇa is personally dancing on your tongue when you chant His holy name.

When you chant alone, it is best to chant on *japa* beads (available at any of the centres listed in the advertisement at the end of this book). This not only helps you fix your attention on the holy name, but also helps you count the number of times you chant the *mantra* daily. Each strand of *japa* beads contains 108 small beads and one large bead, the head bead. Begin on a bead next to the head bead and gently roll it between the thumb and middle finger of your right hand as you chant the full Hare Kṛṣṇa *mantra.*

Then move to the next bead and repeat the process. In this way, chant on each of the 108 beads until you reach the head bead again. This is called one "round" of *japa.* Then, without chanting on the head bead, reverse the beads and start your second round on the last bead you chanted on.

Initiated devotees vow before the spiritual master to chant at least sixteen rounds of the Hare Kṛṣṇa *mantra* daily. But even if you can chant only one round a day, the principle is that once you commit yourself to chanting that round, you should try to complete it every day without fail. When you feel you can chant more, then increase the minimum number of rounds you chant each day — but try not to fall below that number. You can chant more than your fixed number, but you should maintain a set minimum each day. Please note that the beads are sacred and therefore should never touch the ground or be put in an unclean place. To keep your beads clean, it is best to carry them in a special bead bag, also available from any of the temples.

Aside from chanting *japa,* you can also sing the Lord's holy names in *kīrtana.* Although you can sing *kīrtana* on your own, it is generally performed with others. A melodious *kīrtana* with family or friends is sure to enliven everyone. ISKCON devotees use traditional melodies and instruments, especially in the temple, but you can chant to any melody and use any musical instruments to accompany your chanting. As Lord Caitanya said, "There are no hard and fast rules for chanting Hare Kṛṣṇa." One thing you might want to do, however, is to obtain some *kīrtana* and *japa* audiotapes and hear the various styles of chanting.

Setting Up Your Altar

You will probably find that *japa* and *kīrtana* are more effective when done before an altar. Lord Kṛṣṇa and His pure devotees are so kind that they allow us to worship them even through their pictures. It's something like mailing a letter: You can't mail a letter by placing it in just any box; you must use the postbox authorised by the government. Similarly, we cannot concoct an image of God and worship that, but we may worship the authorised picture of God, and Kṛṣṇa accepts our worship through that picture.

Setting up an altar at home means receiving the Lord and His pure devotees as your most honoured guests. Where should you set up the altar? Well, how would you seat a guest? An ideal place would be clean, well lit, and free from draughts and household disturbances. Your guest, of course, would need a comfortable chair, but for the picture of Kṛṣṇa's form a wall shelf, a mantel-piece, a corner table, or the top shelf of a bookcase will do. You wouldn't seat a guest in your home and then ignore him; you'd provide a place for yourself to sit, too, where you could comfortably face him and enjoy his company, so don't make your altar inaccessible.

What do you need to set up your altar? Here are the essentials:

1. A picture of Śrīla Prabhupāda.
2. A picture of Lord Caitanya and His associates.
3. A picture of Rādhā and Kṛṣṇa.

In addition, you may want an altar cloth, water cups (one for each picture), candles with holders, a special plate for offering food, a small bell, incense, an incense holder, and fresh flowers, which you may offer in vases or simply place before each picture. If you're interested in more elaborate Deity worship, ask any of the ISKCON devotees or write to the Bhaktivedanta Book Trust.

The first person we worship on the altar is the spiritual master. The spiritual master is not God. Only God is God. But because the spiritual master is His dearmost servant, God has empowered him to be His representative and therefore he deserves the same respect as that given to God. The spiritual master links the disciple with God and teaches him the process of *bhakti-yoga.* He is God's ambassador to the material world. When the Queen sends an ambassador to a foreign country, the ambassador receives the same respect as that accorded the Queen, and the ambassador's words are as authoritative as the Queen's. Similarly, we should respect the spiritual master as we would God, and revere his words as we would God's.

There are two main kinds of *guru*: the instructing *guru* and the initiating *guru.* Everyone who takes up the process of *bhakti-yoga* as a result of coming in contact with ISKCON owes an immense debt of gratitude to Śrīla Prabhupāda. Before Śrīla Prabhupāda left India in 1965 to spread Kṛṣṇa consciousness abroad, almost no one outside India knew anything about the practice of pure devotional service to Lord Kṛṣṇa. Therefore, everyone who has learned of the process through his books, his *Back to Godhead* magazine, his tapes, or contact with his followers should offer respect to Śrīla Prabhupāda. As the founder and spiritual guide of the International Society for Krishna Consciousness, he is the prime instructing *guru* of all of us.

Devotees should first of all develop this spiritual understanding and their relationship with Śrīla Prabhupāda. However, the Vedic literature encourages us to become connected to the current link of the chain of spiritual masters. Following Śrīla Prabhupāda's departure, this means accepting initiation from one of Śrīla Prabhupāda's senior followers who are acknowledged as spiritual masters within the movement.

The second picture on your altar should be of the *pañca-tattva,* Lord Caitanya and His four leading associates. Lord Caitanya is the incarnation of God for this age. He is Kṛṣṇa Himself, descended in the form of His own devotee to teach us how to surrender to Him, specifically by chanting His holy names and performing other activities of *bhakti-yoga.* Lord Caitanya is the most merciful incarnation, for He makes it easy for anyone to attain love of God through the chanting of the Hare Kṛṣṇa *mantra.*

And of course, your altar should have a picture of the Supreme Personality of Godhead, Lord Śrī Kṛṣṇa, with His eternal consort, Śrīmatī Rādhārāṇī. Śrīmatī Rādhārāṇī is Kṛṣṇa's spiritual potency. She is devotional service personified, and devotees always take shelter of Her to learn how to serve Kṛṣṇa.

You can arrange the pictures in a triangle, with the picture of Śrīla Prabhupāda on the left, the picture of Lord Caitanya and His associates on the right and the picture of Rādhā and Kṛṣṇa, which, if possible, should be slightly larger than the others, on a small raised platform behind and in the centre. Or you can hang the picture of Rādhā and Kṛṣṇa on the wall above.

When you establish an altar, you are inviting Kṛṣṇa and His pure devotees to reside as the most important guests in your home. Carefully clean the altar each morning. Cleanliness is essential in the worship of Kṛṣṇa. You would not neglect to clean the room of an important guest. If you have water cups, rinse them out and fill them with fresh water daily. Then place them conveniently close to the pictures. You should remove flowers in vases as soon as they're slightly wilted, or daily if you've offered them at the base of the pictures. You should offer fresh incense at least once a day, and, if possible, light candles and place them near the pictures while you're chanting before the altar.

Please try the things we've suggested so far. It's very simple really: If you try to love God, you'll gradually realize how much He loves you. That's the essence of *bhakti-yoga.*

Prasādam: How to Eat Spiritually

By His omnipotent transcendental energies, Kṛṣṇa can actually convert matter into spirit. If we place an iron rod in a fire, soon the rod becomes red hot and acts just like fire. In the same way, food prepared for and offered to Kṛṣṇa with love and devotion becomes completely spiritualized. Such food is called Kṛṣṇa *prasādam,* which means "the mercy of Lord Kṛṣṇa."

Eating *prasādam* is a fundamental practice of *bhakti-yoga.* In other forms of *yoga* one must artificially repress the senses, but the *bhakti-yogī* can engage his or her senses in a variety of pleasing spiritual activities, such as tasting delicious food offered to Lord Kṛṣṇa. In this way the senses gradually become spiritualised and bring the devotee more and more transcendental pleasure by being engaged in devotional service. Such spiritual pleasure far surpasses any kind of material experience.

Lord Caitanya said of *prasādam,* "Everyone has tasted these foods before. However, now that they have been prepared for Kṛṣṇa and offered to Him with devotion, these foods have acquired extraordinary tastes and uncommon fragrances. Just taste them and see the difference in experience! Apart from the taste, even the fragrance pleases the mind and makes one forget any other aroma. Therefore, it should be understood that the spiritual nectar of Kṛṣṇa's lips must have touched these ordinary foods and imparted to them all their transcendental qualities."

Eating only food offered to Kṛṣṇa is the perfection of vegetarianism. Refraining from animal flesh out of compassion for innocent creatures is certainly a praiseworthy sentiment, but when we go beyond vegetarianism to a diet of *prasādam,* our eating becomes helpful in achieving the goal of human life — reawakening the soul's original relationship with God. In the *Bhagavad-gītā* Lord Kṛṣṇa says that unless one eats only food that has been offered to Him in sacrifice, one will suffer the reactions of *karma.*

How to Prepare and Offer Prasādam

As you walk down the supermarket aisles selecting the foods you will offer to Kṛṣṇa, you need to know what is offerable and what is not. In the *Bhagavad-gītā,* Lord Kṛṣṇa states, "If one offers Me with love and devotion a leaf, a flower, a fruit, or water, I will accept it." Elsewhere, it is explained that we can offer Kṛṣṇa foods prepared from milk products, vegetables, fruits, nuts, and grains. (Write to the Bhaktivedanta Book Trust for one of the many Hare Kṛṣṇa cookbooks.) Meat, fish and eggs are not offerable. A few vegetarian items are also forbidden — garlic and onions, for example, because they tend to agitate the mind, making meditation more difficult. (Hing, asafoetida, is a tasty substitute for them in cooking and is available at most Indian grocers.) Nor can you offer Kṛṣṇa coffee or tea that contain caffeine. If you like these beverages, purchase caffeine-free coffee and herbal teas.

While shopping, be aware that you may find meat, fish, and egg products mixed with other foods; so be sure to read labels carefully. For instance, some brands of yoghurt and sour cream contain gelatin, a substance made from the horns, hooves, and bones of slaughtered animals. Most hard cheese contains rennet, an enzyme extracted from the stomach tissue of slaughtered calves. Look for such cheese labelled as being suitable for vegetarians.

Try to avoid foods cooked by nondevotees. According to the subtle laws of nature the consciousness of the cook affects the food. The principle is the same as that at work in a painting: a painting is not simply a collection of brush strokes on a canvas but an expression of the artist's state of mind, which affects the viewer. So if you eat food cooked by nondevotees such as processed foods etc., then you are likely to absorb a dose of materialism and *karma.* As far as possible in your own cooking use only fresh, natural ingredients.

In preparing food, cleanliness is the most important principle. Nothing impure should be offered to God; so keep your kitchen very clean. Always wash your hands thoroughly before entering the kitchen. While preparing food, do not taste it, for you are cooking the meal not for yourself but for the pleasure of Kṛṣṇa. Arrange portions of the food on dinnerware kept especially for this purpose; no one but the Lord should eat from those dishes. The easiest way to offer food is simply to pray, "My dear Lord Kṛṣṇa, please accept this food," and to chant each of the following prayers three times while ringing a bell (see the Sanskrit Pronunciation Guide on page 331).

1. Prayer to Śrīla Prabhupāda:

nama oṁ viṣṇu-pādāya kṛṣṇa-preṣṭhāya bhū-tale
śrīmate bhaktivedānta-svāmin iti nāmine

namas te sārasvate deve gaura-vāṇī-pracāriṇe
nirviśeṣa-śūnyavādi-pāścātya-deśa-tāriṇe

"I offer my respectful obeisances unto His Divine Grace A.C. Bhaktivedanta Swami Prabhupāda, who is very dear to Lord Kṛṣṇa, having taken shelter at His lotus feet. Our respectful obeisances are unto you, O spiritual master, servant of Bhaktisiddhānta Sarasvatī Gosvāmī. You are kindly preaching the message of Lord Caitanyadeva and delivering the Western countries, which are filled with impersonalism and voidism."

2. Prayer to Lord Caitanya:

namo mahā-vadānyāya kṛṣṇa-prema-pradāya te
kṛṣṇāya kṛṣṇa-caitanya-nāmne gaura-tviṣe namaḥ

"O most munificent incarnation! You are Kṛṣṇa Himself appearing as Śrī Kṛṣṇa Caitanya Mahāprabhu. You have assumed the golden colour of Śrīmatī Rādhārāṇī, and You are widely distributing pure love of Kṛṣṇa. We offer our respectful obeisances unto You."

3. Prayer to Lord Kṛṣṇa:

namo brahmaṇya-devāya go-brāhmaṇa-hitāya ca
jagad-dhitāya kṛṣṇāya govindāya namo namaḥ

"I offer my respectful obeisances unto Lord Kṛṣṇa, who is the worshipable Deity for all *brāhmaṇas,* the well-wisher of the cows and the *brāhmaṇas,* and the benefactor of the whole world. I offer my repeated obeisances to the Personality of Godhead, known as Kṛṣṇa and Govinda."

Remember that the real purpose of preparing and offering food to the Lord is to show your devotion and gratitude to Him. Kṛṣṇa accepts your devotion, not the physical offering itself. God is complete in Himself — He doesn't need anything — but out of His immense kindness He allows us to offer food to Him so that we can develop our love for Him.

After offering the food to the Lord, wait at least five minutes for Him to partake of the preparations. Then you should transfer the food from the special dinnerware and wash the dishes and utensils you used for the offering. Now you, your family and any guests may eat the *prasādam.* While you eat, try to appreciate the spiritual value of the food. Remember that because Kṛṣṇa has accepted it, it is nondifferent from Him, and therefore by eating it you will become purified.

Everything you offer on your altar becomes *prasādam,* the mercy of the Lord. The flowers, the incense, the water, the food having been offered for the Lord's pleasure become spiritualised. The Lord enters into the offerings, and thus the remnants are nondifferent from Him. So you should not only deeply respect the things you've offered, but you should distribute them to others as well. Distribution of *prasādam* is an essential expression of your devotion to Kṛṣṇa.

Everyday Life: The Four Regulative Principles

Anyone serious about progressing in Kṛṣṇa consciousness must try to avoid the following four sinful activities:

1. **Eating meat, fish, or eggs.** These foods are saturated with the modes of passion and ignorance, and therefore cannot be offered to the Lord. A person who eats these foods participates in a conspiracy of violence against helpless animals and thus curtails his spiritual progress.

2. **Gambling.** Gambling invariably puts one into anxiety and fuels greed, envy, and anger.

3. **The use of intoxicants.** Drugs, alcohol, and tobacco, as well as any drinks or foods containing caffeine, cloud the mind, overstimulate the senses, and make it impossible to understand or follow the principles of *bhakti-yoga.*

4. **Illicit sex.** This is sex outside of marriage or sex in marriage for any purpose other than procreation. Sex for pleasure compels one to identify with the body and prevents from understanding Kṛṣṇa consciousness. The scriptures teach that sex attraction is the most powerful force binding us to the illusions of the material world. Anyone serious about advancing in Kṛṣṇa consciousness should therefore abstain from or regulate sexual activity according to the scriptures. In *Bhagavad-gītā* Kṛṣṇa says that sexual union for conceiving a child to be raised in God consciousness is an act of devotion to Him.

Engagement in Practical Devotional Service

We all must work to earn our livelihood and to maintain home, family, and so on. However, if we try to take the fruits of our labour for ourselves and dependents, we must also accept the karmic reactions incurred because of our work. Kṛṣṇa says in the *Bhagavad-gītā* (3.9), "Work done as a sacrifice for Viṣṇu (Kṛṣṇa) has to be performed. Otherwise work binds one to the material world."

However, it is not necessary to change our occupation, we need to change our attitude. If we are striving for Kṛṣṇa consciousness, if our home has become a temple, and if we share spiritual life with our family members, then what we earn may legitimately be spent for the maintenance of our domestic affairs and the balance engaged in promoting our and others' spiritual lives. Thus, whatever we do we can see it as being part of our devotional service to Kṛṣṇa.

Further, we may also have the opportunity to use our skills and talents directly for Kṛṣṇa. If you're a writer, write for Kṛṣṇa; if you're an artist, create for Kṛṣṇa; if you're a secretary, type for Kṛṣṇa. You may also help a local temple in your spare time, and you could sacrifice some of the fruits of your work by contributing a portion of your earnings to help maintain the temple and propagate Kṛṣṇa consciousness. Some devotees buy Hare Kṛṣṇa literature and distribute it to their friends and associates, or they engage in a variety of services at the temple. There is also a wide network of devotees who gather in each other's homes for chanting, worship, and study. Write to your local temple or the Society's secretary to learn of any such programmes near you.

Additional Devotional Principles

There are many more devotional practices that can help you become Kṛṣṇa conscious. Here are two vital ones:

Studying Hare Kṛṣṇa literature. Śrīla Prabhupāda, the founder-*ācārya* of ISKCON, dedicated much of his time to writing and translating books such as the *Śrīmad-Bhāgavatam.* Hearing the words — or reading the writings — of a realised spiritual master is an essential spiritual practice. So try to set aside some time every day to read Śrīla Prabhupāda's books. You can get a free catalogue of available books and tapes from the Bhaktivedanta Book Trust.

Associating with devotees. Śrīla Prabhupāda established the Hare Kṛṣṇa movement to give people in general the chance to associate with devotees of the Lord. This is the best way to gain faith in the process of Kṛṣṇa consciousness and become enthusiastic in devotional service. Conversely, maintaining intimate connections with nondevotees slows one's spiritual progress. So try to visit the Hare Kṛṣṇa centre nearest you as often as possible.

In Closing

The beauty of Kṛṣṇa consciousness is that you can take as much as you're ready for. Kṛṣṇa Himself promises in the *Bhagavad-gītā* (2.40), "There is no loss or diminution in this endeavour, and even a little advancement on this path protects one from the most fearful type of danger." So bring Kṛṣṇa into your daily life, and we guarantee you'll feel the benefit.

Hare Kṛṣṇa!

STAY IN TOUCH

Now that you've read this book, you may like to further your interest by joining thousands of others as a member of ISKCON.

The International Society for Krishna Consciousness was founded in 1966 by the author of this book, Srila Prabhupada. The Society is dedicated to providing knowledge of Krishna and the science of Krishna consciousness as a means of achieving the highest personal happiness and spiritual fellowship among all living beings. We invite you to join us.

What Does Membership of ISKCON Mean for Me?

For an annual donation of £21 you'll receive a membership package that will keep you fully informed and involved. Here's what you receive (£25 for non UK addresses):

• BACK TO GODHEAD

The Magazine of the Hare Krishna Movement

Each issue of *Back to Godhead* has colorful photos and informative articles on topics such as:

- techniques of *mantra* meditation
- how the spiritual knowledge of the *Vedas* can bring peace, satisfaction, and success in your life
- recipes for a *karma*-free diet
- news of Hare Krishna devotees and devotional projects worldwide
- clear explanations of Vedic science and cosmology
- Krishna conscious perspectives on current affairs... and much more

• THE NAMA HATTA

ISKCON UK's newsletter covering happenings in both UK and Ireland. Articles, letters and lots of news and items of interest.

• VALUABLE DISCOUNTS

All registered members will be sent a valuable 10% Membership Discount Card to use on purchases of books, audio and video tapes, posters, incense, and all other items from UK Hare Krishna shops and the mail order department.

• VAISHNAVA CALENDAR

A beautifully illustrated 12 page wall calendar featuring some of the best of The Bhaktivedanta Book Trust paintings. It will remind you of all the important festivals and celebrations of the Krishna devotee year.

Become a member today and experience the higher taste of *bhakti-yoga.*

Application for Membership

(you can write these details out on a separate piece of paper if you wish)

I wish to be included as a member of ISKCON UK and I have enclosed payment of £21 accordingly for the next years membership. Please send my magazines to:

Surname Mr/Mrs/Ms______________________________

Forenames______________________________

Address______________________________

____

Postcode____________________ County______________

Please make all payments out to ISKCON:

Signed____________________ Date______________

SB 6:1

Please Return this application to:
Membership Service Dept., ISKCON,
2 St. James Rd., Watford, WDI 8EA

BHAGAVAD-GITA AS IT IS

The world's most popular edition of a timeless classic.

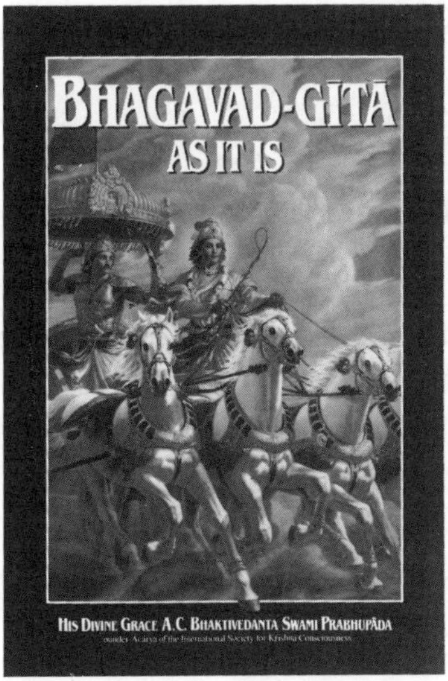

Throughout the ages, the world's greatest minds have turned to the *Bhagavad-gita* for answers to life's perennial questions. Renowned as the jewel of India's spiritual wisdom, the *Gita* summarizes the profound Vedic knowledge concerning man's essential nature, his environment, and ultimately his relationship with God. With more than fifty million copies sold in twenty languages, *Bhagavad-gita As It Is,* by His Divine Grace A.C. Bhaktivedanta Swami Prabhupada, is the most widely read edition of the *Gita* in the world. It includes the original Sanskrit text, phonetic transliterations, word-for-word meanings, translation, elaborate commentary, and many full-colour illustrations.

	Pocket	Vinyl	Hard	Deluxe
UK	**£3.00**	**£5.25**	**£7.95**	**£13.95**
US	$3.90	$8.50	$10.30	$18.00
AUS		$11.00	$14.00	$28.00

EASY JOURNEY TO OTHER PLANETS

One of Srila Prabhupada's earliest books, *Easy Journey* describes how *bhakti-yoga* enables us to transfer ourselves from the material to the spiritual world.

Softbound, 96 pages

UK: £1.00; US: $1.00; AUS: $2.00

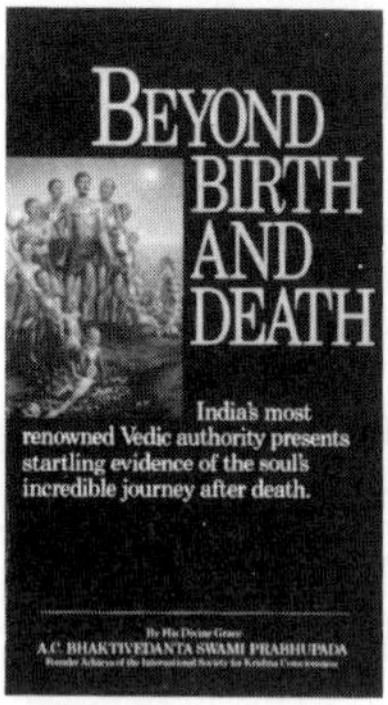

BEYOND BIRTH AND DEATH

What is the self? Can it exist apart from the physical body? If so, what happens to the self at the time of death? What about reincarnation? Liberation? *Beyond Birth and Death* answers these intriguing questions, and more.

Softbound, 96 pages

UK: £1.00; US: $1.00; AUS: $2.00

THE HIGHER TASTE

A Guide to Gourmet Vegetarian Cooking and a Karma-Free Diet

Illustrated profusely with black-and-white drawings and eight full-colour plates, this popular volume contains over 60 tried and tested international recipes, together with the why's and how's of the Krishna conscious vegetarian life-style.

Softbound, 176 pages

UK: £1.00; US: $1.99; AUS: $2.00

RAJA-VIDYA: THE KING OF KNOWLEDGE

In this book we learn why knowledge of Krishna is absolute and frees the soul from material bondage.

Softbound, 128 pages

UK: £1.00; US: $1.00; AUS: $2.00

THE PERFECTION OF YOGA

A lucid explanation of the psychology, techniques, and purposes of *yoga;* a summary and comparison of the different *yoga* systems; and an introduction to meditation.

Softbound, 96 pages

UK: £1.00; US: $1.00; AUS: $2.00

MESSAGE OF GODHEAD

An excerpt: "The influences of various people, places, and terms have led us to designate ourselves as Hindus, Muslims, Christians, Buddhists, Socialists, Bolsheviks, and so forth. But when we attain transcendental knowledge and are established in *sanatana-dharma,* the actual, eternal religion of the living entity, the spirit soul, then and then only can we attain real, undeniable peace, prosperity, and happiness in this world."

Softbound, 68 pages

UK: £1.00; US: $1.00; AUS: $2.00

GREAT

VEGETARIAN DISHES

Featuring over 100 stunning full-colour photos, this new book is for spiritually aware people who want the exquisite taste of Hare Krishna cooking without a lot of time in the kitchen. The 240 international recipes were tested and refined by world-famous Hare Krishna chef Kurma dasa.

240 recipes, 192 pages, coffee table size hardback

UK: £12.95; US: $19.95; AUS: $24.95

THE HARE KRISHNA BOOK OF

VEGETARIAN COOKING

A colourfully illustrated, practical cookbook that not only helps you prepare authentic Indian dishes at home, but also teaches you about the ancient tradition behind India's world-famous vegetarian cuisine.

130 kitchen-rested recipes, 300 pages, hardback

UK: £8.95; US: $11.60; AUS: $15.00

STAY IN TOUCH...

❐ Please send me a free information pack, including the small booklet *Krishna the Reservoir of Pleasure* and a catalogue of available books.

- ❐ Bhagavad-gita As It Is ❐ Pocket ❐ Vinyl ❐ Hard ❐ Deluxe
- ❐ Great Vegetarian Dishes
- ❐ The Hare Krishna Book of Vegetarian Cooking
- ❐ The Higher Taste
- ❐ Raja-Vidya: The King of Knowledge
- ❐ Easy Journey to Other Planets
- ❐ Beyond Birth and Death
- ❐ The Perfection of Yoga
- ❐ Message of Godhead

Please send me the above books. I enclose $/£________ to cover the cost and understand that the prices given include postage and packaging. (All prices offered here are greatly reduced from our normal retail charges!)

Name____

PLEASE PRINT

Address____

______________________________ Postcode________________

SB 6:1

Post this form with payment to:

In Europe: The Bhaktivedanta Book Trust, P.O. Box 324, Borehamwood, Herts, WD6 1NB, U.K.

In North America: The Bhaktivedanta Book Trust, 3764 Watseka Ave., Los Angeles, CA 90034, U.S.A.

In Australasia: The Bhaktivedanta Book Trust, P.O. Box 262, Botany, N.S.W. 2019, Australia